Financial Products

Financial Products provides a step-by-step guide to some of the most important ideas underpinning financial mathematics. It describes and explains interest rates, discounting, arbitrage, risk neutral probabilities, forward contracts, futures, bonds, FRA and swaps. It shows how to construct both elementary and more complex (Libor) zero curves. Options are described, illustrated and then priced using the Black–Scholes formula and binomial trees. Finally, there is a chapter describing default probabilities, credit ratings and credit derivatives (CDS, TRS, CSO and CDO). An important feature of the book is that it explains this range of concepts and techniques in a way that can be understood by those with a basic understanding of algebra. Many of the calculations are illustrated using Excel spreadsheets, as are some of the more complex algebraic processes. This accessible approach makes it an ideal introduction to financial products for undergraduates and those studying for professional financial qualifications.

Bill Dalton was Head of the Mathematics Department at Harrow School, 1978–1998. He retired in 2006 and now writes and lectures part-time in financial mathematics.

Financial Products

An Introduction Using Mathematics and Excel

Bill Dalton

CAMBRIDGE
UNIVERSITY PRESS

CAMBRIDGE UNIVERSITY PRESS
Cambridge, New York, Melbourne, Madrid, Cape Town,
Singapore, São Paulo, Delhi, Tokyo, Mexico City

Cambridge University Press
The Edinburgh Building, Cambridge CB2 8RU, UK

Published in the United States of America by Cambridge University Press, New York

www.cambridge.org
Information on this title: www.cambridge.org/97897805216822220

First published 2008

A catalogue record for this publication is available from the British Library

Library of Congress Cataloguing in Publication data
Dalton, Bill, 1943–
Financial products : an introduction using mathematics and Excel / Bill Dalton.
p. cm.
Includes index.
ISBN 978-0-521-86358-2 (hardback) – ISBN 978-0-521-68222-0 (pbk.)
1. Finance–Mathematical models. 2. Microsoft Excel (Computer file) I. Title.

HG106.D33 2008
332.6320420285554 – dc22 2007044748

ISBN 978-0-521-86358-2 Hardback
ISBN 978-0-521-68222-0 Paperback

Contents

Introduction

This book is an introduction to some of the ways mathematics can be used to obtain useful, profitable and extremely attractive results in finance. It is now widely recognised that the financial world has become a profitable hunting ground for mathematicians. Indeed, without a confident grasp of basic mathematics, many of the most important financial products in the market will not be understood. It is the aim of this book to explain, in simple terms, some of the most important ideas of basic financial mathematics. A significant feature of the book is that Excel spreadsheets are used to assist the reader with the more tricky algebraic manipulations. If the reader is strong in algebra, the spreadsheets act as an aid with the calculations. If the reader is not so strong, these spreadsheets will show, in a numerical framework, what is 'going on' in the algebra. By seeing what the spreadsheet is doing, the reader grasps the purpose of the algebra. An introduction to those parts of Excel used in this book is given in the first chapter. However, this is not meant to be a tutorial in Excel; rather, it is a basic covering of those features of Excel the reader will need. It is important to emphasise that to move ahead with this subject, familiarity and confidence with Excel (or some other programming language) are essential. Some references are given in 'An introduction to Excel'.

One of the really attractive features of financial mathematics is that the subject is so new. The major breakthrough came in 1973 with the classic Black–Scholes result on the pricing of European call and put options. Almost everything in this subject has happened since that fairly recent date. This means that not only are the results new and fresh but so is the thinking that led to these results. We can still see – very clearly – the problems the originators were trying to overcome when they produced these wonderful ideas. Because we are so near the beginning of the subject, there is no long history to absorb before today's ideas can be seen. There is no vast theory to plough through before you can understand today's problems. In Chapter 8, we look at recent developments. There are fewer exercises attached to this chapter. In a sense, the problems that could be attached to Chapter 8 are close to what mathematicians are working on today. In this subject, it is not a long bus ride to the frontier.

So who is the book for?

1. Level of mathematical ability:
   We have aimed the book at:
   - very good GCSE candidates, who are confident enough to try new things in mathematics
   - those who have at least some AS Mathematics experience: ideally in the C1 and C2 pure modules and in the S1 statistics module.
2. Courses, examinations involving the subject matter of the book:
   - Business Studies, Finance, Investment and Economics courses in institutions of higher education and universities.
   - The Securities and Investment Institute: Certificate in Investment Administration; Certificate in Investments; also, the Financial Derivatives Module.
   - The Faculty of Actuaries and Institute of Actuaries Finance and Investment, Specialist Technical B syllabus: Certificate in Derivatives.
   - The CFA Program (Chartered Financial Analyst): Analysis of Debt Investments (VII); Analysis of Derivatives (VIII).

What is the book about?

There are eight chapters.

Chapter 1 describes the building blocks of the subject. We describe interest rates, how they are calculated and how they may be used. Then interest rates are used to describe the present value (or the discounted value) of money. We define and explain the important idea of arbitrage, after which we illustrate risk neutral probabilities. Finally, we take a first look at a curve illustrating the development of interest rates: the zero curve.

Chapter 2 implements some of these ideas and describes in full detail how forward contracts operate and change in value as time passes.

Chapter 3 takes forward contracts into the market place and provides a full description of futures contracts. We describe the mechanics of futures contracts and illustrate how they might be traded. We show how futures contracts can be used for speculation and for hedging risk.

Chapter 4 looks at bonds: what they are and how they are priced. We look at quotations, day count conventions, bond yields and how to compare different bonds. We show how futures contracts and bonds can be used together and, finally, we make a second attempt to construct a zero curve.

Chapter 5 takes forward the idea of interest rates – literally – and considers interest rates over future time periods. We look at forward rate agreements and show how to achieve, over a future time period, an interest rate that is fixed today. We define and describe interest rate swaps and the swap rate and illustrate some applications of swaps. We describe and illustrate caps and floors. We show how to enter a futures contract on an interest rate and, finally, we construct and plot a realistic zero curve.

Chapter 6 takes a pictorial look at options. We describe many options (including call and put options) with their pay-offs and the strategies determining their use. We illustrate put–call parity. We show how the options can be used to hedge risk and for racheting up profits.

Chapter 7 shows how options can be priced. We describe in elegant detail a binomial tree method for pricing European and American options. We describe and illustrate the Black–Scholes formula.

Chapter 8 points to the future. In this chapter, we remove the idea that all debts will be honoured in full on the day they fall due and see what happens. We consider, from two different standpoints, the probability that a company will default on its obligations and look at an outstanding problem in this area. Finally, we describe four ways in which, for a price, risk can be considerably reduced, if not eliminated.

What further help is available?

There are internet sites. We give below some that the author has found helpful, but as can be imagined, in this rapidly developing field where communication is all important, there are many, many more.

Educational (helpful with definitions, explanations and background material):

www.defaultrisk.com	Mainly credit risk and credit derivatives
www.investopedia.com	
www.investorguide.com	
www.investorwords.com	

www.riskglossary.com
en.wikipedia.org

Information and data:

www.moneyextra.com	
www.moneyfacts.co.uk	
yahoo finance	An excellent and really useful site offering both information and large amounts of data.

Exchanges and markets:

www.bankofengland.co.uk	Bank of England
www.cbot.com	Chicago Board of Trade
www.cme.com	Chicago Mercantile Exchange
www.ftse.com	FTSE International
www.liffe.com	London International Financial Futures and Options Exchange
www.londonstockexchange.com	London Stock Exchange

Newspapers and news (also helpful with data and background information):

www.bbc.co.uk	BBC
www.bloomberg.com	Bloomberg
www.ft.com	*Financial Times*
www.reuters.com	Reuters
money.cnn.com	CNN and *Fortune* magazine
yahoo finance	Helpful here, also

And there are books. Again, the choice is large, but again, the list below contains those the author has found particularly helpful.

- **Baxter, Martin and Rennie, Andrew, Financial Calculus: Cambridge University Press**

  A joy. The book starts from basics and moves apparently seamlessly through binomial trees to continuous models to an interesting presentation of interest rate models. This book is both profound and hugely enjoyable.
- **Benth, Fred Espen, Theory with Stochastic Analysis. An Introduction to Mathematical Finance: Springer**

  A good, approachable introduction to the next stage in the subject; deals with stochastic integration and martingales. Shows some VBA programs (Monte Carlo simulation and numerical methods).

- **Choudhry, Moorad, An Introduction to Credit Derivatives: Elsevier (Butterworth-Heinemann)**
  A straightforward introduction to credit derivatives. Case studies, diagrams and pictures of computer screens are helpful.
- **Etheridge, Alison, A Course in Financial Calculus: Cambridge University Press**
  Mathematically much more advanced, but very readable in the introductory sections. For anyone wanting to take the subject further and develop the more mathematical approach, this is a terrific book. (See Benth's book as a possible introduction.)
- **Hull, John C., Options, Futures and Other Derivatives: Prentice Hall (Pearson Education International)**
  Described by many as 'The Bible' of the subject. A first-class book for beginners and experienced practitioners alike.
- **Luenberger, David G., Investment Science: Oxford University Press**
  A very good and broad introduction to the subject.
- **Meissner, Gunter, Credit derivatives: Blackwell Publishing**
  Credit derivatives in a discrete setting.
- **Neftci, Salih N., An Introduction to the Mathematics of Financial Derivatives: Academic Press**
  An excellent introduction to the subject and to the harder mathematics that will follow if the reader wishes to take the subject further.
- **Schönbucher, Philipp J., Credit Derivatives Pricing Models: John Wiley**
  Very good indeed. The early part of the book is more descriptive, with concrete examples; later sections involve more advanced mathematical ideas. The book focuses mainly on credit risk and credit derivatives (Chapter 8).
- **Servigny, Arnaud de and Renault, Olivier, Measuring and Managing Credit Risk: McGraw-Hill**
  Very readable, vast in scope, mainly concerned with credit risk and credit derivatives (Chapter 8).
- **Shreve, Steven E., Stochastic Calculus for Finance I and II: Springer**
  Volume I focuses on the binomial tree method. *Volume II* considers continuous models. Very readable, interesting and beautifully presented. *Volume I* complements and extends Chapter 7.
- **van der Hoek, John and Elliott, Robert J., Binomial Models in Finance: Springer**
  A very clear description of how binomial trees can be used in more advanced modelling. Topics include assets paying dividends, exchange rate

contracts and interest rate derivatives. The authors show how binomial tree models can be constructed to calculate values consistent with market prices.

- **Wilmott, Paul, Derivatives: The Theory and Practice of Financial Engineering: John Wiley**

  A first-class introduction to the subject; very well organised and extremely readable. The Excel diagrams make reader participation almost a certainty.

- **Wilmott, Paul, Howison, Sam and Dewynne, Jeff, The Mathematics of Financial Derivatives: Cambridge University Press**

  Although mathematically more advanced, the book is genuinely an 'introduction' to the subject. Very clear and readable. Probably the best introduction to the subject using the differential equation approach.

For Excel:

Advanced Modelling in Finance using Excel and VBA, Mary Jackson and Mike Staunton: Wiley Finance – an excellent book and really useful for performing calculations in Excel. Includes VBA programming.

Excel 2000/2003 VBA Programmer's Reference, John Green: Wrox – for serious programmers.

Excel 2003, Steve Johnson: Pearson, Prentice Hall

Excel 2003 in Easy Steps, Stephen Copestake: Computer Step

Maran Illustrated Excel 2003: Maran

Microsoft Office, Excel 2003 Quick Steps, John Cronan: McGraw-Hill

Visual Basic 2005 Demystified, Jeff Kent: McGraw-Hill

Assumptions

We assume (almost) throughout the book that the price an asset can be bought for is the same as the price the asset can be sold for. This gives the asset 'one price' which is convenient for pricing theory.

We assume no transaction costs. So when a commodity is bought or sold, there is no charge made by the agent handling the sale. Again, this is not wholly realistic, but this assumption does make it easier to see what is happening in the theory without becoming embroiled in administration.

We assume no costs of storage. This applies mainly in Chapter 2 with forward contracts on commodities.

Short selling is a way to derive profit from a fall in the value of a share or some other security. A 'short seller' will borrow a security and immediately sell it. The short seller hopes the security will then fall in value. If this happens, the short seller will buy the security (at a lower price) and replace what he has borrowed. The difference in prices becomes the short seller's profit.

If this sounds easy, there are strict regulations governing 'short sales'. Two of the non-legal regulations are that any dividends that are paid during the period in which the security has been borrowed must be paid to the rightful owner by the short seller, and if the security is required by the rightful owner, the short seller has to replace the security immediately. There are also dangerous overtones in short selling. There is the potential for unlimited loss. If the security rises in value, the short seller must purchase at the higher price (perhaps the considerably higher price) to replace the security.

We certainly are not advocating that the reader becomes involved in short sales. This is completely a game for the professionals. But we do use the idea of short selling in some of the pricing arguments.

Names of companies, firms and organisations

These are almost entirely fictitious. We have used the names BT and BP: all other names bear no resemblance to any organisation existing now or in the past. The reason for this is that, of course, the share price and the financial standing of a company change over time. So what might be a realistic share price today will almost certainly not be realistic by the time this is being read. Using real companies would mean that with high probability, the data would be inaccurate and possibly misleading. There are no such problems with a fictitious company.

To the reader

But what really matters is that the reader has the enthusiasm and determination to try out the examples and exercises for themselves. Put pen to paper. Try to see what is actually happening. Financial mathematics is not a spectator sport. You need to get involved. And involvement means doing. If the algebra is looking taxing, there are Excel spreadsheets to help you through the worst of it. We hope you enjoy the ideas that lie ahead. This is a beautiful subject: it is important and potentially highly profitable. It is hard to think of more compelling reasons to read a book.

Acknowledgements

With grateful thanks to Gary Cook for his invaluable advice in matters of Excel. To Ian Hammond, who, with his many friendly enquiries – 'How's the book going?' – shamed me into writing, when I would have preferred to be doing other things. To the referee for his/her many helpful, perceptive, well-informed and extremely useful observations. I am grateful to David Buik and Andrew Garrood of Cantor Index for very helpful initial discussions on the content of the book. To the editorial and production staff of Cambridge University Press for all their considerable expertise and their unfailingly helpful and patient advice. To Mike and Tim for listening, being occasionally impressed but always totally supportive. And to Dorothy, for her help with writing and editing, for being calming and encouraging and for providing a reassuringly normal and happy world when the writing was going badly. To all, I offer heartfelt thanks. Theirs was the inspiration. The mistakes, alas, are all mine.

An introduction to Excel

All the calculations in this book can be performed on a calculator. However, they can be performed more efficiently and much faster on a spreadsheet in Excel. If a calculation has to be repeated, then with a spreadsheet in place the repeat calculation is almost immediate. With a calculator, you just have to start again.

In this chapter we present a short introduction to those features of Excel that are used to perform calculations in this book. We recommend, however, that the reader acquires a complete introduction to Excel and learns more about this remarkable facility. To go further with financial mathematics, a knowledge of VBA (Visual Basic for Applications and available through Excel) or some other high-level programming language is essential. (See the texts described in the Introduction.)

The starting point for an Excel calculation is an Excel worksheet (Figure 1).

We have indicated the menu bar, the tool bars and the formula bar. Also, for future reference, we have indicated the chart wizard, the paste function and the name box.

Each cell in a worksheet has a name or a reference. This is **letter** followed by **number**. In Figure 1, the cell B6 is illustrated. Observe that the letter identifies the column (B) and the number identifies the row (6).

To enter a number, words or a formula in a particular cell, left click the required cell. The heavy border indicates that this is now the active cell. (The cell has been 'highlighted').

For a number or words:

type in the number or the words

press Enter

For a formula:

type = followed by the formula

The formula bar now has the symbols shown in Figure 2.

To enter the formula, click the Enter button. Or, press Enter. To cancel, click the cross.

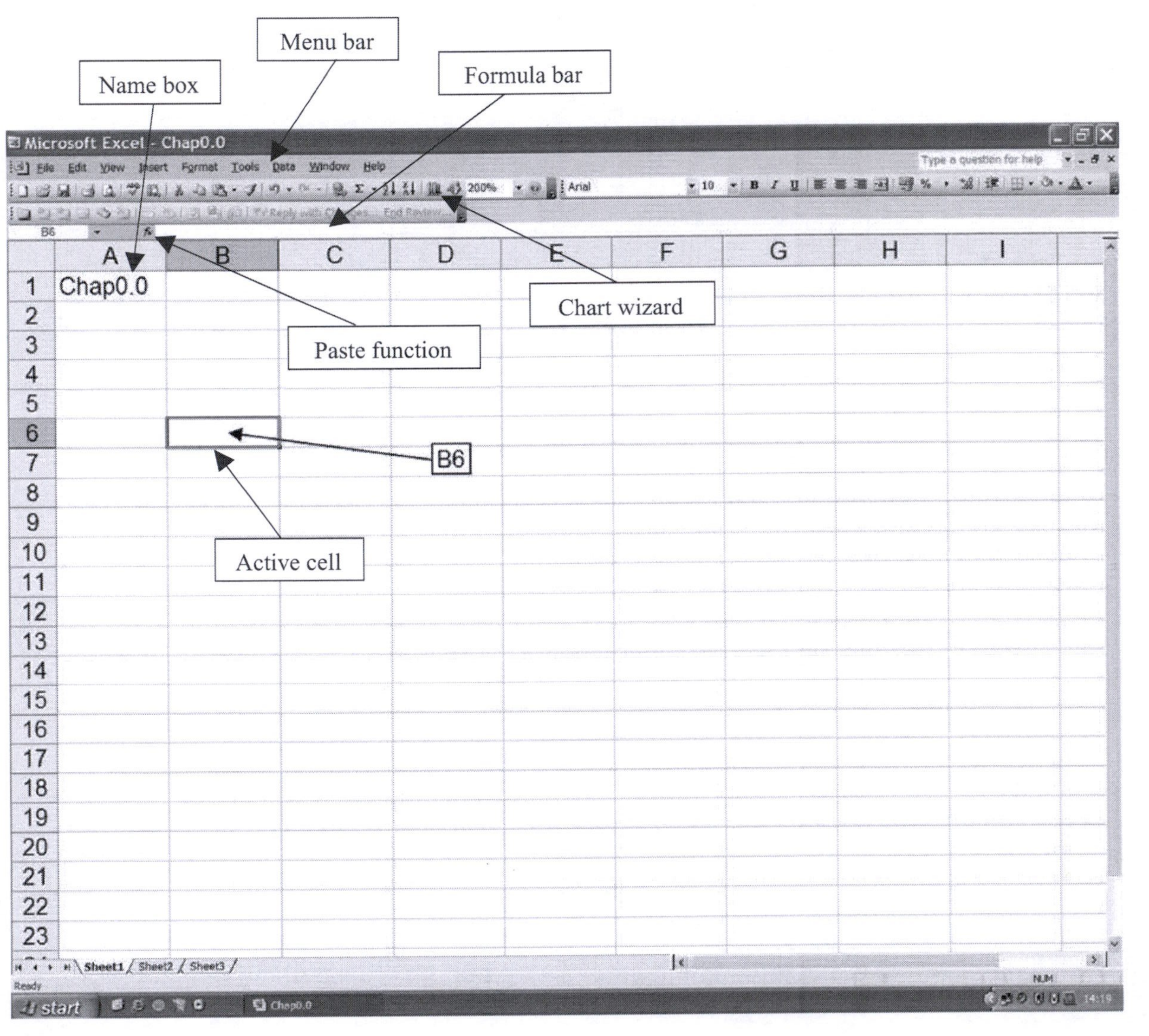
Menu bar
Name box
Formula bar
Microsoft Excel - Chap0.0
Chart wizard
Paste function
Chap0.0
B6
Active cell
Sheet1
Sheet2
Sheet3

Figure 1

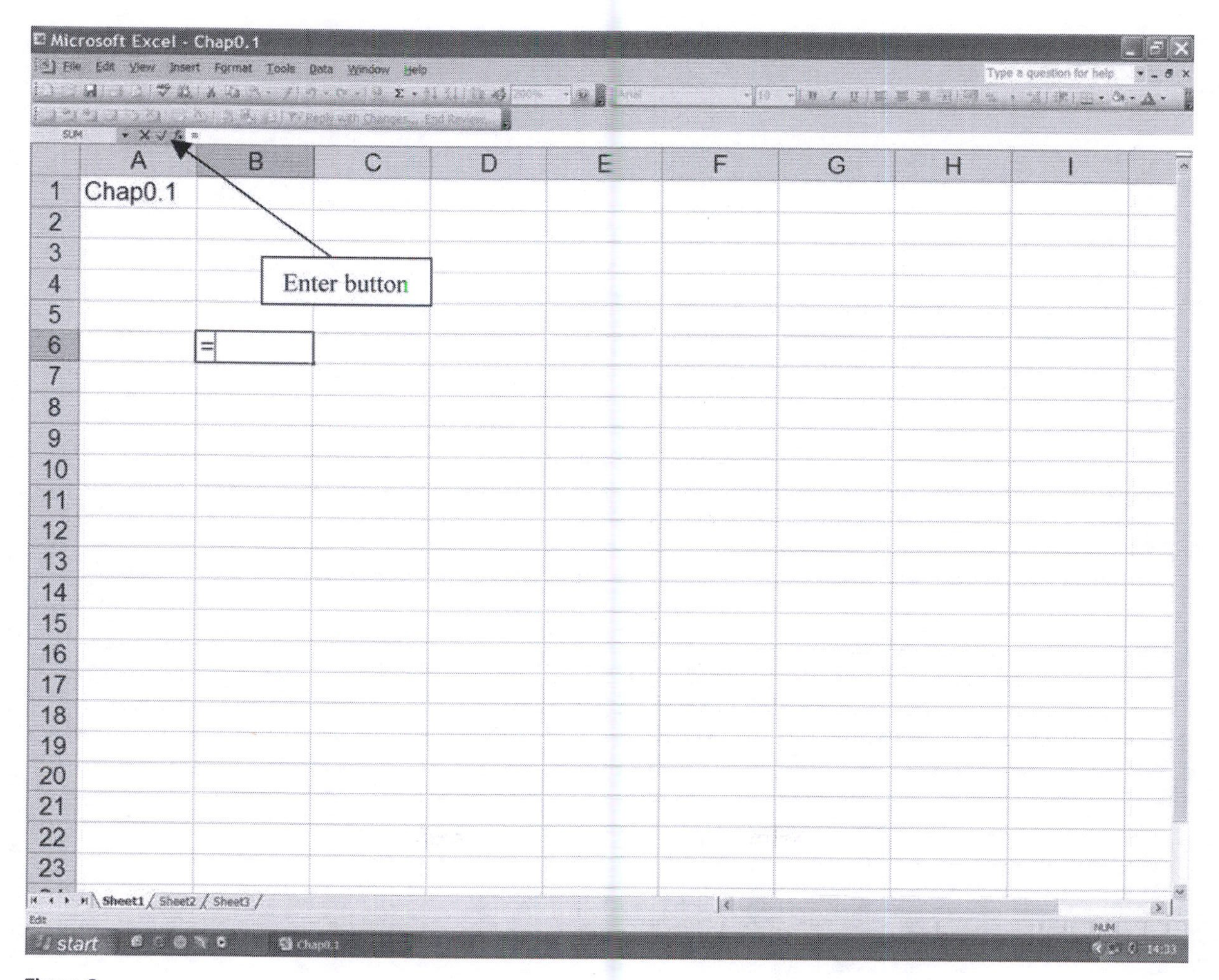
Microsoft Excel - Chap0.1
File Edit View Insert Format Tools Data Window Help
Type a question for help
A B C D E F G H I
Chap0.1
Enter button
=
Sheet1 Sheet2 Sheet3
start

Figure 2

Exercise

Enter 'asset value' in cell A5 (enter words)
Enter 10.3 in cell A6 (enter a number)
Enter 8.1 in cell A7
Now enter a formula to add these two numbers and store the sum in A8.
Click A8: type = A6 + A7: click the Enter button or press Enter.
The result should be as in Figure 3.

Note: from now on, to enter a formula we will write only 'press Enter'. But the option to click the Enter button is always there.

The way ahead

Excel has an easy way of entering expressions (e.g. $3x^2 - 4x + 1$) and then calculating the value of the expression for as many values of the underlying variable as are needed. We will illustrate the important techniques involving 'creating formulas', 'dragging down' and 'graph drawing' by calculating the value of $3x^2 - 4x + 1$ for x values $x = -5, -4.5, -4, \ldots 4.5, 5$ and then drawing the graph $y = 3x^2 - 4x + 1$ for x values $-5 \leq x \leq 5$. We then show this can be achieved more conveniently by using 'absolute cell referencing' and 'range names'. Then we point to the vast number of **functions** available in Excel. Finally, we will illustrate 'Goal Seek' by solving the equation $5e^{2R+1} = 37$.

(a) Creating formulas

We want to calculate the value of $3x^2 - 4x + 1$ for $x = -5$, $x = -4.5$, $x = -4, \ldots x = 4.5$, $x = 5$.

(i) Select the cell that is to contain the x value. Let this be D3.
Click D3. Enter −5. Press Enter.

(ii) Select the cell that is to contain the formula. Let this be E3.
Click E3: type = 3*D3*D3 − 4*D3 + 1: press Enter.
In E3, we have $3x^2 - 4x + 1$ evaluated at $x = -5$. (= 96)
This is good, but we can do much better.

(b) Drag down (evaluating formula in a range of cells and highlighting)

Click D4: type = D3 + 0.5: press Enter.

(We have entered a formula to add 0.5 to the number in the cell immediately above. You will see −4.5 appear in D4.)

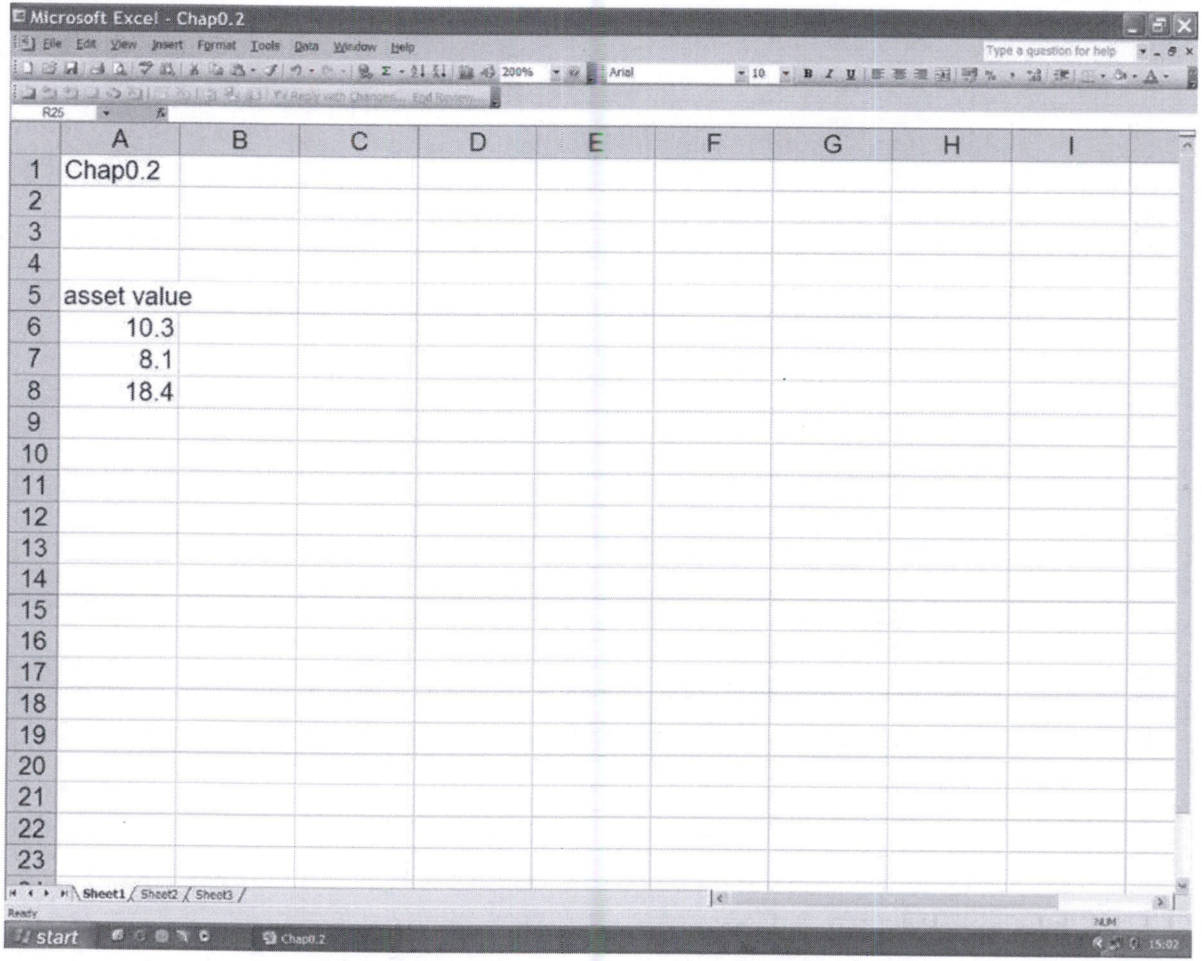

Microsoft Excel - Chap0.2

File Edit View Insert Format Tools Data Window Help

Type a question for help

200% Arial 10

R25

	A	B	C	D	E	F	G	H	I
1	Chap0.2								
2									
3									
4									
5	asset value								
6	10.3								
7	8.1								
8	18.4								
9									
10									
11									
12									
13									
14									
15									
16									
17									
18									
19									
20									
21									
22									
23									

Sheet1 / Sheet2 / Sheet3

Ready NUM

start Chap0.2 15:02

Figure 3

See a small black square in the bottom right-hand corner of the heavy border. This is called the **drag handle**.

Click on the drag handle and holding down the mouse button, drag down column D19 cells (to D23).

Release the mouse button.

You will see Figure 4.

These are the 'x values'.

We repeat the drag down procedure with E3.

Click E3.

See the drag handle in the bottom right-hand corner of the heavy border.

Click on the drag handle and holding down the mouse button, drag down column E twenty cells (to E23).

Release the mouse button.

You will see Figure 5.

In E3:E23 we see the result of evaluating $3x^2 - 4x + 1$ at the different x values shown in column D.

Click E10. In the formula bar, you will see 3*D10*D10 – 4*D10 + 1, which is our formula evaluated at D10.

The words 'drag down' are used also in **highlighting**. When a cell is clicked, the cell becomes shaded and we say the cell has been 'highlighted'. If a range of cells is to be highlighted, click the top cell and without releasing the mouse button, drag down to the bottom cell in the range. Release the mouse button. You will see that the range of cells has been 'highlighted'.

Note that when a calculation is being 'dragged down' through a range of cells, it is the drag handle that is clicked before the mouse drags the calculation through the cells. When a range of cells is being highlighted, the top cell in the range is clicked before the mouse is dragged to the bottom cell in the range.

(c) Graph drawing

Click D3. Hold down the mouse button and drag down to D23. Release the mouse button. You will see D3:D23 highlighted.

Press CTRL and keep this button depressed. Click E3. Drag down to E23. This will highlight E3:E23 (*now you will see both columns highlighted*).

Release the mouse button and CTRL.

Click 'Chart Wizard' on tool bar (see Figure 1).

You will see Figure 6.

Click 'XY (scatter)'. Click the highlighted graph (as shown).

Click Next.

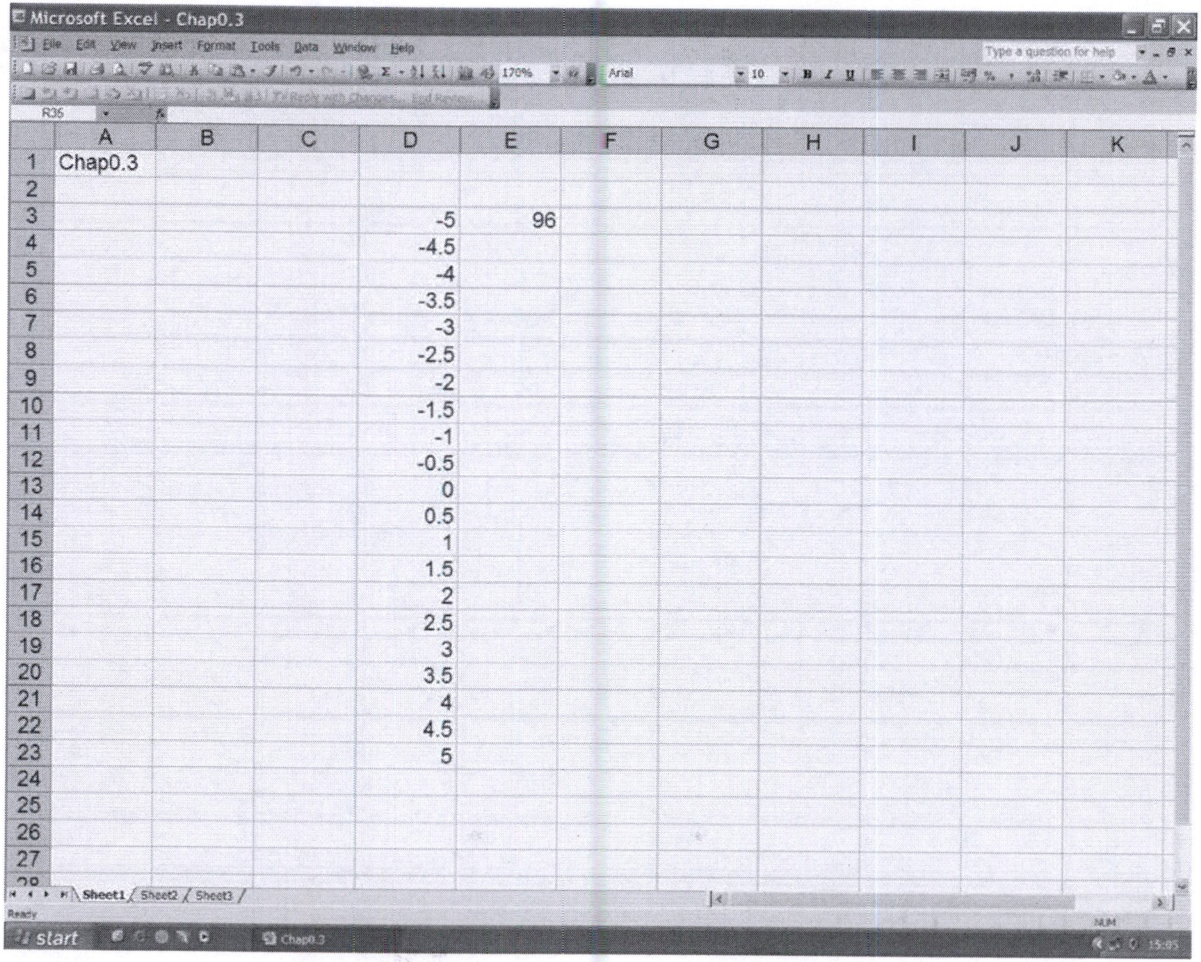

Microsoft Excel - Chap0.3

	A	B	C	D	E	F	G	H	I	J	K
1	Chap0.3										
2											
3				-5	96						
4				-4.5							
5				-4							
6				-3.5							
7				-3							
8				-2.5							
9				-2							
10				-1.5							
11				-1							
12				-0.5							
13				0							
14				0.5							
15				1							
16				1.5							
17				2							
18				2.5							
19				3							
20				3.5							
21				4							
22				4.5							
23				5							
24											
25											
26											
27											

Sheet1 / Sheet2 / Sheet3

Figure 4

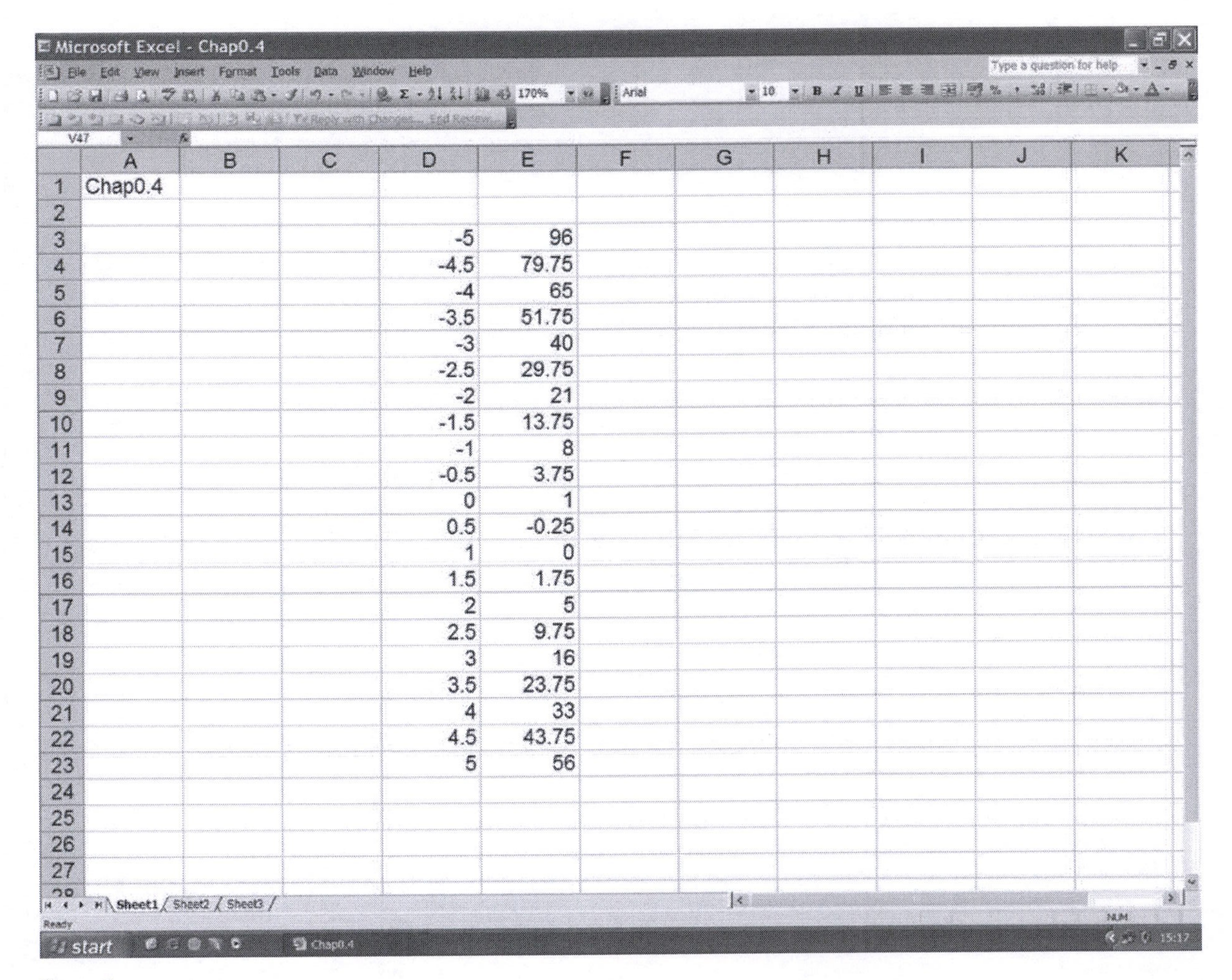
Microsoft Excel - Chap0.4
File Edit View Insert Format Tools Data Window Help
Type a question for help
170%
Arial
10
V47
A
B
C
D
E
F
G
H
I
J
K
Chap0.4
-5 96
-4.5 79.75
-4 65
-3.5 51.75
-3 40
-2.5 29.75
-2 21
-1.5 13.75
-1 8
-0.5 3.75
0 1
0.5 -0.25
1 0
1.5 1.75
2 5
2.5 9.75
3 16
3.5 23.75
4 33
4.5 43.75
5 56
Sheet1
Sheet2
Sheet3
Ready
NUM
start
Chap0.4
15:17

Figure 5

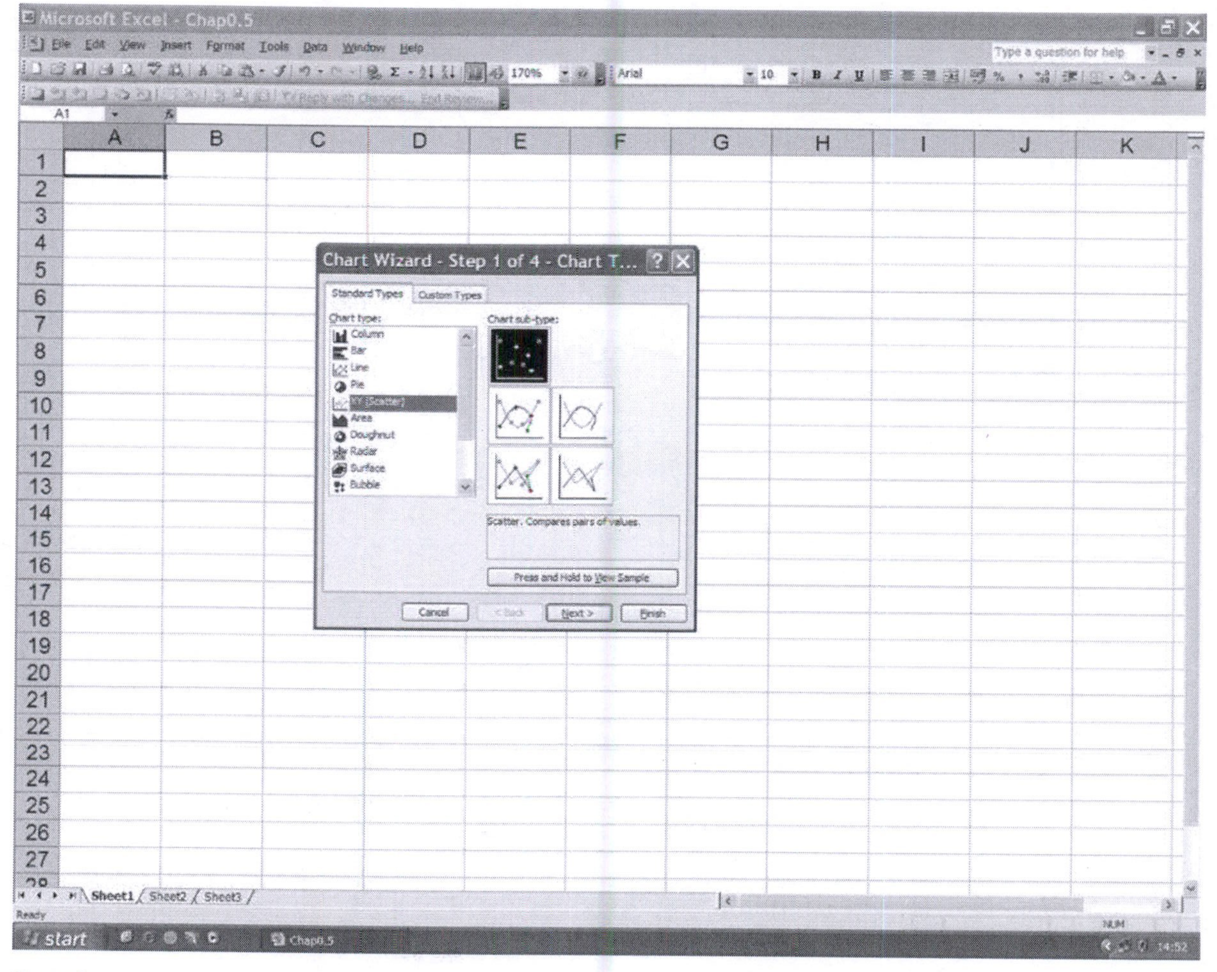
Microsoft Excel - Chap0.5
File Edit View Insert Format Tools Data Window Help
Type a question for help
170%
Arial
10
A1
Chart Wizard - Step 1 of 4 - Chart T...
Standard Types
Custom Types
Chart type:
Column
Bar
Line
Pie
XY (Scatter)
Area
Doughnut
Radar
Surface
Bubble
Chart sub-type:
Scatter. Compares pairs of values.
Press and Hold to View Sample
Cancel
< Back
Next >
Finish
Sheet1
Sheet2
Sheet3
Ready
NUM
start
Chap0.5
14:52

Figure 6

Add title and titles for X and Y axes if you wish.

Click Next.

Click Finish.

And there is the graph $y = 3x^2 - 4x + 1$ – Figure 7.

Note. You could have clicked on D3 and dragged down and across until D3:E23 were highlighted. Then click 'Chart Wizard' and continue as above. The process of highlighting one column at a time is useful when the required columns are not adjacent. Such data is known as noncontiguous data.

(d) Absolute cell referencing

If you wanted to draw another quadratic graph, you would have to re-enter the equation in E3. A neater way of doing this would be to store the numbers in the equation (3, −4, 1) in a separate area of the worksheet and just change these numbers when you wanted to change the equation. We will store the numbers in B3, B4, B5, as shown in Figure 8.

(Note that we have put in some descriptive headers to give the worksheet some meaning.)

To enter the calculations in E3:E23, it might be tempting to proceed as follows:

Click E3: type = B3*D3*D3 − B4*D3 + B5: press Enter. Drag down to E23.

If you do enter this, you will get Figure 9.

This is clearly wrong.

The error occurred when we dragged down. With the E3 entry as shown, the B3, B4 and B5 cells were also dragged down. So what was calculated in E4 was $-4{*}x^2 + 1{*}x + 0$ and in E5 we have $1{*}x^2 + 0{*}x + 0$ and so on. To prevent this happening we can use absolute cell referencing. Putting $ signs in front of the letter and the number ($B$3) will fix the number to be the entry in B3 no matter how often we drag down or whenever we refer to this cell. Inclusion of the dollar sign is known as absolute cell referencing. We have done this in Figure 10.

Notes:

(i) Putting a $ sign in front of the letter only ($B3) will 'anchor' that column. So $B3 means that column B is fixed and will not change when the drag handle is moved across columns. Similarly, putting a $ sign in front of the number only (B$3) will anchor that row, so B$3 means that row 3 is fixed and will not change when the drag handle is moved across rows. In the above example, we could have used B$3, B$4 and B$5 to fix the three coefficients.

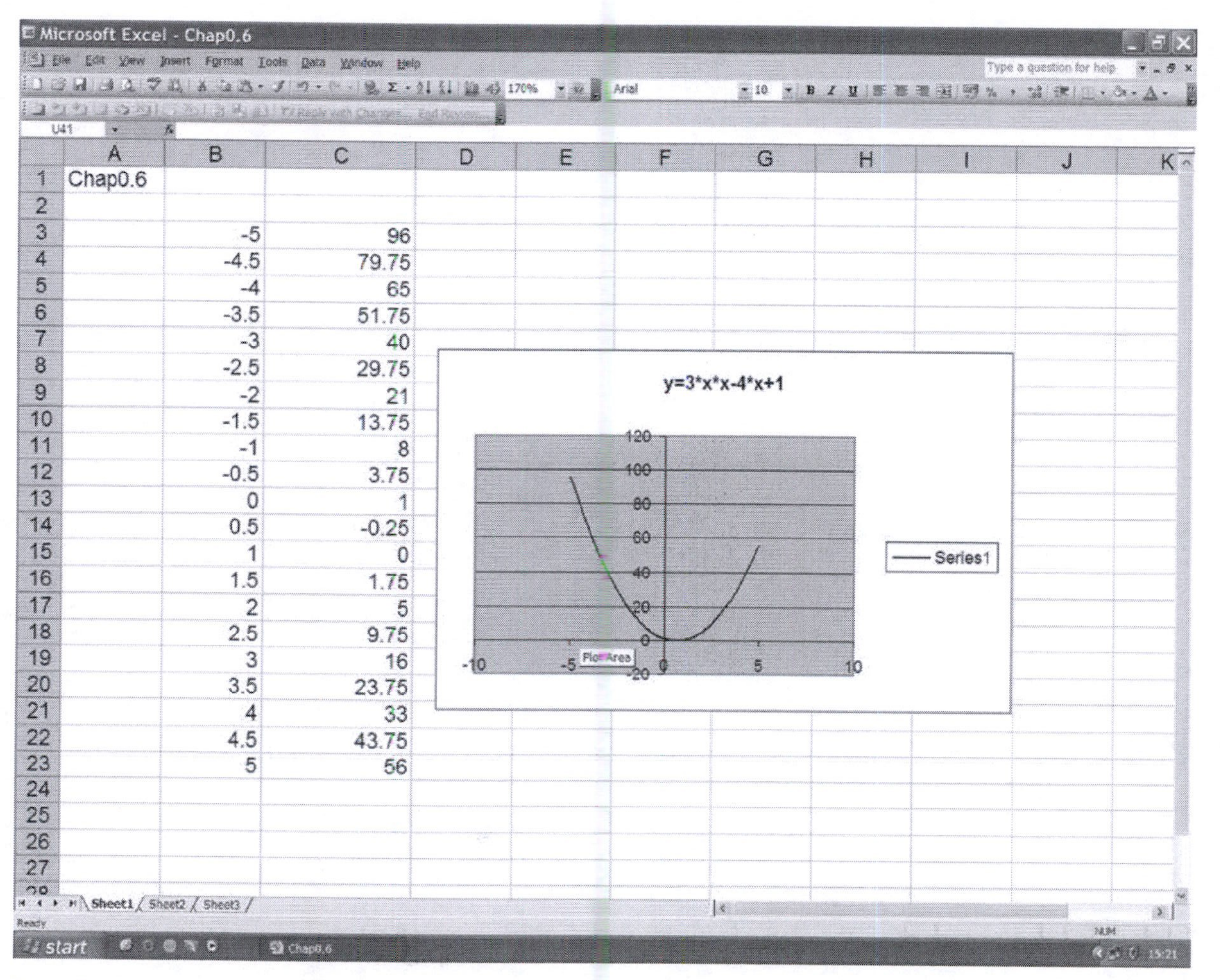
Microsoft Excel - Chap0.6
File Edit View Insert Format Tools Data Window Help
Type a question for help
170%
Arial
10
U41
A B C D E F G H I J K
Chap0.6
-5 96
-4.5 79.75
-4 65
-3.5 51.75
-3 40
-2.5 29.75
-2 21
-1.5 13.75
-1 8
-0.5 3.75
0 1
0.5 -0.25
1 0
1.5 1.75
2 5
2.5 9.75
3 16
3.5 23.75
4 33
4.5 43.75
5 56
y=3*x*x-4*x+1
120
100
80
60
40
20
0
-20
-10
-5
0
5
10
Series1
Sheet1
Sheet2
Sheet3
Ready
NUM
start
Chap0.6
15:21

Figure 7

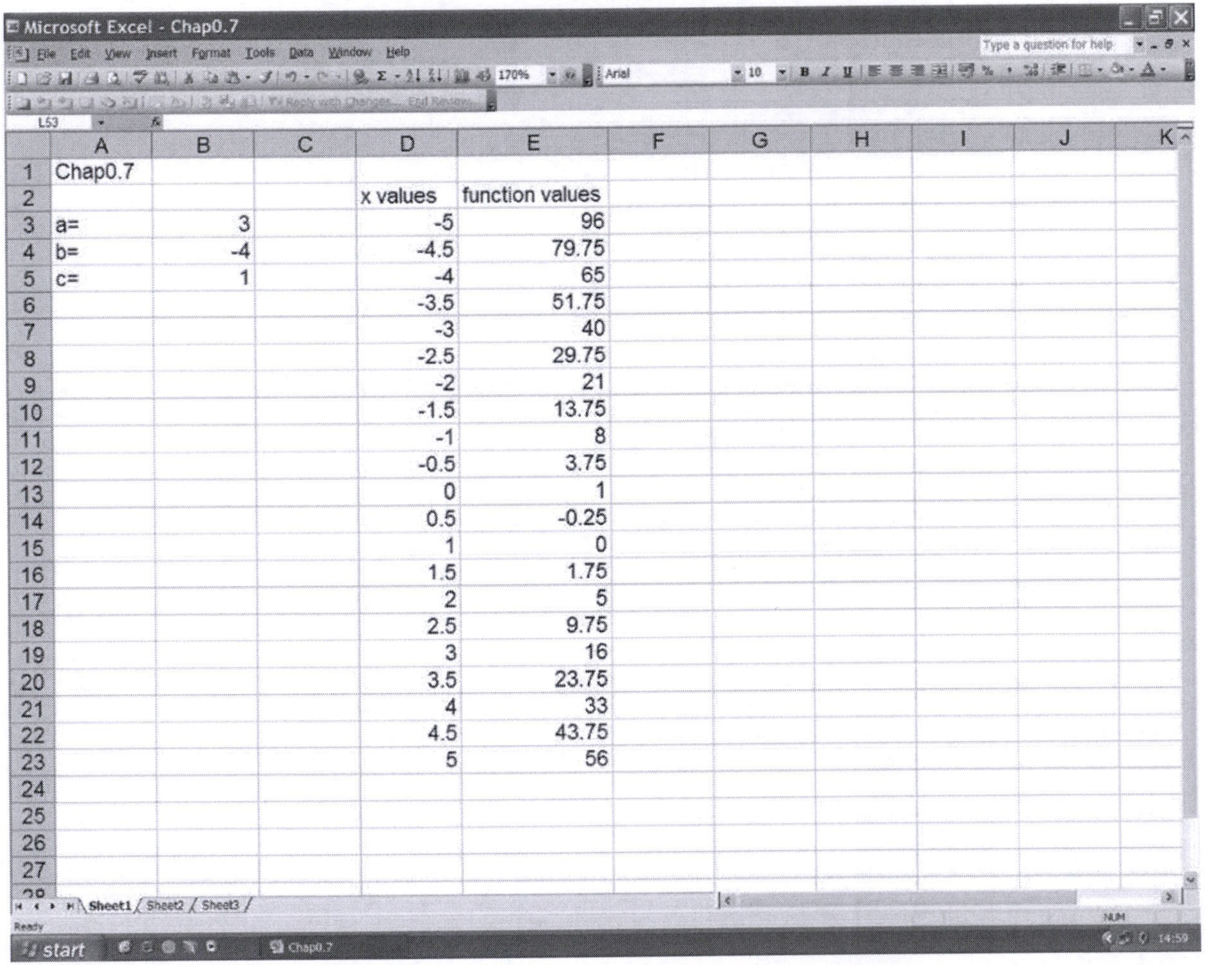

Microsoft Excel - Chap0.7

File Edit View Insert Format Tools Data Window Help

	A	B	C	D	E
1	Chap0.7				
2				x values	function values
3	a=	3		-5	96
4	b=	-4		-4.5	79.75
5	c=	1		-4	65
6				-3.5	51.75
7				-3	40
8				-2.5	29.75
9				-2	21
10				-1.5	13.75
11				-1	8
12				-0.5	3.75
13				0	1
14				0.5	-0.25
15				1	0
16				1.5	1.75
17				2	5
18				2.5	9.75
19				3	16
20				3.5	23.75
21				4	33
22				4.5	43.75
23				5	56

Sheet1 / Sheet2 / Sheet3

Figure 8

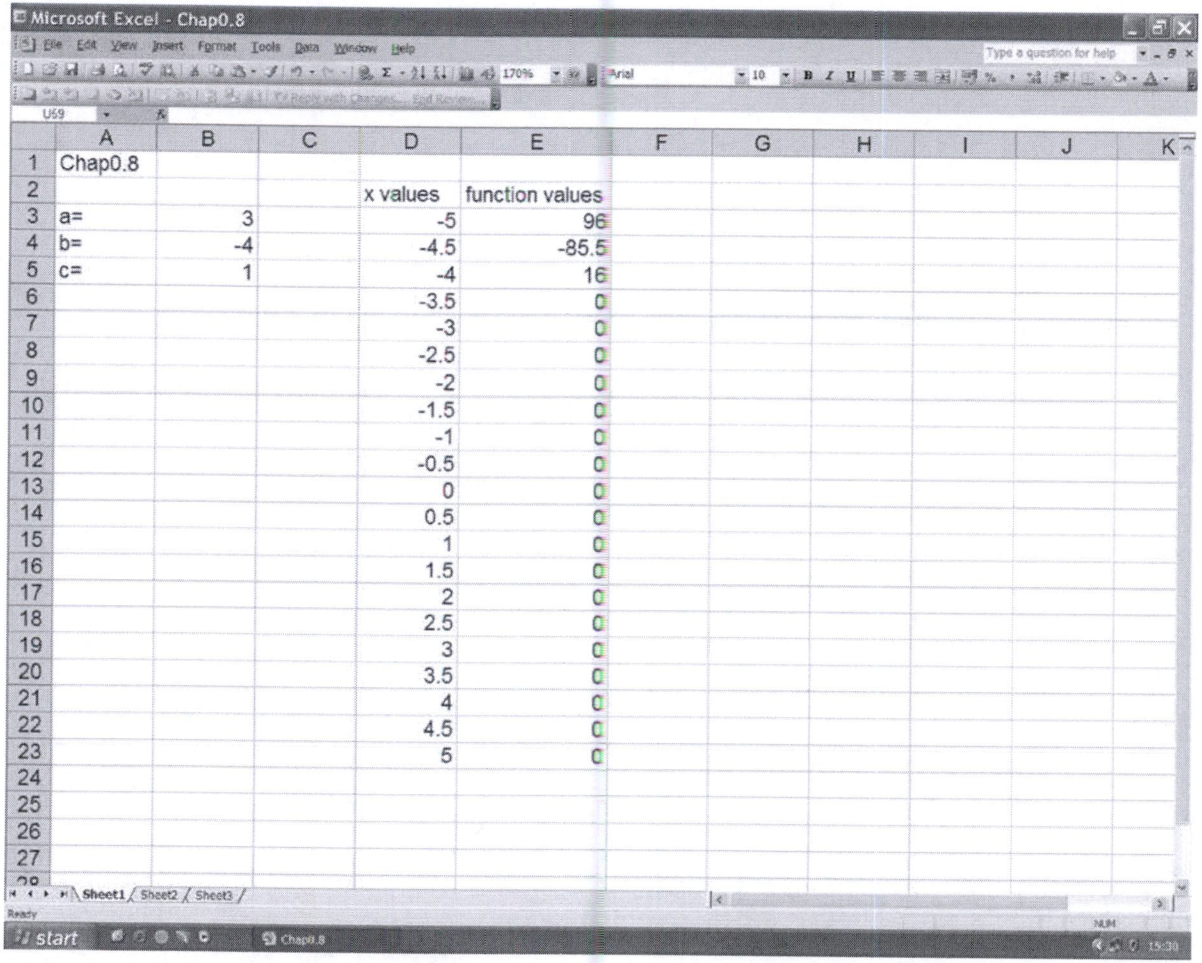

Microsoft Excel - Chap0.8

	A	B	C	D	E
1	Chap0.8				
2				x values	function values
3	a=	3		-5	96
4	b=	-4		-4.5	-85.5
5	c=	1		-4	16
6				-3.5	0
7				-3	0
8				-2.5	0
9				-2	0
10				-1.5	0
11				-1	0
12				-0.5	0
13				0	0
14				0.5	0
15				1	0
16				1.5	0
17				2	0
18				2.5	0
19				3	0
20				3.5	0
21				4	0
22				4.5	0
23				5	0

Sheet1 / Sheet2 / Sheet3

Figure 9

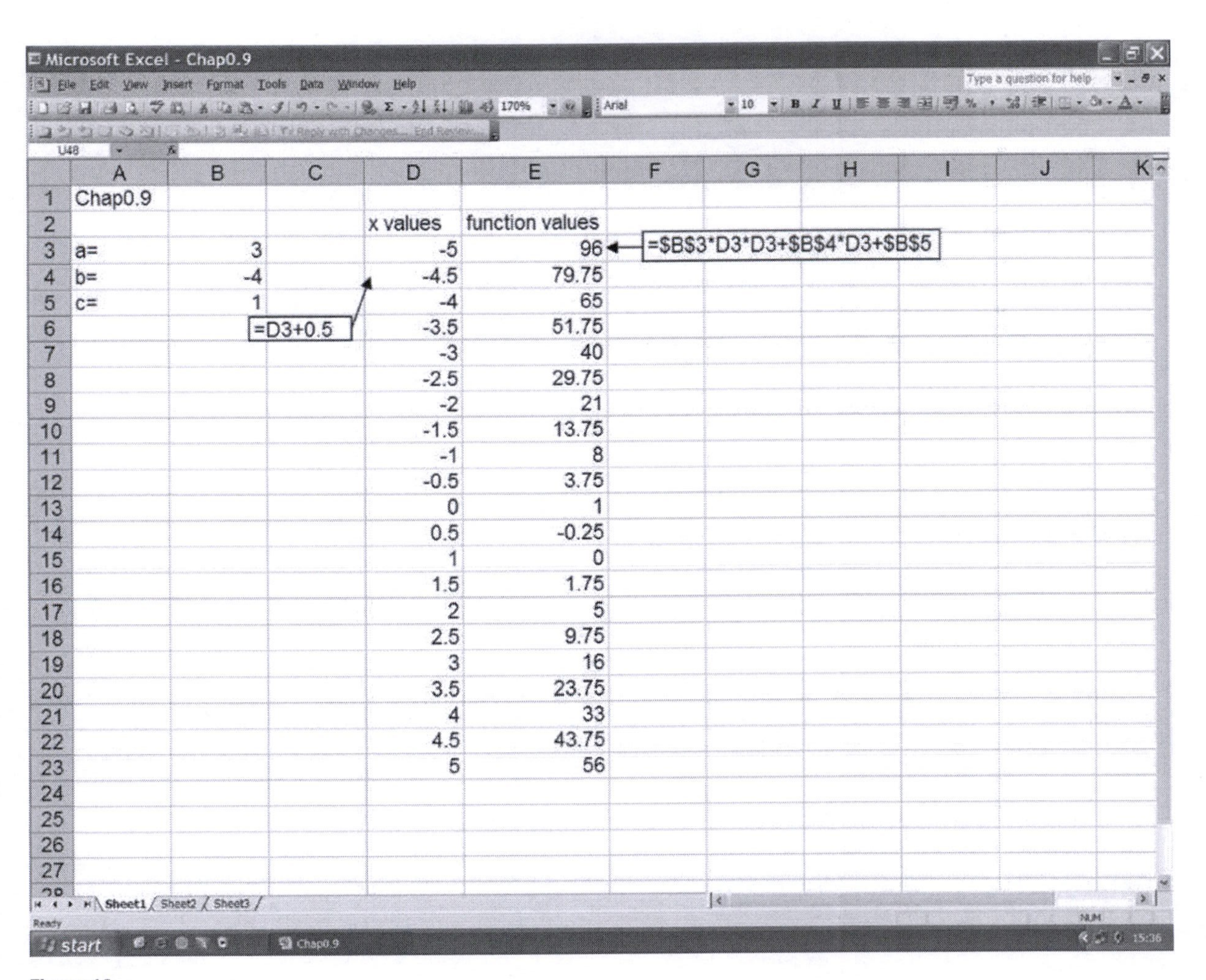

Microsoft Excel - Chap0.9
Chap0.9
a=
3
b=
-4
c=
1
=D3+0.5
x values
function values
=$B$3*D3*D3+$B$4*D3+$B$5
-5
96
-4.5
79.75
-4
65
-3.5
51.75
-3
40
-2.5
29.75
-2
21
-1.5
13.75
-1
8
-0.5
3.75
0
1
0.5
-0.25
1
0
1.5
1.75
2
5
2.5
9.75
3
16
3.5
23.75
4
33
4.5
43.75
5
56
Sheet1
Sheet2
Sheet3

Figure 10

(ii) In the worksheets in the book, whenever there is a column of numbers and a formula addressing the top cell in the column (as in columns D and E in Figure 10) we will usually have **dragged down** and the formula at the top of the column will contain either absolute cell referencing or range names (described below). This is a very useful way of performing calculations quickly. We have used it frequently in the following chapters.

(e) Range names

Most of the spreadsheets in this book will use a formula to calculate the numerical entry in one or more cells. If we use absolute cell referencing, as shown in Figure 10, it will not always be easy to see immediately what the terms in the formula represent. One way of making formulas more easily recognisable is to use 'range names'. First, we describe how to give a single cell, or a range of cells, a name. Then we will show how this process leads to greater clarity.

To name a cell or a range of cells:

(a) Click the cell (or highlight the range of cells).
(b) Click the name box on the menu bar.
(c) Type in a name for the cell or for the range of cells. The name can include upper- and lower-case letters, numbers and some punctuation, but no spaces. (Some words, e.g. intrate, are key words used elsewhere in Excel and might not be accepted.) Since the purpose is greater clarity, it makes sense to choose names that reflect the information contained in the cell(s).
(d) Press Enter.

The range name will appear in the name box whenever the cell or the range of cells is highlighted.

Note: in the following, it might be helpful to know whether a name is being used to represent a single quantity or a set of quantities. If a name represents a single quantity, it will be called a **cell name** (the single quantity will reside in a single cell). If the name represents a set of quantities, it will be called a **range name** (the set will occupy a range of cells).

Example

The annual interest rate is 5.5%. An investor wishes to deposit £10 000 and wants to know what her investment will be worth at the end of each of the following ten years. Construct a spreadsheet that will calculate this information.

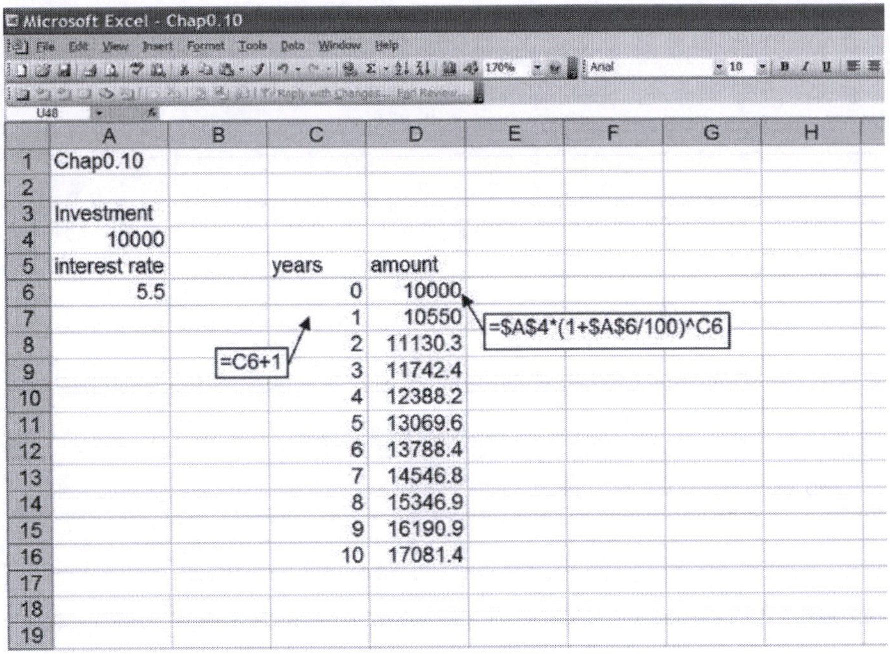

Microsoft Excel - Chap0.10

	A	B	C	D	E	F	G	H
1	Chap0.10							
2								
3	Investment							
4	10000							
5	interest rate		years	amount				
6	5.5		0	10000				
7			1	10550				
8			2	11130.3				
9			3	11742.4				
10			4	12388.2				
11			5	13069.6				
12			6	13788.4				
13			7	14546.8				
14			8	15346.9				
15			9	16190.9				
16			10	17081.4				
17								
18								
19								

=C6+1

=$A$4*(1+$A$6/100)^C6

Figure 11

Solution

We will do this twice: once using absolute cell referencing and again using range names.

In Figure 11, the investment (10 000) is stored in A4, the interest rate (5.5) in A6 and the times at which the amount of the investment has to be calculated are stored in the range of cells C6:C16. We want the amount of the investment, after the corresponding number of years, to be stored in D6:D16. The amount, after (for example) two years will be $10\,000^*(1+\frac{5.5}{100})^2$. This suggests that we click D6: type $= \$A\$4^*(1+\$A\$6/100)\hat{}C6$: press Enter.

Dragging down gives the required amounts.

Now give names to the investment, the interest rate and the time of the investment. (See Figure 11).

Click A4. Click the name box: type investment: press Enter.

Click A6. Click the name box: type rate: press Enter.

Click C6 and holding down the mouse key, drag down to C16. (This highlights C6:C16.) Click the name box: type years: press Enter.

Click D6. Type = investment*(1 + rate/100)^years: press Enter.

Drag this calculation down to D16.

Microsoft Excel - Chap0.11

	A	B	C	D	E	F	G	H
1	Chap0.11							
2								
3	Investment							
4	10000							
5	interest rate		years	amount				
6	5.5		0	10000				
7			1	10550				
8			2	11130.3	=investment*(1+rate/100)^years			
9		=C6+1	3	11742.4				
10			4	12388.2				
11			5	13069.6				
12			6	13788.4				
13			7	14546.8				
14			8	15346.9				
15			9	16190.9				
16			10	17081.4				
17								

Figure 12

We have the same result. But now, when the formula is printed, it is perfectly clear what has been calculated.

Alternatively, rather than typing in 'investment', 'rate', 'years', you could highlight the cell or the range of cells containing these quantities. Excel will then enter the range name in the formula (Figure 12).

Note that investment is a cell name while years is a range name.

Because range names are used extensively in the book, we provide a second example where both variables are stored in cell ranges.

Example

The table gives the probabilities associated with six x values.

x	5	7	8	10	12	15
prob	0.1	0.05	0.3	0.15	0.25	0.15

Calculate: $0.1 \times 5+0.05 \times 7+0.3 \times 8+0.15 \times 10+0.25 \times 12+0.15 \times 15$

(This gives the 'Expected value' of the x values, or, as it is written in statistics books, E(x).)

Solution

Again, we perform this calculation twice, once with absolute cell referencing and a second time with range names.

Enter the x values in A4:A9 and the corresponding probabilities in B4:B9.

Click C4: type = B4:A4: press Enter. Drag down to C9.

To add these products, use the SUM function in Excel.

Click C10: type = SUM(C4:C9): press Enter. (This simply adds the contents of cells C4 through to C9.)

We have Figure 13.

Click A4 and drag down to A9. Click the name box: type x: press Enter.

Click B4 and drag down to B9. Click the name box: type prob: press Enter.

Click C4: type = prob*x: press Enter. Drag down to C9.

Highlight C4:C9. Click the name box: type = probtimesx: press Enter.

To add the products, click C10: type = SUM(probtimesx): press Enter.

Alternatively, instead of typing 'x' and 'prob' and 'probtimesx', you could have highlighted the cell or range of cells and allowed Excel to write these names in the formula for you.

The calculations are identical, but the formula boxes explain much more clearly what has been calculated (Figure 14).

It is important to be aware that most of the spreadsheets in this book contain data and formulas carrying range names. To recreate one of these spreadsheets on your computer, note that each formula will contain (usually) several named quantities. For each name:

- Highlight the cell or the range of cells corresponding to that name.
- Click the name box and type in that name. Press Enter.

Then:

- Click the cell containing the formula. Type = followed by the formula as written. Press Enter.
- If necessary, drag down the calculations.
- If these calculations are to be used in another formula, highlight the cells, click the name box and name this cell range, as indicated in the spreadsheet.

To illustrate, consider Figure 15 (which calculates the forward price of a dividend paying asset).

To implement this spreadsheet:

Click B2: click the name box: type spot: press Enter.

Click B3: click the name box: type rate: press Enter.

Click B4: click the name box: type comp: press Enter.

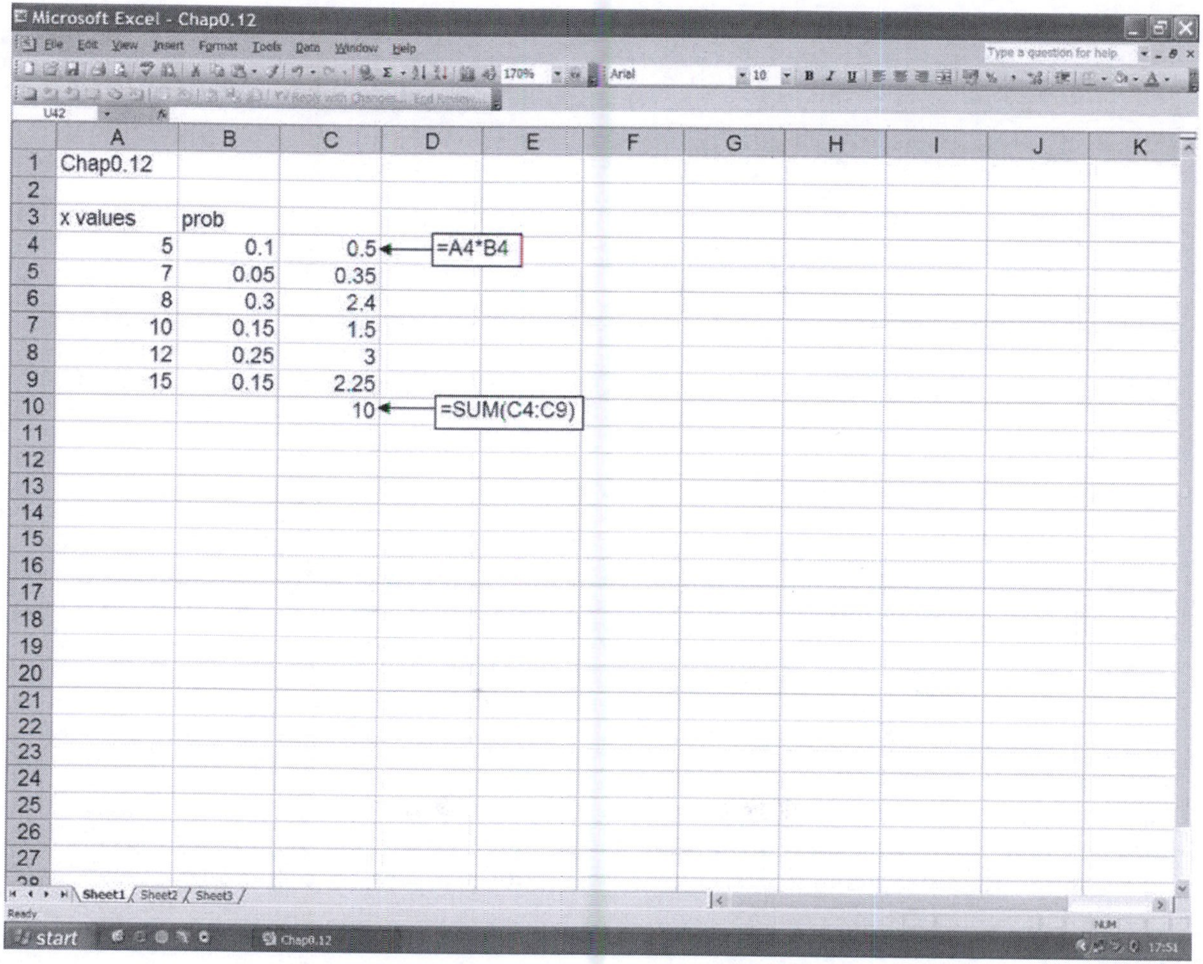

Microsoft Excel - Chap0.12

	A	B	C	D	E
1	Chap0.12				
2					
3	x values	prob			
4	5	0.1	0.5	← =A4*B4	
5	7	0.05	0.35		
6	8	0.3	2.4		
7	10	0.15	1.5		
8	12	0.25	3		
9	15	0.15	2.25		
10			10	← =SUM(C4:C9)	

Sheet1 / Sheet2 / Sheet3

Figure 13

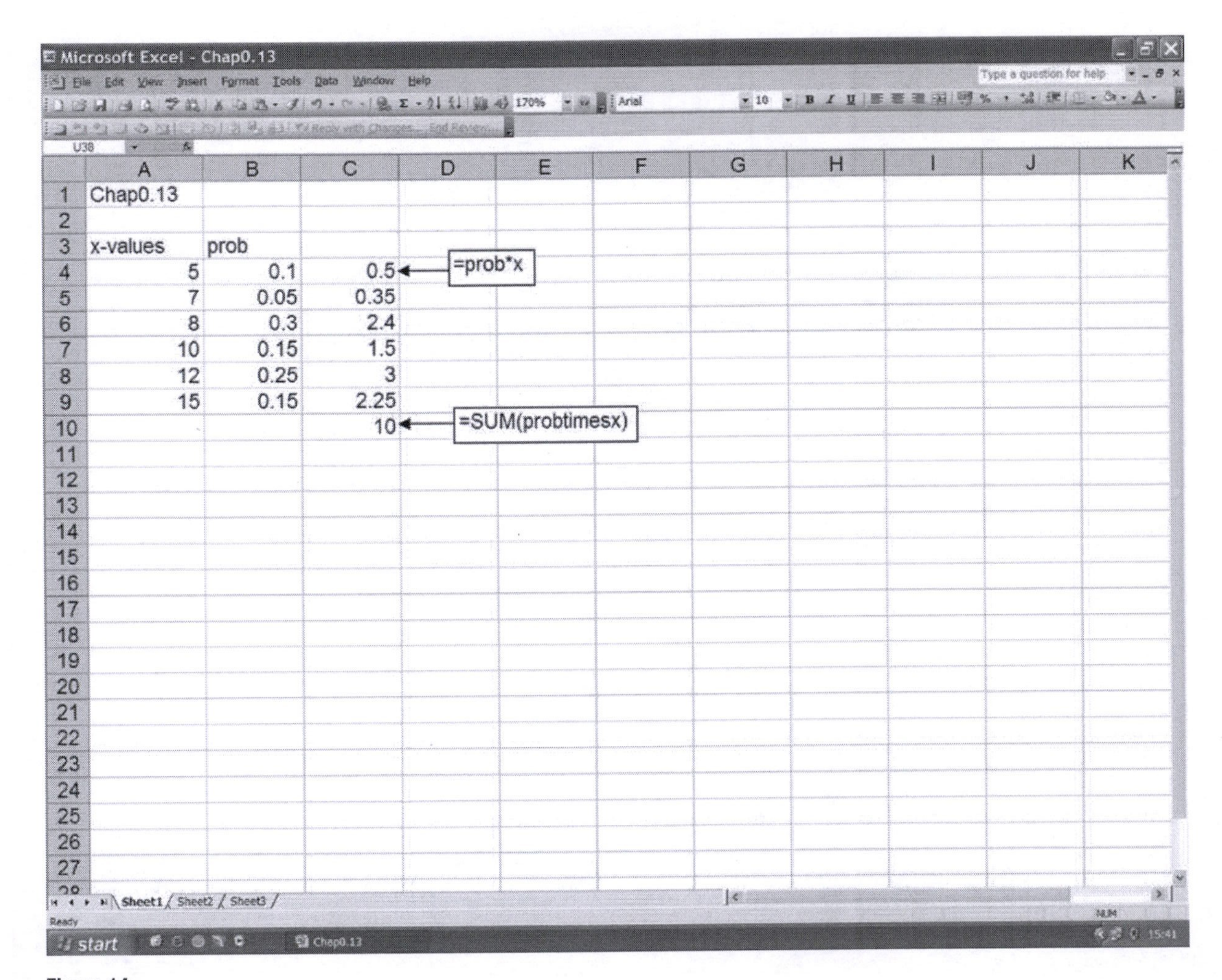
Microsoft Excel - Chap0.13
Chap0.13
x-values
prob
5
0.1
0.5
7
0.05
0.35
8
0.3
2.4
10
0.15
1.5
12
0.25
3
15
0.15
2.25
10
=prob*x
=SUM(probtimesx)
Sheet1
Sheet2
Sheet3

Figure 14

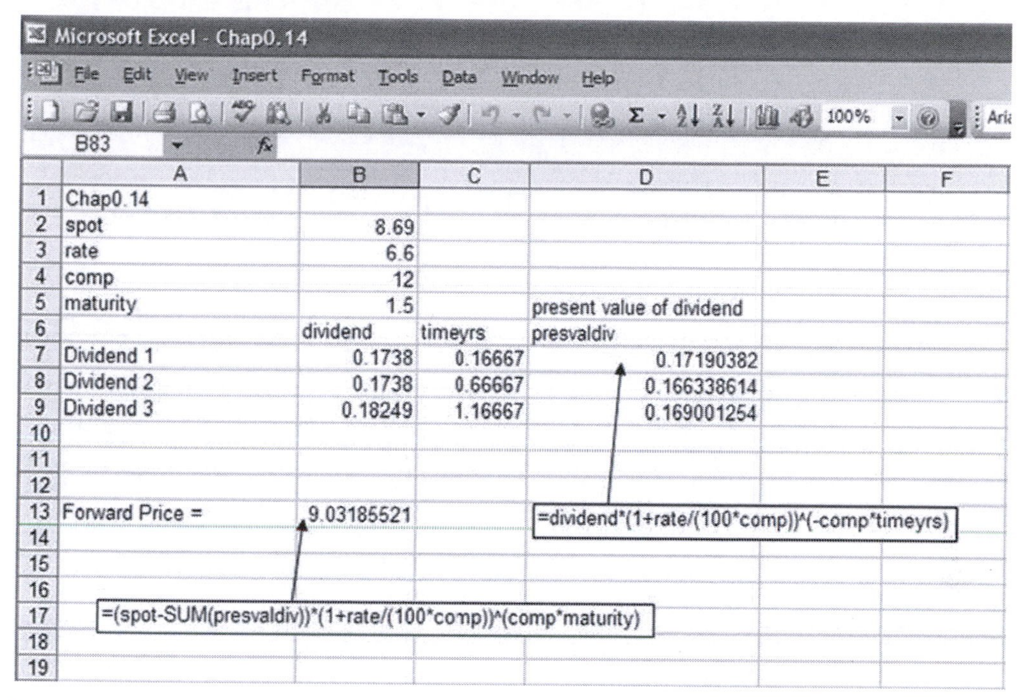

Figure 15

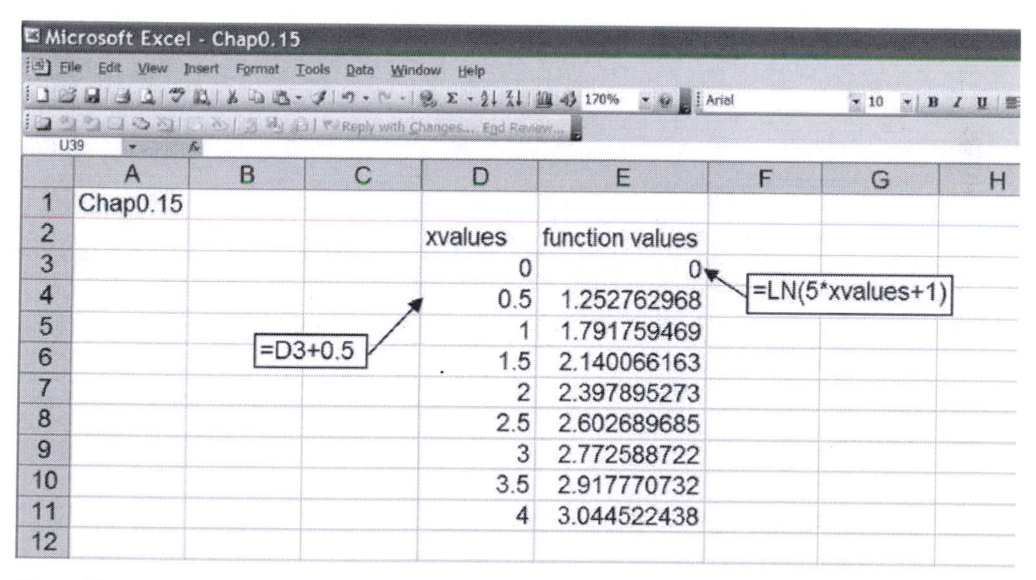

Figure 16

Click B5: click the name box: type maturity: press Enter.
Click B7 and highlight B7:B9: click the name box: type dividend: press Enter.
Click C7 and highlight C7:C9: click the name box: type timeyrs: press Enter.
Click D7: type = dividend*(1 + rate/(100*comp))^(−comp*timeyrs): press Enter.
(Or you could highlight the relevant cells to avoid having to type all this.)
Drag down to D9.
Click D7 and highlight D7:D9: click the name box: type presvaldiv: press Enter.
Click B13: type
= (spot – SUM(presvaldiv))*(1 + rate/(100*comp)) ^(comp* maturity): press Enter.

The calculations are complete. (But note again: the typing could be reduced by highlighting the relevant cells.)

(f) Functions

Excel contains many (bewilderingly many) built-in functions. To see these, click the paste function.

Most functions require arguments and these are asked for by Excel when you click the paste function and select the function you require. However, you can also just type in the function from the keyboard. If you type in exactly what is shown in the worksheets that follow, the calculations will go through perfectly well. This is illustrated in the following.

Example

Draw the graph $y = \ln(5x + 1)$ for values of x satisfying $0 \le x \le 4$ and taking $x = 0$, $x = 0.5$, $x = 1$, ... $x = 4$. (Here, ln represents the natural logarithm. This function will be used a great deal in this book.) Find the mean of the y values calculated from these values of x.

Solution

Click D3: enter 0: press Enter.
Click D4: type = D3 + 0.5: press Enter.
Drag down to D11.
Highlight D3:D11.
Click name box: type xvalues: press Enter.
Click E3: type = LN(5*xvalues + 1): press Enter.

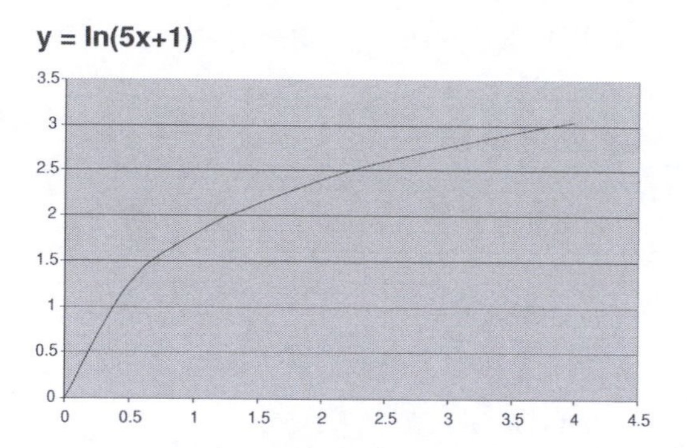

Figure 17

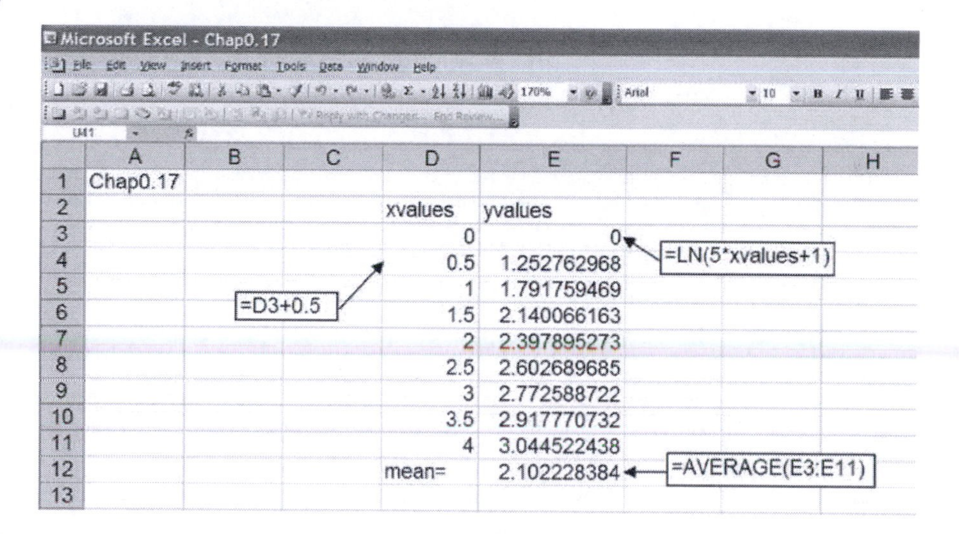

	A	B	C	D	E	F	G	H
1	Chap0.17							
2				xvalues	yvalues			
3				0	0			
4				0.5	1.252762968			
5				1	1.791759469			
6				1.5	2.140066163			
7				2	2.397895273			
8				2.5	2.602689685			
9				3	2.772588722			
10				3.5	2.917770732			
11				4	3.044522438			
12				mean=	2.102228384			
13								

Figure 18

Drag down to E11 and you will see Figure 16.

Highlight D3:D11 and E3:E11 as shown in (c) Graph drawing. Click Chart Wizard and follow the graph drawing procedure described in section (c) (Figure 17).

To calculate the mean of the y values, we use the AVERAGE function.

Click E12: type = AVERAGE(E3:E11): press Enter.

Or, highlight E3:E11: click the name box and type yvalues: press Enter.

Click E12: type = AVERAGE(yvalues): press Enter (Figure 18).

In this book, the functions used most are LN and EXP [EXP calculates e^x and requires one argument: e.g. e^{-2} becomes EXP(−2)] But we use also (Chapter 7) NORMSDIST. This gives Prob($X \leq x$) where X is distributed

N(0,1). NORMSDIST requires one argument, e.g. Prob($X \leq 1$) is entered as NORMSDIST(1)

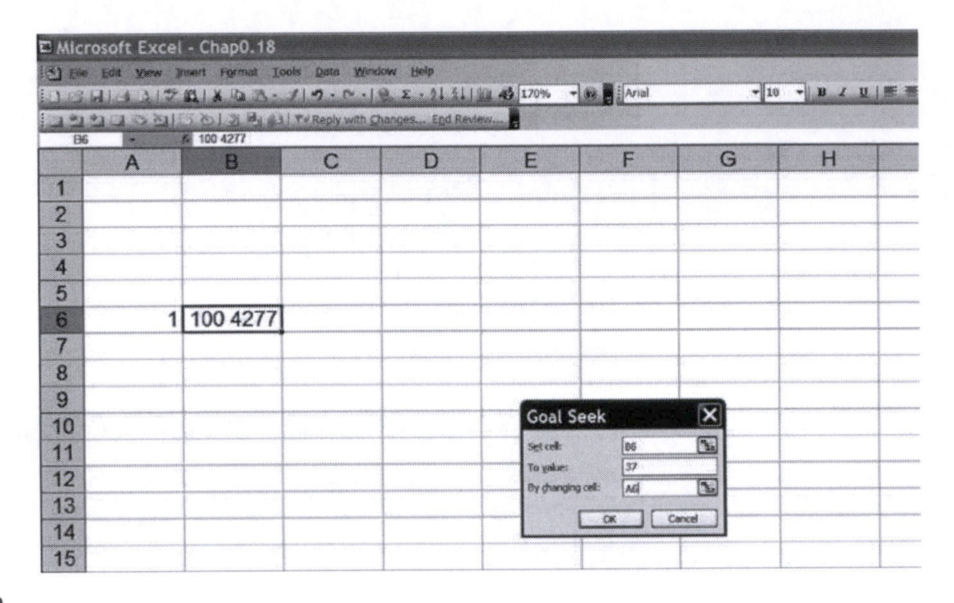

Figure 19

(g) Goal Seek

We might want to solve equations (Chapters 4 and 5). Goal Seek is ideal.

Example

Solve $5e^{2R+1} = 37$.

Solution

Select a cell (the goal cell) which will contain the formula [$5e^{2R+1}$] which is to be put equal to a numerical value [37]. We nominate B6. The aim is to find a value for R which will force $5e^{2R+1} = 37$. Select a cell that will contain the proposed value of R. We nominate A6.

Click A6. Enter 1 (or some other number of your choice).

Click B6. Enter = 5*EXP(2*A6 + 1).

Click Tools, Goal Seek (if Goal Seek is not shown, you might have to click 'Add ins' and include Goal Seek from the menu that appears).

The Goal Seek dialog box appears. (See Figure 19)

In Set cell, enter B6.

In To value, enter 37 (note: you must enter a numerical value here and not a cell reference).

In By changing cell, enter A6.
Press OK.
Up flashes Goal Seek Status.
Goal Seek has found a solution. (The target value and the current value give a measure of the accuracy of the solution.)
Click OK.
The Goal Seek solution is 0.50074 and this is stored in A6.
Neat.

1 A foundation

In this chapter we introduce some of the basic ideas that appear in the book. First, an overview of the chapter.

Interest rates

Interest rates are the life-blood of financial mathematics. To set up a new business, or to develop or diversify an existing business, you need to borrow money. To invest in a new idea, you need cash. To buy a home or an expensive item, such as a car, most people need to take out a loan. And when money is loaned, the person lending the money charges interest on the loan. This is:

(a) to compensate the lender for the inconvenience of being parted from his/her cash.

(b) because there is always a chance that not all the money will be re-paid, the lender is rewarded for exposing themselves to risk; the interest payments are that reward.

Variations in interest rates

In general, there will be a different interest rate for loans extending over short periods than for loans over longer periods. Over a longer period, the owner of the money has to manage without that money for a longer time and the risk of default on the loan becomes greater. So generally, loans over longer periods carry a higher interest rate. However, some loans carry far greater risk than others. A loan of £10 000 to a school mathematics teacher, married with children, might carry less risk than a loan of the same amount to a one-legged trapeze artiste. More risky loans, over any time period, will generally involve higher interest rates. Loans from different sources may also carry different interest rates. As I write, money can be borrowed from banks and building societies for 8%–9% per year while some store cards are charging interest at almost 30% per year. So interest rates vary widely.

Safe interest rates and their uses

Most people believe that investing money with a large international bank represents a safe investment. Money invested will be returned and interest that is promised will be paid. The investment is safe: the interest rate will reflect this by being low. Such an investment will reveal the rate at which money can grow, safely, with no effort or risk on the part of the investor. This interest rate will then reflect the safe, risk-free growth rate of money. An investor planning something more risky can observe this risk-free rate and compare the expected return on his proposed investment. If this expected return falls below what could be received from a safe investment, the investor might look again, rather more critically, at the project. In this way, the interest rate offered by a reputable bank or institution stands as a measure of what can (almost certainly) be achieved. The return on more risky investments can then be compared with this safe rate. This represents an important purpose for interest rates.

Borrowing money might not be entirely voluntary. A credit card holder who does not pay off the full amount each month is effectively borrowing money from the credit card company and will, therefore, be charged interest on the amount that remains. Anyone who goes overdrawn at the bank is liable for interest rate charges, as is a tax payer who does not complete their tax return on time. A motorist convicted by a court and fined who does not pay what she owes by the date payment is due will also be liable for interest charges. The list goes on. Since most of us fall into one (or more) of these categories, we all ought to know something about how interest rates are calculated. This will be discussed in section 1.1.

One of the most important ideas in finance is that of **discounting** or finding **the present value of money**. This idea is illustrated by the question: what will you give me today for my promise to give you $100 in six months' time? (The amount, $100, and the time can be varied at will.) My promise is good. The money will be delivered in six months' time. So the question is asking: what amount of money today will have a value of $100 in six months' time? The question suggests that money has a time value. $1 today is not the same as $1 tomorrow or in six months' time. This question could be described as one of the fundamental questions of finance and this topic forms the subject matter of section 1.2.

In section 1.3, we will make some comments on how interest rates are set. This will include a brief introduction to the extremely important LIBOR interest rate.

In section 1.4, we discuss **arbitrage**. Broadly speaking, an arbitrage opportunity is a situation that allows money to be created from nothing. You start with nothing; your fortune is zero. (Let us say you have borrowed a sum of money and have then invested every penny you have borrowed in some scheme.) An arbitrage opportunity occurs if a short time later, your fortune cannot possibly be negative and, with positive probability, your fortune is positive. (So there is no possibility of the scheme losing money and with positive probability, the scheme returns more than the amount you have to repay.) Such situations exclude the possibility of loss and ensure a positive probability of profit. These are very desirable but rarely attainable situations – for the reasons given in section 1.4.

Probability has been mentioned. That was to be expected. Probability is how the human race responds to uncertainty. There is plenty of uncertainty in the money markets, hence there will be plenty of probability in financial mathematics. But not, perhaps, the probability you might have expected. Some thoughts on creative probability appear in section 1.5.

Finally, in section 1.6, we will make a first attempt to construct the **zero curve**. This is hugely important in the financial world: it aims to provide bankers, dealers and analysts with an unfolding picture of interest rates. We will return to the zero curve, for a more sophisticated treatment, in Chapters 4 and 5.

1.1 Interest rates – the basic rules

Ada McPhee won £5 000 000 in the national lottery. Her advisors told her the money would be invested in one month's time in a carefully designed portfolio, but in the meantime she should put the money in a high-interest bank account. There were many suitable accounts to choose from, she was told.

Ada was beginning to get the hang of this. 'Yes, but how do I know which account offers the best interest rate?' she asked.

There was a short silence. 'That's a good question,' one advisor replied.

(See problem 8 in Exercise 1.)

Interest charged (or paid) is usually proportional to the amount you lend (or borrow) and clearly, the more you lend, the greater the interest you would expect to receive. The **interest rate**, r, determines how much interest you will receive on an investment of £P.

Notation To simplify the writing, we will assume we are investing cash. The calculations involved in making a cash loan are identical.

Principal: The sum of money invested is called the principal and will be denoted by P.

Duration: The duration of an investment is the period of time the money is invested. The time at which an investment is cashed in is called the **maturity**.

Amount: We shall use the word 'amount' to represent the total value of the cash investment. Initially, the amount of the investment is P. Subsequently, interest will be calculated. If the interest is added to the investment, then we have 'new amount' = 'old amount' + interest.

Interest rate: The interest rate r determines how much interest will be paid. The interest rate will usually be given as a percentage, e.g. 6.5%, and this, unless it is stated otherwise, will represent an *annual* interest rate. Generally, the larger the principal and/or the longer the duration, the greater the interest that accrues.

Compounding period: In practice, there are many ways in which interest can be calculated. The methods in this book differ only in the period of time that passes before the interest on the amount of an investment is calculated. This period of time is called the compounding period.

We consider four ways of calculating interest.

In each case, an annual interest rate is given.

1 Simple compounding

The interest over any time period is the product of the time period (in years), the interest rate (as a percentage) divided by 100 and the amount invested.

Example 1

Charlie invests £10 000 in an account that pays interest of 6.5% per year (simply compounded) for four months. Find the interest he will receive at the end of the four months.

Solution

The interest over one year would be $1 \times \frac{6.5}{100} \times 10\,000$

The interest (simply compounded) over four months will be

$$\frac{4}{12} \times \frac{6.5}{100} \times 10\,000 = 216.7$$

Generally: if £P is invested at r% per year with simple compounding, for a period of time t (in years)

$$Interest = t \times \frac{r}{100} \times P \qquad Amount = P + t \times \frac{r}{100} \times P$$

This method of calculating interest is often called **simple** interest. Perhaps it is the word, 'simple', or possibly it is comparison with its more glamorous competitor (compound interest, described below), but simple interest is often regarded merely as an elementary introduction to the way that 'real' interest rates work. In fact, simple interest is the basis of the LIBOR interest rate (described in section 1.3), one of the most important interest rates from both a practical and a theoretical point of view.

In the next three cases, we will assume that the interest generated is re-invested immediately. No cash payments are made from this investment until maturity. (These methods of calculating interest are often called compound interest.)

2 Annual compounding

£P is invested at an annually compounded rate. After one year, the interest is calculated and added to the amount of the investment at the beginning of that year. This sum becomes the amount of the investment at the beginning of the second year. At the end of this year, the interest is calculated and added to the amount of the investment at the beginning of this year. And so on. Until maturity.

Example 2

Mike Roach invests £10 000 in a savings account that pays interest at 6.5% per year (annually compounded). Mike makes no withdrawals and all the interest is paid immediately into the account. Find the interest and the amount he will have in the account after (a) one year and (b) ten years.

Solution

(a) After one year, the interest is $\frac{6.5}{100} \times 10\,000 = £650$

The amount at the end of one year $= 10\,000 + 650$

$= £10\,650.$

(b) To discover what has happened to the account after ten years, we could proceed on a year-by-year basis, calculating the interest at the end of each year and adding it to the amount of the investment at the beginning of that year. But this is unnecessarily time consuming. To derive an extremely useful formula, look again at what had happened at the end of the first year. But now, write the fraction $\frac{6.5}{100}$ in decimal form as 0.065.

(Interest rates are usually given as percentages; for calculation purposes, we usually work with the decimal form. We will call the decimal form a **rate**.)

$$\begin{aligned}\text{Amount at end of first year} &= 10\,000 + 0.065 \times 10\,000\\ &= 10\,000\,(1 + 0.065)\\ &= 10\,000 \times 1.065\end{aligned}$$

This gives:

amount at the end of the year is obtained by multiplying the amount at the beginning of the year by 1.065

For this reason, 1.065 is often called a multiplying factor.

$$\begin{aligned}\text{Amount at end of second year} &= \text{amount at beginning of second year} \times 1.065\\ &= (10\,000 \times 1.065) \times 1.065\\ &= 10\,000 \times 1.065^2\end{aligned}$$

(No interest and no other cash is withdrawn and no cash is paid in. Hence the amount at the beginning of the second year is precisely the amount at the end of the first year.)

$$\begin{aligned}\text{Amount at the end of third year} &= \text{amount at beginning of third year} \times 1.065\\ &= (10\,000 \times 1.065^2) \times 1.065\\ &= 10\,000 \times 1.065^3\end{aligned}$$

The pattern is now established.

$$\begin{aligned}\text{Amount at the end of ten years} &= 10\,000 \times 1.065^{10}\\ &= 18\,771.37\end{aligned}$$

This is such a fundamental result that we state it formally.

£P is invested at r% per year, compounded annually, for T years.
Assuming that all the interest is immediately reinvested and that no other cash is paid in or withdrawn,
after T years, the amount of the investment will be $P(1+\frac{r}{100})^T$
or: if the annual rate is $R=\frac{r}{100}$:
Amount after T years $= P(1+R)^T$ Interest $= P(1+R)^T - P$ **

The calculation is identical if the money is being borrowed.

Example 3

Alan borrowed £50 000 at 8.15% per year (compounded annually) for 18 months. Assuming he made no repayments before maturity, what will Alan have to pay to settle the debt at the end of the 18 months? How much interest will he pay, altogether, on this loan?

Solution

$P = £50\,000,\ R = \frac{8.5}{100} = 0.085,\ T = 1.5$ years.

Alan will have to pay $P(1+R)^T$

$$= 50\,000(1+0.085)^{1.5}$$
$$= £56\,508.61$$

Total interest $= 56\,508.61 - 50\,000$
$$= £6\,508.61$$

3 m-times a year compounding

Not all investments (loans) use a one-year compounding period. Investments with a compounding period of six months are common, as are investments that are compounded quarterly (compounding period = three months), monthly and daily. The argument with a compounding period of any length is as described above. At the end of the first compounding period, interest is calculated and immediately added to the amount. This sum becomes the amount at the beginning of the second compounding period. At the end of the second compounding period, interest is calculated and immediately added to the amount and so on. The idea will be to find a rate and a duration written not in units of one year but in the unit of the compounding period. Then, using these units, (**) may be applied. We illustrate with some examples before providing a formula.

Example 4

Gerald Pugh needs £1200 each year to endow a sports scholarship. The highest interest rate he can find will pay 7.5% per year with interest compounded monthly. Gerald invests £16 000. Is this sufficient to pay for the scholarship?

Solution

The rate and the duration must be written in the unit of the compounding period, in this case one month.

An annual interest rate of 7.5% gives an annual rate (decimal) of $\frac{7.5}{100} = 0.075$. We will take this to imply that the rate R per month is given by $R = \frac{0.075}{12} = 0.00625$.

In one year, there are 12 compounding periods, so $T = 12$.

Using (**): with R and T measured relative to the compounding period of one month, we have:

$$\text{Amount} = P(1 + R)^T$$

$$\text{Amount at the end of one year} = 16\,000(1 + 0.00625)^{12} = 17\,242.12$$

So Gerald receives interest of £1242.12 each year. This will pay for the sports scholarship and leave Gerald an extra £42.12 each year. Perhaps this could pay for an annual Pugh Cup.

Example 5

Simone invests £500 at 4.5% per year for four years. Interest is compounded quarterly. Find the value of Simone's investment after the four years.

Solution

1. Annual rate $= \frac{4.5}{100} = 0.045$
2. Rate R per quarter $= \frac{0.045}{4} = 0.01125$
3. There are $4 \times 4 = 16$ quarters (compounding periods) in four years. So $T = 16$.
4. Using ** with three months as the unit time period,
   $\text{Amount} = 500 \times (1 + 0.01125)^{16}$
   $= £598.01$

Generally, there are four important points to observe.

1. The interest rate (e.g. 6.5%) will be an **annual** interest rate. This will sometimes be given as a rate (decimal) $= \frac{percentage}{100}$
2. Interest rates will always be given relative to a specific **compounding period.** It is vital that the compounding period be properly identified and used as the basic unit in interest rate calculations.
3. The interest rate (rate) over the time of the compounding period is the relevant fraction of the annual interest rate (rate).
4. The **duration** of the investment (loan) T is expressed as a multiple of the compounding period.

We can now give a general result:

P is invested (or borrowed) at r% per year compounded m times per year, for T years

$R = \frac{r}{100}$ = *rate per year with interest compounded m times a year*

$\frac{R}{m}$ = *rate per unit of compounding period*

mT = *number of compounding periods in T years*

Then, assuming no money is withdrawn and no money (other than interest) is paid in,

$$\text{Amount after } T \text{ years} = P\left(1 + \frac{R}{m}\right)^{mT} \qquad \text{Interest} = P\left(1 + \frac{R}{m}\right)^{mT} - P$$

Observe that if m = 1, we have annual compounding. Hence, [3] is a special case of [2].

Example 6

Rocky borrows $6000 for a holiday. He pays interest at 5.75% per year compounded semi-annually. Assuming that Rocky makes no repayments during the first six years, how much would he owe after six years?

Solution

P = $6000 Rate (per year) = 0.0575

Rate (per half year) $= \frac{0.0575}{2} = 0.02875$

Number of compounding periods $= 2 \times 6 = 12$

Amount (after six years) $= P\left(1 + \frac{R}{2}\right)^{2\times 6} = 6\,000(1 + 0.02875)^{12} = 8430.81$

In Figure 1.1 we show an Excel spreadsheet giving the value of an investment (or the amount of a debt) after a number of years. This spreadsheet can be used to see how any investment, or debt, with known compounding period can grow. The principal (£100) is entered in A6 and the rate (8%) in B6. These are given the cell names, principal and rate, respectively. In C6

Microsoft Excel - Chap1.1

	A	B	C	D	E	F	G	H
1	Chap1.1							
2			DISCRETE					
3	Principal	rate	comp	maturity	amount	interest		
4								
5								
6	100	8	2	4	136.856905	36.8569		
7				4.5	142.331181	42.3312		
8				5	148.024428	48.0244		
9				5.5	153.945406	53.9454		
10				6	160.103222	60.1032		
11				6.5	166.507351	66.5074		
12				7	173.167645	73.1676		
13				7.5	180.094351	80.0944		
14				8	187.298125	87.2981		
15				8.5	194.79005	94.79		
16				9	202.581652	102.582		
17				9.5	210.684918	110.685		
18								
19								
20								
21								
22								
23								
24								

=amount-Principal

=Principal*(1+rate/(100*comp))^(comp*maturity)

Figure 1.1

is entered the number of times interest is compounded during one year (this carries the cell name comp). Figure 1.1 illustrates a situation where interest is compounded semi-annually (twice each year). The times to maturity appear in D6:D17 (with the range name maturity); the corresponding amounts appear in E6:E17 (range name amount) and interest in F6:F17 (range name interest). Cell and range names are used (see Excel introduction) to simplify the formulae.

For some investments/loans, the compounding period is one day. An unauthorised bank overdraft will charge interest by the day on an overdrawn account. Some credit card companies charge interest by the day on credit card debt. Often in finance there will be 'overnight' borrowing. Since a compounding period of one day occurs frequently, we will investigate more closely.

Example 7

Harshad owes £6500 on his credit card. Interest is charged at 21.5% per year with interest compounded daily. If he does not repay any of this debt in the following six months, how much will Harshad owe on this debt six months later?

Solution

$$P = 6500 \quad R = 0.215 \quad m = 365 \quad T = \tfrac{6}{12}$$

$$\text{Hence: Amount after six months} = 6500\left(1 + \tfrac{0.215}{365}\right)^{365\times\frac{6}{12}}$$
$$= 7237.46$$

This type of calculation is so common that it will be helpful to have a simple method that provides an accurate approximation to this value. This leads to continuous compounding.

4 Continuous compounding

To introduce this, consider what happens when the compounding period becomes very small (one second, say) or, equivalently, when the number of compounding periods in one year becomes very large (3 153 600, say).

The effect of increasing the number of compounding periods is shown in Figure 1.2. Here, the effect of investing or borrowing a principal of $1000 at a

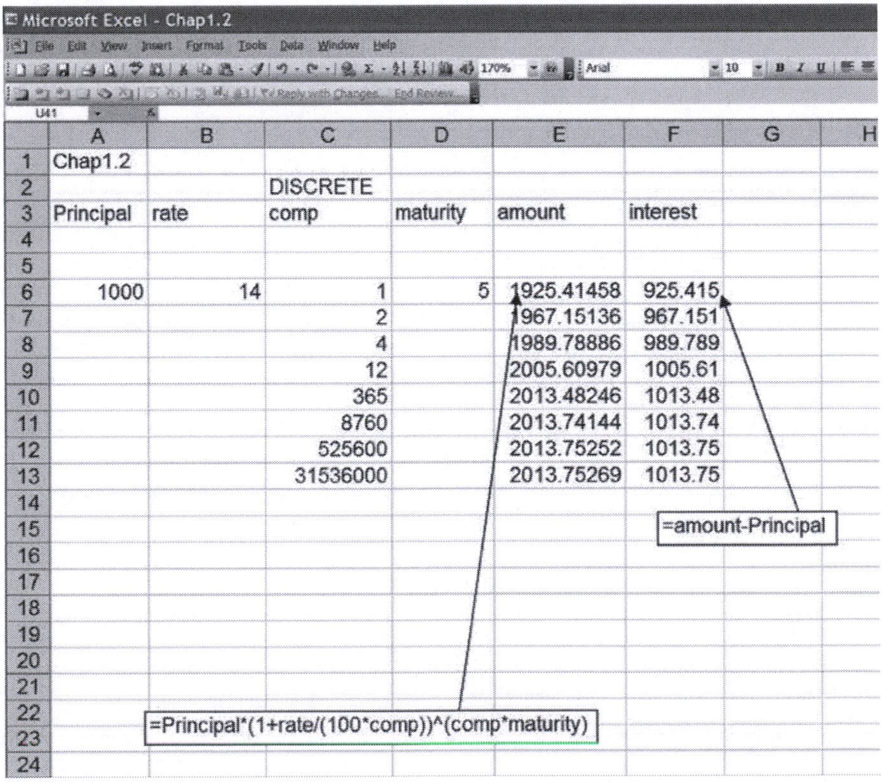

Microsoft Excel - Chap1.2

	A	B	C	D	E	F	G	H
1	Chap1.2							
2			DISCRETE					
3	Principal	rate	comp	maturity	amount	interest		
4								
5								
6	1000	14	1	5	1925.41458	925.415		
7			2		1967.15136	967.151		
8			4		1989.78886	989.789		
9			12		2005.60979	1005.61		
10			365		2013.48246	1013.48		
11			8760		2013.74144	1013.74		
12			525600		2013.75252	1013.75		
13			31536000		2013.75269	1013.75		

=amount-Principal

=Principal*(1+rate/(100*comp))^(comp*maturity)

Figure 1.2

rate of 14% with a maturity of five years with varying compounding periods (comp) is shown. Principal, rate and maturity are each cell names; comp is a range name. The 365 in C10 indicates a compounding period of one day, 8760 in C11 gives a compounding period of one hour and so on until the 31 536 000 in C13 gives a compounding period of one second. The amount for the varying compounding periods is entered as a range name.

Notice how the amount (E6:E13) and the interest (F6:F13) both seem to tend to a limit as the number of compounding periods per year becomes very large. Also, these limits (2013.75 and 1013.75) are not very different to the amount and interest for the daily rate (2013.48 and 1013.48). So this limit, whatever it is, provides a very good approximation to daily compounding. To get this limit, we let there be infinitely many compounding periods in each year. So the duration of each compounding period will become infinitely small. This will give continuous compounding.

Below, we show how this happens and find the limit. But if this ferocious display of algebra displeases you, cut to the next example and look at the spreadsheet in Figure 1.4.

We know that the amount (investment/loan) is $P(1+\frac{R}{m})^{mT}$

The key is to look closely at $(1+\frac{R}{m})^{mT}$

Since mT $= \frac{m}{R} \times RT$, we can write:

$$\left(1+\frac{R}{m}\right)^{mT} = \left(1+\frac{R}{m}\right)^{\frac{m}{R}\times RT}$$

Now consider $(1+\frac{R}{m})^{\frac{m}{R}}$

R is fixed. Only m can change and m (the number of compounding periods in one year) is very, very large. Look at the Excel spreadsheet in Figure 1.3.

R = 0.06 but this is a token value. We see that as m becomes very large, $(1+\frac{R}{m})^{\frac{m}{R}}$ is approaching the value 2.718281828. This number is famous and, better than that, very useful. Rather like π, it appears, unexpectedly, in all manner of places. So it has been given a name. This number is the fundamental constant e (written in Excel as EXP(1)). From the spreadsheet we see that as m $\to \infty$ $(1+\frac{R}{m})^{\frac{m}{R}} \to$ e

$$\text{so} \quad \left(1+\frac{R}{m}\right)^{mT} = \left[\left(1+\frac{R}{m}\right)^{\frac{m}{R}}\right]^{RT} \text{ becomes } e^{RT}$$

This is a remarkable and a remarkably useful piece of simplifying.

Microsoft Excel - Chap1.3

File Edit View Insert Format Tools Data Window Help

	A	B	C	D	E	F	G
1	Chap1.3						
2							
3							
4	R =	m =		(1+R/m)^(m/R)			
5	0.06	100000		2.718281013			
6		200000		2.71828142			
7		400000		2.718281624			
8		800000		2.718281726			
9		1600000		2.718281777			
10		3200000		2.718281803			
11		6400000		2.718281847			
12		12800000		2.718281789			
13		25600000		2.718281921			
14		51200000		2.718281923			
15		102400000		2.718281924			
16		204800000		2.718281924			
17		409600000		2.718281924			
18							
19			e =	2.718281828			
20							
21							

Figure 1.3

Example 8

Sergi borrows £1 000 000 at 5% per year, interest compounded continuously, for three months. If he repays the entire amount at the end of the three months, how much will Sergi have to repay?

Solution

$$P = 1\,000\,000 \quad R = 0.05 \quad T = \tfrac{3}{12}$$

$$\text{Amount (after three months)} = Pe^{RT} = 1\,000\,000 \times e^{0.05 \times \frac{3}{12}} = 1\,012\,578.45$$

Generally:

If P is invested or borrowed

R = rate per year with interest compounded continuously

T = time, in years

Then assuming interest is re-invested and that no other money is taken out or paid in

Amount after T years = Pe^{RT}

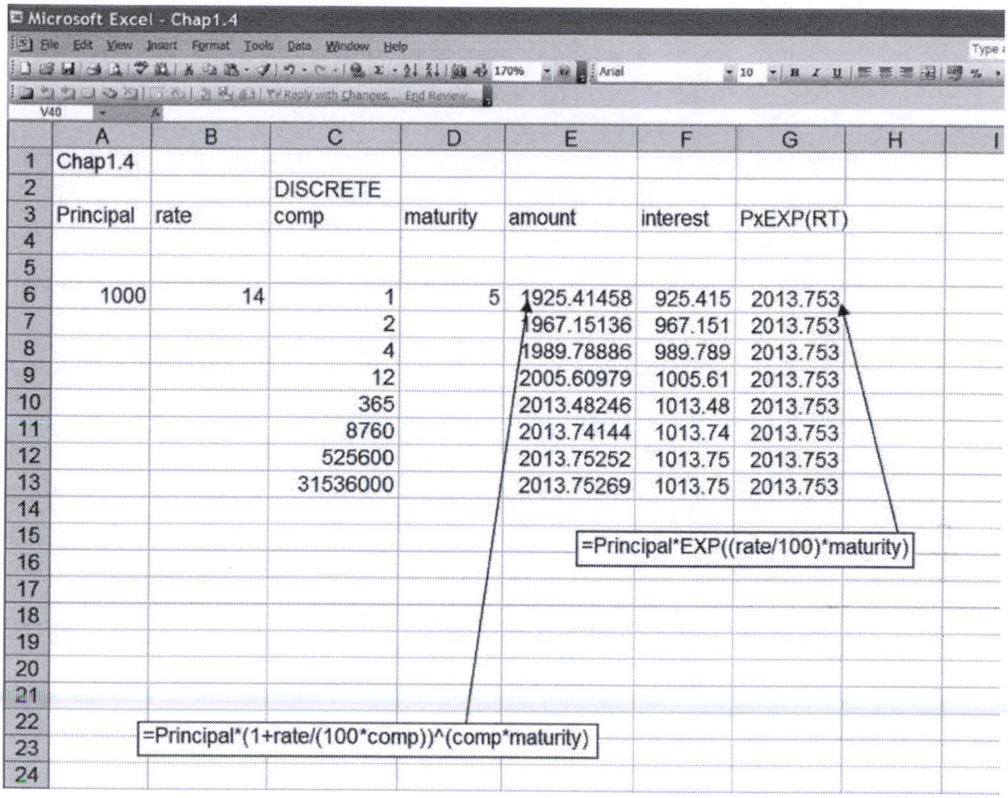

Microsoft Excel - Chap1.4

	A	B	C	D	E	F	G	H	I
1	Chap1.4								
2			DISCRETE						
3	Principal	rate	comp	maturity	amount	interest	PxEXP(RT)		
4									
5									
6	1000	14	1	5	1925.41458	925.415	2013.753		
7			2		1967.15136	967.151	2013.753		
8			4		1989.78886	989.789	2013.753		
9			12		2005.60979	1005.61	2013.753		
10			365		2013.48246	1013.48	2013.753		
11			8760		2013.74144	1013.74	2013.753		
12			525600		2013.75252	1013.75	2013.753		
13			31536000		2013.75269	1013.75	2013.753		
14									
15									
16									
17									
18									
19									
20									
21									
22									
23									
24									

=Principal*EXP((rate/100)*maturity)

=Principal*(1+rate/(100*comp))^(comp*maturity)

Figure 1.4

Now look at Figure 1.4.

This is Figure 1.2 with an additional column giving the result of continuous compounding. Notice how, as the number of compounding periods becomes very large, the amount (column E) becomes very close indeed to the amount resulting from continuous compounding (column G). The limit, as the number of compounding periods becomes infinite, is Pe^{RT}. Notice again how close the continuously compounded amount (2013.75) is to the daily compounding amount (2013.48). Continuous compounding does indeed provide a good approximation to daily compounding.

Notation It is convenient to describe compounding that occurs a finite number of times each year as **discrete compounding**. So semi-annual compounding, quarterly compounding and daily compounding are all discrete. If the compounding takes place continuously, then we refer to **continuous compounding**.

For anyone intending to invest or borrow money, there is a very wide range of interest rates available. The annual rate as well as the compounding period will vary from bank to bank and with circumstances. Clearly, the potential investor wants to maximise the interest they will receive and the intending borrower will be very keen to minimise the interest they will pay. So the question will be asked: *How can different interest rates be compared?*

One approach is to consider equivalent interest rates.

Definition Two or more interest rates are *equivalent* if on identical investments, they return identical amounts after an investment of one year.

To illustrate how equivalent interest rates can be calculated, consider three problems:

(1) I have become overdrawn at the bank. My bank charges 13.9% per year with interest compounding daily. My dad, looking smug, tells me that on overdrafts, his bank charges 14.95% per year with annual compounding. Should I change banks?

(2) Stella wants to invest £20 000. Bank A offers 4.5% per year with interest compounded monthly; bank B offers 4.7% with interest compounded semi-annually. Which bank will give better value?

(3) A2Z Securities knows it can borrow money at 6.6% per year compounded continuously. It would prefer to invest in an account that compounds quarterly. What rate with quarterly compounding is equivalent to 6.6% compounded continuously?

Problem 1

Assume the overdraft is £100. We will calculate the rate with annual compounding (R) that is equivalent to 13.9% per year with daily compounding. To do this, we will calculate the amount of debt, under both interest rate schemes, after one year:

(a) Interest compounded daily:

$$\text{Amount after one year} = 100 \times \left(1 + \frac{0.139}{365}\right)^{365}$$

(b) Interest compounded annually (R is the (unknown) annual rate)

$$\text{Amount} = 100 \times (1 + \text{R})$$

For the rates to be equivalent, we need:

$$100 \times (1 + \text{R}) = 100 \times \left(1 + \frac{0.139}{365}\right)^{365}$$

We see now that the size of the overdraft is unimportant. The 100 cancels giving

$$1 + R = \left(1 + \frac{0.139}{365}\right)^{365}$$

$$R = \left(1 + \frac{0.139}{365}\right)^{365} - 1$$

$$= 0.1491$$

Hence the equivalent annually compounded interest rate is $R = 14.91\%$.

I explained this to my dad as he struggled, again, with the DVD. I did not change banks.

Problem 2

We calculate the rate with semi-annual compounding that is equivalent to 4.5% per year with monthly compounding. The amounts of the investment under both schemes after one year are shown below.

(a) 4.5% per year, compounded monthly:

$$\text{Amount} = 20\,000 \times \left(1 + \frac{0.045}{12}\right)^{12}$$

(b) Rate R, compounded semi-annually:

$$\text{Amount} = 20\,000 \times \left(1 + \frac{R}{2}\right)^{2}$$

For the rates to be equivalent, $(1 + \frac{R}{2})^2 = (1 + \frac{0.045}{12})^{12}$ (Observe that the principal cancels. In future, we will not include this amount.)

$$\left(1 + \frac{R}{2}\right) = \left(1 + \frac{0.045}{12}\right)^{6} \qquad \text{(square root both sides)}$$

$$\frac{R}{2} = \left(1 + \frac{0.045}{12}\right)^{6} - 1$$

$$R = 2\left[\left(1 + \frac{0.045}{12}\right)^{6} - 1\right]$$

$$= 0.04542$$

Or, the equivalent semi-annual rate is 4.542% per year.

Since bank B is offering 4.7% and the equivalent rate is 4.542%, go, go, go with bank B.

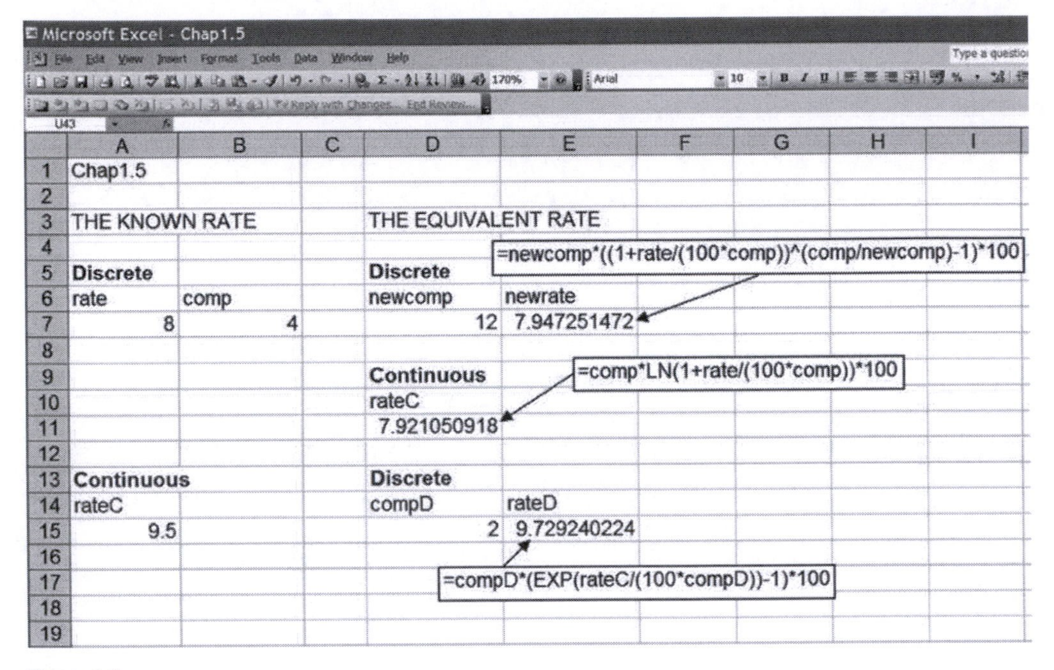

Figure 1.5

Problem 3

After one year

(a) 6.6% per year, with interest compounded continuously:

$$\text{Amount} = \text{P}e^{0.066\times 1}$$

(b) Rate R per year, compounded quarterly:

$$\text{Amount} = \text{P}\left(1 + \frac{R}{4}\right)^4$$

Therefore, $(1 + \frac{R}{4})^4 = e^{0.066}$

$$1 + \frac{R}{4} = e^{\frac{0.066}{4}} \quad \text{(fourth root of both sides)}$$

$$R = 4 \times \left[e^{\frac{0.066}{4}} - 1\right]$$

$$= 0.06655$$

The equivalent quarterly rate is = 6.655% per year.

An easy way of calculating equivalent rates is shown in the spreadsheet in Figure 1.5. Here, the known rate is entered in A7 (if compounding is discrete) or as rateC in A15 (if compounding is continuous). The known number of (discrete) compounding periods per year (comp) is entered in B7. To find the equivalent rate, enter the number of compounding periods (for a discrete, equivalent rate) in D7 or in D15. The equivalent rates are then shown in E7 (newrate), D11 (rateC) and E15 (rateD).

1.2 Discounting or the 'present value' of money

On her 18th birthday, Smilla was told she had been left £20 000 in her grandmother's will. The problem for Smilla was that she would not receive the money until her 25th birthday.

'What does it feel like to be worth £20 000 at the age of 18?' asked her friend. Smilla studied mathematics. 'I really wouldn't know,' she sighed.
(See problem 14 on Exercise 1.)

We have seen how interest rates cause investments (and debts) to grow. This work (if interest rates remain constant) answers the question: *If I invest £P today, what sum of money will I have at a given time in the future?*

The reverse problem is possibly even more important in financial mathematics: *What sum of money, invested today, will yield £P at a given time in the future?*

Using the techniques we have developed so far and a little algebra, the reverse problem is easily solved.

We illustrate with a simple example.

Example 9

In two years' time, I will need to find £100 000. I can invest money at 4.5% per year with interest compounded quarterly. What amount must I invest today to ensure that I have £100 000 in two years' time?

Solution

If I invest £P today, then with $R = 0.045$, $m = 4$ and $T = 2$, in two years' time my investment will be worth:

$$P \times \left(1 + \frac{0.045}{4}\right)^{4\times 2} = P \times (1.01125)^8$$

To achieve the aim, this expression must equal £100 000.

Hence: $P \times (1.01125)^8 = 100\,000$

So: $P = \frac{100000}{(1.01125)^8}$

$= 91\,439.054$

So £91 439.054 invested today will yield £100 000 in two years' time.

Putting this another way, £100 000 in two years' time is worth £91 439.054 today. This is an example of how the value of money changes over time. Investment possibilities, interest rates, inflation and other changing economic circumstances all mean that 'the pound nestling deep in your pocket today will not have the same value, comparatively, if it is still there tomorrow, or next week, or next year'. Money has a time value. The old phrase 'time is money' has been recast. 'Money is a function of time.' Such thoughts are extremely important in financial mathematics.

Observe that from $P \times (1 + \frac{0.045}{4})^{4\times 2} = 100\,000$, we could have written: $P = (1 + \frac{0.045}{4})^{-8} \times 100\,000$. We shall tend to use this form more and more in the remainder of the book.

Consider now a second problem.

Example 10

A finance director knows that she will have to settle an account for $1 000 000 in four months' time. Her bank will pay interest on dollar investments of 5.2% per year with interest compounded daily for a four-month period. If the financial director used continuous compounding to calculate the amount she must invest, how much money (in dollars) should she invest today?

Solution

Let \$P be the amount she invests today. $R = 0.052$, $T = \frac{4}{12}$.

In four months' time, the value of the investment (using continuous compounding) will be $P \times e^{RT}$

So we need: $P \times e^{RT} = P \times e^{0.052\times\frac{4}{12}} = 1\,000\,000$

This gives:

$$P = e^{-0.052\times\frac{4}{12}} \times 1\,000\,000$$
$$= 982\,816.02$$

She should invest $982 816.02 today.

So her $1 000 000 bill in four months' time is a bill for $982 816.02 today. The time value of money is evident again.

The process of finding what amount today will, T years in the future, yield £P is important enough to merit a name. This process is known as **discounting** or **finding the present value of money**. The sum needed today to yield £P in the future is called the **discounted value** of P or **the present value** of P.

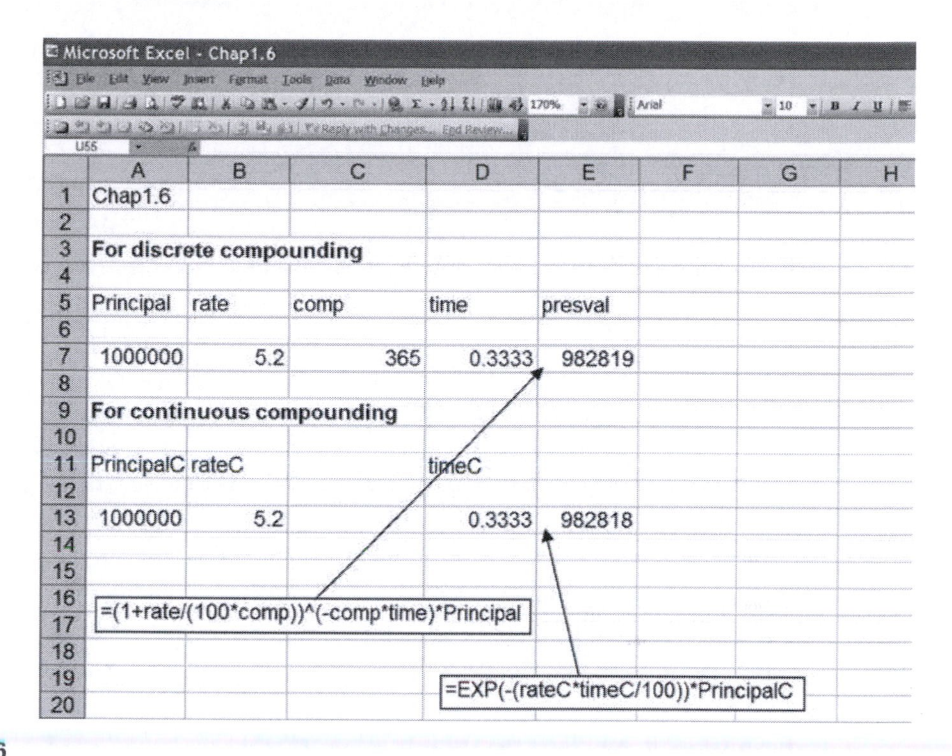

Figure 1.6

Important result

The amount today that will become £P in T years' time (assuming a constant annual interest rate r) is given by:

Discrete compounding:

For an annual rate R, compounded m times a year:

$$\text{Discounted value of P} = \left(1 + \frac{R}{m}\right)^{-mT} \times \text{P}$$

Continuous compounding:

For an annual rate R, compounded continuously:

$$\text{Discounted value of P} = \text{e}^{-RT} \times \text{P}$$

The calculations are carried out very conveniently in an Excel spreadsheet. In Figure 1.6, we illustrate such a spreadsheet. The calculation shown in the discrete case is not the amount shown in Example 10. In the spreadsheet, the time to maturity is given as 0.3333. In the example, this time was given, exactly, as $\frac{4}{12}$. Rounding errors can create difficulties when large numbers are involved and the reader is advised to be careful when entering approximations. Again, observe that the amount derived from continuous compounding,

$982 816.02, is very close to the figure derived from daily compounding ($982 818.9).

1.3 How are interest rates set?

Each month, the Bank of England's Monetary Policy Committee meets to set the Official Dealing Rate. This is the rate at which the Bank of England is prepared to lend to commercial banks. In the US, the Federal Reserve Board, through the Federal Open Market Committee, sets the Discount Rate at which commercial banks can borrow money from Federal Reserve Board banks. A loan from both the Bank of England and the Federal Reserve Board to a commercial bank is regarded as safe: the interest payments will be made and the capital will be repaid. Hence, there is no additional premium in these interest rates to cover the cost of default. The Official Dealing Rate (in England) and the Discount Rate (in the US) represent a 'minimum' national interest rate.

Businesses and the public borrow money from the commercial banks and other institutions. The yardstick interest rates quoted by the commercial banks are often called 'base rates' and loans from commercial banks to small businesses and the public are set in relation to base rates.

But now there is a risk of default on the payments. The risk is low with a creditworthy institution and high for a barefoot trapeze artist with verrucas. So the commercial banks will charge a number of percentage points above base rate. For a creditworthy institution, this might be 2–3 percentage points above base rate; for a loan to which a large amount of risk is attached, this could be 8–10 percentage points above base rate. So if base rate was 5%, a creditworthy company/individual might pay 7% or 8% on their loan. A borrower with a poor credit history might pay 13% to 15%, or more. Sometimes, the percentage is expressed in **basis points**. One basis point is $\frac{1}{100}$th of 1%. So 0.5% above base rate might be described as 'base rate plus 50 basis points'.

Banks will not extend the same interest rate to investors and borrowers. The rate they will pay to those depositing funds in the bank is called the **bid** rate. The rate they will charge for lending money is the **offer** rate. The bid rate will be lower than the offer rate. (In business, the amount you pay out should be less than the amount you receive.)

The LIBOR rate

Large international banks are heavily involved in lending and borrowing money in all currencies from other large international banks. The rate used in these transactions is based on the LIBOR rate (London Interbank Offered Rate). LIBOR is the rate at which banks can borrow money from other banks in the London interbank market. Since there is a small risk of default in these transactions, LIBOR rates will be above the Official Dealing Rate. But banks are usually more creditworthy than small businesses and private citizens so LIBOR will be below those rates offered by commercial banks.

The LIBOR rate is set by the British Bankers' Association (BBA) at 11.00 am on each business day. LIBOR is the most widely used reference rate for short-term interest rates. It is used as the basis for the settlement of interest rate contracts on many of the world's major futures and options exchanges. The table below gives LIBOR rates for 27 July 2004.

Maturity	Interest rate
Over night	4.66125
One month	4.72000
Three months	4.91875
Six months	5.08625
One year	5.3375

To set the LIBOR rate, the British Bankers' Association, acting with the advice of senior market practitioners, refers to a panel of at least eight contributor banks. These banks are chosen to reflect the composition of the market. In selecting its panel, the BBA might consider a bank's reputation, expertise, size of market activity and in particular the involvement of the bank in the currency whose LIBOR rate is to be determined. BBA LIBOR rates are set daily for nine international currencies: pound sterling, US dollar, Japanese yen, Swiss franc, Canadian dollar, Australian dollar, euro, Danish krone and the New Zealand dollar.

The LIBOR rate is quoted in the financial press as annual rate, but it should be remembered that LIBOR is a **simply compounded** interest rate.

So if the one-month LIBOR rate is 4.72000% then on an investment of £10 000,

$$\text{Amount after one month} = 10\,000\left(1 + \frac{1}{12} \times 0.0472\right) = 10\,039.33$$

If the three-month LIBOR rate is 4.91875% then

$$\text{Amount after three months} = 10\,000\left(1 + \frac{3}{12} \times 0.0491875\right) = 10\,122.97$$

Note: For completeness, we refer here to a topic described fully in Chapter 4: day count conventions. LIBOR rates are calculated using the day count convention actual/360, except for the pound sterling, which is calculated using an actual/365-day count convention.

A great deal of useful information on LIBOR rates can be obtained from:
The British Bankers' Association website: www.bba.org.uk
The Bank of England website: www.bankofengland.co.uk/statistics
Useful websites for interest rates generally are:
www.moneyextra.com
www.moneyfacts.co.uk
www.moneynet.co.uk

1.4 Arbitrage

The telephone rings. A confident voice tells you how, by making an investment of £1000, you can buy into a proven investment scheme. Expert traders, having access to information unavailable to private citizens, are constantly seeking out investment opportunities. These experts scrutinise world markets 24 hours a day. Now, should prices fall in the UK, they must, in the nature of things, rise somewhere else, and with their expert traders on hand to spot and capitalise on these investment opportunities, you can be sure that your investment will grow *at least* at the level of the current interest rate. And, the voice goes on, there is a real chance that the growth of your investment will outpace interest rate growth and perform better than your safe investment in a bank or a building society.

You waver. It seems an unbelievably good offer, but you are not certain.

There is more. The voice continues. In fact, you do not need to put up any money yourself. The company will arrange, on your behalf, a loan of £1000 repayable at the current interest rate. They will invest the sum you borrow and your investment will then increase in value rising to, well, at the very least the amount you will have to repay on the loan. And there is a real chance that your investment will be worth more than you will have to repay. So how can you refuse, the voice asks, very confidently. You cannot lose money and there is a real chance that you will make money.

The offer described above is an example of an **arbitrage opportunity**. An arbitrage opportunity is a situation where, under all market conditions, the growth of an investment is at least as great as the growth of an identical amount invested at the current interest rate. And there is a chance (a positive probability) that the value of the investment at maturity will exceed the value of an identical amount invested at the current interest rate.

This is the first scenario outlined by the telephone salesperson. Because arbitrage opportunities are extremely important in the theory of financial mathematics, we give a more precise definition.

Notation Consider a portfolio. This might consist of shares, cash or other financial instruments (bonds, futures contracts, options, all to be considered later in the book). We let this portfolio have value V and we add a superscript if we want to indicate the time.

Let V_0 = initial ($t = 0$) value of a portfolio. (So in the example above, $V_0 = £1000$.)
Let R = current interest rate (per year) between $t = 0$ and $t = T$ (assume that R is continuously compounded and constant).
If a sum of money equal to V_0 (£1000 in the example) is invested today at the interest rate R, then at time T the investment will have value $e^{RT} \times V_0$.
Let V_T = value of the portfolio at time T (V_T is the value of the portfolio at maturity).

Definition *An arbitrage opportunity is the existence of a portfolio having the properties*

(i) $V_T \geq e^{RT} V_0$ *for all possible movements of the market (so the portfolio always performs at least as well as a safe investment)*
(ii) $V_T > e^{RT} V_0$ *for at least one outcome of the possible market changes (there is a real chance (a positive probability) that the portfolio will perform better than a safe investment).*

In an arbitrage opportunity, there is a risk-free chance of making a profit. This scenario is a dream shared by many and lived by only a few. There are groups of traders called arbitrageurs, whose (highly paid) job it is to spot and then exploit such opportunities. Precisely because risk-free profit is every trader's dream, such opportunities do not last long. Once an arbitrage opportunity is observed, the currency prices, shares, bonds, etc. involved are the objects of heavy trading as traders try to exploit this opportunity. This will tend to drive down a price that is too high or drive up a price that is too low. In this way, in an arbitrage opportunity, prices adjust very quickly and so close the arbitrage opportunity.

We will assume throughout this book that arbitrage opportunities, if they occur, vanish almost immediately. **So we will assume, as a general principle, that no arbitrage opportunities exist**. This is, in fact, a very powerful idea. We are using a form of 'financial equilibrium'. And just as equilibrium in engineering is used to balance forces and so derive information about the situation, so the absence of arbitrage is used in financial engineering to balance contracts and so derive useful information about prices.

Arbitrage opportunities are sometimes described in a slightly different form. This alternative form has the advantage of being easier to work with. We describe this alternative form below and then show how an arbitrage opportunity under the first definition implies an arbitrage opportunity under this second definition. The second definition is the situation described in the fallback position adopted by the telephone salesperson. In this situation, starting from nothing and with no chance of losing money, there is a positive chance of making money.

Definition *An arbitrage opportunity is the existence of a portfolio having the properties:*

(iii) The initial value of the portfolio is zero.

(iv) The value of the portfolio at maturity is greater than or equal to zero for all possible movements of the market.

(v) There is a real chance (a positive probability) that the value of the portfolio at maturity is strictly greater than zero.

We now show that this definition follows from the first definition.

Initially, the investor borrows a sum of money, **all** of which she then invests in the asset. So the portfolio consists of the asset and an amount (negative) of cash. This leaves no money in hand and the initial value of the investor's portfolio is zero. In symbols, the initial value of the portfolio is $1000 - V_0 = 0$. This gives (iii).

At maturity, the investor pays back the loan and cashes in the investment. So an amount $e^{RT}V_0$ is paid out and V_T is received. The value of the portfolio at maturity is $V_T - e^{RT}V_0$.

But if, from (i) in the first definition, for all movements of the markets $V_T \geq e^{RT}V_0$, then $V_T - e^{RT}V_0 \geq 0$. This gives (iv).

But if, from (ii) in the first definition, for at least one possible market movement,
$V_T > e^{RT}V_0$, then $V_T - e^{RT}V_0 > 0$. This gives (v).

Useful result

Suppose the value of the portfolio at maturity (V_T) does not depend on uncertain fluctuations in the value of the asset(s). In this case (assuming a known interest rate), V_T is a function only of T – and when T is known, so is V_T.

Suppose now that we use the second form of the definition. So $V_0 = 0$.

If $V_T > 0$ then an arbitrage opportunity occurs (perhaps for the person buying the portfolio).

If $V_T < 0$ then an arbitrage opportunity occurs (perhaps for the person selling the portfolio).

So for the 'no arbitrage' condition to hold, we need $V_T = 0$.

(This will be used and explained further in Chapter 2 when this idea will be used to price a forward contract.)

We give an example of an arbitrage opportunity.

It is 2.00 pm. The pound US dollar exchange rate is £1 = $1.76. A trader in London notices that the price of a BP share in London is £5.82. Further, the price quoted for this share on the New York Stock Exchange is $10.29. The trader borrows £1 000 000 and buys 171 821 BP shares $[\frac{1\,000\,000}{5.82} = 171\,821.31]$.

The trader sells the shares in New York for $171\,821 \times 10.29 = \$1\,768\,038.09$.

Now the trader sells the dollars at £1 = $1.76 and receives $\frac{1\,768\,038.09}{1.76} = 1\,004\,567.10$.

This is an arbitrage opportunity. The initial value of the portfolio is zero. The trader borrows £1 000 000 and immediately spends £1 000 000 buying BP shares. This gives (iii).

After selling the BP shares and the dollars she received from the sale and returning the £1 000 000, the value of the portfolio (£4567.10) will be greater than zero. This establishes (v).

Of course, this example ignores transaction costs, but the purpose is to illustrate an arbitrage opportunity.

Most likely, the trader would not have been alone in spotting this arbitrage opportunity. Others would have bought BP shares in London (driving up the price) and sold them in New York (driving down the price) and the arbitrage opportunity would have closed.

Of course, we are not saying that in the absence of arbitrage it is impossible to make a profit. We are saying that in a no-arbitrage market, when there is the chance of taking a profit there is also the chance of taking a loss. So it is luck or a skilful appreciation of probabilities that leads to profit. *In an arbitrage-free market, there are no opportunities for profit without there being also the potential to make a loss.*

1.5 Probability

In the remarks on arbitrage, there appeared the word 'probability'. Experience tells us that the price of a share goes up and down. The FTSE rises and falls; there is uncertainty in the financial world. Of course probability is going to enter the discussion.

The price of a buyhappyapples.com share at the opening of the market is £5.34. What is the probability that by the close of the market today the price of this share will have risen? Who knows? Does the internet company know? Do the traders know? I suspect that if you asked them, all you would get would be a slightly rueful smile.

Probability does play a huge role in financial mathematics but not, perhaps, in quite the way you might have imagined. We will look at this more closely in Chapter 7, but to introduce a very important idea, we will think about horse racing.

In the Accrington Gold Cup, running today, there are three horses. Suppose that after considering form, the state of the course, the success rate of the jockey, a punter gives Arbitrage Annie a probability of $\frac{6}{10}$ of winning. Then there is a probability of $\frac{4}{10}$ that Arbitrage Annie will not win. These probabilities are transformed into 'odds' by writing '6 to 4 on' (to win) or '4 to 6 against' (to lose). The odds 'against' are what we want to look at because these tell us that for every £6 bet on Arbitrage Annie to win, £4 (plus the return of the stake) will be paid out. Or, for every £1 spent backing Arbitrage Annie to win, $\frac{4}{6}$ or $\frac{2}{3}$ of a pound (plus the return of the stake) is paid out to the holder of the ticket. For this reason, it is useful to us to write the odds against in the form x:1.

The probabilities and odds against on two other horses are as given below.

Horses	Probability of winning	Probability of losing	Odds (against)	Money
Arbitrage Annie	$\frac{6}{10}$	$\frac{4}{10}$	4 to 6 or $\frac{2}{3}$ to 1	5000
Bountiful Bond	$\frac{1}{10}$	$\frac{9}{10}$	9 to 1	10 000
Cash Flow	$\frac{3}{10}$	$\frac{7}{10}$	7 to 3 or $\frac{7}{3}$ to 1	15 000

If Arbitrage Annie wins, then for each £1 bet, the holder of a winning ticket receives £$(\frac{2}{3} \times 1 + 1)$.

If Cash Flow wins and I backed this horse to win, I would receive £$(\frac{7}{3} \times 1 + 1)$ for each £1 that I bet.

So let us look at what the **bookie receives** in the case of each horse winning.

Arbitrage Annie wins	Bountiful Bond wins	Cash Flow wins
$\frac{2}{3} \times (-)5000 + 25\,000$ $= 21\,666\frac{2}{3}$	$9 \times (-)10\,000 + 20\,000$ $= -70\,000$	$\frac{7}{3} \times (-)15\,000 + 15\,000$ $= -20\,000$

The bookie's expected gain =

$$\frac{6}{10} \times 21\,666\frac{2}{3} + \frac{1}{10} \times (-70\,000) + \frac{3}{10} \times (-20\,000) = 0$$

So in the long run, the bookie will break even, but there could be some heavy losses on the way.

Could the bookie do better? Could he 'engineer' a set of probabilities that will remove the risk of these heavy losses? One suggestion is that he calculate the probabilities (his odds) by looking at the possible cash pay-outs. So the bookie sets up the probabilities according to *the amount bet on each horse.*

Horses	Probability of winning	Probability of losing	Odds (against)	Money
Arbitrage Annie	$\frac{1}{6}$	$\frac{5}{6}$	5 to 1	5000
Bountiful Bond	$\frac{1}{3}$	$\frac{2}{3}$	2 to 1	10 000
Cash Flow	$\frac{1}{2}$	$\frac{1}{2}$	1 to 1 (evens)	15 000

So let us look again at what the **bookie receives** in the case of each horse winning.

Arbitrage Annie wins	Bountiful Bond wins	Cash Flow wins
$5 \times (-)5000 + 25\,000$ $= 0$	$2 \times (-)10\,000 + 20\,000$ $= 0$	$1 \times (-)15\,000 + 15\,000$ $= 0$

Now this is very much better. By changing the probabilities the bookie has eliminated his risk. Such a set of probabilities is known as **risk neutral probabilities.** These are not probabilities that relate to real-world events; they do not give winners and losers. They are much more useful than that. These probabilities create an environment in which risk is eliminated. By removing risk, we can calculate 'fair' prices. We shall see how these probabilities are calculated and used in finance in Chapter 7.

1.6 The zero curve

As mentioned earlier, interest rates permeate every area of finance. Most new ideas and a distressingly large number of old ideas need injections of cash to service developments and stimulate growth. Every loan carries with it the requirement to make interest payments. When interest rates rise, borrowers might have to pay more and this can cause real problems if budgets have been fixed with a certain range of interest payments in mind. If interest rates fall, the lenders will generally receive less money and this, too, can cause anxieties. Also, the return offered by various financial products can usefully be compared with a basic interest rate. It is vital, then, for those involved in the money markets to have some idea of future interest rates. The zero curve is constructed to provide such information and, loosely speaking, the zero curve is a graph that plots interest rate against varying maturities.

The interest rate plotted in the zero curve is chosen with considerable care. It is *not* the Official Discount Rate, or bank base rate, or the rate High Street banks charge or pay for loans or deposits. The interest rate plotted in the zero curve gives, for any maturity t, the interest rate that is implied by current trading in the market.

This might sound very sensible, if a little short on detail. Exactly how the zero curve should be plotted is a topic on which there is much disagreement. All international banks will plot, each day, a version of the zero curve and probably most will use a (slightly) different method to construct the curve. But there is some agreement. *Most zero curves follow the convention that interest rates plotted on the zero curve are continuously compounded.* Hence, if we are using a rate which is compounded quarterly to construct the zero curve, first we must calculate the equivalent continuously compounded rate. It is this equivalent continuously compounded rate that is used to plot the curve. Conversely, if we take a reading from an existing zero curve, the reading will be of a continuously compounded rate. If a semi-annually compounded rate is required, the equivalent semi-annual rate will then have to be calculated.

We shall make a first attempt to construct the zero curve for Thursday 31 July 2003. Consider LIBOR rates up to one year. These are as shown in Figure 1.7.

To produce a zero curve from these LIBOR rates, we must first calculate the equivalent continuously compounded rates. This is done in the spreadsheet shown in Figure 1.7. Then, the equivalent continuous rates are plotted against

Microsoft Excel - Chap1.7

	A	B	C	D	E
1	Chap1.7				
2					
3		rate	days	comp	rateC
4					
5	Over night	3.11031	1	365	3.110177487
6	1 month	3.43625	30	12	3.43133945
7	3 month	3.44625	90	4	3.431488925
8	6 months	3.45164	182	2	3.422193763
9	12 months	3.54016	365	1	3.478937078

=comp*LN(1+rate/(100*comp))*100

Figure 1.7

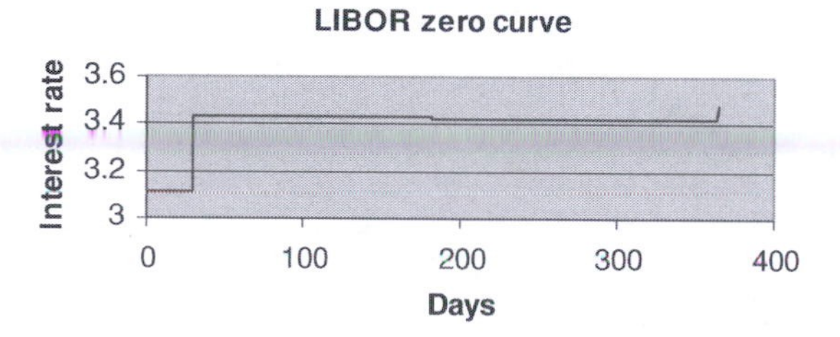

Figure 1.8

maturity. The points are joined by a sequence of straight lines and the result is the zero curve shown in Figure 1.8.

There are problems with this curve. It extends for only one year and there are no data to help us see what is happening in the large gaps between three months and six months and between six months and one year. But it is the best zero curve we can produce at the moment. So we shall regard this as a first approximation to a meaningful zero curve.

The zero curve forms a common thread in this book. In Chapters 4 and 5, we will produce more efficient and more accurate zero curves. Finally (in Chapter 5) we shall arrive at a zero curve commonly used in practice.

Exercise 1

1. Joe invests £2000 at 3.9% per annum with interest compounded twice yearly. What is the equivalent rate with the interest compounded annually?

2. Interest is charged at 3.67% per year, compounded monthly. What is the equivalent annually compounded rate?

3. Sarah can borrow £20 000 and pay interest at 6% per year (compounded annually). What is the equivalent rate when interest is compounded quarterly?

4. An investment company offers investors a rate of 4.75% per year compounded quarterly. What would be the equivalent rate with interest compounded twice yearly?

5. If interest is paid at 5.2% per year compounded annually, what will be the equivalent continuously compounded rate?

6. When £5000 is invested for six months, the interest is £200. (i) What is the (annually compounded) rate of interest? (ii) What would be the equivalent continuously compounded rate?

7. Which of the following two annual rates would be more attractive to an investor, 6.4% compounded daily or 6.395% compounded continuously?

8. Amy McPhee wishes to invest £5 000 000 for one month. Which interest rate should she choose?
   (i) AAABank offering 6.13% per year, simply compounded.
   (ii) FriendlyBank offering 6.3% per year compounded annually.
   (iii) InvestandGrow offering 6.2% per year compounded semi-annually.
   (iv) MoneyValue offering 6.11% per year compounded continuously.

9. I am offered interest rates of:
   5.5% per annum compounded quarterly
   5.49% per year compounded monthly
   5.6% per year compounded semi-annually
   5.48% per year compounded continuously.
   Which rate should I choose if I plan to (i) invest money, (ii) borrow money?

10. Alan owes £5000 on his credit card. At the end of the first week, the company charges interest of £20.19. If the company is charging a compounding

rate and Alan did not pay off any part of the debt in the meantime, how much did the company charge at the end of the fourth week?

11. Oleg owes £100 000. The interest charged is 15% (per year) compounded daily. How many days before Oleg's debt is more than £1 000 000? (Assume no repayments are made until the £1 000 000 has been reached.)

12. The interest rate today is 6.5% per year (annually compounded). What is the value today of:
    (i) £5000 to be received in two years' time?
    (ii) £10 000 to be received in six months' time?
    (iii) £10 000 000 to be received in five years' time?

13. PJ Furnishings has to pay $100 000 in two years' time. The interest rate today (continuously compounded) is 5.5%. How much should the company set aside today?

14. Smilla is to receive £20 000 in seven years' time. The interest rate is 6.5%, compounded semi-annually. What is the value today of this legacy?

15. Andrew will be paid £8500 in two years' time. What is the value of this amount today if the interest rate (compounded quarterly) is 6.8% per year?

16. FirstInvestors wants to invest a sum of money today to ensure it will have £100 000 in two years' time. Several interest rates are available:

Interest rate (per year)	Compounded
6.88	Annually
6.75	Semi-annually
6.68	Monthly
6.65	Continuously

Which interest rate should it choose?

17. An investment company will receive $15 000 in one year, $17 000 in two years, $21 000 in three years, $5000 in four years and $3000 in five years.

The interest rates with these maturities are as shown in the table:

Maturity (years)	Interest rates (per year) compounded annually
1	6.6
2	6.8
3	6.95
4	7.1
5	7.2

What is the value today of these future payments?

18. Mary invests £9956 today and in three months' time she will have £10 000. What semi-annually compounded interest rate has she used?

19. A bank will receive $10 000 in two years' time and $20 000 in four years' time. The interest rate with a two-year maturity is 5.8% per year with quarterly compounding. The bank would like to borrow $24 000 today and use the money it is to receive in two years and in four years to pay off the loan. What interest rate (compounded quarterly) with a maturity of four years will it need?

20. A share in XAY company costs £7.38 on the London Stock Exchange. This share is selling for $13.14 on the New York Stock Exchange. The exchange rate is £1 = $1.775. What should I do? What assumptions have you made to calculate your answer?

21. The value of 1 000 000 yen on the London currency market is £5000. On the Frankfurt market, 1 000 000 yen is quoted at €7376.21. Today, €1 = £0.6826. What should I do? What is likely to happen next?

22. In New York, the sterling exchange rate is £1 = $1.73. In Moscow, £1 = 51.752 Russian rubles (RUB). In Moscow, one US dollar will buy 27.98 Russian rubles. Is this an arbitrage opportunity?

23. Today, a car in Brussels costs €17 500. It will cost Asha €300 to transport the car to England. Today, Asha confirmed the sale of this car for £13 000. The exchange rate is £1 = €1.464. Is this an arbitrage opportunity? If so, give Asha's risk-free profit.

24. I can borrow money at 6.53% per year compounded semi annually. A bond will pay me £100 in nine months' time. I can buy this bond for £95.50. Should I buy the bond? Outline a strategy and describe the profits from the strategy.

25. (i) On the Tokyo market, £1 = 198.738 yen. In Hamburg, €1 = 135 yen and in London, £1 = €1.4715.
    (a) Why is the product $198.738 \times \frac{1}{135} \times \frac{1}{1.4715}$ of interest?
    (b) Evaluate this product. What do you deduce?

    (ii) Today, £1 = a yen, 1 yen = €b, €1 = £c.
    What would you do if:
    (i) $abc > 1$?
    (ii) $abc = 1$?
    (iii) $abc < 1$?

26. Show that if two portfolios give rise to identical values at maturity, then in a world free of arbitrage, they must have the same value today.

27. In the Queen Anne stakes, the strongly fancied BoomAnBust meets the ever reliable SoarinInflation (there are no other horses). On race day, the odds are:

    BoomAnBust: 5 to 2 against
    SoarinInflation: 5 to 2 on.

    On race day, £4000 is bet on BoomAnBust to win and £8000 is bet on SoarinInflation to win.
    (i) Write down the probabilities that each horse might win.
    (ii) Calculate the bookies' expected gain.
    (iii) From the bookies' viewpoint, what is the worst that can happen?
    (iv) Suggest how the bookies could shift the odds (and create a new set of probabilities) to produce a risk-free race.

28. An interest rate R (R is an annual rate) is compounded m times a year. An equivalent interest rate Q is an annual rate compounded n times a year. Show that $Q = n[(1+\frac{R}{m})^{\frac{m}{n}} - 1]$. If U is an equivalent rate compounded continuously, show that $R = m \times [e^{\frac{U}{m}} - 1]$.

29. Mike borrows £10 000 at 6% per year (compounded annually) for one year. After four months, he pays £2000 to the company from which he took the

loan. This amount is not immediately deducted from what he owes – the £2000 will be deducted from the amount he owes at the maturity of the loan. At the end of the year, Mike pays off the remainder of what he owes. What rate of interest did Mike pay on this loan?

Suppose now that Mike pays a further £2000 to the company after eight months. This amount also will not be deducted immediately from what he owes but will be deducted at maturity. What interest rate did Mike pay on this loan? (Note: you might find it useful to use Goal Seek in Excel to solve this part of the problem.)

2 Forward contracts

Let's take three situations.

A. A farmer growing organic crops has invested heavily this year in the production of frozen organic peas. The freezing plant cost the farmer a great deal of money. There is little surplus in his budget and it is important that, this year, he gets a good price for his frozen peas. Today is 1 March and the price he would get for one unit (16 ounces) of frozen peas is \$2.37. There are signs of a wonderful spring and the farmer is concerned that a bumper harvest might force down prices. He would like to avoid this uncertainty. Could the farmer agree **today** a price for his peas that would be enforceable when he comes to sell his harvest in September?

B. A company is close to completing a large construction contract in Japan. The agreement is that the company will be paid in yen and the financial director knows that in four months' time, she will receive 3.5 billion yen. The pound/yen exchange rate today is £1 = 187.93 yen, so if the yen were to be sold for pounds today, the company would receive $£\frac{3500000000}{187.93} = £18.623956$ million. The financial director is concerned, however, that in the short term, the yen might weaken against the pound. This would cause the company to lose money in the settlement of the contract. Clearly, she would like to avoid this uncertainty. Is there a way that she could agree **today** a pound/yen exchange rate that would be applicable in four months' time?

C. The price of a ULS share, today, 8 March, is £10.75. These shares are paying, this year, an annual dividend of 6% in two instalments: the first instalment will be paid in one month's time, the second six months later. Stella's financial advisor recommends that she enters a contract to purchase 1000 ULS shares on 8 November. Stella can borrow money at 5% per year, compounded annually, and she enters a contract to buy the shares on 8 November. What price should Stella agree, **today**, to pay for the shares on 8 November?

On 8 May, the share price had fallen to £9.25 and Stella wanted to sell the contract. On this day, what would be the value of the contract?

In this chapter, these questions will be answered and the answer will involve a forward contract.

2.1 The forward contract

Definition A forward contract is an agreement, made today, for the sale/purchase of an asset for an agreed price on an agreed future date. It costs nothing to enter a forward contract, so no money changes hands today. This means that the value of a forward contract, at the time it is entered, is zero. The two parties to the contract exchange the asset and the agreed price on the agreed future date.

Notes:

(1) The asset might be a commodity (cereal, meat, gold, etc.), a security (stock in a company, bonds) or a currency (yen, dollars, krona). The parties must agree the precise nature of the asset to be sold. For example, if the asset is gold, there has to be agreement over purity; if the asset is wheat or cattle, agreement over quality is essential. If the asset is stock, there must be agreement over which company issues the stock and over the type and class of share.

(2) The delivery date is specified. With some assets, there are clear seasonal variations (turkeys, wheat, fruit) and in many important cases, contracts are available only for delivery in certain months (in particular, see Chapter 3).

(3) There must be agreement on the method and manner of delivery of the asset. If the contract is to buy money in a certain currency, there must be an agreement on where (into which bank account) the currency is to be paid. There might be occasions when currency is handed over directly to the buyer. In such a case, as well as agreeing where and when the exchange will occur, there might be a requirement for the currency to be in certain denominations (in $100 bills, say). If the contract is to buy wheat, both sides must agree on where, and how, the wheat should be delivered (Upper Hill Farm, Stroud, Shropshire, say, or A1 Warehouse, A1 Industrial Estate, Wapping and packed in standard-sized bales).

An overview of the chapter

The farmer in A would take out a forward contract to sell his frozen peas (the asset) at an agreed price on 1 September. But how can we agree today a price that will be fair when the exchange takes place on a date in the future? Answering this question will be the subject of the first part of the chapter. An agreement that puts a fixed future price on an asset will, as time passes, gain monetary value. In the second part of the chapter, we show how to calculate the value over time of a forward contract. Finally, we will show how to apply these methods to assets that pay a dividend.

First, we clarify the meaning of some terms in the definition of a forward contract, then we provide a list of some notation used in the chapter and later in the book.

Notation **Maturity** (T) The date specified in a forward contract for the exchange of the asset and cash is called the **maturity** of the contract. The time that must elapse before maturity is called the **duration** or the **time to maturity** of the contract. When no date is specified, we write T to represent the time at maturity. If the contract is entered today ($t = 0$), the time to maturity is T years. If the contract is entered at time t, the time to maturity is $T - t$ years.

Delivery price (K) The money handed over, at maturity, in exchange for the asset is called the **delivery price**. We will denote this by K. The delivery price is fixed on the day the contract is set up. The value K will not change during the life of the contract.

Spot price (S_0) The value of the asset today is S_0. This is called the **spot price** (S_0 for SpOt). The value of the asset at time t is S_t. The value of the asset at maturity is S_T.

Interest rate (R) We will assume that the **interest rate** R is constant throughout the contract. Since most contracts are of a shortish duration, this is not too severe a restriction. As usual, the annual **rate** will be written as $R = \frac{r}{100}$.

A person who enters a forward contract to **buy** the asset is said to be entering a **long** forward contract. A person who enters the forward contract to **sell** the asset is said to be entering a **short** forward contract. So, in the financial world, going **long** means you **buy**; going **short** means you are **selling**.

Portfolio A **portfolio** is a collection of assets. Some of the assets might be commodities (wheat, sugar, gold), some might be securities (shares in Abbey National, bonds) and some might be cash (pounds, dollars, rubles). The value of the portfolio will change with time. We shall write:

V_0 = value of a portfolio today ($t = 0$)

V_T = value of a portfolio at time T.

Our pricing strategy will invoke the 'no arbitrage' principle.

Recall that this says that there cannot exist a portfolio having the property:
$V_0 = 0$ and $V_T \geq 0$ for all possible market outcomes
$V_T > 0$ for at least one possible market outcome.

To recap: a six-month long forward contract on 1000 BT shares with delivery price £2.50 per share means that you are contracting to buy 1000 BT shares for £2500 in six months' time. No money is paid today. The contract, initially, has zero value. At maturity, you hand over the delivery price (£2500) in exchange for the 1000 shares.

2.2 To calculate the delivery price (on an asset that does not pay any dividends)

In a forward contract, the asset and the maturity are determined largely by external conditions. (What do you want to buy or sell? When do you need it? When can you sell it?) It is the delivery price that is of real interest and we shall require the delivery price to satisfy two conditions:

(i) The delivery price must be set to preclude the possibility of any arbitrage opportunities.
(ii) The delivery price must reflect current market conditions and must be, demonstrably, the 'right price' for the asset at maturity.

To calculate a delivery price satisfying these conditions, we establish a portfolio (V). This portfolio will consist of some cash, the asset, and a forward contract. The portfolio will be set up so that initially (at $t = 0$) the value of the portfolio will be zero ($V_0 = 0$). The portfolio will be designed so that its value at maturity will be independent of the value of the asset. So V_T will be dependent only on T and, by the Useful Remark in section 1.4, to avoid arbitrage, we must have $V_T = 0$. This condition will force out an arbitrage-free, market-sensitive value for the delivery price.

We illustrate the method for Example A given at the beginning of the chapter.

Example 1

A farmer (call him Farmer A) grows and freezes organically cultivated peas. He is worried that the price of peas might fall. Today is 1 March and the price he would get today for one unit (16 ounces) of frozen peas is \$2.37. The farmer plans to sell his crop in September and if the price for peas fell significantly, the farmer would have financial problems. He would like to avoid this uncertainty. Today, the farmer enters a forward contract to sell 10 000 units of frozen peas on 1 September. The interest rate is 6.5% per year, compounded annually.

What is the delivery price in this contract? Or, to put it another way, what is the price, agreed today, that the farmer will receive for his frozen peas on 1 September?

Solution

Strategy
Set up a portfolio V as follows:

Today: (t = 0)

Borrow the cash needed to buy one unit of the asset. The farmer borrows $2.37.

Buy one unit of the asset (one unit of frozen peas).

Enter a forward contract to sell one unit of the asset, at maturity, for £K (the delivery price).

What was borrowed has been spent. The value of a forward contract, initially, is zero. Hence, the value of the portfolio is: $V_0 = 2.37 - 2.37 + 0 = 0$.

At maturity: (in six months' time; $T = \frac{1}{2}$)

Repay the loan: so hand over $\$2.37 \times (1 + 0.065)^{\frac{1}{2}} = \$2.45$.

Hand over one unit of the asset (one unit of frozen peas).

Receive the delivery price £K.

The contract has been discharged: the value of the forward contract is zero.
The value of the portfolio at time T is: $V_T = -\$2.45 + K + 0 = K - 2.45$

The portfolio was constructed so that its value at maturity is independent of the value of the asset. V_T depends only on T. So as with the Useful Remark in section 1.4:

If $V_T > 0$ an arbitrage opportunity exists (the holder makes a guaranteed profit).

If $V_T < 0$ an arbitrage opportunity exists (the other party makes a guaranteed profit).

So under the assumption of no arbitrage, $V_T = 0$.

This gives $K - 2.45 = 0$.

Therefore $K = \$2.45$.

Clearly, the 'no arbitrage' condition is satisfied and (as we now show) the value found for the delivery price is demonstrably the right price.

(i) Suppose the delivery price > 2.45.

Suppose, in fact, it was 2.47.

On 1 March:

Borrow $2.37 at 6.5% for six months.

Buy one unit of frozen peas.

Enter a forward contract to sell one unit of frozen peas on 1 September for \$2.47.

On 1 September:

Repay the loan: pay out $2.37 \times 1.065^{\frac{1}{2}} = \$2.45$.

Sell one unit of frozen peas (under the forward contract) for \$2.47.

This gives a guaranteed profit of $2.47 - 2.45 = \$0.02$ per unit. But in this world, arbitrage opportunities do not exist. So we cannot have a delivery price greater than \$2.45.

(ii) Suppose the delivery price < 2.45.

Suppose it was \$2.41.

On 1 March:

Borrow one unit of frozen peas.

Sell the peas and receive \$2.37.

Invest \$2.37 at 6.5% for six months.

Enter a forward contract to buy one unit of frozen peas on 1 September.

On 1 September:

Receive (from the investment) $2.37 \times 1.065^{\frac{1}{2}} = 2.45$.

Buy one unit of frozen peas (under the forward contract) for \$2.41.

Return the unit of peas.

This gives the farmer a guaranteed profit (of \$0.04 per unit) and so represents an arbitrage opportunity. Hence, the delivery price cannot be less than \$2.45.

We are running out of options. The only delivery price that will not permit an arbitrage opportunity is \$2.45. This is demonstrably the right price.

Since the farmer wants to sell 10 000 units of frozen peas, this 'contract' would be 'repeated' 10 000 times. The farmer would then receive \$24 500 for his 10 000 units. It is easier, however, to work with one unit of the asset and this we will continue to do.

To express the delivery price in terms of S_0, R and T (there are no dividend payments in this example) we explain the strategy in general terms.

Strategy

Assume that the current interest rate is r% per year; we will assume annual compounding. R is the annual rate.

Set up a portfolio V consisting of cash, the asset and a forward contract, as follows:

Today: ($t = 0$).

Borrow the spot price S_0. This is the cash needed to buy one unit of the asset.

Buy one unit of the asset.

Enter a forward contract to sell one unit of the asset, on the delivery date, for £K.

What was borrowed has been spent. The initial value of a forward contract is zero. The value of the portfolio at $t = 0$ *is:* $V_0 = S_0 - S_0 + 0 = 0$

At maturity: ($t = T$).

Repay the loan: so pay out $S_0 \times (1 + R)^T$.

Hand over one unit of the asset.

Receive the delivery price £K.

The contract has been discharged: the value of the forward contract is now zero.

The value of the portfolio at time T is:

$$V_T = -S_0 \times (1 + R)^T + K + 0 = K - S_0 \times (1 + R)^T$$

V_T depends only on T. To prohibit an arbitrage opportunity, we require that $V_T = 0$.

This gives: $K - S_0 \times (1 + R)^T = 0$.

Therefore $K = S_0 \times (1 + R)^T$.

The delivery price (for a maturity T years hence)
$= S_0 \times (1 + R)^T$.

2.3 Delivery price and the forward price

The delivery price represents the perceived value of the asset, T years in the future. This is a useful idea. Knowing how to use conditions known today to calculate the future value of an asset is very appealing. We use a forward contract to define the **forward price** of an asset.

The delivery price ($2.45) in the farmer's forward contract could, very reasonably, be called the six-month forward price of frozen peas. More generally, the T year forward price of an asset is the delivery price in a forward contract on the asset set up today and with maturity in T years' time. With a view towards forward rate agreements and swaps in Chapter 5, we could also say that the forward price on an asset is that value of K (the delivery price) that gives the corresponding forward contract an initial value of zero.

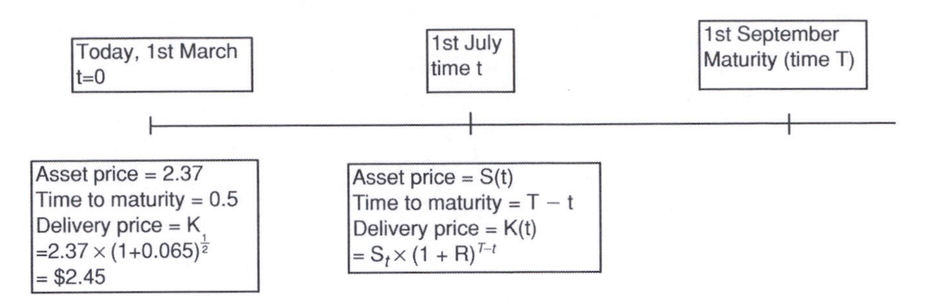

Figure 2.1

To obtain the three-month forward price of gold, examine the delivery price on a forward contract in gold, set up today, with maturity in three months' time.

But be careful: 'delivery price' on a forward contract of duration T years and 'T year forward price' are not necessarily the same. The delivery price on a forward contract, once fixed, cannot be changed. But as time passes and the asset changes value, the T year forward price of the asset will change.

Example 2

The delivery price on the farmer's six-month forward contract is \$2.45. Today, 1 March, the six-month forward price of frozen peas is \$2.45. But suppose that on 1 April the spot price of one unit of frozen peas is \$2.33. A six-month forward contract taken out on 1 April will have delivery price $2.33 \times (1 + 0.065)^{\frac{1}{2}} = 2.40$. So on 1 April, the six-month forward price of frozen peas is \$2.40. But the delivery price on the farmer's forward contract is still \$2.45.

It is time for a definition. Observe that forward price is defined in terms of a forward contract. Hence the definition of forward price must involve the time the contract is set up and the time of maturity.

Definition We are at time t. An asset X has value S_t. Enter a forward contract (maturity time T) on X. The duration of the forward contract is $T - t$ and the delivery price is K.

Then the $T - t$ forward price on X (at time t) $= S_t \times (1 + R)^{T-t}$ (see Figure 2.1).

Notes:

1. This definition builds on the above remarks.
   If $t = 0$ (the present time is today), then:
   The $T - 0$ forward price $= S_0 \times (1 + R)^T$

So the T forward price has the same value as the delivery price on a forward contract with duration T years.

2. The term 'forward price' is widely used in practice and in the literature. Also, we shall use the forward price when we investigate the value of a forward contract.

Example 3

A company knows it will have to buy 100 000 barrels of crude oil, in the market, in one month's time. The situation in the Middle East is turbulent and the company fears that the price of crude oil could rise considerably. The market price, today, for one barrel of crude oil is \$68.05. The company enters a long one-month forward contract on 100 000 barrels of oil.

(a) What is the one-month forward price for this type of crude oil?
(b) After one week, the company's fears are confirmed. The price of one barrel of oil has risen to \$69.75. What is the three-week forward price for one barrel of this oil?

Solution

(a) The company wishing to buy 100 000 barrels of crude oil in one month's time should enter 100 long (to buy) forward contracts on 1000 barrels of crude oil. On each contract, $S_0 = \$68\,050$, $T = \frac{1}{12}$. Assuming a constant interest rate r = 7.85% per year (interest compounded annually), the one month forward price of 1000 barrels of crude oil will be $S_0 \times (1 + R)^T = 68\,050 \times 1.0785^{\frac{1}{12}} = \$68\,479.90$.
(b) The three-week forward price involves a spot price of $S_t = \$69.75$ and a time to maturity of $T - t = \frac{3}{52}$.

$$\begin{aligned}\text{The three-week forward price} &= S_t \times (1 + R)^{T-t} \\ &= 69.75 \times 1.0785^{\frac{3}{52}} \\ &= \$70.05\end{aligned}$$

In many instances, it is convenient to assume that the interest rate is continuously compounded. In this case, the money to be repaid on a loan to cover the spot price, S_0, is $S_0 \times e^{RT}$

Following through the argument, using continuous repayment, gives:
When interest is continuously compounded:
The delivery price K (for a maturity of T years)

$$\mathbf{K = S_0 \times e^{RT}}$$

The $T - t$ forward price F_t at time t ($t > 0$)

$$F_t = S_t \times e^{R(T-t)}$$

There is symmetry in this argument: when someone sells, someone buys. So the forward price in a long forward contract is identical to that in a short forward contract.

Example 4

A company wishes to buy 200 ounces of gold in three months' time. The interest rate is 3.9% per annum (continuously compounded).

(i) If the spot price for gold of this purity is \$600 per ounce, find the three-month forward price of gold.
(ii) One month later, the spot price is \$601.5 per ounce. If the interest rate is unchanged, find, on this date, the two-month forward price of gold.

Solution

(i) $S_0 = 600 \quad R = 0.039 \quad T = \frac{1}{4}$

$$\begin{aligned} \text{The three-month forward price} &= S_0 \times e^{RT} \\ &= 600 \times e^{0.039 \times 0.25} \\ &= 605.88 \end{aligned}$$

(ii) One month later, $S_0 = 601.5 \quad R = 0.039 \quad T = \frac{1}{6}$

$$\begin{aligned} \text{The two-month forward price} &= S_0 \times e^{RT} \\ &= 601.5 \times e^{0.039 \times \frac{1}{6}} \\ &= 605.42 \end{aligned}$$

2.4 The value of a forward contract

Introduction

Forward contracts can be used to reduce uncertainty. But markets do not exist to help people cope with their anxieties. Markets exist to make money. We show now that forward contracts change in value over time and so can be thought of speculatively.

Consider Farmer A in the above example. On 1 March, he took out forward contracts because he was concerned that a bumper harvest would cause the price of peas to fall. It turns out that he was right. On 1 April, pea prices were down on their 1 March value. And again on 1 May, prices were below the level of the previous month. But remember: the farmer owned a contract which guaranteed a price for frozen peas based on the 1 March spot price and on 1 March the value of this contract was zero. Then, over successive months, as the price of peas fell, the value of Farmer A's contract must have risen. In this section, we calculate the value of this forward contract over time.

The value of a forward contract (the calculations)

Suppose the spot price of one unit of frozen peas over the six months 1 March to 1 September is as shown in the table.

Date	1 March	1 April	1 May	1 June	1 July	1 August	1 September
Spot price	2.37	2.33	2.29	2.27	2.26	2.27	2.28

We assume that the interest rate, r, is constant at 6.5% with annual compounding. By entering a forward contract on 1 March, Farmer A ensured that for each of the 10 000 units he had agreed to sell on 1 September, he would receive $2.45 – or $24 500 in all.

A second farmer (Farmer B) did not realise until 1 April that the price of peas was dropping. So on 1 April, he entered a forward contract to sell on 1 September 10 000 units of frozen peas. For this contract, the spot price (S_0) is $2.33 and the time to maturity (T) is $\frac{5}{12}$. The delivery price K is given by:

$$K = 2.33 \times (1 + 0.065)^{\frac{5}{12}} = 2.39$$

On 1 September, Farmer B will receive $2.39 for each of his 10 000 units, or $23 900 in all. This is $600 less than Farmer A will receive. It would seem that on 1 April, the forward contract held by Farmer A ought to have a monetary value.

We will use f to represent the value of Farmer A's contract (f will represent the value per unit). On 1 March this value is f_0. Since forward contracts initially have zero value, $f_0 = 0$. On 1 April the value of this contract is f_1. By comparing the values of the contracts held by Farmer A and Farmer B, we will show how to calculate f_1.

	1 March ($t = 0$)	1 April ($t = \frac{1}{12}$)	1 September ($t = \frac{1}{2}$)
Farmer A	value $f_0 = 0$	value $= f_1$	Receives 2.45 per unit
Farmer B	–	value $= 0$	Receives 2.39 per unit

Difference in value between the contracts on 1 September

$= 2.45 - 2.39 = 0.06.$

Difference in value between the contracts on 1 April = $f_1 - 0 = f_1$

So a difference of f_1 becomes, five months later, a difference of 0.06.

To ensure that no arbitrage opportunities are allowed to creep in, these differences must mirror exactly an investment in a bank account. (See the first definition of an arbitrage opportunity, in section 1.2.) Or, to put it another way, f_1 must be the present value of 0.06 (discounted over five months at 6.5% per year).

Hence the value of Farmer A's contract on 1 April is:

$$f_1 = \frac{0.06}{(1+0.065)^{\frac{5}{12}}} = 0.0584$$

On 1 May, Farmer C noticed that the price of peas was falling. On that day, he entered a forward contract to sell 10 000 units of frozen peas on 1 September. For this contract, the spot price (S_0) is $2.29 and the time to maturity (T) is $\frac{4}{12}$. The delivery price is K.

$$K = 2.29 \times (1+0.065)^{\frac{4}{12}} = 2.34$$

So on 1 September, Farmer C will receive $23 400 for his 10 000 units of frozen peas. This is $1100 less than Farmer A will receive. Let f_2 represent the value of Farmer A's contract on 1 May.

	1 March	1 April	1 May	1 September
Farmer A	value $f_0 = 0$	value $f_1 = 0.0584$	value = f_2	Receives 2.45
Farmer C			value = 0	Receives 2.34

Now, the difference in values on 1 September = 2.45 − 2.34 = 0.11

The difference in values on 1 May = $f_2 - 0 = f_2$

So a difference of f_2 becomes, four months later, a difference of 0.11.

Again, to exclude the possibility of arbitrage opportunities, these differences must match, exactly, an investment at the 'safe' rate, r. So f_2 must be (or face arbitrage) the present value of 0.11 (discounted at 6.5% per year over four months).

$$\text{So} \quad f_2 = \frac{0.11}{(1+0.065)^{\frac{4}{12}}} = 0.1077$$

The Excel spreadsheet in Figure 2.2 illustrates further calculations.

Observe that maturity (column B) and spot (column C) have range names, while rate (D6) carries a cell name.

The increasing value of Farmer A's forward contract is illustrated in Figure 2.3.

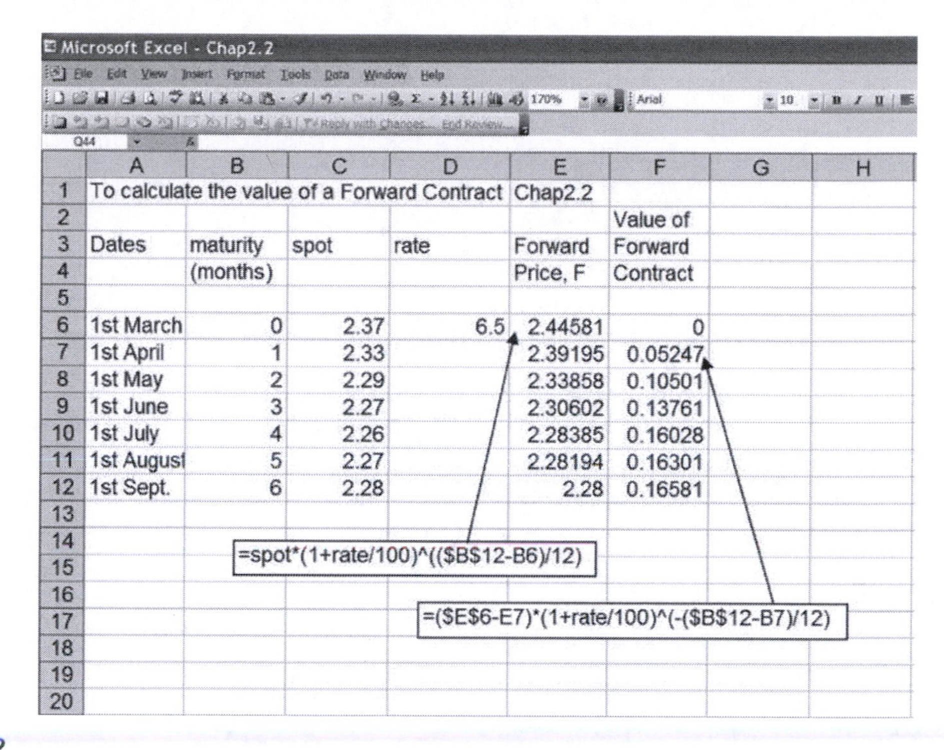

	A	B	C	D	E	F	G	H
1	To calculate the value of a Forward Contract				Chap2.2			
2						Value of		
3	Dates	maturity	spot	rate	Forward	Forward		
4		(months)			Price, F	Contract		
5								
6	1st March	0	2.37	6.5	2.44581	0		
7	1st April	1	2.33		2.39195	0.05247		
8	1st May	2	2.29		2.33858	0.10501		
9	1st June	3	2.27		2.30602	0.13761		
10	1st July	4	2.26		2.28385	0.16028		
11	1st August	5	2.27		2.28194	0.16301		
12	1st Sept.	6	2.28		2.28	0.16581		

=spot*(1+rate/100)^(($B$12-B6)/12)

=($E$6-E7)*(1+rate/100)^(-($B$12-B7)/12)

Figure 2.2

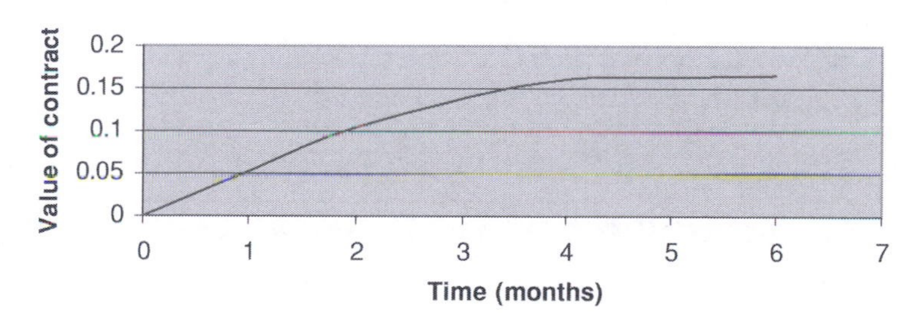

Figure 2.3

Notice how the forward price converges to the spot price at maturity (as would be expected).

The general formula

Consider two short (to sell an asset) forward contracts A and B. The contracts are written on the same asset and mature on the same date. Contract A is entered today ($t = 0$); contract B is entered later at time t ($0 < t < T$).

Contract A: delivery price (the T forward price of the asset) = K.
Contract B: delivery price (the T − t forward price of the asset) = F_t.
At time t: value of contract A = f_t.
value of contract B = 0.

	time = 0	time = t	Maturity: time = T
A	value = $f_0 = 0$	value = f_t	Receives K
B		value = 0	Receives F_t

So the difference in the contracts at maturity = $K - F_t$
The difference in the contracts at time t = f_t
To avoid arbitrage opportunities, the difference at time t must be the discounted value of the difference at maturity. Discounting at the annually compounded rate R over time T − t gives

$$f_t = \frac{K - F_t}{(1 + R)^{T-t}}$$

This is often written as:

$$f_t = (K - F_t) \times (1 + R)^{-(T-t)}$$

If the safe interest rate R is compounded continuously, this becomes:

$$f_t = (K - F_t) \times e^{-R(T-t)}$$

So we have found the value f_t at time t of a short forward contract.
For the corresponding long forward contract, we have:

$$f_t = (F_t - K) \times (1 + R)^{-(T-t)}$$ for an annually compounded rate R.

$$f_t = (F_t - K) \times e^{-R(T-t)}$$ for a continuously compounded rate R.

These equations will be useful (in section 2.7) where we calculate the value of a forward contract on an asset that pays a dividend.
The remainder of this chapter could be postponed until a second reading. The ideas have all gone before, but the calculations become more intricate.

2.5 Assets paying dividends

Dividends are financial rewards paid to the holders of certain kinds of assets. From our point of view, dividends are a sequence of regular and predictable payments based on the value of the asset. We will assume that the value of each dividend payment is known in advance. Dividends are paid in one of two ways.

1 Discrete dividend payments

Cash payments are made to the holder of the asset at regular intervals throughout the year. Shares and bonds come into this category.

Shares

Each year, or several times a year, the board of directors of a company will decide how much of the profits are to be paid out to the share holders in the form of dividends. The purpose of paying a dividend is to reward the share holders for investing their money in the company (buying their shares). Share holders might expect to make money by seeing the value of the shares they hold rise at a faster rate than the safe interest rate. But if a company is not experiencing a reasonable rise in the value of its shares, generous dividend payments might have the effect of keeping the share holders happy. Dividend payments are made to share holders on the basis of a certain amount of cash to be paid per share held and a dividend is paid (usually) twice a year in the UK and four times a year in the US. Although, strictly speaking, the value of a share dividend is not known in advance of the board's decision, in practice, companies like to keep the cash per share amount much the same, year to year. So the insistence that dividend payments are known in advance is not, in practice, unduly restrictive.

Bonds

The dividend (often called a coupon) is a stated percentage (e.g. 6%) of the face value of the bond (e.g. $100). This is usually paid twice yearly (e.g. a payment of $3 every six months).

2 Continuous dividend payments

The asset pays a dividend continuously.

Examples:

Currency: A person holding a foreign currency can receive interest at the current risk-free rate of that foreign country. The holder of the currency could invest the money in a bond issued by the foreign country. We will assume that this foreign risk-free rate is compounded continuously.
Gold: Over a certain period, the value of gold will rise. The increase in value could be viewed as a continuously paid dividend.

To cope with continuous dividend payments, we define the **dividend yield** of an asset

$$\text{dividend yield} = \frac{\text{dividend or income}}{\text{value of asset}} \times 100$$

So the dividend yield is the dividend/income from an asset expressed as a percentage of the value of the asset.

Example 5

A stock currently priced at £28.50 pays a dividend of £3. The dividend yield is $\frac{3}{28.5} \times 100 = 10.53\%$.

2.6 Forward contracts on assets that pay discrete dividends

Forward contracts on dividend-paying assets are priced and valued in the same way as non-dividend-paying assets. But the flow of cash from the asset during the existence of the contract causes some differences in the detail. The overall plan is as before: first we outline the strategy, then we show how this is implemented.

Strategy

Today ($t = 0$): Set up a portfolio V consisting of cash, the asset and a forward contract.

Borrow precisely the amount of cash needed to ensure you have possession of one unit of the asset at maturity.
Buy one unit of the asset.
Enter a forward contract to sell one unit of the asset for £K at maturity.

Maturity ($t = T$):
Pay off the existing loan on the contract.
Hand over one unit of the asset.
Receive the delivery price, £K.

Implementation

The devil, they say, is in the detail. If the asset pays out a dividend before maturity, this dividend can be used to pay off part of the loan. We shall arrange matters so that **each** dividend, as it is paid, pays off a separate loan. Since the dividends pay off loans taken out to buy the asset, there is less cash to be paid out at maturity. The technique is illustrated in the example that follows.

Example 6

The share price today (S_0) of AirC is £6.75. The share will pay a dividend of £0.20 after four months and after ten months. I enter a forward contract to sell one unit of the asset (1 share) in 14 months' time. I can borrow money at 4.5% per year with interest compounded annually. What is the delivery price on this contract? Or, equivalently, what is the 14-month forward price of an AirC share?

Solution

Today ($t = 0$):

Borrow £6.75.

Buy one share.

Enter a forward contract to sell one share for £K in 14 months' time ($t = \frac{14}{12}$).

We do this. But now, by owning one share, we receive the dividends the share pays out. So we receive £0.20 after four months and £0.20 after ten months. *We shall arrange to borrow the £6.75 so that a part of the loan will be paid off by these dividends.* This is a real bonus. At maturity, we will not have to pay off the entirety of the loan: the dividends from the share will pay off a part of the loan. In this way, the dividend payments will reduce the amount we have to repay at maturity. Now we show, in detail, how the strategy is put into practice.

Today ($t = 0$)

(1) Find the present value of the first dividend payment (discount £0.20 at 4.5% over four months).

$$R = 0.045 \quad \text{and} \quad t = \frac{4}{12}$$

Present value $= £0.20 \times (1 + 0.045)^{-\frac{4}{12}} = 0.1971$

Borrow this amount today at 4.5% for four months. 0.1971

(2) Find the present value of the second dividend payment (discount £0.20 at 4.5% over ten months).

$$R = 0.045 \quad \text{and} \quad t = \frac{10}{12}$$

Present value $= £0.20 \times (1 + 0.045)^{-\frac{10}{12}} = 0.1928$

Borrow this amount today at 4.5% for ten months. 0.1928
(We have borrowed, in total, £(0.1971 + 0.1928) = £0.3899.
This amount will be paid off in part after four months, with the first dividend payment, with the remainder paid off after ten months by the second dividend payment.)

To acquire one share, it remains to borrow £6.75 – £0.3899 = £6.3601.

(3) **Borrow** £6.3601 at 4.5% per year for 14 months. 6.3601
(4) **Buy** one share.
(5) **Enter a forward contract** to sell one share for £K at maturity.
What was borrowed has been spent. The forward contract has an initial value of zero. The initial value of the portfolio is: $V_0 = 0$.

On delivery day (t = T)

(1) **Pay off** the existing loan:
This is $6.3601 \times (1 + 0.045)^{\frac{14}{12}} = £\,6.6952$.
(2) **Hand over** the share.
(3) **Receive** the delivery price, £K.
The contract has been discharged: the value of the forward contract is zero and the value of the portfolio is: $V_T = K - 6.6952$.

As with the non-dividend-paying asset, since $V_0 = 0$, to prohibit arbitrage, we require $V_T = 0$. This forces K = £6.6952. The 14-month forward price for an AirC share is £6.70.

These calculations are made very conveniently in an Excel spreadsheet. We illustrate the method in the next example, then give a general result, followed by a possible Excel spreadsheet.

The aim is to calculate the forward price for a dividend-paying asset. Clearly, for every sale there has to be a purchase. To calculate the forward price using a forward contract to buy the asset, simply use the above strategy and calculate the forward price using an otherwise identical forward contract to sell the asset.

Example 7

Today is 4 June. The price of a EuroP share is £8.69. The share is paying a dividend of 4% per year, twice yearly, with dividends due in two months' and in eight months' time. It is thought the dividend for the following year will be slightly higher at 4.2% per year. A dividend at this new rate will be paid in 14 months' time. I enter a forward contract to buy 5000 EuroP shares in 18 months' time. I can borrow money at 7.1% per year with semi-annual compounding. Calculate the 18-month forward price of the 5000 shares.

Solution

We calculate the forward price using the corresponding forward contract to buy the asset.

Observe:

(1) Prior to maturity, the share will make three dividend payments.

In the first year, the total annual dividend will be $0.04 \times 8.69 = 0.3476$. Hence the dividends in two months and in eight months will each pay $0.5 \times 0.3476 = 0.1738$.

In the second year, the total annual dividend will be $0.042 \times 8.69 = 0.3650$. (Assume, for the purposes of calculation, that the share price is unchanged.) So the third dividend, in 14 months, will pay $0.5 \times 0.3650 = 0.1825$.

(2) For discounting and interest rate calculations we will use a rate of 0.071 per year compounded twice yearly.

(3) We will work, as before, with one unit of the asset (one share). When the forward price of one share has been calculated, we will multiply this price by 5000 to get the forward price of 5000 shares.

Step 1

Today ($t = 0$), set up the loans which will be paid off (in three cases) by the dividends and in the fourth case at maturity. The calculations are illustrated in Table 2.1.

(1) **Borrow** 0.1718 at 7.1% per year (compounded twice yearly) for two months.

(2) **Borrow** 0.1659 at 7.1% per year (compounded twice yearly) for eight months.

Table 2.1

Spot price =	8.69		
Interest rate =	0.071		
Comp. periods per year =	2		
	Dividend	Time	Discounted dividend (DD)
Dividend 1	0.1738	$\frac{2}{12}$	$0.1738 \times (1 + \frac{0.071}{2})^{-2\times\frac{2}{12}} = 0.1718$
Dividend 2	0.1738	$\frac{8}{12}$	$0.1738 \times (1 + \frac{0.071}{2})^{-2\times\frac{8}{12}} = 0.1659$
Dividend 3	0.1825	$\frac{14}{12}$	$0.1825 \times (1 + \frac{0.071}{2})^{-2\times\frac{14}{12}} = 0.1682$
		Sum (DD)	$0.1718 + 0.1659 + 0.1682 = 0.5059$
Spot price − Sum (DD)	$8.69 - 0.5059 =$	8.1841	
Forward price =	$8.1841 \times (1 + \frac{0.071}{2})^{2\times\frac{18}{12}} =$	9.0870	

(3) **Borrow** 0.1682 at 7.1% per year (compounded twice yearly) for 14 months. *(This gives a total borrowing of 0.1718 + 0.1659 + 0.1682 = 0.5059)*
(4) **Borrow** 8.69 − 0.5059 = 8.1841 at 7.1% per year (compounded twice yearly) for 18 months.
(5) **Buy** one share.
(6) **Enter a forward contract** to sell one share in 18 months' time.

Step 2

Calculate the amount to be repaid on delivery day. (The first three loans, of course, will be paid off by the dividend payments.)

On delivery day

Repay $8.1841 \times \left(1 + \frac{0.071}{2}\right)^{2\times\frac{18}{12}} = £9.0870$

Receive $£K$

For there to be no arbitrage opportunities, K = £9.0870 or £9.09.

Hence, the 18-month forward price on 5000 EuroP shares is:

5000 × 9.0870 = £45 435

To calculate the forward price of an asset paying a discrete dividend

To produce a formula we will assume that the rate R is compounded m times a year. Maturity is at time T and the asset is valued today at S_0.

At time t_1 the asset pays a dividend D_1. At time t_2 the asset pays a dividend D_2 and so on until time t_n when the asset pays the last dividend D_n. The T-forward price F_0 of the asset is calculated as follows.

(i) Calculate the present value of all dividend payments.
(ii) Find the sum of all present values calculated in (i). Subtract this sum from the spot price.
(iii) Calculate the amount to which this quantity will grow under investment at the present interest rate. The result is the forward price of the asset.

Table 2.2 gives the forward price, $F_0 = (S_0 - D) \times (1 + \frac{R}{m})^{m\times T}$.

Figure 2.4 shows this calculation in a spreadsheet.

Spot (B2), rate, comp (the number of compounding periods in one year) and maturity are entered as cell names. The dividend payments (dividend in B7: B9), the time to their payment (timeyrs in C7:C9) and the present value of the dividend payments (presvaldiv in D7:D9) are entered as range names.

In practice, of course, there will be a wide choice of available interest rates. You might be offered 6.8% per year compounded semi-annually, or 6.6% per year with interest compounded monthly. Which one should you choose?

Table 2.2

Spot price =	S_0		
Interest rate =	R		
Comp. periods per year =	m		
	Dividend	Time (years)	Discounted dividend (DD)
Dividend 1	D_1	t_1	$D_1 \times (1+\frac{R}{m})^{-m\times t_1}$
Dividend 2	D_2	t_2	$D_2 \times (1+\frac{R}{m})^{-m\times t_2}$
Dividend n	D_n	t_n	$D_n \times (1+\frac{R}{m})^{-m\times t_n}$
		Sum (DD) =	D
Spot price − Sum (DD)	$S_0 - D$		
Forward price =	$(S_0 - D)(1+\frac{R}{m})^{m\times T}$		

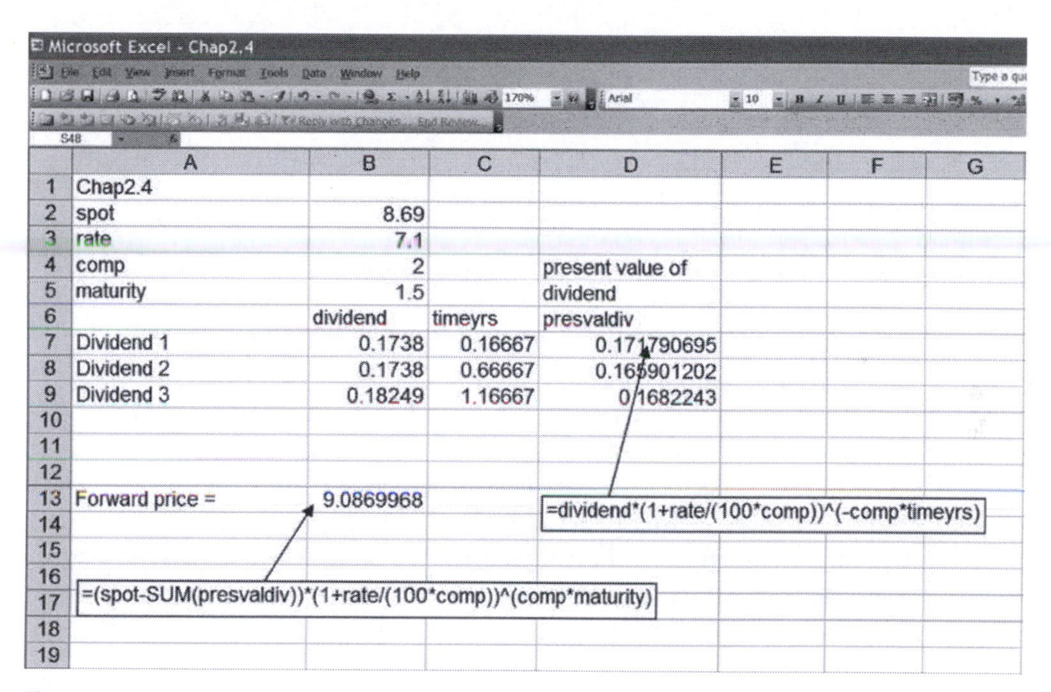
Microsoft Excel - Chap2.4

	A	B	C	D
1	Chap2.4			
2	spot	8.69		
3	rate	7.1		
4	comp	2		present value of
5	maturity	1.5		dividend
6		dividend	timeyrs	presvaldiv
7	Dividend 1	0.1738	0.16667	0.171790695
8	Dividend 2	0.1738	0.66667	0.165901202
9	Dividend 3	0.18249	1.16667	0.1682243
13	Forward price =	9.0869968		

=dividend*(1+rate/(100*comp))^(-comp*timeyrs)

=(spot-SUM(presvaldiv))*(1+rate/(100*comp))^(comp*maturity)

Figure 2.4

Since the forward price is what it costs to pay off a loan, we ought to choose the interest rate that makes this pay-off as small as possible. The amount that we borrow in this loan is $S_0 - D$. The larger the value of D, the smaller the value of $S_0 - D$: consequently, the less we have to borrow and the less we have to pay back. So ideally, we should make D as large as possible. Since each of the dividends pays off one individual loan, each of these 'dividend loans' pays for itself. To make D large, choose the lowest available interest rate for each of

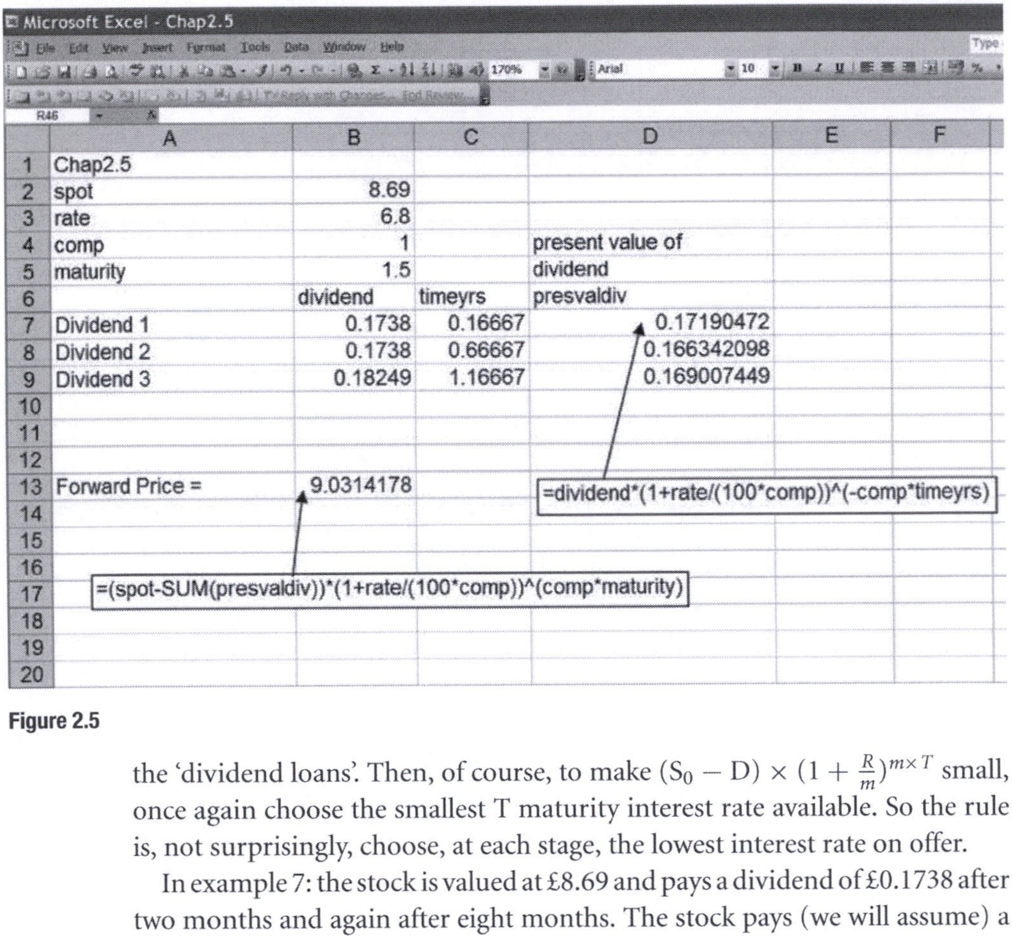

Microsoft Excel - Chap2.5

	A	B	C	D	E	F
1	Chap2.5					
2	spot	8.69				
3	rate	6.8				
4	comp	1		present value of		
5	maturity	1.5		dividend		
6		dividend	timeyrs	presvaldiv		
7	Dividend 1	0.1738	0.16667	0.17190472		
8	Dividend 2	0.1738	0.66667	0.166342098		
9	Dividend 3	0.18249	1.16667	0.169007449		
10						
11						
12						
13	Forward Price =	9.0314178				
14						
15						
16						
17						
18						
19						
20						

=dividend*(1+rate/(100*comp))^(-comp*timeyrs)

=(spot-SUM(presvaldiv))*(1+rate/(100*comp))^(comp*maturity)

Figure 2.5

the 'dividend loans'. Then, of course, to make $(S_0 - D) \times (1 + \frac{R}{m})^{m \times T}$ small, once again choose the smallest T maturity interest rate available. So the rule is, not surprisingly, choose, at each stage, the lowest interest rate on offer.

In example 7: the stock is valued at £8.69 and pays a dividend of £0.1738 after two months and again after eight months. The stock pays (we will assume) a further dividend of £0.18249 after 14 months. Consider two available interest rates, 6.8% per year (compounded annually) and 6.6% per year (compounded monthly). The latter is equivalent to a rate of 6.8034%, compounded annually. So 6.8% per year (compounded annually) is the lower rate and this is the rate we should choose.

The spreadsheets in Figures 2.5 and 2.6 illustrate the calculations.

2.7 Forward contracts on assets paying a continuous dividend

This model is useful when an asset pays out a dividend continuously (or very frequently) and *this dividend is immediately reinvested in the asset.* There are three situations where the model might be particularly useful:

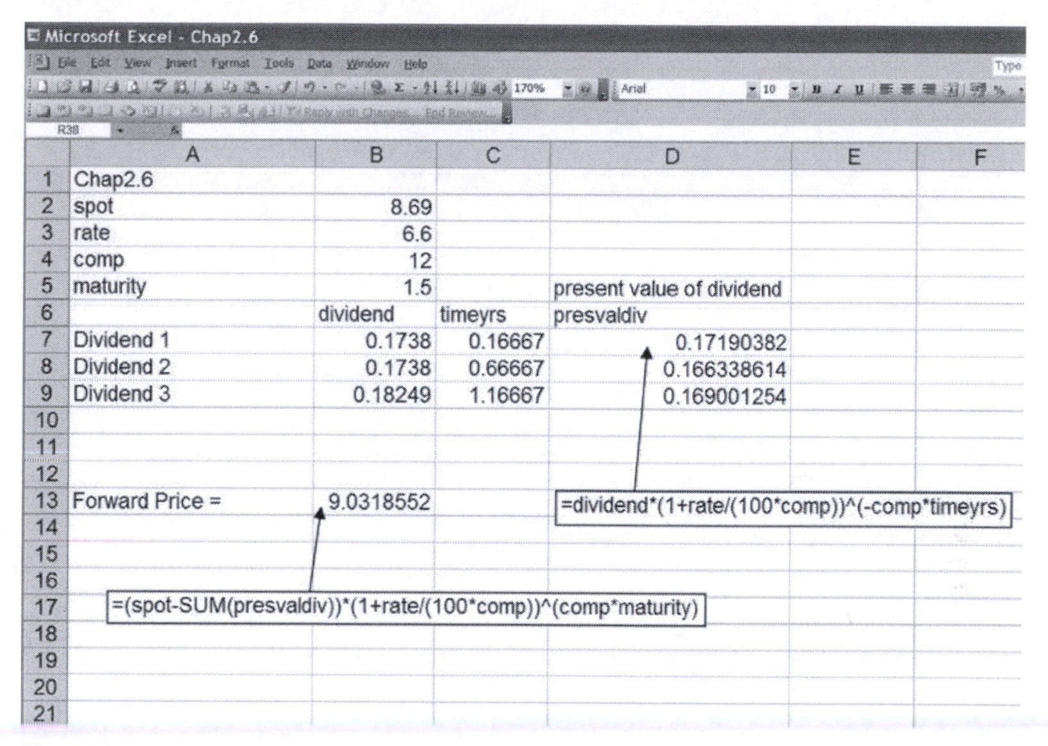

Figure 2.6

(i) The asset is a foreign currency. The 'dividend' is the growth rate of the economy issuing the currency. If, for example, the currency is invested in a bond issued by the government of that country, the asset will achieve the (continuous) growth of that nation's economy.

(ii) The asset pays a dividend 'very frequently' (so the asset could be gold or copper) and the dividend is reinvested in the asset. We saw in Chapter 1 how continuous compounded interest rates provided a good approximation to a situation where interest was compounded (and reinvested) very frequently.

(iii) An asset pays a dividend of, say, 4.5% per year, compounded semi-annually, with reinvestment. By calculating the equivalent continuously compounded rate (see Chapter 1), use can be made of the simple and widely used formula to be derived in this section.

Notation Observe that we have two rates: the dividend paid out by the asset (the dividend yield) and a rate at which cash can be safely borrowed and invested.

The dividend yield will be denoted by Q. The safe interest rate will be denoted by R. Both Q and R will be rates (decimals) and both will be written as continuously compounded, annual rates.

It will always be assumed that the dividend yield is reinvested in the asset.

Again, we use the strategy outlined in section 2.2. For convenience we repeat it here.

Strategy

Today (t = 0): Set up a portfolio consisting of cash, the asset and a forward contract.

Borrow precisely the amount of cash needed to ensure you have possession of one unit of the asset at maturity.

Buy one unit of the asset.

Enter a forward contract to sell one unit of the asset for £K at maturity.

Maturity (t = T):

Pay off the existing loan on the contract.

Hand over one unit of the asset.

Receive the delivery price, £K.

Since the strategy is identical to that where discrete dividends are paid, the delivery price must be the 'continuously compounded' equivalent of:

$$\text{Delivery price} = (S_0 - D) \times \left(1 + \frac{R}{m}\right)^{m \times T}$$

$S_0 - D$ is the amount of cash borrowed today which, when the investment from the dividends is taken into account, ensures that one unit of the asset is held at maturity.

The key is the following: if an amount e^{-QT} is invested at the continuously compounded annual rate Q, then, after T years, the investment will be worth $e^{-QT} \times e^{QT} = 1$. So after T years, the portion $e^{-QT} \times 1$ of the asset will have grown into one unit of the asset.

This is good. To own one unit of the asset at maturity, we need a portion $e^{-QT} \times 1$ of the asset, today. Suppose that S_0 is the cost, today, of one unit of the asset. It will cost $S_0 \times e^{-QT}$ today to buy a portion $e^{-QT} \times 1$ of the asset. So $S_0 \times e^{-QT}$ is the amount we must borrow, today, to own one unit of the asset at maturity. $S_0 \times e^{-QT}$ is the continuous equivalent of the discrete expression $S_0 - D$. Writing $S_0 \times e^{-QT}$ in place of $S_0 - D$ gives:

$$\text{the delivery price} = S_0 \times e^{-QT} \times \left(1 + \frac{R}{m}\right)^{mT}$$

Or, if R is also a continuously compounded rate,

$$\text{the delivery price} = S_0 \times e^{-QT} \times e^{RT}$$
$$= S_0 \times e^{(R-Q)T}$$

This delightfully compact formula is widely used in finance.

Example 8 (Problem B at the beginning of the chapter)

The financial director of a large company knows that her company will receive a payment in four months' time of 3.5 billion yen. She is concerned about fluctuations in the currency markets and would like to know today the price she will get, in sterling, if she sold the yen on the day they were received.

We will assume that the rate at which the financial director can borrow pounds (the domestic rate) is 6.05% (compounded continuously). The Japanese interest rate, almost certainly, will be different. Assume the Japanese interest rate is 3.3% (also continuously compounded).

The pound/yen exchange rate is, today, £1 = 187.4983 yen:

so 1 yen $= £\frac{1}{187.4983} = £\,0.005333$

Solution

We want to calculate the four-month forward price of the yen.

We have: the asset is 1 yen.

S_0 = spot price of one unit of the asset

So $S_0 = £\,0.005333$

$Q = 0.033, \quad R = 0.0605, \quad T = \frac{4}{12}$

To implement the strategy:

We ask: what amount of the asset must be purchased today to ensure that with continuous compounding (at rate Q) and reinvestment we will have, in four months' time, exactly one unit of the asset (1 yen)?

The amount is: $e^{-QT} \times 1 = e^{-0.033 \times \frac{4}{12}} \times 1 = 0.9891$ yen.

We need to borrow exactly the amount needed to buy e^{-QT} $(= 0.9891)$ of the asset. The spot price of one unit of the asset is S_0 (= £0.005333). Hence we need to borrow, today, $£S_0 \times e^{-QT} = £0.005333 \times 0.9891 = £0.005275$.

Today: (t = 0)

Borrow $£S_0 \times e^{-QT} = £0.005275$ at rate R (= 0.0605) per year, compounded continuously for $T = \frac{4}{12}$ years.

Buy $e^{-QT} = 0.9891$ yen.

Invest this amount in the Japanese market at rate Q (= 0.033) per year compounded continuously for $T = \frac{4}{12}$ years.
Enter a forward contract to sell 1 yen for £K in four months' time.

At maturity: $(t = \frac{4}{12})$
Pay off the loan.
Repay $£S_0 \times e^{-QT} \times e^{RT} = £0.005275 \times e^{0.0605 \times \frac{4}{12}} = £0.005383$.
Hand over the asset.
The investment e^{-QT} will grow, in T years, to 1 yen. Hand over 1 yen.
Receive £K.
The usual argument now kicks in. $V_0 = 0$. $V_T = K - 0.005383$. To avoid arbitrage opportunities, $V_T = 0$ giving $K = 0.005383$ $(= S_0 \times e^{(R-Q)T})$.
The financial director can then sell her 35 000 000 000 yen for £35 000 000 000 × 0.005383 = £188 405 000.

In general terms:
Suppose that today spot price of asset = S_0.
The domestic interest rate is r% with rate $R = \frac{r}{100}$.
The foreign interest rate is q% with foreign rate $Q = \frac{q}{100}$. (Note that both R and Q are continuously compounded rates.)
Time to maturity = T years.
The delivery price (and the T forward price F_0) of an asset paying a dividend yield rate Q is:

$$F_0 = S_0 \times e^{(R-Q)T}$$

Note: for consistency, we have taken the spot price to be the price of one unit of the asset in pounds or dollars. In the financial markets the usual way of showing the relative value of currencies is to quote the number of units of a currency that are equivalent to \$1. For example: 0.7944 euro = \$1 and 2144.2251 Belarus rubles = \$1. The exception to this is the pound/dollar ratio – this is given as the number of dollars that have the same value as one pound. For example, £1 = \$1.7243.

The equation $F_0 = S_0 \times e^{(R-Q)T}$ is important in finance. **It is common practice to convert all interest rates into their equivalent continuously compounded rate. This formula, with its great simplicity, can then be applied.** But whenever an asset shows continuous growth and that growth is immediately reinvested in the asset (e.g. currencies, gold, crude oil), this equation is applicable. The equation represents, in particular, a fundamental relationship in the currencies market.

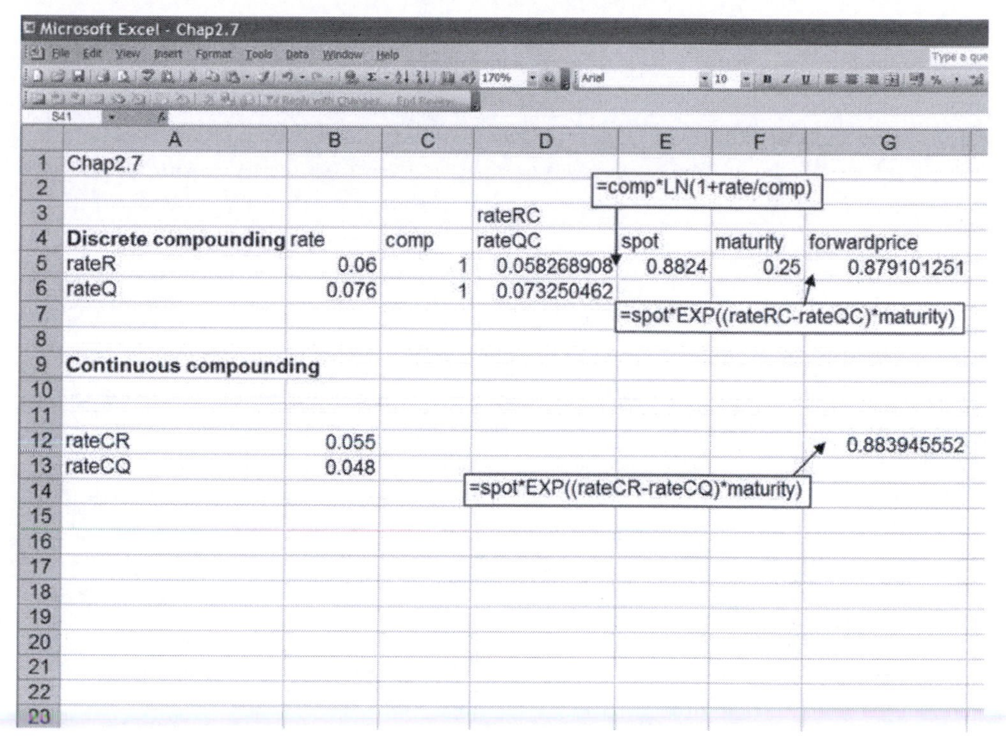

Figure 2.7

Example 9

The interest rate in the UK for a three-month loan is 6% per annum compounded annually. In Brazil, the interest rate for a three-month loan is 7.6%, compounded annually. The spot price of one Brazilian real is £1 = 0.8824 BR. What is the three-month forward price of the Brazilian real?

Solution

$S_0 = 0.8824$
$R = 0.06$ (annually compounded)
$Q = 0.076$ (annually compounded)
To find the equivalent continuously compounded rate:
$e^{R\times 1} = 1.06$: giving $R = \ln(1.06) = 0.05827$
$e^{Q\times 1} = 1.076$: giving $Q = \ln(1.076) = 0.07325$
The three-month forward price is $S_0 e^{(R-Q)T}$
$= 0.8824 \times e^{(0.05827-0.07325)\times \frac{3}{12}}$
$= 0.8791$

This is an important calculation. In Figure 2.7 we give a spreadsheet illustrating the calculation.

Note that in C5 and C6 there is an option to consider discrete interest rates which compound interest several times in one year. If the interest is compounded annually, enter 1 here. As usual the number of compounding periods in one year is denoted by comp. Observe that rate (B5:B6) and comp (C5:C6) are entered as range names. The equivalent continuously compounded rates are given cell names, rateRC and rateQC. The forward price (forwardprice) appears in G5.

If continuously compounded rates are given for R and Q, enter these in B12 and B13 (with cell names rateCR and rateCQ). The three-month forward price (0.8824) is shown in G12.

A neat 'add in'

We have a neat, compact and efficient equation. It would be wasteful not to try to extend its use. We can use this equation with discrete dividend yields so long as the dividend payments are immediately reinvested in the asset. An example will show how this can be done. Then we give the general result and a spreadsheet illustrating the calculations.

Example 10

A stock valued today at £5.24 pays a dividend yield of 3.5% after two months and five months and a dividend yield of 3.6% after eight months. Each dividend is immediately reinvested in the asset. Assuming a continuously compounded annual interest rate of 5.5%, find the nine-month forward price of the stock.

Solution

The idea is to find a single continuously compounded rate $\hat{Q}$ that is equivalent to the dividend yields.

1st dividend This adds 3.5% of the asset to the value of the asset. Hence:

Value of asset after 1st dividend payment $= 5.24 \times (1 + 0.035)$

2nd dividend This adds 3.5% of the asset to the value of the asset. Hence:

Value of asset after 2nd dividend payment =

$5.24 \times (1 + 0.035) \times (1 + 0.035)$

3rd dividend This adds 3.6% of the asset to the value of the asset.

Value of the asset after 3rd dividend payment =

$5.24 \times (1 + 0.035) \times (1 + 0.035) \times (1 + 0.036)$

Let Q be the single equivalent rate.

$$\text{Then } 1 + Q = (1 + 0.035) \times (1 + 0.035) \times (1 + 0.036)$$
$$= 1.1098$$

But we need an equivalent rate where the interest is compounded continuously over nine months. Let this rate be $\hat{Q}$.

$$\text{Then } e^{\hat{Q}\times\frac{9}{12}} = 1.1098$$

$$\hat{Q} \times \frac{9}{12} = \ln(1.1098)$$

$$\hat{Q} = \frac{12}{9} \times \ln(1.1098)$$

$$= 0.1389 \text{ (or } 13.9\%)$$

Now the nine-month forward price on the asset is $S_0 \times e^{(R-\hat{Q})T}$.

$S_0 = 5.24, \ R = 0.055, \ \hat{Q} = 0.1389, \ T = \frac{9}{12}$

$$\text{Forward price} = 5.24 \times e^{(0.055-0.1389)\times\frac{9}{12}}$$

$$= £4.92$$

Notice that the forward price is less than the spot price. This is because ownership *now* carries entitlement to three generous dividend payments. This makes ownership now more valuable than entering ownership *after* the payment of these three dividends. But see the note below.

General result

Let dividend yields $Q_1, Q_2, \ldots Q_n$ be paid and reinvested in the asset at times $t_1, t_2, \ldots t_n$ during the life of the contract (although the times of the payments are not important for the calculation).

We need to find a rate Q that is equivalent to these discrete payments with reinvestment of the dividends.

Then Q is such a rate where $1 + Q = (1 + Q_1)(1 + Q_2) \ldots (1 + Q_n)$.

We need to find a continuously compounded rate $\hat{Q}$ that is equivalent to Q over the life of the contract, T.

$$\hat{Q} \text{ is such a rate where } e^{\hat{Q}T} = 1 + Q$$

$$\hat{Q}T = \ln(1 + Q)$$

$$\text{Giving: } \hat{Q} = \frac{\ln(1 + Q)}{T}$$

The T year forward price is $S_0 \times e^{(R-\hat{Q})T}$

Example 11

The spot price of 1 ounce of gold is $278. The gold increases in value in succeeding months, as shown:

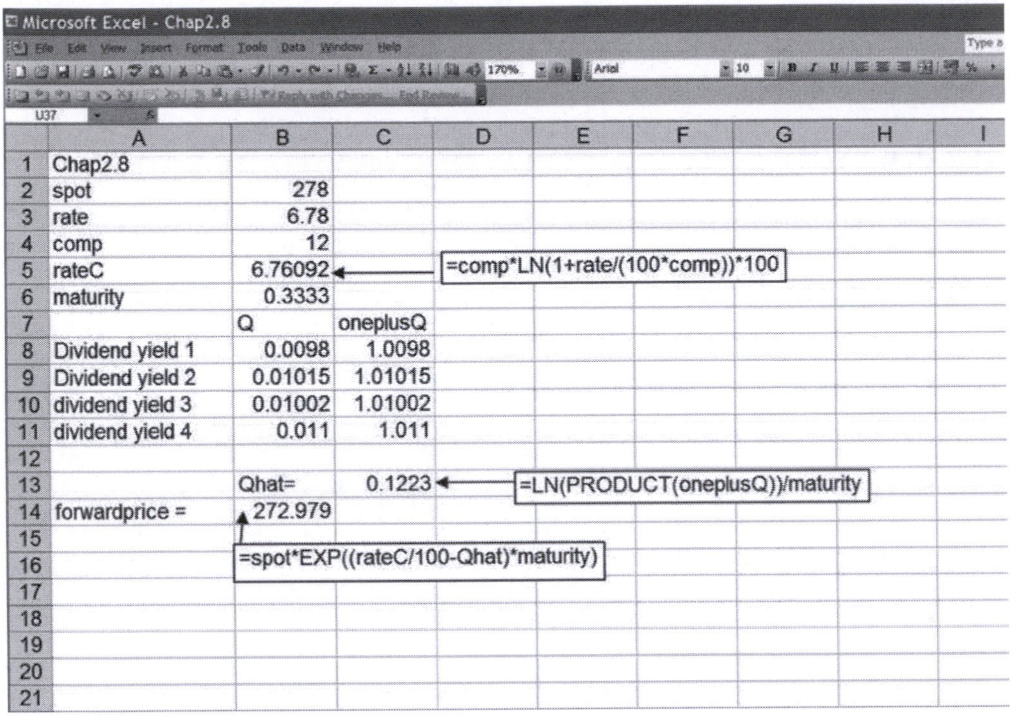

Microsoft Excel - Chap2.8

	A	B	C	D	E	F	G	H	I
1	Chap2.8								
2	spot	278							
3	rate	6.78							
4	comp	12							
5	rateC	6.76092							
6	maturity	0.3333							
7		Q	oneplusQ						
8	Dividend yield 1	0.0098	1.0098						
9	Dividend yield 2	0.01015	1.01015						
10	dividend yield 3	0.01002	1.01002						
11	dividend yield 4	0.011	1.011						
12									
13		Qhat=	0.1223						
14	forwardprice =	272.979							
15									
16									
17									
18									
19									
20									
21									

B5: =comp*LN(1+rate/(100*comp))*100

C13: =LN(PRODUCT(oneplusQ))/maturity

B14: =spot*EXP((rateC/100-Qhat)*maturity)

Figure 2.8

After 1 month	0.98%
After 2 months	1.015%
After 3 months	1.002%
After 4 months	1.1%

The current interest rate is 6.78%, compounded monthly. Find the four-month forward price of the gold.

Solution

See Figure 2.8.

Observe that the current interest rate 6.78%, compounded monthly, has to be converted into the equivalent continuously compounded rate before the formula can be used. This calculation appears in cell B5 in the spreadsheet (where the result is given the cell name rateC). The four dividend yields and the dividend yields+1 are given range names Q and oneplusQ. The four-month forward price of gold is given in cell B14. This is calculated as $S_0 \times e^{(R-\hat{Q})T}$ where (we repeat) R and $\hat{Q}$ are continuously compounded rates. The calculation that ensures $\hat{Q}$ is a continuously compounded rate appears

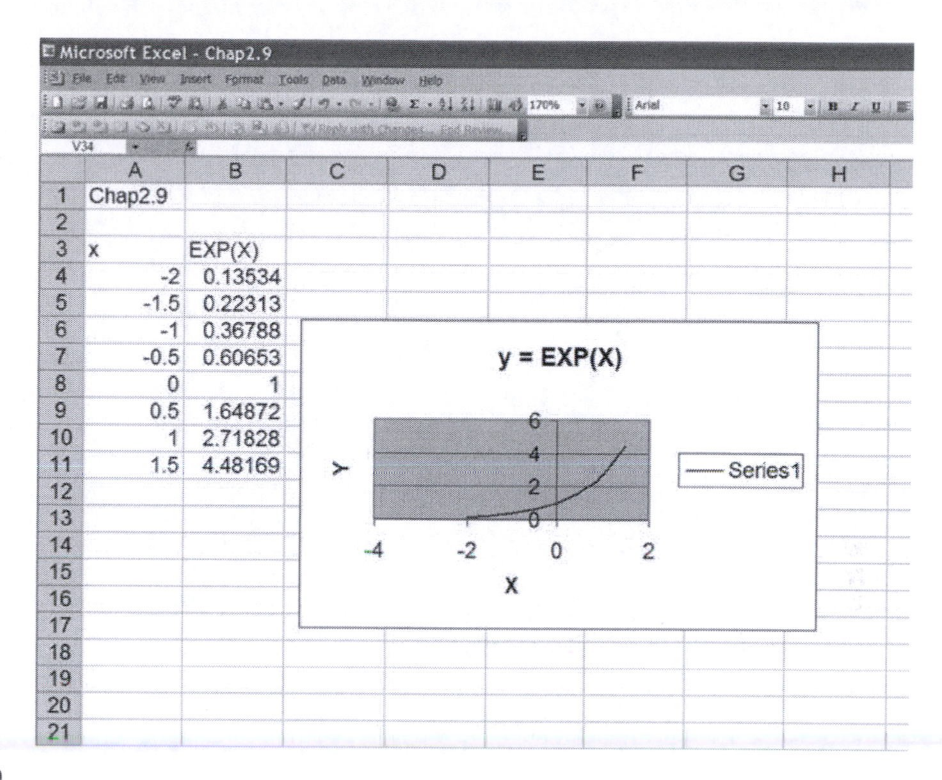

	A	B
1	Chap2.9	
2		
3	x	EXP(X)
4	-2	0.13534
5	-1.5	0.22313
6	-1	0.36788
7	-0.5	0.60653
8	0	1
9	0.5	1.64872
10	1	2.71828
11	1.5	4.48169

Figure 2.9

in cell C13. This process, the remaining calculations and the solution are illustrated in the spreadsheet.

Note: on some occasions, the forward price F_0 will be less than the spot price S_0. On other occasions, F_0 will be greater than S_0. An explanation for this can be seen from the equation $F_0 = S_0 \times e^{(R-Q)T}$.

We can write this equation as $F_0 = S_0 \times e^X$ where $X = (R - Q)T$. The graph of $y = e^x$ will show us the relationship between F_0 and S_0. See Figure 2.9.

If $R - Q < 0$:

then $R < Q$ and the dividend yields are outperforming the safe interest rate. So it makes good sense to acquire the asset now and take advantage of the generous dividend yields. We would expect, in this case, that $F_0 < S_0$. But if $(R - Q) < 0$ then $(R - Q)T < 0$ and $X < 0$. From the graph, we can see that $e^X < 1$. Hence $e^{(R-Q)T} < 1$ and this gives $F_0 < S_0$, as expected.

If $R - Q > 0$:

then $R > Q$ and the dividend yield Q is less than the safe rate R. In this case the dividend yield fails to excite and there is no rush to buy now. We would expect that $F_0 > S_0$. But if $(R - Q)T > 0$, then $X > 0$ and from the graph, $e^X > 1$, giving $e^{(R-Q)T} > 1$. This gives $F_0 > S_0$, as expected.

2.8 Value of a forward contract

Finally, we calculate the value over time of a forward contract on an asset making dividend payments.

The value of a forward contract at a time t after it was set up was considered in section 2.4. There, it was shown that for an asset paying no dividends, the value of a forward contract is given by:

	Interest rate R (compounded annually)	Interest rate R (compounded continuously)
Short	$f_t = \frac{K - F_t}{(1+R)^{T-t}}$	$f_t = (K - F_t)e^{-R(T-t)}$
Long	$f_t = \frac{F_t - K}{(1+R)^{T-t}}$	$f_t = (F_t - K)e^{-R(T-t)}$

These results and the method of proof remain valid when the asset pays a dividend. What has to change are the values taken by K and by F_t. As shown in section 2.5, K and F_t carry different forms with different dividend structures.

K and F_t are calculated according to the dividend paid by the asset. It is useful to observe that since $K = F_0$, we can write for a short forward contract:

$$f_t = \frac{F_0 - F_t}{(1+R)^{T-t}} \qquad \text{when R is compounded annually}$$

and

$$f_t = (F_0 - F_t)e^{-R(T-t)} \qquad \text{when R is compounded continuously}$$

with similar expressions for a long forward contract.

Now, F_0 and F_t are calculated as shown in section 2.3 (for assets not paying a dividend) and sections 2.5 and 2.6 (for assets which pay dividends). An example will illustrate the procedure.

Example 12 (Example C at the beginning of the chapter)

Today is 8 March. ULS shares are selling today at £10.75. The share pays a dividend of 6% per year in two equal dividend payments, made on 8 April and 8 October. Stella wants to enter a forward contract to buy 1000 shares on 8 November. She can borrow money at 5% per year, compounded annually.

(i) Find the eight-month forward price on ULS shares.

(ii) On 8 May, the share price has fallen to £9.25. On this day, what is the value of Stella's forward contract?

Solution

Dividends are paid. The dividends are discrete. The interest rate is compounded annually. So $F_t = (S_t - D_t) \times (1 + R)^{(T-t)}$

(i) $S_0 = 10.75$

$T = \frac{8}{12}$

$R = 0.05$

Two dividends are paid before maturity.

Dividend 1 = 0.3225

Time to payment = 0.08333: Present value $= 0.3225 \times (1 + 0.05)^{-0.08333} = 0.3212$

Dividend 2 = 0.3225

Time to payment = 0.5833: Present value $= 0.3225 \times (1 + 0.05)^{-0.5833} = 0.3135$

Present value of dividend payments (D) = 0.3212 + 0.3135 = 0.6347

$S_0 - D = 10.75 - 0.6347 = 10.1153$

$F_0 = (S_0 - D)(1 + R)^{\frac{8}{12}} = 10.1153 \times 1.05^{\frac{8}{12}} = 10.4497$

The eight-month forward price of the share is £10.45.

On 8 May:

(ii) $S_t = 9.25$

There are six months to maturity: $T - t = \frac{6}{12}$

$R = 0.05$

One dividend payment is made before maturity.

Dividend 1 = 0.3225

Time to payment $= \frac{5}{12}$: Present value $= 0.3225 \times (1 + 0.05)^{-\frac{5}{12}} = 0.3160$

$S_t - D_t = 9.25 - 0.3160 = 8.9340$

$F_t = (S_t - D_t)(1 + R)^{T-t} = 8.9340 \times 1.05^{\frac{6}{12}} = 9.1546$

This is a long forward contract.

$$\text{Hence:} \quad f_t = \frac{F_t - F_0}{(1 + R)^{\frac{6}{12}}} = \frac{9.1546 - 10.4497}{1.05^{0.5}} = -1.2639$$

If the interest rate R (in the example, 5% per year, compounded annually) had in fact been a continuously compounded rate, we would have used the

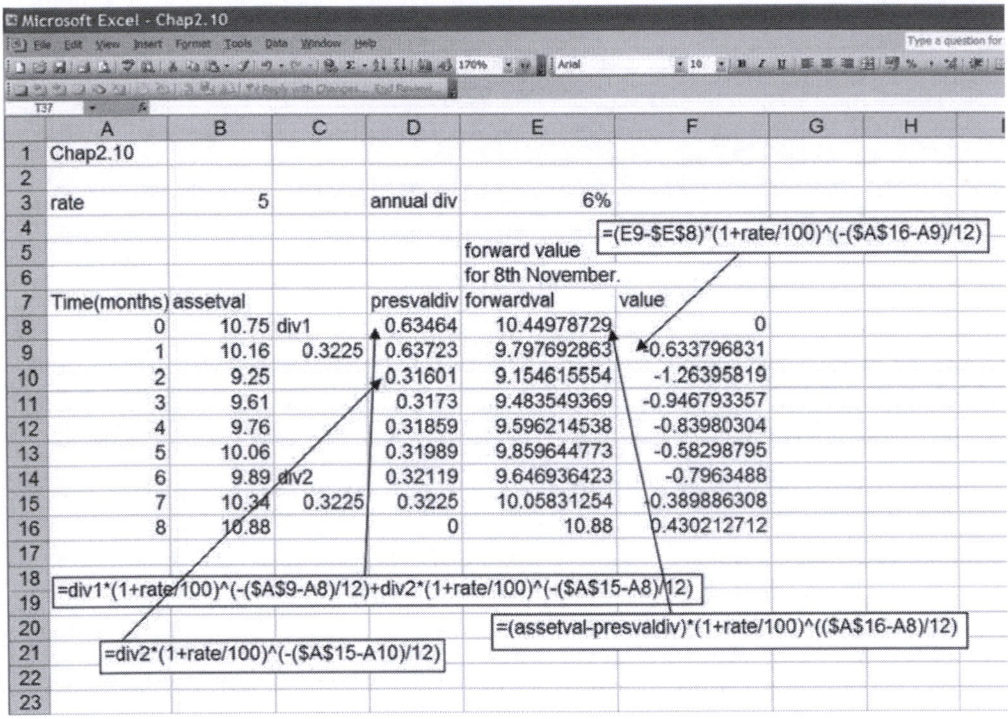

Microsoft Excel - Chap2.10

	A	B	C	D	E	F
1	Chap2.10					
2						
3	rate	5		annual div	6%	
4						
5					forward value	
6					for 8th November.	
7	Time(months)	assetval		presvaldiv	forwardval	value
8	0	10.75	div1	0.63464	10.44978729	0
9	1	10.16	0.3225	0.63723	9.797692863	0.633796831
10	2	9.25		0.31601	9.154615554	-1.26395819
11	3	9.61		0.3173	9.483549369	-0.946793357
12	4	9.76		0.31859	9.596214538	-0.83980304
13	5	10.06		0.31989	9.859644773	-0.58298795
14	6	9.89	div2	0.32119	9.646936423	-0.7963488
15	7	10.34	0.3225	0.3225	10.05831254	0.389886308
16	8	10.88		0	10.88	0.430212712

=(E9-$E$8)*(1+rate/100)^(-($A$16-A9)/12)

=div1*(1+rate/100)^(-($A$9-A8)/12)+div2*(1+rate/100)^(-($A$15-A8)/12)

=(assetval-presvaldiv)*(1+rate/100)^(($A$16-A8)/12)

=div2*(1+rate/100)^(-($A$15-A10)/12)

Figure 2.10

form: $F_t = (S_t - D_t) \times e^{R(T-t)}$ and D_t would be calculated using the continuously compounded rate, R. Also, $f_t = \dfrac{F_t - F_0}{e^{R(T-t)}}$.

If R was a continuously compounded interest rate and the asset paid a continuous dividend Q, we would have used: $F_t = S_t \times e^{(R-Q)(T-t)}$ with $f_t = \frac{F_t - F_0}{e^{R(T-t)}}$. See Exercise 21.

Finally, as time passes, what is the relationship between the value of an asset, the forward price of the asset and the value of a (short) forward contract based on that asset? If we know, or can project, future values of the asset, then a succession of forward prices and forward contract values can be calculated.

We illustrate this for Example 12 in the spreadsheet shown in Figure 2.10.

The interest rate is entered in B3 with the cell name rate.

Column A gives the time, in months, after 8 March.

Column B gives the value of the asset in succeeding months (entered with range name assetval).

Column C shows the two dividend payments made by the asset (entered with cell names div1 and div2).

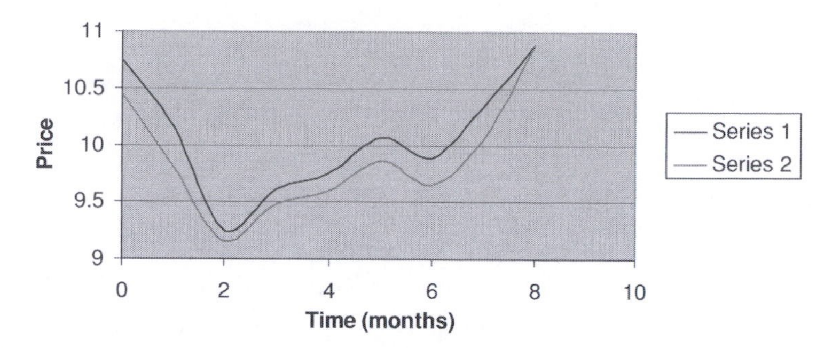

Figure 2.11

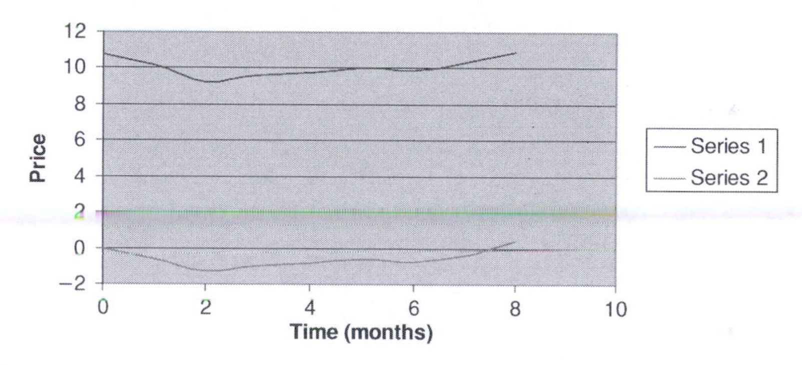

Figure 2.12

Column D shows the present values of the dividend payments (entered with range name presvaldiv).

Column E shows successive forward prices (range name forwardval).

E8 shows the eight-month forward price (10.45).

E9 shows the seven-month forward price one month later (9.80).

E10 shows the six-month forward price two months later (9.15).

Column F gives the values of a long forward contract at the times given in column A.

In Figure 2.11 we show graphs, over time, of the asset price and the forward price (through to maturity). Note the high correlation between these values and the fact that at maturity, the forward price coincides with the asset value.

In Figure 2.12 we plot, over time, the asset price and the corresponding value of the (long) forward contract. The graphs indicate a strong positive correlation in these two sets of values.

Exercise

Use the spreadsheet in Figure 2.10 to calculate successive monthly values of the corresponding short forward contract. How do these values relate to the values of the asset? Could we have predicted this result?

Observing the changing value over time of a forward contract (Figure 2.10 and the Exercise) makes it reasonable to assume that people might want to buy (and others sell) forward contracts. There is, however, no obvious market in which forward contracts may be bought and sold. Trading in contracts of this kind does take place, but to protect buyer and seller, strict regulations are imposed on all concerned. The change in value of these contracts is recorded daily and when contracts are traded under these conditions, they are called futures contracts. These are the subject of Chapter 3.

Exercise 2

1. George has 10 000 litres of fuel. He sells the fuel for £900 and invests the money he receives for three months at the current safe rate of 5% per year, compounded annually. He enters a forward contract to buy 10 000 litres of fuel for £K in three months' time.

   Three months to the day, he buys 10 000 litres of fuel for £K and receives the pay-off from the investment. George has cash and 10 000 litres of fuel. Describe how arbitrage considerations (Chapter 1) can be used to find a 'fair value' for K.

2. A bushel of corn is valued today at $3.49. The annual safe rate is 6.3% (compounded annually). A forward contract is entered to sell the corn in four months' time. What is the delivery price in the contract?

3. An ounce of gold today is priced at $110.70. The interest rate is 5.8% (compounded twice yearly). A forward contract is entered to buy 20 ounces of gold in three months' time. What is the delivery price in this contract?

4. A horse David would like to buy, High Jinks, has been winning most of his races this season. David will have the money to buy High Jinks in two months' time, but he is concerned about a steep rise in the value of the horse in those two months. Today, High Jinks is valued at £100 000 and the interest rate is 7.4% per annum, compounded twice yearly. Explain, with details, how David could remove the risk of a sudden price rise.

5. An asset is valued today at \$20.00. What is meant by the three-month forward price of the asset? How is the three-month forward price calculated?

6. A Bebop share is valued today at £10.50. The interest rate is 7.2%, compounded continuously. Find (i) the four-month forward price, (ii) the six-month forward price on a Bebop share. I enter a six-month forward contract on Bebop shares. What is the delivery price in this contract?

7. A football team is valued at £35 million. Things have not been going too well and the owner decides to sell the team at the end of the season, four months away. He enters a forward contract to sell the team in four months' time. The interest rate is 4.8% per year, compounded semi-annually.
   (i) What is the delivery price on this forward contract? What is the four-month forward price on the team?
   (ii) One month later, the team is valued at £32.5 million.
      (a) What is the delivery price in the forward contract in part (i)?
      (b) What is the three-month forward price of the team?

8. A one-year forward contract to buy a non-dividend-paying stock is entered when the price of the stock is £15. The risk-free interest rate is 7.5% per year with continuous compounding.
   (i) What is the initial value of the forward contract?
   (ii) What is the one-year forward price on the stock?
   (iii) In six months' time, the stock is trading at £17.70 and the interest rate is unchanged. What is the delivery price on the original forward contract? What is the six-month forward price on the stock?

9. A six-month forward contract to buy a non-dividend-paying stock (a long forward contract) is entered when the stock sells at £18.50. The current safe interest rate is 8.7% per year compounded annually.
   (i) What is the six-month forward price on the stock?
   (ii) After one month, the stock is valued at £19.98. What is the five-month forward price? What, today, is the value of the forward contract?
   (iii) One month later, the stock was selling at £19.50. Calculate the four-month forward price. What is now the value of the forward contract?

10. An asset pays a dividend of £5.50 twice each year. The first dividend payment is due in one month's time. The asset is valued at £150. If the

interest rate is 6% per year (compounded annually), find the delivery price in a forward contract with delivery date in one year's time.

11. A share is priced today at £10.00. The share pays a dividend of 5% per year, in two equal instalments: the first dividend payment is due in four months' time. The interest rate is 6% per year, continuously compounded. I enter a forward contract on the share with delivery date in 14 months' time. Find the delivery price.

12. An asset is valued today at \$20.00. The asset pays a dividend of \$1 twice each year. The first dividend is due in three months' time. The interest rate is 6.5% per year compounded continuously. A ten-month short forward contract is entered.
    (i) What is the ten-month forward price and what, today, is the value of the contract?
    (ii) One month later, the value of the stock has fallen to \$17. What is the nine-month forward price on the stock and what is now the value of the forward contract?
    (iii) After a further month, the stock is selling at \$25. What is the eight-month forward price and what is the value of the forward contract?

13. The interest rate is 7.3% compounded annually. A stock paying a dividend of £2.50 every six months (the next dividend payment is due in three months' time) is valued at £35. The six-month forward price on the stock is £34.00. Is this an arbitrage opportunity? If so, how precisely would you respond?

14. The interest rate in the UK is 4.8% per year compounded continuously. The interest rate in the US is 5.3% per year, compounded continuously. Today, £1 = \$1.87. Calculate, in pounds, the six-month forward price of the dollar. Why is the six-month forward price of the dollar less than the spot price?

15. The interest rate in the UK is 4.75% (continuously compounded) and in the US the interest rate is 4.50% (continuously compounded). Today, £1 = \$1.8233. Use the spreadsheet (Figure 2.7) to calculate the three-month forward price of the dollar. Repeat for different interest rates R and Q and with different times to maturity. Convince yourself that the note at the end of section 2.7 is correct.

16. The interest rate in London is 4.35% per year compounded annually. In Cyprus, the interest rate is 6.16% (compounded annually). One Cypriot pound (CYP) = £1.1981. In four months' time, how many pounds might I expect to buy for 10 000 CYP?

17. In Australia, the interest rate is 4.23% (compounded continuously). The interest rate in the US is 4.78% (compounded continuously). Today, one Australian dollar (AUD) = \$0.7632. Describe carefully what a currency dealer in New York might do if the six-month forward price of the AUD was (i) \$0.7700, (ii) \$0.7600.

18. BBR is a company which was a late arrival on the BBQ scene. The BBR share price today is £5.70 and the company will pay a dividend of 2% of today's share price in three months and again in nine months. The interest rate is 4.5% compounded quarterly.
    (i) Calculate the equivalent continuously compounded annual rate for (a) the safe interest rate (call the continuously compounded rate R), and (b) the two dividend payments (call this continuously compounded rate Q).
    (ii) Use the formula $F = S_0 \times e^{(R-Q)T}$ to calculate the one-year forward price of the BBR share.

19. Polyfew chemical shares cost, today, £15.50. The shares pay an annual dividend of 6% in two six-monthly dividend payments. The next dividend is to be paid in four months' time. It is thought that next year the annual dividend will be 6.1%. (Assume the share price next year remains at £15.50.) The interest rate is 5.5% compounded annually.
    Use the formulas (i) $(S_0 - D)(1 + R)^T$ for discrete dividend payments, and (ii) $S_0 e^{(R-Q)T}$ with equivalent continuously compounded rates to calculate the 18-month forward price on the shares.

20. The interest rate in the UK is 4.87% (compounded annually). Today, £1 = 3767.676 Belarus rubles (BYR). The six-month forward price on the BYR is £1 = 3925.831 BYR. Estimate the interest rate (annually compounded) in Belarus.

21. Complete the table – assume a continuously compounded safe interest rate R.

Asset pays	Forward price	Value of short forward contract with delivery price K
No dividend	S_0e^{RT}	
Discrete (known dividend)	$(S_0 - D)e^{\cdots\cdots}$	
Continuous yield		

22. An asset is valued today at £55.00. The asset pays a dividend of £2.50 every six months, with the first dividend due in two months' time. The interest rate is 5.0%, compounded continuously.
    (i) Calculate the 12-month forward price of the asset. A long 12-month forward contract on the asset (the delivery price is the 12-month forward price) is entered today. What is the value of this forward contract today?
    (ii) The value of the asset in one month's time, two months' time and so on are given in the table below. Calculate the value of the forward contract described in (i) on each of these dates. Draw a graph of the value of the forward contract against asset value. The spreadsheet in Figure 2.10 might be useful.

Month	Asset value	Value of contract
0	55.00	
1	59.32	
2	64.15	
3	62.70	
4	60.08	
5	58.44	
6	54.88	
7	51.90	
8	48.60	
9	44.70	
10	46.88	
11	50.80	
12	52.50	

3 The futures market

Forwards become futures (a bit of history)

Forward contracts were known, apparently, to the Ancient Greeks. But the modern development of this market began in the 1840s, in Chicago. The early settlers in the American Mid West were farmers and they needed a market for their produce. Initially, scarcities and then surpluses of livestock, corn, wheat, animal feed and the like caused huge and chaotic swings in prices. There was a need for a market to regulate and stabilise sales in all such products. Chicago, at the base of the Great Lakes and close to the farmlands of the Mid West, was a natural centre for transportation and distribution. In 1848, the Chicago Board of Trade (CBOT) was formed and the first forward contract (on corn) was written in March 1851.

It soon became apparent that an existing forward contract could, with a favourable movement of the market, become a thing of value. A forward contract could be sold, or bought, to generate a profit. Thus the idea of buying and selling forward contracts, purely for profit, was born. In 1865 a system for trading forward contracts was set up. This we shall describe shortly. These new, tradable contracts were called futures contracts and in time the futures markets would develop into new areas and far outstrip their agricultural beginnings. In 1972, the International Money Market (IMM), a division of the Chicago Mercantile Exchange (CME), was established to trade futures contracts on foreign currencies. Later in the 1970s, futures contracts trading on the future value of interest rates began. Perhaps the most important of these are the 90-day Eurodollar contracts, which began trading in 1981. These interest rate contracts had a huge impact on the financial world and contributed to the development of the now enormous interest rate swap market. We will describe the 90-day Eurodollar contract and the interest rate swap in Chapter 5, but first, let us give some idea of the huge growth in futures trading. On just one day (8 March 2002) over 3.5 million futures contracts were traded through just one exchange – the Chicago Board of Trade. The underlying value of these contracts was around $26 trillion.

One reason for the enormous popularity of the futures markets is the belief that there is more money to be made in these markets than in, say, the stock market. Futures prices generally tend to change more quickly than stock prices. Also, the futures markets are highly leveraged. As we shall see, the trader puts up only a small percentage (10–15%) of the value of the contract, yet the trader reaps the full reward of any rise in the value of the contract. The downside, of course, can be equally dramatic. There are, potentially, unlimited gains to be made in futures trading; by the same argument, there is also the potential for unlimited losses, as Barings Bank discovered in 1995 (see Chapter 6, Exercise 20).

In the first part of this chapter, we describe the mechanics of futures trading. We then illustrate how futures contracts can be used for speculation and describe how futures can be used to hedge against risk.

Notation (reminder)

Long (short) position: a person taking a long (short) position is entering a contract to buy (sell) an asset for an agreed price on an agreed date.

3.1 Futures contracts

A futures contract is an agreement that one party will buy and the other will sell an asset at a certain time and for a certain price. There is no cost attached to entering a futures contract (but see margin requirements in (ii) below).

This sounds very like a forward contract. The differences between a forward contract and a futures contract are contained in the following.

Futures contracts are managed through an exchange. The role of the exchange is:

(i) to regulate the contract, and
(ii) to ensure, as far as possible, that no one defaults on their financial obligations.

We discuss these two roles separately.

(i) Regulation

(a) The exchange lays down the specific rules concerning the precise nature of the asset to be traded. For cattlefeed, for example, a clear description of what cattlefeed actually is, in terms of content, is laid down. If the asset was gold, the purity of the gold to be traded would be specified. If the asset was orange juice, the exchange would specify what percentage of the juice had actually seen an orange. Both parties must know exactly what they are buying/selling.

(b) The exchange specifies contract size. Wheat, for example, is traded in contracts of 5000 bushels by the Chicago Board of Trade; cattlefeed is traded in contracts of 50 000 lbs on the Chicago Mercantile Exchange; gas oil is traded in contracts of 100 metric tons on the International Petroleum Exchange, London.

(c) The exchange lays down delivery arrangements. For many commodities, only certain delivery months are available. For example, futures contracts in cocoa, arranged through the Coffee, Sugar & Cocoa Exchange, New York, are available with delivery dates only for September, December, March, May and July. Contracts for corn, quoted on the Chicago Board of Trade, are available only for the months of September, December, March, May and July, while futures contracts on Brent Crude (International Petroleum Exchange) are available for any month. The exchange will also specify the last day on which trading can take place for a particular contract. (All such information is widely available – see, for example, the *Financial Times* or *The Wall Street Journal*.)

(d) The exchange will specify where delivery will take place. This is extremely important when the asset is a commodity. A farmer buying 100 000 lbs of cattlefeed must know the delivery point so he can make immediate arrangements, if necessary, to transport the cattlefeed to his farm.

Example 1

Jack Hardy was worried about having enough cattlefeed for his herd the coming winter. In August, Jack decided to buy 100 000 lbs of cattlefeed for delivery in November. Jack called his broker. The broker knew that futures contracts, each one for 50 000 lbs of cattlefeed, with delivery in November, are traded on the CME. The broker called a trader on the floor of the CME and requested a long position in two futures contracts for November delivery.

At roughly the same time, D. J. Easton company in Illinois, marketing cattlefeed, instructed its broker to sell 200 000 lbs of cattlefeed each month throughout the winter. This broker spoke to his trader on the floor of the CME. The two traders met and agreed a price of 70 cents per lb (or $35 000 per contract). Brokers were informed and the deal was done. Jack had entered a long futures position, the cattlefeed company had entered a short futures position, and the price agreed on the floor of the CME is the current futures price for November cattlefeed.

The details and timing of delivery of the cattlefeed were agreed in the contract.

(ii) To protect both parties against default

The exchange will insist that on the day a futures contract is entered, both parties are required to deposit an amount of cash (but this could, by agreement, include other securities) with their broker. This cash is called **margin** and the money is kept by the broker in a **margin account.** Initially, a person entering a futures contract is expected to put up, as margin, approximately 10% of the value of the contract. The amount that is deposited with the broker at the time the contract is entered into is called the **initial margin.**

During the course of a trading day, the price of a futures contract will change. Suppose that, during the day, the price rises. At the end of the day, anyone holding a contract to buy (a long contract) will make a gain (they are contracted to buy at the lower price); anyone holding a contract to sell (a short contract) will make a loss (they are contracted to sell at the lower price). If the price falls, positions are reversed. At the end of each trading day, the exchange will calculate the gains and losses made by each futures contract. Everyone holding a futures contract that has made a loss on the day's trading will have a sum of money equal to the day's loss deducted from their margin account. This money is paid into the exchange. The exchange then pays a sum equal to the day's gains into the margin accounts of those who, correspondingly, made a gain on the day's trading. In this way, debts and credits on each contract are settled daily. This process is called **marking to market**. By means of this device, changes in the value of futures contracts are settled daily from available resources and hence the risk of default by either party is reduced considerably.

To illustrate the process, we look again at Jack's November futures contract in Example 1.

At the end of the first day, the price of a November cattlefeed contract had risen to 71.2 cents per lb. Jack, holding a contract to buy at 70 cents per lb, had made a profit of 1.2 cents per lb. This made a gain of $600 on a contract for

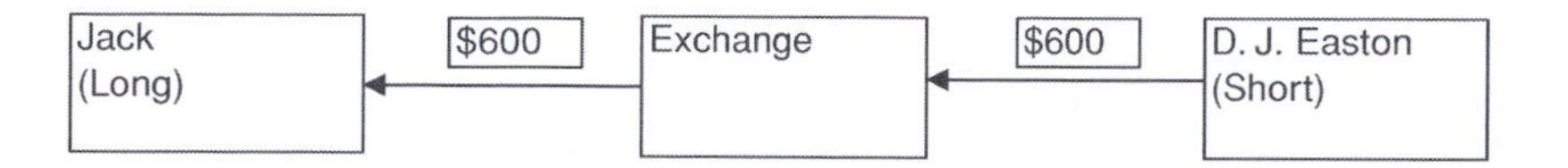

Figure 3.1

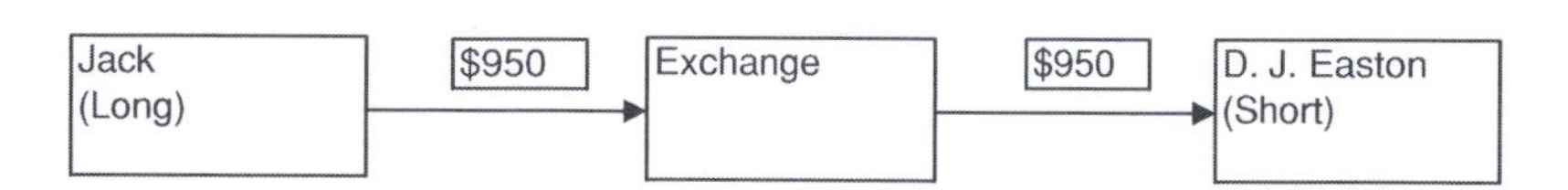

Figure 3.2

50 000 lbs. The party holding a contract to sell at 70 cents per lb made a loss on the day of 1.2 cents per lb, or $600 per contract. Hence, $600 (per contract) is removed from D. J. Easton's margin account and paid into the exchange; the exchange pays $600 (per contract) into Jack's margin account (see Figure 3.1).

At the end of the second day, the price of a November futures contract in cattlefeed fell to 69.3 cents per lb. Jack made a loss of 71.2 – 69.3 = 1.9 cents per lb. This represented a loss of $950 per contract on the day's trading. D. J. Easton made, correspondingly, a gain of $950 per contract (see Figure 3.2).

The holder of a futures contract is allowed to withdraw from their margin account any funds in excess of the initial margin. However, the initial margin is only 10% of the value of the asset and it is not inconceivable that following a run of adverse movements in the market, the initial margin could become seriously depleted. To guard against this, an amount called the **maintenance margin** is set. The maintenance margin is usually less than the initial margin. (As a rough guide, the maintenance margin is often 75% of the initial margin.) If funds in the margin account fall below the level of the maintenance margin, the holder receives a **margin call** from the broker. This margin call requires the holder of the futures contract to top up the margin account to the level of the initial margin and to do this within a very short period of time. The additional funds deposited into the margin account are called **variation margin.** If the holder does not provide the variation margin within the time stipulated, the broker sells the futures contract. Minimum levels for initial and maintenance margins are set by the exchange. Brokers are allowed to require margins greater than those specified by the exchange; they are not allowed to require less.

By the use of these rules, there are few defaults in the futures markets.

We illustrate the use of margins by continuing Example 1.

Day 1: on the day he entered the futures contract, Jack was required to put up an **initial margin** of £3500 per contract (10%) or $7000 in all. The **maintenance margin** was set at $5500. As described, at the end of that day the futures price had risen to 71.2 cents per lb. Jack, potentially, is in a position to make a profit of 1.2 cents per lb. This would give Jack a profit, on the day, of:

$$\$\frac{1.2 \times 100\,000}{100} = \$1200$$

End of Day 1: the exchange deducts $1200 from the margin account of D. J. Easton and pays this amount into Jack's margin account. At the end of Day 1, Jack's margin account contains $(7000 + 1200) = $8200. (The margin account of D. J. Easton would decrease by $1200.)

Day 2: on the second day, the price of cattlefeed fell and the futures price, at the close of trading, was 69.3 cents. Jack is 1.9 cents per lb down on the previous day. On Day 2, Jack lost:

$$\$\frac{1.9 \times 100\,000}{100} = \$1900$$

End of Day 2: the exchange deducts $1900 from Jack's margin account and pays this into D. J. Easton's account. Jack's margin account contains $(8200 – 1900) = $6300. (D. J. Easton's margin account would increase by $1900.)

Jack's margin account is still above the maintenance margin level, so no margin call.

Day 3: the bad news continued and when the markets closed on the third day, the futures price of cattlefeed (November delivery) was 68.4 cents. This was 0.9 cents down on the previous day and Jack lost a further:

$$\$\frac{0.9 \times 100\,000}{100} = \$900$$

End of Day 3: $900 is deducted from Jack's account and $900 is paid into D. J. Easton's account. Jack's margin account contains $(6300 – 900) = $5400. The margin account has now dipped below the maintenance level and Jack will receive a margin call from his broker. Within 24 hours, Jack will have to provide **variation margin** of $1600 to restore the margin account to $7000, the maintenance margin.

The table below shows the futures price on six consecutive trading days. Also shown are the daily gain, the cumulative gain, the funds in the margin account and the occasions when a margin call was received.

	Futures price	Daily gain	Cumulative gain	Margin account	Margin call
	70.0 (on entry)			7000	
Day 1	71.2	1200	1200	8200	
Day 2	69.3	−1900	−700	6300	
Day 3	68.4	−900	−1600	5400	1600
Day 4	68.5	100	−1500	7100	
Day 5	66.6	−1900	−3400	5200	1800
Day 6	67.9 (on leaving)	1300	−2100	8300	

Day 4: the futures price rises 0.1 cents. Jack gains $100 on the day. His margin account, having been restored to $7000 by the margin call, now stands at $7100.

Day 5: the futures price falls by 1.9 cents. Jack loses $1900 and his margin account falls to $5200. This again triggers a margin call and Jack has to place $1800 in his margin account within 24 hours to restore the account to the maintenance level of $7000.

Day 6: Jack decides to leave the market. The futures price at the time he leaves is 67.9. This is 1.3 up on the starting price for the day. Jack gains $1300 and his margin account rises to $8300.

3.2 Closing out a position

The process of leaving the market is as easy as entering. All that is required is that you instruct your broker to assume the opposite position in the same asset with the same delivery date. So if you were in a long position (you were buying), you instruct your broker to assume a short position (to sell). If you were in a short position, you instruct your broker to go long. But the asset and the delivery date must be the same. This process is extremely important. It is called **closing out a position**. The vast majority of futures contracts entered do not proceed to maturity. Mostly, the aim is speculation (see section 3.5), but hedging risk (sections 3.6–3.8) is another important use for futures contracts. Speculators and hedgers would probably prefer not to have 100 000 lbs of cattlefeed dumped in their drives – closing out positions is important, necessary and a frequent occurrence.

Jack entered the futures market to buy 100 000 lbs of cattlefeed for 70 cents a lb, in November. When he closed out his position, his broker entered a contract to sell 100 000 lbs of cattlefeed in November for 67.9 cents a lb. Thus, someone else, in a sense, was contracting to take delivery of those 100 000 lbs

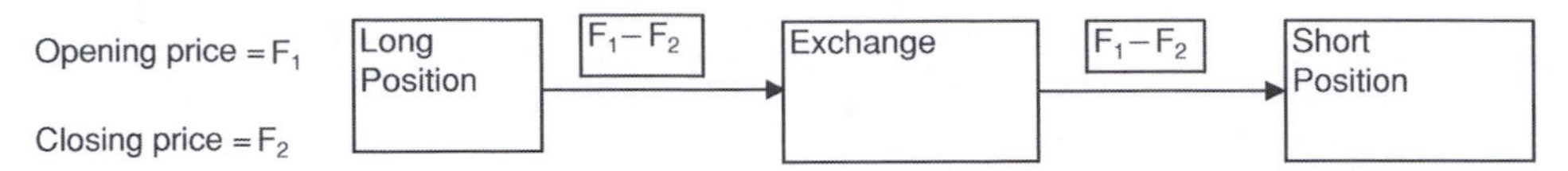

Figure 3.3

of cattlefeed in November. The exchange would handle the details and Jack was out of the market.

Overall, Jack lost $2100 from his venture into the futures market.

It will be useful to express profit/loss created from holding a futures contract in terms of futures prices.

3.3 Profit or loss when a position is closed out

The overall profit or loss created from a futures contract is the sum of the daily gains/losses over the number of days the contract is held.

For Jack, this would be:

$$+1200 - 1900 - 900 + 100 - 1900 + 1300 = -2100$$

(and the cumulative gains column records how much in total has been gained or lost by holding the contract).

Recall that the holder of a long futures contract, at the end of the working day, pays to the exchange (i.e. losses) an amount, $F_1 - F_2$ where:

F_1 = futures price at the opening of the market

F_2 = futures price when the market closes.

It might be that $F_1 - F_2$ is negative, in which case the holder of the long contract receives this amount of money from the exchange. Similarly, the holder of a short futures contract, at the end of the working day, will receive from the exchange $F_1 - F_2$ (see Figure 3.3).

Suppose, then, that the table below records opening and closing prices for a particular futures contract. We have:

Day	Closing futures price	Holder of *long* pays exchange	Holder of *short* receives from exchange
	F_1 (on entry)		
1	F_2	$F_1 - F_2$	$F_1 - F_2$
2	F_3	$F_2 - F_3$	$F_2 - F_3$
n	F_{n+1} (on closing out)	$F_n - F_{n+1}$	$F_n - F_{n+1}$
		Accumulated total $= F_1 - F_{n+1}$	Accumulated total $= F_1 - F_{n+1}$

(We assume that the closing price on Day 1 is the opening price on Day 2 and so on.) The amount paid to the exchange by the holder of a long contract over the number of days the contract is held is the sum of the amounts shown in column 3. This sum is:

$$F_1 - F_2 + F_2 - F_3 + F_3 - F_4 + \cdots + F_n - F_{n+1}$$

and this sum collapses neatly into an amount $F_1 - F_{n+1}$

The holder of a short futures contract will receive from the exchange an identical sum.

This gives the important result:

> Long futures contract: on closing out the position, the holder pays the exchange $F_1 - F_{n+1}$

> Short futures contract: on closing out the position, the holder receives from the exchange $F_1 - F_{n+1}$

Using this result, when Jack entered the long futures contract, the price per lb was \$0.70. When he closed out his position, the price was \$0.679. Jack paid the exchange (lost)

$$\$(0.70 - 0.679) \times 100\,000 = \$2100$$

and this is the amount given above.

Note that in the futures market, the buyer does not know the seller and the seller does not know the buyer. And neither do they need to know each other. The details, the administration, the organisation are all handled by the exchange. Inevitably, there will be transaction costs. But with the aim of describing the essential structure of futures, we have ignored these.

3.4 Two important points

1. As delivery date approaches, the futures price F will approach the spot price S. So we have a diagram similar to Figure 3.4.

   To see why this must be so, at maturity suppose F > S. Then an enterprising dealer could short a futures contract on the asset (enter a futures contract to sell the asset for F). On delivery day, the dealer buys the asset

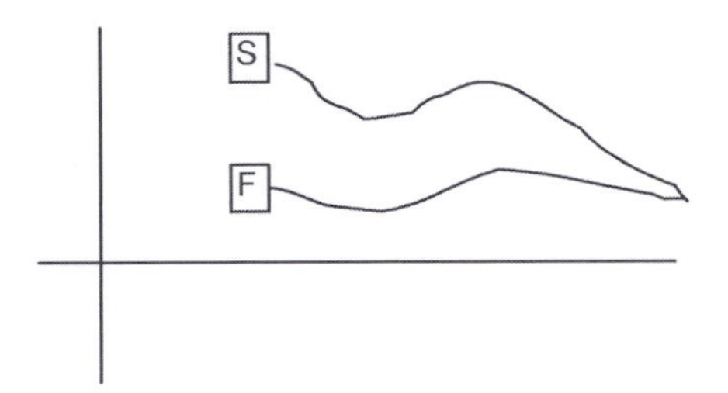

Figure 3.4

(S), hands over the asset and receives F. Since F > S, this is a clear arbitrage opportunity.

Suppose F < S. Then during the delivery period, a dealer could enter a long forward contract on the asset. On delivery day, the dealer hands over F and receives the asset, which he immediately sells for S. Since S > F, this, too, represents a guaranteed profit.

Hence, in the delivery period, to avoid arbitrage, we must have F = S. (Observe that in Figure 2.11, we saw that the forward price (F) approached the spot price (S) at maturity.)

2. Forward prices and futures prices are equal when interest rates are constant. A proof of this result appears in the appendix to this chapter.

   This result is useful when the contract lasts only a few months. Over that period of time, it is not unreasonable to suppose that interest rates will remain at least roughly the same. Over longer periods, this result should not be used. We will consider interest rate futures contracts in Chapter 5; these futures contracts might have maturities as far ahead as ten years and in such cases this result will not hold. In the real world, issues such as transaction costs, margin requirements and taxes might have an effect on prices. Also, futures contracts are easier to trade than forward contracts and this too might affect prices. Nevertheless, there are good grounds for believing that in the short term, futures prices and forward prices, against a background of a constant interest rate, are equal. The time spent in valuing forward contracts in Chapter 2 was not wasted.

3.5 Uses of futures contracts – speculation

As we have mentioned, the vast majority of futures contracts do not go through to maturity. Most are closed out before that time and most (it is thought in excess of 90%) are entered for purposes of speculation.

The usual advice, in finance, is: buy low, sell high. If you believe that the value of an asset (shares in a company, corn, oil, gold, etc.) is going to rise, you could enter a long futures contract on the asset. If you are right and the value of the asset increases, the futures price will increase also. When you have observed a reasonable rise in the futures price, close out the position. The difference in the futures prices becomes your profit. You have bought low and sold high.

In the same way, if you believe that the value of the asset will fall, you could enter a short forward contract (sell high) and then, when the value of the asset and the futures price have fallen, close out the contract (buy low) and pocket the difference in the futures prices.

There are two good reasons why it might be more sensible to buy (or sell) futures contracts rather than the asset itself.

(i) It might be difficult/inconvenient to buy a perishable commodity. Where and how would it be stored? How much would it cost to store the asset? What would be the additional costs in transportation?

(ii) Futures are a highly leveraged tool. All that you need when entering a futures contract is the initial margin to be deposited with your broker. Since this is generally around 10% of the value of the asset, you are deriving the full value of any increase/decrease in the value of the asset for only 10% of the value of the asset.

We illustrate how this works.

Example 2

You have \$100 000 to invest. Today is 1 July and you believe that the value of gold is going to fall. The three-month futures price of gold is \$314.60 per troy oz and the contracts traded on the New York Mercantile Exchange (Comex Division) are for 100 troy oz. Each contract will cost \$31 460. With \$100 000 you could buy just three contracts. However, with a futures contract, you are required to put up only 10% of the value, so you have to put up \$3146 per contract. Hence, you can buy $\frac{100000}{3146}$ or 31 three-month short futures contracts on gold at a cost of $31 \times 3146 = \$97\,526$. This you do.

The following day, the price of an October delivery short futures contract in gold is \$314.51. You enter a long October futures contract in gold and close out your position. Your profit is $(314.60 - 314.51) \times 31 \times 100 = \$279$.

The futures price of gold has fallen by $\frac{0.09}{314.60} \times 100 = 0.0286\%$. Your percentage profit (on an outlay of \$97 526) is $\frac{279}{97526} \times 100 = 0.286\%$. So by operating in the futures market, your profit percentage is ten times greater than if you had been dealing in gold. (This assumes that the futures price of gold is highly correlated with the price of gold.)

Look at this another way. Suppose the safe interest rate is 5%. Then, an investment of $97 526 for one day would yield interest of

$\frac{0.05}{365} \times 97\,526 = \$13.36$. But a movement of 0.0286% in the futures price of gold has yielded $279, which is more than 20 times the amount yielded by the safe interest rate.

Dealing in futures can yield large rewards. However, what works wonderfully well when fortune is smiling can create disasters when fortune looks the other way. Exactly the same mechanism, with an incorrect guess, can generate enormous, unlimited losses (as with Nick Leeson and the Barings Bank 'problem' in 1995). Speculating in the futures market is probably best left to those who know what they are doing.

3.6 Hedging

1. A company owns (or expects soon to own) an asset which it intends to sell, at the current market price, in two months' time. The company is exposed to risk through the possibility of a fall, over the following two months, in the value of the asset.
2. A second company expects to buy an asset in three months' time, the price being the market price on the day of purchase. This company is exposed to risk from a rising market.

Hedging is the process of neutralising risk or at least reducing the risk in a financial contract. By entering a futures contract which makes a gain in precisely the circumstances where the risky contract will make a loss, the hedger is neutralising (reducing) the risk inherent in the original contract.

Example 3

Today is 14 May and the spot price of gold is $296 per troy oz. A company expects to receive on or shortly before 30 July (in settlement of an account) 500 troy oz of gold. The company wants to sell the gold, in the open market, as soon as it is received. The company is exposed to risk through a possible fall in the price of gold. If it enters, today, a short futures contract (to sell gold) and the price of gold does fall, the company will make a loss from the sale of the gold but make a gain from the futures contract. If, however, the price of gold rises, it will make a profit from the sale of the gold and a loss from the futures contract. We show how this strategy can be used to remove (or lessen) the risk from a falling market and provide the company, today, with an approximate price it will receive from the sale of the gold.

Futures contracts in gold are available for any delivery month on the NYME (Comex Division). Each contract is for 100 troy oz. The price (per troy oz) for an August futures contract in gold is $299. The company enters five short August futures contracts, which it closes out on the day the gold is sold. (Since this day is likely to be late in July, an August futures contract is used for the hedge.)

We show now that this strategy will guarantee the company a price of approximately $299 per troy oz.

On 30 July:

There are two possibilities.

(i) The spot price on 30 July is greater than or equal to $299.
Suppose the spot price on this day is $301. Since, at maturity, the spot price and the futures price converge, the closing out price on the futures contracts should be approximately $301. Since the futures contracts are to sell for $299, the company **loses** $(301 − 299) per troy oz on the futures contracts. From the sale of its gold, the company **receives** $301 per troy oz. Hence the company achieves (approximately)
$301 − $(301 − 299) = $299 per troy oz.

(ii) The spot price on 30 July is less than $299.
Suppose the spot price on 30 July is $290. The closing out price on the futures contracts should be approximately $290, so the company makes a **profit** of $(299 − 290) per troy oz from the futures contracts. From the sale of its gold, the company realises $290 per troy oz. Hence, overall the company achieves (approximately) $290 + $(299 − 290) = $299 per troy oz.

The aim has been to balance (or hedge) a loss in one contract by a gain in the other and as the arithmetic shows, this has been successful. By such means, the company has been able to realise a price that was known on 14 May. By this means, the uncertainty associated with this deal has been reduced considerably.

Definition This situation, where the risk associated with a **sale** in the open market is neutralised by entering a **short** futures contract on an identical or closely related asset, is called a **short hedge**.

A second company expects to **buy** a certain asset in three months' time, the purchase price being the market price on the day of the purchase. The company is exposed to risk from a rising market.

Example 4

It is 23 July. A company knows it will have to buy 1000 metric tons of gas oil on 1 October. The spot price per metric ton on 23 July is \$214.65. A long October futures contract in gas oil is priced at \$219.70 per metric ton. (Futures contracts, each for 100 metric tons, are traded for every delivery month on the International Petroleum Exchange.) The company enters ten long October futures contracts. The aim will be to guarantee a purchase price to the company of around \$219.70 per metric ton.

On 1 October, again there are two possibilities (all prices are per metric ton).

(i) The spot price on 1 October is greater than or equal to \$219.70.
Suppose the spot price is \$220.50. Since, at maturity, the spot price and the futures price converge, the futures price on this day will be close to \$220.50. The futures contracts are to buy the gas oil for \$219.70, so by closing out its futures contracts, the company will make a **profit** of (approx) \$(220.50 − 219.70). The company will pay \$220.50 for the gas oil. Hence, the company will be paying
\$220.50 − \$(220.50 − 219.70) = \$219.70 per metric ton, as hoped for.

(ii) The spot price on 1 October is less than \$219.70.
Suppose the spot price is \$218.30. By closing out the futures contracts, the company loses (approx) \$(219.70 − 218.30). In the purchase, the company pays out \$218.30. So in total, the company pays out (approximately) \$218.30 + \$(219.70 − 218.30) = \$219.70.

Again a hedging strategy has fixed a price that was known to the company on 23 July.

Definition The process of neutralising the risk associated with a **purchase** in the open market by entering a **long** futures contract on an identical or closely related asset is called setting up a **long hedge.**

In these two examples, the hedge worked extremely well. Too well. In the real world, events are not so tidy. There are two things that can make a hedge less than perfect.

Problem 1

The asset underlying the hedge is not the same as the asset to be bought or sold.

A company might wish to buy or sell a commodity not traded in the futures market, e.g. coal, jet fuel, tomatoes, steel, horses, bricks, cement, or the asset might be gold or silver, of a purity inferior to that specified in a futures contract.

In these cases, the usual procedure is to identify an asset whose price movements are highly correlated with the price movement of the asset to be sold/bought and on which futures contracts are traded. Futures contracts on this asset are then used to hedge the purchase/sale. If the correlation really is high, then an efficient (but probably not perfect) hedge is possible. Examples of this method will be given in sections 3.7 and 3.8.

Problem 2

It might not be possible to find a delivery date that matches the date of the sale/purchase. Futures contracts in corn, traded on the Chicago Board of Trade, for example, have delivery dates only in March, May, July, September and December.

There are sound reasons why in any hedge a futures contract should be chosen which has a delivery date **after** the date of the purchase/sale. First, prices of some futures contracts in the delivery month fluctuate widely. Second, the hedger wants to close out his futures positions on or around the date of the sale/purchase. He does not want to risk going to the delivery date and then having to (a) sell an asset he does not own, (b) buy an asset he doesn't want. So the delivery date of the futures contract chosen to hedge the sale/purchase should, ordinarily, be the nearest available delivery date **after** the date of the sale/purchase. If, for example, delivery dates in March, June, September and December were available and the date of the sale/purchase was late September, October or November, then a futures contract with a December delivery date would be chosen.

3.7 Hedge ratio

With the hedges considered so far, the idea has been to enter as many futures contracts as are necessary to match as closely as possible the size of the asset being hedged. When 500 oz of gold were being sold and each futures contract in gold was for 100 oz, the strategy was to enter five short futures contracts. When

1000 metric tons of gas oil were to be purchased and each futures contract in gas oil was for 100 metric tons, the plan was to enter ten long futures contracts.

Definition Hedge ratio (h) $= \dfrac{\text{size of position in futures contracts}}{\text{size of asset to be hedged}}$

Each of the hedges considered so far has had a hedge ratio of 1.0. Let S be the asset to be hedged by N futures contracts, each having value F. The size of the futures position is NF and so far we have tried to ensure that NF = S. This gives a hedge ratio h $= \frac{NF}{S} = 1$.

The hedge ratio does not have to be 1. Aiming to achieve parity in this way might not always be the best policy. But before we consider another way of calculating the hedge ratio, observe: once the hedge ratio is known, we can calculate the number of futures contracts necessary for the hedge.

Example 5

A company plans to invest \$2 000 000 in a new soft drink. The company believes that the price of frozen orange juice and sales of the new drink will have a high correlation. So it uses long futures contracts in frozen orange juice to hedge its expenditure. Futures contracts (on 15 000 lbs of frozen orange juice) are available on the New York Board of Trade (NYBOT). The futures price today of frozen orange juice is 82.15 cents per lb. Each contract will have a value of $\$0.8215 \times 15\,000 = \$12\,322.5$. It is thought that a hedge ratio of 0.85 would be appropriate. How many long futures contracts should the company buy to hedge its expenditure?

Solution

S = \$2 000 000
F = \$12 322.5
h = 0.85

Using h $= \dfrac{NF}{S}$

$$0.85 = \frac{N \times 12\,322.5}{2\,000\,000}$$

$$\text{And N} = \frac{0.85 \times 2\,000\,000}{12\,322.5} = 137.96$$

So (rounding to the nearest whole number) 138 long futures contracts should be entered.

Generally:
Let S = value of asset to be hedged
F = value of one futures contract being used to hedge the asset
N = number of futures contracts to be used in the hedge
Then the hedge ratio equation becomes: $\frac{NF}{S} = h$
This gives the number of futures contracts to be used in the hedge: $N = \frac{hS}{F}$
Consequently, if we know the hedge ratio, h, then we can calculate the number of futures contracts, N.

3.8 Practical hedging: the optimal hedge ratio

Now the question is, if we are not going to take h = 1.0, how can a meaningful value for h be calculated? Suppose that (problem 1) the asset underlying the futures contract (F) is not the asset (S) whose variation we are trying to hedge. F will be highly correlated with S but could be subject to greater (or less) variation than S.

We would like h to measure changes in the movement of the asset value relative to changes in the movement of the futures contract. We consider three ways of calculating such a value for h. The three methods are equivalent and lead to the same result.

Definition This value of h found by all three methods is known as **the optimal hedge ratio.**

Each method will be illustrated using the data in Figure 3.5.

Time	F value	S value
0	4.9	10.428
0.083333	4.985	10.502
0.166666	5.023	10.796
0.249999	5.1	10.801
0.333332	5.099	10.903
0.416665	5.078	10.66
0.5	5.045	10.47
0.583333	5.271	11.063
0.666666	5.25	10.878

Figure 3.5

Each method will compare changes in the asset value S with changes in the futures contract value F. So the first step will be to calculate these changes. We look at successive differences in F values and successive differences in S

Time	F value	S value	x (difference in F)	y (difference in S)
0	4.9	10.428		
0.083333	4.985	10.502	0.085	0.074
0.166666	5.023	10.796	0.038	0.294
0.249999	5.1	10.801	0.077	0.005
0.333332	5.099	10.903	−0.001	0.102
0.416665	5.078	10.66	−0.021	−0.243
0.5	5.045	10.47	−0.033	−0.19
0.583333	5.271	11.063	0.226	0.593
0.666666	5.25	10.878	−0.021	−0.185

Figure 3.6

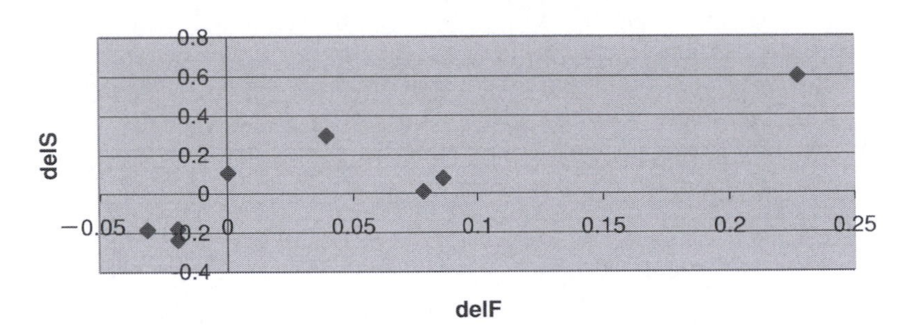

Figure 3.7

values. We will call these differences x and y respectively. (The first x value is $4.985 - 4.9 = 0.085$; the first y value is $10.502 - 10.428 = 0.074$ – see Figure 3.6.)

Method 1

Plot a scatter graph of y against x (Figure 3.7). h is to measure changes in S values relative to changes in F values. Drawing the (straight) line of best fit (in the above scatter graph) will achieve this. It turns out that the gradient of this line of best fit is precisely the value we require for h. In Excel, the function SLOPE (y values, x values) calculates the gradient of the line of best fit. We use SLOPE in Figure 3.8 to calculate h. The F value differences are entered with the range name x. Similarly with y. (The INTERCEPT of the line of best fit is thrown in for good measure.)

The hedge ratio h is 2.815281. We will round to the nearest integer. Enter three futures contracts.

Methods 2 and 3, while leading to the same result, are more technical.

x and y measure successive changes in F and in S. We would like h, in some way, to minimise the variation between changes in S and changes in

Microsoft Excel - Chap3.8

File Edit View Insert Format Tools Data Window Help

	A	B	C	D	E	F	G	H
1	Chap3.8							
2							=INTERCEPT(y,x)	
3								
4	Time	F value	S value	x	y			
5						-0.06692		
6						2.81528		
7	0	4.9	10.428					
8	0.08333	4.985	10.502	0.085	0.074	=SLOPE(y,x)		
9	0.16667	5.023	10.796	0.038	0.294			
10	0.25	5.1	10.801	0.077	0.005			
11	0.33333	5.099	10.903	-0.001	0.102			
12	0.41667	5.078	10.66	-0.021	-0.243			
13	0.5	5.045	10.47	-0.033	-0.19			
14	0.58333	5.271	11.063	0.226	0.593			
15	0.66667	5.25	10.878	-0.021	-0.185			
16								
17								
18								
19								
20								
21								
22								
23								
24								
25								
26								

Figure 3.8

F (between y and x). We would like h to make the variation in $y - h \times x$ as small as possible.

By variation we mean variance. So the problem is:

choose h to minimise $\mathrm{var}(y - h \times x)$

Methods 2 and 3 use a technical result, a standard result from statistics, which we give without proof.

$$\mathrm{var}(y - h \times x) = \mathrm{var}(y) + h^2\mathrm{var}(x) - 2h\rho\sqrt{\mathrm{var}(y) \times \mathrm{var}(x)} \qquad **$$

where ρ = correlation coefficient between y and x

Method 2

From the data in Figure 3.6, we can calculate (in Excel) var(y), var(x) and the correlation coefficient ρ (Figure 3.9).

Again, the F value differences are entered with range name x.

Microsoft Excel - Chap3.9

File Edit View Insert Format Tools Data Window Help

U42

	A	B	C	D	E	F	G	H
1	Chap3.9							
2								
3						var (x)		
4	Time	F value	S value	x	y			
5						0.00748		
6						0.07972		
7	0	4.9	10.428			var (y)		
8	0.08333	4.985	10.502	0.085	0.074			
9	0.16667	5.023	10.796	0.038	0.294			
10	0.25	5.1	10.801	0.077	0.005	0.86213		
11	0.33333	5.099	10.903	-0.001	0.102			
12	0.41667	5.078	10.66	-0.021	-0.243	=CORREL(x,y)		
13	0.5	5.045	10.47	-0.033	-0.19			
14	0.58333	5.271	11.063	0.226	0.593			
15	0.66667	5.25	10.878	-0.021	-0.185			
16								
17								
18								
19								
20								
21								

Figure 3.9

Substitute these values in **

$$\begin{aligned} \text{var}(y - h \times x) &= 0.079722 + h^2 \times 0.007476 \\ &\quad - 2 \times h \times 0.862133 \times \sqrt{0.079722 \times 0.007476} \\ &= 0.007476h^2 - 0.0420947567h + 0.079722 \end{aligned}$$

The right-hand side is a quadratic expression in h. Plot the graph of this quadratic (in Excel) and observe the value of h that produces a minimum value for var(y − h × x) (Figure 3.10a).

From the graph, minimum value occurs when h = 2.8.

Optimal hedge ratio = 2.8. Buy three futures contracts.

Method 3

This method uses calculus to find the minimum value of the quadratic in h.

(1) Differentiate the quadratic expression with respect to h.

(2) Put the resulting derivative equal to zero and solve for h.

(3) Check that this value for h does give a minimum by showing that the second derivative is positive for this value of h.

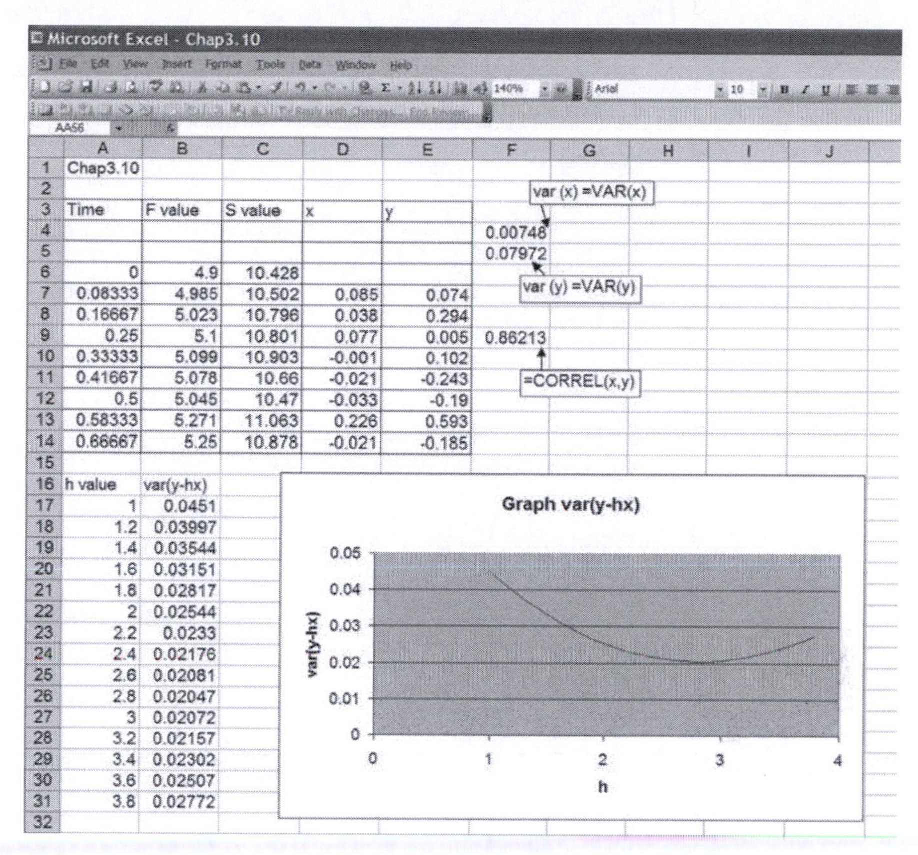

Microsoft Excel - Chap3.10

	A	B	C	D	E	F
1	Chap3.10					
2						var (x) =VAR(x)
3	Time	F value	S value	x	y	
4						0.00748
5						0.07972
6	0	4.9	10.428			var (y) =VAR(y)
7	0.08333	4.985	10.502	0.085	0.074	
8	0.16667	5.023	10.796	0.038	0.294	
9	0.25	5.1	10.801	0.077	0.005	0.86213
10	0.33333	5.099	10.903	-0.001	0.102	
11	0.41667	5.078	10.66	-0.021	-0.243	=CORREL(x,y)
12	0.5	5.045	10.47	-0.033	-0.19	
13	0.58333	5.271	11.063	0.226	0.593	
14	0.66667	5.25	10.878	-0.021	-0.185	
15						
16	h value	var(y-hx)				
17	1	0.0451				
18	1.2	0.03997				
19	1.4	0.03544				
20	1.6	0.03151				
21	1.8	0.02817				
22	2	0.02544				
23	2.2	0.0233				
24	2.4	0.02176				
25	2.6	0.02081				
26	2.8	0.02047				
27	3	0.02072				
28	3.2	0.02157				
29	3.4	0.02302				
30	3.6	0.02507				
31	3.8	0.02772				
32						

Figure 3.10a

Microsoft Excel - Chap3.10b

	A	B	C	D	E	F
1	Chap3.10b					
2						
3						var (x) =VAR(x)
4	Time	F value	S value	x	y	
5						0.00748
6						0.07972
7	0	4.9	10.428			
8	0.083333	4.985	10.502	0.085	0.074	var (y) =VAR(y)
9	0.166666	5.023	10.796	0.038	0.294	
10	0.249999	5.1	10.801	0.077	0.005	0.86213
11	0.333332	5.099	10.903	-0.001	0.102	
12	0.416665	5.078	10.66	-0.021	-0.243	=CORREL(x,y)
13	0.5	5.045	10.47	-0.033	-0.19	
14	0.583333	5.271	11.063	0.226	0.593	2.81528
15	0.666666	5.25	10.878	-0.021	-0.185	
16						
17			Optimal hedge ratio = correl(x,y)*SQRT(var(y))/SQRT(var(x))			
18						

Figure 3.10b

(1) $\dfrac{d[\text{var}(y - hx)]}{dh} = 2\text{var}(x)h - 2\rho\sqrt{\text{var}(y) \times \text{var}(x)}$

(2) $2\text{var}(x)h - 2\rho\sqrt{\text{var}(y) \times \text{var}(x)} = 0$ gives:

$$h = \frac{2\rho\sqrt{\text{var}(y) \times \text{var}(x)}}{2\text{var}(x)} = \rho\sqrt{\frac{\text{var}(y)}{\text{var}(x)}}$$

(3) The second derivative is 2var(x). This is clearly positive: we have a minimum.

Using the data in Figure 3.9, we have:

$$h = 0.862133 \times \sqrt{\frac{0.079722}{0.007476}} = 2.81532616$$

See Figure 3.10b. The optimal hedge ratio is 2.815: buy three futures contracts.

As we have seen, to calculate a value for h (and to make sure there is a high correlation between S and the asset underlying the futures contracts), we need past data in S and F. One more example.

Example 6

HeatingHomes wants to buy 1 000 000 MMBtu units of a specialised heating gas in September. It is planning to use natural gas futures contracts for hedging. Natural gas futures are traded every month on the New York Mercantile Exchange (NYME) in units of 10 000 MMBtu. The values over the past 12 months of one MMBtu unit of the heating gas and the value per MMBtu of natural gas futures are given in Figure 3.11.

(i) Investigate whether natural gas futures might be a realistic choice for hedging.

(ii) If it is reasonable to set up a hedge using natural gas futures, calculate the number of contracts needed to hedge the purchase of 1 000 000 MMBtu units of the heating gas.

Solution

(i) For a successful hedge, we want the futures prices to be highly correlated with the values of the asset. So we need to calculate the correlation coefficient between the two columns in Figure 3.11. This calculation (and

Heating Gas y values	Natural Gas Futures x values
12.74	6.012
12.93	6.134
12.91	6.1
12.85	5.987
12.65	5.842
12.59	5.777
12.58	5.823
12.68	5.941
12.88	6.029
12.99	6.089
13.42	6.174
13.74	6.283

Figure 3.11

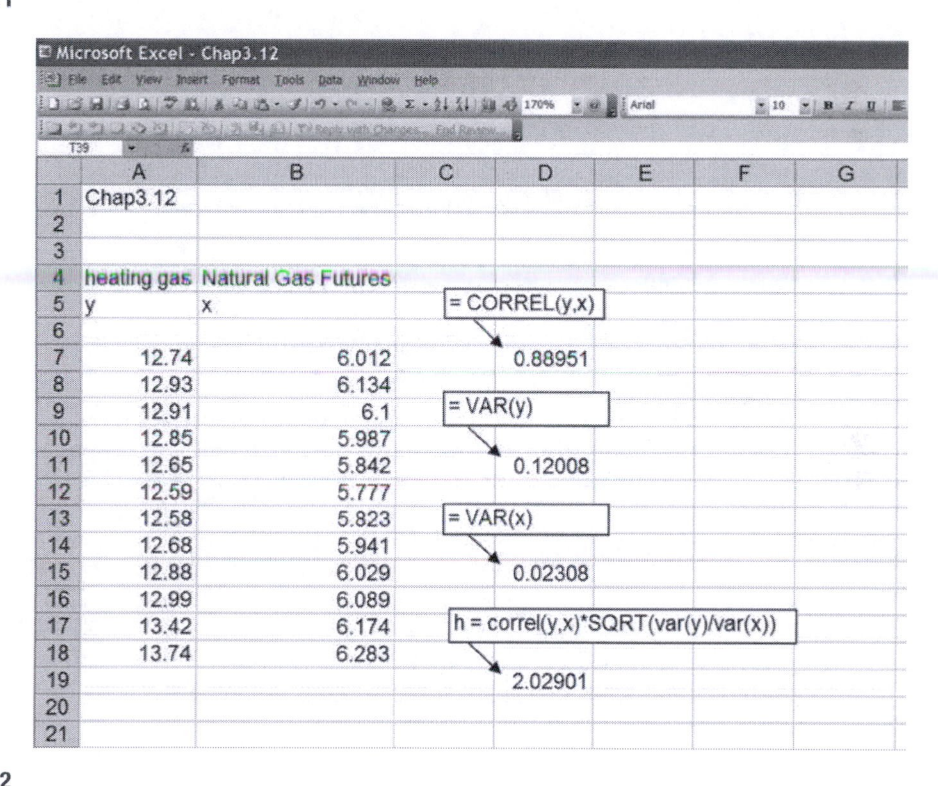

Figure 3.12

all the calculations we shall need) is carried out in the spreadsheet in Figure 3.12.

The correlation coefficient is calculated in D7. A correlation coefficient of 0.889512 suggests that there is high correlation between natural gas futures prices and values of the asset. It is reasonable to use natural gas futures to hedge the purchase of 1 000 000 MMBtu units of the specialised heating gas in September.

(ii) The optimal hedge ratio h is calculated in D19.

$$\text{We have: } h = \frac{\text{size of position in futures contracts}}{\text{size of asset to be hedged}} = \frac{N \times 10\,000}{1\,000\,000}$$

$$\text{The (optimal) number of contracts, } N = \frac{h \times 1\,000\,000}{10\,000} = \frac{2.029014 \times 1\,000\,000}{10\,000} = 203 \text{ (nearest whole number)}$$

Finally, when should a hedge ratio of 1.0 be used and when should we take the trouble to calculate the optimal hedge ratio? The answer depends on the relative variability of asset values (S) and futures prices (F). If the variances of S and F are similar, then a hedge ratio of 1.0 is usually adequate. If, however, the variances are significantly different, then an optimal hedge ratio should be calculated.

Useful websites:

www.cbot.com	Chicago Board of Trade
www.eurexchange.com	Eurex: European Electronic Exchange
www.FT.com	The Financial Times
www.liffe.com	London International Financial Futures and Options Exchange

Appendix

If interest rates are constant, the futures price and the forward price (on the same asset and with the same delivery date) are the same.

Proof

This proof was first given by Cox, Ingersoll and Ross (*Journal of Financial Economics*, December 1981).

For an asset S and a maturity of contract n days hence:

Let S_n be the value of the asset at the end of the nth day.

Let F_1 be the futures price on entry (sometime during Day 1).

$F_2, F_3, \ldots F_{n+1}$ are the futures prices at the close of the market on Days 1 to n.

Let $\hat{F}_1$ be the n day forward price of the asset.

Let R be the interest rate per day. (We could take an interest rate per year and express the daily rate in terms of this rate, but life is about to get complicated. We will try to keep the notation straightforward.)

The overall plan will be to set up two portfolios, one containing futures contracts and the other containing forward contracts. Through an elaborate construction, the two portfolios will be shown to have the same value at the end of day n. Using the usual argument, we then argue that the portfolios must have the same value initially. This will give the result we require.

The 'elaborate construction' is a procedure for buying futures contracts in each of the n days. Buy $1 + R$ futures contracts on the first day. Increase the holding to $(1 + R)^2$ futures contracts on the second day, increase the holding to $(1 + R)^3$ futures contracts on the third day and so on until the portfolio contains $(1 + R)^n$ futures contracts at the end of the nth day. At the end of each day, there will be a gain (possibly a negative gain). Consider the value at the end of day n of the sum of all the gains over the n days. This will be the value of the investment strategy at maturity. It will be shown that this value is $(S_n - F_1)(1 + R)^n$.

The portfolio involving forward contracts consists simply of entering $(1 + R)^n$ forward contracts on Day 1.

Construction

Day 1	Day 2	Day n
Initially:	**At start of trading:**	**At start of trading:**
The futures price is F_1	The futures price is F_2	The futures price is F_n
Enter $1 + R$ futures contracts on the asset	Increase the number of futures contracts to $(1 + R)^2$	Increase the number of futures contracts to $(1 + R)^n$
At close of trading:	**At close of trading:**	**At close of trading:**
Futures price $= F_2$	Futures price $= F_3$	Futures price $= F_{n+1}$
Gain on $(1 + R)$ contracts on the day's trading is:	Gain on $(1 + R)^2$ contracts on the day's trading is:	Gain on $(1 + R)^n$ contracts on the day's trading is:
$(F_2 - F_1)(1 + R)$	$(F_3 - F_2)(1 + R)^2$	$(F_{n+1} - F_n)(1 + R)^n$

See Figure 3.13.

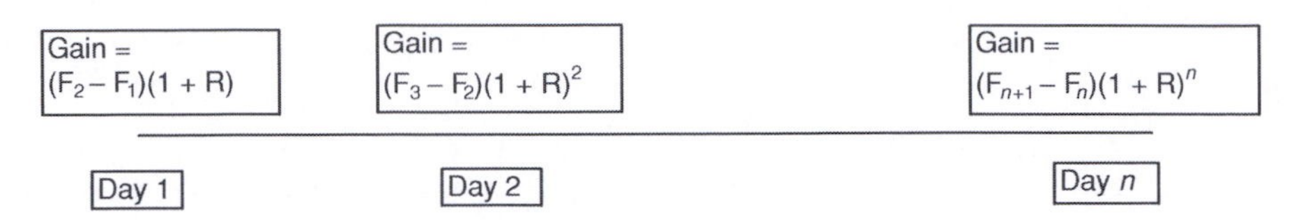

Figure 3.13

If each GAIN is regarded as a dividend and discounted back to the start of trading ($t = 0$), we have:

	Day 1	Day 2	Day 3	Day n
Sum of discounted gains is:	$F_2 - F_1$ +	$F_3 - F_2$ +	$F_4 - F_3$ + ··· +	$F_{n+1} - F_n$

This sum collapses to $F_{n+1} - F_1$.

$F_{n+1} - F_1$ at $t = 0$ will have a value: $(F_{n+1} - F_1)(1 + R)^n$ at $t = n$. Since the futures price F_{n+1} converges to the spot price S_n at maturity, we have $F_{n+1} = S_n$ and this expression becomes $(S_n - F_1)(1 + R)^n$.

Consider two portfolios:

Portfolio A: this portfolio will consist of cash and futures contracts.

At $t = 0$:

You have an amount of cash, F_1.
Invest F_1 at the safe daily rate R for n days.
Begin the sequence of investments in the futures markets described in the above construction.

At $t = n$:

At maturity, the portfolio is worth:
$F_1(1 + R)^n$ (from the cash investment)
$(S_n - F_1)(1 + R)^n$ (from the futures investments).
In total, the portfolio is worth: $S_n(1 + R)^n$.

Portfolio B: this portfolio contains cash and forward contracts.

At $t = 0$:

You have an amount of cash $\hat{F}_1$.
Invest $\hat{F}_1$ at the risk-free daily rate R.
The asset has an n day forward price of $\hat{F}_1$.
Enter $(1 + R)^n$ long forward contracts,
each with delivery price $K = \hat{F}_1$ and delivery date $t = n$.

At $t = n$:

At maturity the cash investment has value $\hat{F}_1(1 + R)^n$.

In settlement of the $(1 + R)^n$ forward contracts,
hand over $\hat{F}_1(1 + R)^n$ and receive $S_n(1 + R)^n$.
The portfolio will be worth:

$$\begin{aligned} &\hat{F}_1(1 + R)^n && \text{(from the cash investment)} \\ &S_n(1 + R)^n - \hat{F}_1(1 + R)^n && \text{(from the forward contracts)} \\ &= S_n(1 + R)^n. \end{aligned}$$

Hence, at time $t = n$, both portfolios are worth $S_n(1 + R)^n$. To avoid arbitrage (see Useful Result, section 1.4), the two portfolios must be worth the same amount at time $t = 0$. This gives, $\hat{F}_1 = F_1$.
That is:

forward price = futures price in a market where the interest rate is constant

Note that it really does not matter that the constant interest rate was the daily rate. The argument goes through for a constant rate over any period.

Exercise 3

1. Why is the holder of a futures contract less likely to default on the contract than the holder of a similar forward contract?

2. What are initial margin, maintenance margin and variation margin? Give an example to illustrate each of these three types of margin.

3. Why might you enter a long futures contract and when might you enter a short futures contract?

4. Today is 11 November 2004. Usha enters a short June 2005 futures contract in gold. What is she contracting to do in June 2005? What does she have to do, on 11 November, to set up this contract?
   On 13 January 2005, Usha decides to close out the contract. How does she do this?

5. On 7 September, Martin enters three long futures contracts in corn with December delivery. One contract is to buy 5000 bushels of corn and today the price of a December futures contract in corn is 268 cents per bushel. Initial margin is set at $1300 per contract. Maintenance margin is 75% of the initial margin. The futures price on successive days is:

Day	Futures price (close of trading)	Daily gain	Cumulative gain	Margin account	Margin call
1	265				
2	261				
3	254				
4	259				
5	263				
6	262				
7	257				

Martin closes out the contract at the close of trading on Day 7. Complete the table. What is Martin's overall gain or loss?

6. In Figure 3.14, the details of nine days' trading in a long futures contract are shown. There is something wrong with this table. What is it?

Ex3.6							
Contract							
		Futures	Contract	Daily	Cumulative	Margin account	Margin
No. contracts	Day	price $	value	gain	gain	balance	call
3	1	15.37	76850			22000	
	2	16.29	81450	4600	4600	26600	0
Contract size	3	18.83	94150	12700	17300	39300	0
5000	4	17.42	87100	−7050	10250	32250	0
	5	16.51	82550	−4550	5700	27700	0
	6	15.29	76450	−6100	−400	22000	400
Initial margin	7	14.64	73200	−3250	−3650	22000	3250
22000	8	13.88	69400	−3800	−7450	22000	3800
	9	14.55	72750	3350	−4100	25350	0
Maintenance margin							
16500							

Figure 3.14

7. In Figure 3.15 the details of eight days' trading in a short futures contract are shown. Prices are in pounds. Complete the table. What was the overall gain or loss over the eight days of trading?

8. Figure 3.16 shows the results of eight days' trading in a long futures contract. Prices are in dollars. Complete the table. Find the overall gain or loss over the eight days.

9. In Figure 3.17 the figures from seven days' trading in a short futures contract can be seen. Prices are in pounds. Complete the table. What was the overall gain or loss over the seven days' trading?

Ex3.7							
		Futures	Contract	Daily	Cumulative	Margin account	Margin
No. contracts	Day	price	value	gain	gain	balance	call
5	1	4.78					
	2	4.5					
Contract size	3	4.36					
10000	4	4.47					
	5	4.59					
	6	4.78					
Initial margin	7	4.96					
5000	8	5.16					
Maintenance margin							
3750							

Figure 3.15

Ex3.8							
		Futures	Contract	Daily	Cumulative	Margin account	Margin
No. contracts	Day	price	value	gain	gain	balance	call
3	1	0.9513	39954.6			12000	
	2	0.9011					
Contract size	3	0.8798					
42000	4	0.8948					
	5	0.8909					
	6	0.8371					
Initial margin	7	0.8049					
12000	8	0.9713					
Maintenance margin							
9000							

Figure 3.16

Ex3.9							
		Futures	Contract	Daily	Cumulative	Margin account	Margin
No. contracts	Day	price	value	gain	gain	balance	call
3	1	0.8537	21342.5			2000	
	2	0.8481	21202.5	140	140	2140	0
Contract size	3	0.8948					
25000	4	0.8911					
	5	0.8792					
	6	0.8899					
Initial margin	7	0.8219					
2000							
Maintenance margin							
1500							

Figure 3.17

10. Borrow £100. Take out a one-week subscription to the *Financial Times.* Invest the remaining amount in a long (or short, if you prefer) futures contract in wheat. Observe daily gains and losses. Close out the contract five trading days later. Pay off the loan (at the current LIBOR rate). Are you better or worse off?

11. You have $50 000 to invest and you believe the price of copper is about to rise. Shares in a copper mining company cost $15.50 each. A December copper futures contract (traded on Cmx.Div.NYM with each contract for 25 000 lbs of copper) is priced at 81.52 cents per lb. Assume an initial margin of 10% of contract value.
    (i) What are you going to do?
    (ii) In seven days' time, the shares are priced at $15.97 and the December futures contract in copper is priced at 81.84 cents per lb. Calculate your profit from your answer to (i).

12. Today is 2 July and the cost of one troy oz of silver is $5.91. A jewellery company expects to buy 10 000 troy oz of silver in the middle of September. It seems the price of silver might rise over the next few months and a sharp rise would cause the company difficulties with existing contracts. A December futures contract in silver (on 5000 troy oz of silver) is priced at $5.97 per troy oz.
    (i) Explain how the company can use a futures contract to hedge its risk.
    (ii) Describe the company's strategy and describe the price per troy oz the company can expect to pay, after hedging.

13. Hothomes buys today (23 April) 90 000 gallons of heating oil. It has agreed a price of $0.87 per gallon. This will be delivered in July and sold immediately to Hothomes' customers at the July price. There is a worry that the price of heating oil might fall before July. But then the financial director sees in her *Financial Times*:

    Heating oil No2 (NYM) 42 000 galls: $ per gall.

April	0.87
May	0.89
June	0.91
July	0.93
August	0.94

What should she do to hedge the risk? Describe her strategy carefully.

What price (approximately) will she get for her heating oil in July? Why might this be an approximation?

14. (i) Describe a short hedge. When and why might you use a short hedge?
 (ii) Describe a long hedge. When and why might you use a long hedge?

15. (i) Define what is meant by hedge ratio.
 (ii) A bakery is marketing a new type of biscuit. Over the next six months, it plans to spend $5 000 000 and is, understandably, nervous. The bakery believes that biscuit sales will be highly correlated with the price of wheat. A six-month futures contract on 5 000 bushels of wheat costs $4.05 per bushel. It is believed that a hedge ratio of 0.8 would be appropriate. How many long futures contracts should the company buy?

16. SoupsInc is planning to invest $ 5 000 000 in marketing a new range of soups. The cost of a packet of (it believes) comparable soup over the past ten months is shown in the table below. The company believes it can hedge the cost by buying soyabean meal futures contracts. Each futures contract is for 100 tons and the price is given in $ per ton. These prices are also given in the table.

Soyabean meal futures contract ($ per ton)	Cost of packet of soup (cents)
148.45	32.78
149.54	33.5
150.32	33.97
150.04	33.98
149.55	33.05
148.97	32.69
147.79	32.13
148.23	32.75
148.74	32.80
150.07	33.18

 (i) Is there a justification for believing that soyabean meal futures can hedge the manufacturing costs of the soup?
 (ii) If there is, use a method of your choosing to calculate the optimal hedge ratio.
 (iii) How many futures contracts should be used in the hedge?

17. A clothing firm plans to import cotton jackets to the value of $10 000 000. It believes sales will be highly correlated to the price of cotton. The price of a jacket of this type and the futures price of cotton (each contract is for 50 000 lbs; the price is given in cents per lb) over the past eight months are given in the table:

Cost of cotton jacket	Futures price of cotton (cents per lb)
14.85	45.67
14.97	47.94
15.12	48.25
15.01	46.74
14.11	44.26
13.27	41.38
13.25	42.61
13.70	44.01

(i) How would the firm decide whether or not cotton futures prices might sensibly be used to hedge cotton jacket sales?

(ii) Using each of the methods 1, 2 and 3 described in Chapter 3, calculate the hedge ratio and hence the number of cotton futures contracts that should be bought to hedge sales in the cotton jacket.

4 Bonds

ABC Airlines needs £50 million to re-equip and update its online booking system. One board member suggested borrowing the £50 million from a bank.

'Sales are down a bit at the moment,' the financial director said. 'We are not looking as prosperous as we have in the past. The bank would charge a very high interest rate.'

'What about floating a share option and selling more shares in the company?' someone else suggested. 'That would bring in plenty of cash.'

The chairman looked grumpy. 'It would bring in a lot of new share holders too,' he said. 'Too many people think they run this company already.'

'We could issue a bond,' someone else suggested. 'That would bring in money, but it would be cash without any interference from the bond holders.'

And that is what they did.

In this chapter, we shall describe various bonds. We will show how to find the value of a bond and why the value of a bond might change. We will show how to measure the yield of a bond and how to compare two (or more) apparently very different bonds. Finally, we show how known bond prices can be used to construct a zero curve.

4.1 Bonds

When an organisation issues a bond, it is promising to make a sequence of predetermined payments to the owner of the bond. The bond will have a **principal** or a **face value** (e.g. $100 or £1000) and a **maturity** (e.g. one year, five years, ten years). We shall consider two types of bond.

1. Zero coupon bond

A zero coupon bond makes just one payment. The face value of the bond is paid out at maturity. There are no other payments.

Figure 4.1

Example 1

A six-month zero coupon bond with face value $100 will pay out $100 six months after the bond was issued (see Figure 4.1).

2. Coupon bearing bond

A coupon bearing bond pays out, each year, a fixed percentage of the face value. Each payment is called a **coupon** and the timing of the coupon payments is a feature of the bond. Some bonds make one coupon payment each year (e.g. 6% of the face value), others make two equal payments (e.g. 3% of the face value every six months), others make four payments (e.g. 1.5% of the face value every three months). These payments continue up to and including the maturity date, when the bond pays out also the face value. These bonds are also known as fixed income bonds.

(With some bonds, the percentage the bond pays is liked to an index (e.g. the Retail Price Index). These are known as index linked bonds. We shall not consider these in this book.)

Example 2

A $1000 two-year coupon bearing bond paying 10% per year might pay out $50 after six months, a further $50 after 12 and 18 months and $1050 after 24 months. The bond pays out $100 per year (or 10%). Each of the $50 payments is called a coupon (see Figure 4.2).

A coupon bearing bond should be more valuable than a zero coupon bond having the same maturity and face value. (A coupon bond delivers more cash to its owner.) It is possible to think of a coupon bearing bond as a sequence of zero coupon bonds.

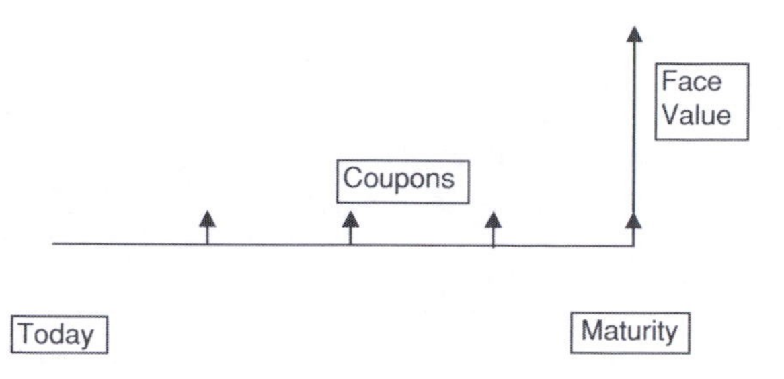

Figure 4.2

In Example 2:

Coupon bond		
Time	Coupon	Four zero coupon bonds
t = 0	0	
t = 0.5	50	Six-month zero coupon bond: face value $50
t = 1	50	Twelve-month zero coupon bond: face value $50
t = 1.5	50	Eighteen-month zero coupon bond: face value $50
t = 2	1050	Two-year zero coupon bond: face value $1050

Bonds are issued mainly by governments (which, similarly, do not relish interference from the share holders), municipal authorities and financial institutions. Government bonds generally are regarded as very safe. Bonds issued by stable governments (e.g. US Treasury bonds, etc.) are backed, in full, by the government issuing the bond and are regarded as risk-free securities. Municipal bonds (munis) are issued by towns and cities (and, in the US, states and counties). These, too, are regarded as safe. Bonds issued by banks and companies are sometimes called corporate bonds. These do have a measure of risk attached; the size of risk will depend on the creditworthiness of the issuing company. We shall largely ignore questions of default and assume that all bonds will make all due payments on the due date.

Thus a bond is a promise of money in the future. Like all such promises, the bond carries a value. This value will depend on the payments made by the bond and on the creditworthiness of the institution issuing the bond. This leads us to consider the value of a bond.

4.2 The value of a bond

A bond pays out cash at fixed times. The **value of a bond**, today, is the present value of all future cash payments made by the bond.

Example 3

A zero coupon bond with face value £100 has two years to maturity. This bond will make one payment, of £100 in two years' time. The interest rate is 6.5%, compounded semi-annually. What is the value of this bond today?

Solution

Present value of £100 in two years' time $= 100 \times (1 + \frac{0.065}{2})^{-2\times 2} = £87.99$. This bond has a value of £87.99 today.

Example 4

A £100 bond has one year to maturity. The bond pays 6% per year with coupon payments made quarterly. The interest rate is 5.8% per year with interest compounded semi-annually. Calculate the value of the bond.

Solution

This bond makes four payments: three coupon payments of £1.5 and one payment at maturity (coupon + face value) of £101.5. Interest is 5.8% per year, compounded twice a year. This gives:

Payment	Time (years)	Present value
1.5	0.25	$1.5 \times (1 + \frac{0.058}{2})^{-0.25\times 2} = 1.4787$
1.5	0.5	$1.5 \times (1 + \frac{0.058}{2})^{-0.5\times 2} = 1.4577$
1.5	0.75	$1.5 \times (1 + \frac{0.058}{2})^{-0.75\times 2} = 1.4370$
101.5	1	$101.5 \times (1 + \frac{0.058}{2})^{-1\times 2} = 95.8595$
	sum =	100.23

The value of this bond is £100.23 today.

Example 5

A $1000 coupon bearing bond with 18 months to maturity pays 8.5% per year in semi-annual instalments. The interest rate per year, continuously compounded, over successive six-monthly intervals is given in the table:

Maturity (years)	Annual interest rate for the maturity shown in column 1
0.5	7.2
1	7.3
1.5	7.35

Find the value of the bond today.

Solution

The bond makes three payments:

Payment	Time (years)
42.5	0.5
42.5	1
1042.5	1.5

The value of the bond is the sum of the present values of these three payments.

Payment	Time	Interest rate (per year, continuously compounded)	Present value
42.5	0.5	7.2	$42.5 \times e^{-0.072\times 0.5} = 40.997$
42.5	1	7.3	$42.5 \times e^{-0.073\times 1} = 39.508$
1042.5	1.5	7.35	$1042.5 \times e^{-0.0735\times 1.5} = 933.674$
		sum =	1014.18

Value of the bond today = £1014.18.
The spreadsheet in Figure 4.3 gives the calculations.

In this spreadsheet, paymentno, paymentval and presval are range names, as are their continuously compounded equivalents, paymentnoC, paymentvalC and presvalC. Also, rateC is a range name. Coupfreq records the number of coupon payments per year and couprate gives the coupon rate of the bond.

4.3 How bond prices change

A bond does not keep its initial value through to maturity. We saw in Chapter 2 how the value of a forward contract changed as circumstances altered. And

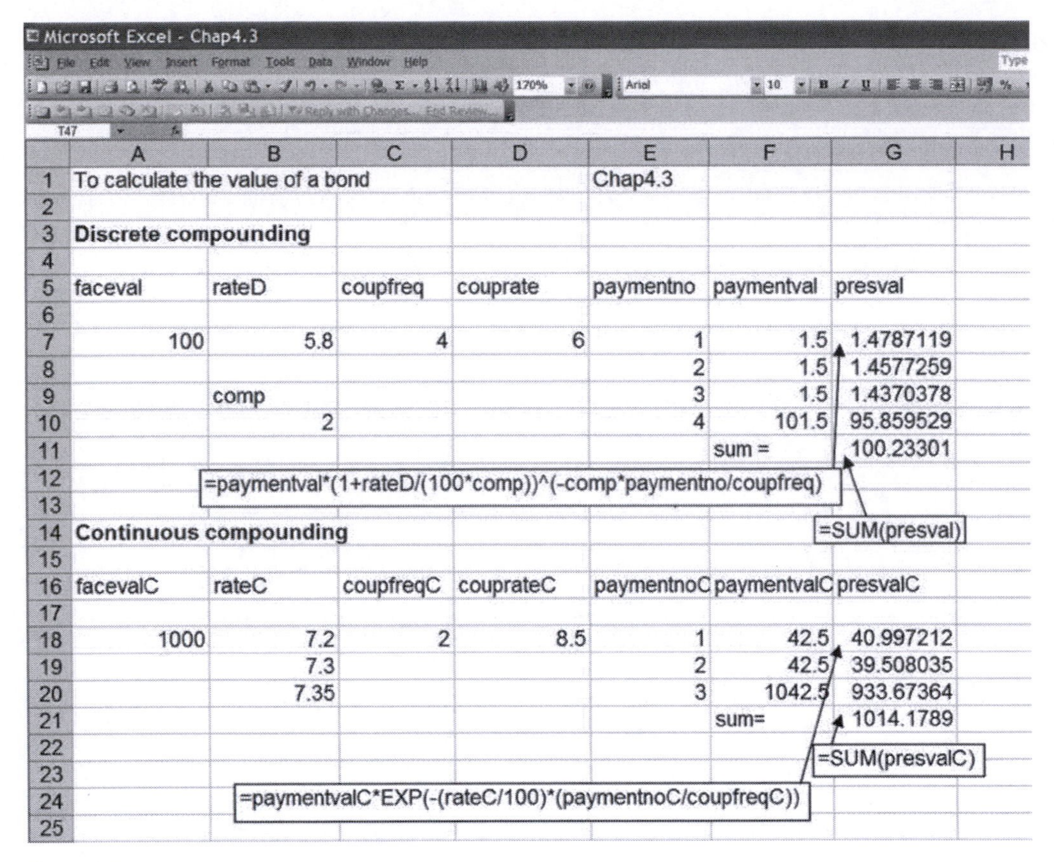

	A	B	C	D	E	F	G	H
1	To calculate the value of a bond				Chap4.3			
2								
3	**Discrete compounding**							
4								
5	faceval	rateD	coupfreq	couprate	paymentno	paymentval	presval	
6								
7	100	5.8	4	6	1	1.5	1.4787119	
8					2	1.5	1.4577259	
9		comp			3	1.5	1.4370378	
10		2			4	101.5	95.859529	
11						sum =	100.23301	
12		=paymentval*(1+rateD/(100*comp))^(-comp*paymentno/coupfreq)						
13								
14	**Continuous compounding**						=SUM(presval)	
15								
16	facevalC	rateC	coupfreqC	couprateC	paymentnoC	paymentvalC	presvalC	
17								
18	1000	7.2	2	8.5	1	42.5	40.997212	
19		7.3			2	42.5	39.508035	
20		7.35			3	1042.5	933.67364	
21						sum=	1014.1789	
22								
23							=SUM(presvalC)	
24		=paymentvalC*EXP(-(rateC/100)*(paymentnoC/coupfreqC))						
25								

Figure 4.3

bond prices too vary over time. There are three major reasons why the value of a bond might change.

(1) Look again at the bond described in Example 4 and the spreadsheet in Figure 4.3. If we change the interest rate (in B7) from 5.8(%) to 4(%), the value of the bond increases to £101.97 (see Figure 4.4).

Similarly, if we have an interest rate of 5% (put 5 in B7), the value of the bond is £101.00. The reader is encouraged to calculate the bond value for other interest rates. However, in the table below, we give the value of the bond for interest rates 4% to 10% and we see something very interesting.

Interest rate	4	5	6	7	8	9	10
Value of bond	101.97	101.00	100.04	99.10	98.17	97.25	96.35

As the interest rate **increases**, the value of the bond **decreases**. Similarly, when the interest rate **decreases**, the value of the bond **increases**. So

Microsoft Excel - Chap4.4

	A	B	C	D	E	F	G
1	To calculate the value of a bond				Chap4.4		
2							
3	**Discrete compounding**						
4							
5	faceval	rate	coupfreq	couprate	paymentno	paymentval	presval
6							
7	100	4	4	6	1	1.5	1.4852213
8					2	1.5	1.4705882
9		comp			3	1.5	1.4560993
10		2			4	101.5	97.558631
11						sum =	101.97054
12							
13							
14							
15							
16							
17							
18							

=paymentval*(1+rate/(100*comp))^(-comp*paymentno/coupfreq)

=SUM(presval)

Figure 4.4

interest rates and bond values move in opposite directions. This pattern of behaviour persists throughout the life of the bond.

Why should this happen? The answer is that at any moment in the life of a bond, all future payments are determined. You know exactly what you are going to get and you know exactly when you are going to get it. The percentage return on your outlay is fixed. (This is why bonds are called fixed income assets.) If interest rates rise (above the rate of return offered by a bond), an investor would get a better return by putting her money in an asset carrying the higher interest rate. Speculators and investors will tend to sell this bond and reinvest at the higher rate. Hence, the bond price will fall. If interest rates were to fall (below the rate offered by bonds), bonds would offer better value than assets carrying the lower interest rate: people would buy the bonds and bond prices would rise.

(2) The government or company issuing the bond becomes less creditworthy. This might happen, for example, if a country experienced a dramatic change in the direction of government (a coup, perhaps) or a company announced a set of very poor trading figures, or experienced a significant and damaging fall in its share price. The news, whatever it might be, could cause traders to suspect that the company had increased the risk of defaulting on its financial responsibilities. In such a case, the price of a bond issued by the country or the company will probably fall.

(3) The bond moves towards its maturity. Since the owner will receive the face value of the bond at maturity, there is little point in paying $105 today for a bond paying out $100 tomorrow. So in a region of the maturity date, the value of a bond will move towards its face value.

As with futures contracts, the potential for a bond to become more (or less) valuable under changing circumstances ensures that bonds are traded extensively. Information on bond prices and performance is quoted in, among others, the *Financial Times* and *The Wall Street Journal.* Yahoo Finance is a website offering a great deal of information on bonds. In the next sections we establish some notation and explain the terms used to describe a bond's performance.

4.4 Notation

US bonds of maturity less than one year are called **bills**. Bills are usually zero coupon bonds. A **note** is a coupon bearing bond (a coupon is paid every six months) with a maturity two years through to ten years. Bonds with maturity greater than ten years are called **bonds**. Bonds issued by the UK government are called **gilts**.

We shall, however, make little attempt to use this notation. We shall call them all bonds.

Quotations

The price quoted in the press is known as the **clean price** of the bond. The clean price is akin to the price calculated in section 4.2. The clean price, however, is not the price you would pay if you bought the bond. Unless you bought the bond on the day a coupon was paid, a period of time (a number of days) towards the payment of the next coupon will have elapsed. During this time, the owner of the bond will have earned a proportion of that next coupon payment. If you want to buy the bond, you must pay the present owner his entitlement to that next coupon payment. This is called **accrued interest**. The accrued interest is the interest on the coupon that has accumulated since the date of the last coupon payment.

To calculate the accrued interest, we need to know:

the coupon payment
the number of days since the last coupon payment
the number of days between coupon payments.

Then:

$$\text{Accrued interest} = \text{coupon} \times \frac{\text{number of days since last coupon payment}}{\text{number of days between coupon payments}}$$

The price that you pay for the bond is the quoted price (clean price) plus the accrued interest and this is known as the **dirty price** of the bond.

Price you pay (dirty price) = quoted price (clean price) + accrued interest

In practice, there are several ways in which accrued interest is calculated. These have to do with what are known as the day count conventions and are very important in the financial world. When two parties enter a contract (to buy or sell bonds, for example), both sides need to agree on how interest (accrued interest) is to be calculated. Stating (and agreeing) the day count convention to be used solves this problem. With certain kinds of bonds, the day count convention is part of the structure of the bond. There are four day count conventions in common and current use and these we now describe.

Day count conventions

The purpose is to calculate the accrued interest. There are four methods. In each method, the **first** date **is** counted as one day; the **last** date **is not**.

1. **Actual/Actual**

We use:

$$\text{Accrued interest} = \text{coupon} \times \frac{\text{number of days since last coupon payment}}{\text{number of days between coupon payments}}$$

The factor:

$$\frac{\text{number of days since last coupon payment}}{\text{number of days between coupon payments}}$$ is called the **accrual factor**

In the accrual factor: in the numerator and in the denominator, the actual number of days between the two dates is used. Leap years count for 366 days: non-leap years count for 365 days.

Example 6

A bond pays a semi-annual coupon of \$3.5 on 7 February 2005. Today is 16 June 2005. Find the accrual factor and the accrued interest.

Solution

Between 7 February and 16 June in 2005 there are 129 days (count 7 February; do not count 16 June).

In February	22 days
In March	31 days
In April	30 days
In May	31 days
In June	15 days (do not count the last day)
Total: 129	

The next coupon will be paid on 7 August. Between 7 February and 7 August 2005 there are 181 days.

The accrual factor $= \frac{129}{181}$. The accrued interest $= 3.5 \times \frac{129}{181} = 2.4945$. Or \$2.49.

The day count convention actual/actual is exact and is used in certain US Treasury bonds.

In the next three day count conventions, the calculations are simplified. In each, a set period of one year is considered. The method calculates the fraction of one year since the last coupon payment. This is also called the accrual factor (for that particular day count convention). To calculate the accrued interest, multiply the **annual** return from the bond by the fraction calculated under the correct day count convention.

2. Actual/365 fixed

$$\text{Accrued interest} = \text{annual return} \times \frac{\text{number of days since last coupon payment}}{365}$$

In the accrual factor: in the numerator, the actual number of days between the two dates is used; the denominator is 365 regardless of whether or not it is a leap year.

Using the data of Example 6, the accrual factor (in the actual/365 convention) is $\frac{129}{365}$. The annual return from the bond is \$7.

$$\text{Accrued interest} = 7 \times \frac{129}{365} = 2.4740. \text{ Or } \$2.47.$$

Actual/365 is used with certain US Treasury bonds.

3. Actual/360

$$\text{Accrued interest} = \text{annual return} \times \frac{\text{number of days since last coupon payment}}{360}$$

In the accrual factor: in the numerator, the actual number of days between the two dates is used. To simplify matters further, in this convention each year is assumed to have 360 days. The denominator is 360.

Using the data of Example 6, the accrual factor (in the actual/360 convention) is $\frac{129}{360}$. The annual return from the bond is \$7.

$$\text{Accrued interest} = 7 \times \frac{129}{360} = 2.5083. \text{ Or } \$2.51.$$

Actual/360 is used in the very important LIBOR rate and with certain bank deposits.

4. 30/360

$$\text{Accrued interest} = \text{annual return} \times \frac{\text{number of days since last coupon payment}}{360}$$

But in this method, a further simplification assumes 30 days in each **complete** month and 360 days in each year.

Example 6 again:

February	22 days (as before)
March	30 days (a complete month)
April	30 days
May	30 days
June	15 days
	= 127

The accrual factor (in the 30/360 convention) is $\frac{127}{360}$. The annual return on the bond is \$7.

$$\text{Accrued interest} = 7 \times \frac{127}{360} = 2.4694. \text{ Or } \$2.47.$$

30/360 is used in many municipal and corporate bonds.

Example 7

A bond has face value \$100. Coupon payments are made on 8 April 2005 and again on 8 October 2005. The bond pays 6% per year. If the price quoted in the press on 24 June 2005 is \$93, find the dirty price of the bond on 24 June using (a) actual/actual, and (b) 30/360 day count conventions.

(a) Actual/Actual There are $23 + 31 + 23 = 77$ actual days between 8 April and 24 June. There are $23 + 31 + 30 + 31 + 31 + 30 + 7 = 183$ actual days between 8 April and 8 October (remember: count the first date; do not count the last date).

$$\text{Accrued interest} = 3 \times \frac{77}{183} = 1.2623$$

Dirty price $= 93 + 1.2623 = \$94.2623$. Or \$94.26.

(b) 30/360 In this convention there are $23 + 30 + 23 = 76$ days between 8 April and 24 June.

$$\text{Accrued interest} = 6 \times \frac{76}{360} = 1.2667$$

Dirty price $= 93 + 1.2667 = \$94.2667$. Or \$94.27.

4.5 Bond performance

Bonds exist in many different forms. It has been suggested that there are something like 157 million different municipal bonds in existence. There are bonds with different face values, different maturity dates, without coupons, with coupons and those that carry coupons carry different coupon rates and different coupon dates. We want to measure the performance of a bond so that we will know (a) what return we will get from that bond, and (b) how that bond compares with other bonds. We might be thinking of buying a bond. So how, from the enormous range of those on offer, are we to decide which particular bond it would be most advantageous to buy? One way of comparing bonds is to calculate an average rate of return offered by each bond. This is usually known as some form of bond yield. Then we describe an average time over which the initial investment in the bond is balanced by payments from the bond. This is the duration of the bond.

Bond yield

There are many ways of calculating a yield. We describe four in common use.

(1) Coupon rate. This is the amount the bond pays out annually expressed as a percentage of the face value of the bond.

(2) Current yield. This is the total annual coupon income expressed as a percentage of the current price of the bond.

In (3) and (4) we deal with the relationships between three quantities:

D: the sum of the present values of all cash payments made by the bond. So D is the 'value of the bond' as calculated in section 4.2.

P: the face value of the bond.

B: the current market value of the bond (the amount you would pay to buy the bond).

(3) Par yield. This is the coupon rate that forces $D = P$.

(4) Yield to maturity or bond yield or redemption yield. This is the **continuously compounded** (annual) rate Y that forces $D = B$.

We now illustrate these four bond yields.

(1) Coupon rate

We have met this before. A coupon rate of 6% will pay out 6% of the face value of the bond in one year. This payment will be made in one, two or four equal instalments (the coupon dates).

(2) Current yield

The current yield is defined to be: $\dfrac{\text{total annual coupon income}}{\text{bond price}} \times 100$

Example 8

Suppose a five-year bond has face value \$50 and pays a coupon of \$2.5 four times a year. Today's market value for this bond is \$44.50. Find the current yield.

Solution

The current yield is $\dfrac{4 \times 2.5}{44.5} \times 100 = 22.47\%$

For (3) we shall use the interest rates for differing maturities as shown in the table.

Interest rate (per year, compounded annually)	Maturity (years)
6	0.5
6.6	1
7	1.5
7.3	2

(3) Par yield

A bond matures in two years' time, has a face value of £1000 and pays a coupon every six months. Let C = par yield. So C is the coupon paid annually. Clearly, $\frac{1}{2}C$ is the coupon paid every six months.

The cash payments from the bond are as shown in the table below:

Cash payment	Time of payment (years)	Present value of payment
$\frac{1}{2}C$	0.5	$\frac{1}{2}C \times (1+0.06)^{-0.5}$
$\frac{1}{2}C$	1	$\frac{1}{2}C \times (1+0.066)^{-1}$
$\frac{1}{2}C$	1.5	$\frac{1}{2}C \times (1+0.07)^{-1.5}$
$1000+\frac{1}{2}C$	2	$(1000+\frac{1}{2}C) \times (1+0.073)^{-2}$

For C to be the par yield of the bond, we need the sum of the present values to equal the face value of the bond.

$$\frac{1}{2}C \times (1+0.06)^{-0.5} + \frac{1}{2}C \times (1+0.066)^{-1} + \frac{1}{2}C \times (1+0.07)^{-1.5} + (1000+\frac{1}{2}C) \times (1+0.073)^{-2} = 1000$$

This equation can be solved quite easily.

Multiply out the last term on the right-hand side.

$$\frac{1}{2}C \times (1+0.06)^{-0.5} + \frac{1}{2}C \times (1+0.066)^{-1} + \frac{1}{2}C \times (1+0.07)^{-1.5} + 1000 \times (1+0.073)^{-2} + \frac{1}{2}C \times (1+0.073)^{-2} = 1000$$

Take out the common factor $\frac{1}{2}C$ from the first, second, third and fifth terms and take the term not having a factor $\frac{1}{2}C$ across to the right-hand side.

$$\frac{1}{2}C \times [(1+0.06)^{-0.5} + (1+0.066)^{-1} + (1+0.07)^{-1.5} + (1+0.073)^{-2}] = 1000 - 1000 \times (1+0.073)^{-2}$$

$$\frac{1}{2}C \times [3.68143] = 131.439$$

Giving $C = 71.4065$

This represents a coupon rate of 7.14065%.

(4) Yield to maturity (bond yield, redemption yield). This is always a continuously compounded rate

This is more complicated. We illustrate first with a zero coupon bond (although yield to maturity is usually applied only to coupon bearing bonds). In this case, the yield to maturity can be obtained explicitly by solving (in a fairly straightforward way) a simple equation. We then show how to calculate the

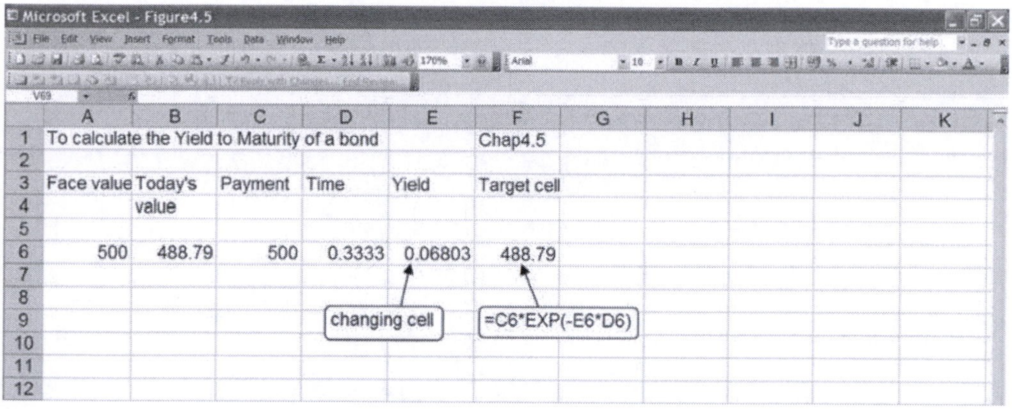

Microsoft Excel - Figure4.5

	A	B	C	D	E	F	G	H	I	J	K
1	To calculate the Yield to Maturity of a bond					Chap4.5					
2											
3	Face value	Today's	Payment	Time	Yield	Target cell					
4		value									
5											
6	500	488.79	500	0.3333	0.06803	488.79					
7											
8											
9					changing cell	=C6*EXP(-E6*D6)					
10											
11											
12											

Figure 4.5

yield to maturity for a coupon bearing bond. In this case, the yield to maturity has to be calculated using a numerical method.

(a) *Zero coupon bonds*

A zero coupon bond with face value \$500 will mature in four months' time. Today, the bond is selling for \$488.79. The bond will make one payment, of \$500 at maturity. The yield to maturity (Y) is the continuously compounded annual rate that will make the present value of this payment equal to today's price \$488.79.

Payment	Time	Present value	Today's price
500	$\frac{4}{12}$	$500 \times e^{-Y\times\frac{4}{12}}$	488.79

So: $$500 \times e^{-Y\times\frac{4}{12}} = 488.79$$

Now solve this equation for Y.

With an eye to the more complicated situation involving coupon bonds, we solve the equation in two ways. First we solve for Y numerically using Goal Seek in Excel. Then we produce the explicit solution (see Figure 4.5).

The face value of the bond is in A6. Today's value is in B6. The one payment made by this bond appears in C6 and the time to payment lies in D6. E6 is where the yield to maturity will appear. (It might be useful to enter a value, 0.5 say, initially in E6.) F6 contains the present value of the payment made by the bond.

Click Tools.
Click Goal Seek.
In 'Set cell' enter F6.
In 'To value' enter 488.79 (not B6).
In 'By changing cell' enter E6.
Click OK.
The yield to maturity 0.068032 appears in E6.
For an analytical solution:

$$e^{-Y\times\frac{4}{12}} = \frac{488.79}{500}$$

Take the ln of both sides: $-Y \times \frac{4}{12} = \ln\left(\frac{488.79}{500}\right)$

Solve for Y: $Y = -\frac{12}{4} \times \ln\left(\frac{488.79}{500}\right)$

$= 0.068025$ or 6.803%

In general a zero coupon bond has face value P. The bond has T years to maturity and B(0, T) is the value of the bond today.

Present value of payment at maturity $= P \times e^{-YT}$

$$P \times e^{-YT} = B(0, T)$$

So: $e^{-YT} = \frac{B(0, T)}{P}$

Ln both sides: $-YT = \ln\left(\frac{B(0, T)}{P}\right)$

$$Y = -\frac{\ln(B(0, T)/P)}{T}$$

Example 9

Consider a zero coupon bond that pays out $20 in four years' time. The value of the bond, today, is $13.65. Calculate the yield to maturity.

Solution

Value of bond today = present value of $20 and this must equal the market value of the bond.

$$20 \times e^{-Y\times 4} = 13.65$$

$$e^{-Y\times 4} = \frac{13.65}{20}$$

$$-Y \times 4 = \ln\left(\frac{13.65}{20}\right)$$

$$Y = -\frac{\ln(13.65/20)}{4} = 0.095498, \qquad \text{or } 9.55\%$$

(*b*) *Coupon bonds*

A £250 coupon bearing bond pays out 7% per year in semi-annual coupon payments. The bond matures in two years' time. Today, the bond is selling for £264.89. What is the yield to maturity?

Let Y be the yield to maturity. Remember that yield to maturity is a continuously compounded rate. The payments made by the bond are as shown in the table below.

Payment	Time	Present value
8.75	0.5	$8.75 \times e^{-Y \times 0.5}$
8.75	1	$8.75 \times e^{-Y \times 1}$
8.75	1.5	$8.75 \times e^{-Y \times 1.5}$
258.75	2	$258.75 \times e^{-Y \times 2}$

Today's value = £264.89.

Present value of all cash payments

$$= 8.75 \times e^{-Y \times 0.5} + 8.75 \times e^{-Y \times 1} + 8.75 \times e^{-Y \times 1.5} + 258.75 \times e^{-Y \times 2}$$

Today's value = 264.89.

For Y to be the yield to maturity, we need:

$$8.75 \times e^{-Y \times 0.5} + 8.75 \times e^{-Y \times 1} + 8.75 \times e^{-Y \times 1.5} + 258.75 \times e^{-Y \times 2} = 264.89.$$

There is no analytical method for solving this equation and we need a numerical method to find Y. Again, Goal Seek comes to our aid. This is illustrated in Figure 4.6.

The face value is in A6. Today's value is in B6. The payments by the bond have the range name payment and appear in C6:C9. The times at which payments are made have the range name timeyrs and appear in D6:D9. E6 is the cell where the yield to maturity will appear. It might be useful to enter a value (0.5, say) in E6 initially. The present values of the payments have the range name presval: these appear in F6:F9. These are summed in F10.

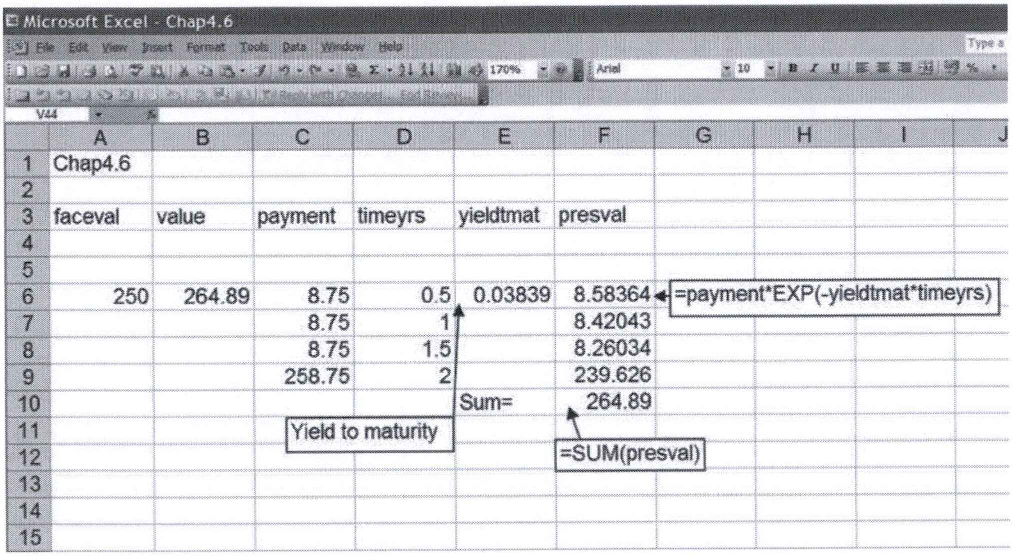

Microsoft Excel - Chap4.6

	A	B	C	D	E	F
1	Chap4.6					
2						
3	faceval	value	payment	timeyrs	yieldtmat	presval
4						
5						
6	250	264.89	8.75	0.5	0.03839	8.58364
7			8.75	1		8.42043
8			8.75	1.5		8.26034
9			258.75	2		239.626
10					Sum=	264.89

=payment*EXP(-yieldtmat*timeyrs)

Yield to maturity

=SUM(presval)

Figure 4.6

Click Tools.
Click Goal Seek.
In 'Set cell' enter F10.
In 'To value' enter 264.89 (not B6).
In 'By changing cell' enter E6.
Click OK.
The yield to maturity appears in E6.
The yield to maturity of this bond is 0.038392. Or 3.8392%.

In general a bond has face value P and pays coupons C at time t_1, C at time t_2, ... P + C at time t_n ($T = t_n$).

Payment	Time	Present value
C	t_1	$C \times e^{-Y \times t_1}$
C	t_2	$C \times e^{-Y \times t_2}$
P + C	t_n	$(P + C) \times e^{-Y \times t_n}$

The sum of the present values of all payments by the bond is:

$$C \times e^{-Yt_1} + C \times e^{-Yt_2} + \cdots + (P + C) \times e^{-Yt_n}$$

If the value of the bond today is B(0, T), then:

$$C \times e^{-Yt_1} + C \times e^{-Yt_2} + \cdots + (P + C) \times e^{-Yt_n} = B(0, T)$$

This equation must be solved for Y and this is done numerically. Goal Seek in Excel is ideal for this purpose.

Duration

We know when we buy a bond the time at which the bond will mature. But is there an average time (before maturity) at which the payments made by the bond in some way match the price paid for the bond?

We know that the price of a bond will fall with a rise in interest rates and rise when interest rates fall. But is there a way of measuring how much the bond price will fall when interest rates rise by (say) 1%?

Duration provides an answer to both these questions.

Definition The **duration** of a bond is a weighted average of the times at which the bond makes a payment. The weights are the present values of the payments made by the bond (using the yield to maturity to discount the payments) divided by the sum of all such discounted payments.

Example 10

A two-year £100 bond pays 7% per year semi-annually. The value of the bond is £101.11. Calculate the duration of the bond.

Solution

The yield to maturity is calculated as in Figure 4.6. The yield to maturity of this bond is 0.063.

The calculations are illustrated in the Excel spreadsheet in Figure 4.6a. The duration is 1.9015 years.

Observe that

(i) the sum of the payments discounted at the yield to maturity rate is the value of the bond, B.

(ii) by construction, the weights must add to 1.

Now note that:

$$\circ \quad \frac{3.3915}{B} \times 0.5 + \frac{3.2863}{B} \times 1 + \frac{3.1844}{B} \times 1.5 + \frac{91.2471}{B} \times 2 = \text{Duration}$$

So:

$$3.3915 \times 0.5 + 3.2863 \times 1 + 3.1844 \times 1.5 + 91.2471 \times 2 = B \times \text{Duration}$$

The left-hand side is: payment times weighted by discounted payments.
The right-hand side is: duration (time) weighted by the bond's value.

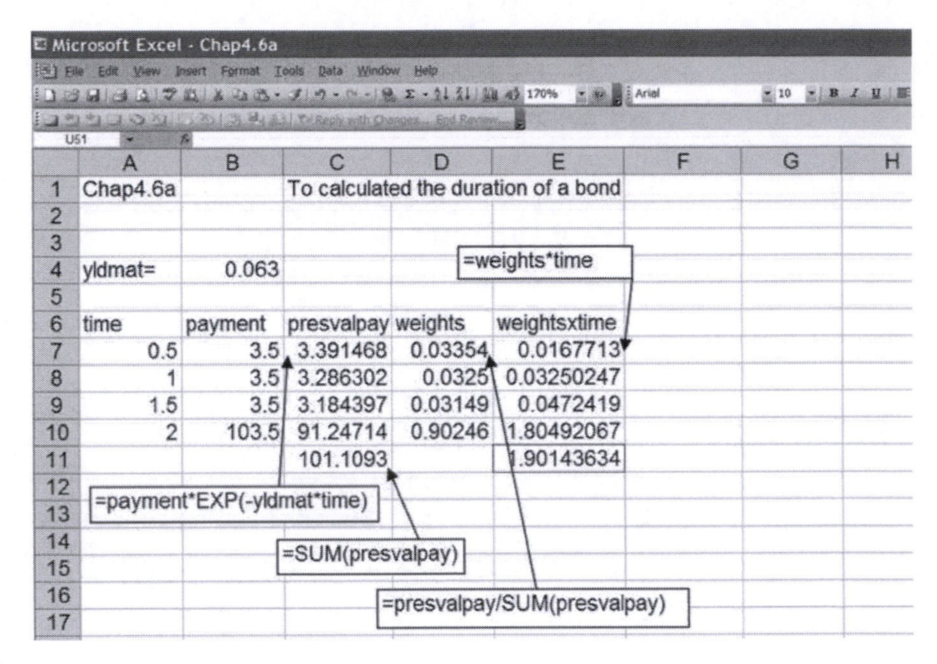
Microsoft Excel - Chap4.6a

	A	B	C	D	E
1	Chap4.6a		To calculated the duration of a bond		
2					
3					
4	yldmat=	0.063			
5					
6	time	payment	presvalpay	weights	weightsxtime
7	0.5	3.5	3.391468	0.03354	0.0167713
8	1	3.5	3.286302	0.0325	0.03250247
9	1.5	3.5	3.184397	0.03149	0.0472419
10	2	103.5	91.24714	0.90246	1.80492067
11			101.1093		1.90143634

Figure 4.6a

This supports the idea that duration is the time at which the bond payments match the bond's value.

- The duration is always less than or possibly equal to the maturity of the bond. In a zero coupon bond, the duration is the maturity of the bond. (There is just one payment – at maturity.)
- The longer the duration, the greater the risk attached to the bond and the more volatile the price of the bond.
- Higher coupon rates (and higher yields) give rise to lower durations.
- The change in the value of a bond due to a change in the yield is given by:

$-$bond price $\times$ duration $\times$ change in the yield.

For example, suppose a bond, priced at £90.30 has duration 9.5 years. If the yield falls by 0.02, the bond price will rise by $90.30 \times 9.5 \times 0.02 =$ £17.16.

If the yield rises by 0.0012, the bond price will fall by $90.30 \times 9.5 \times 0.0012 =$ £1.03.

Comparison of bonds

We will use yield to maturity and duration to decide which of several bonds might be the most attractive for investment.

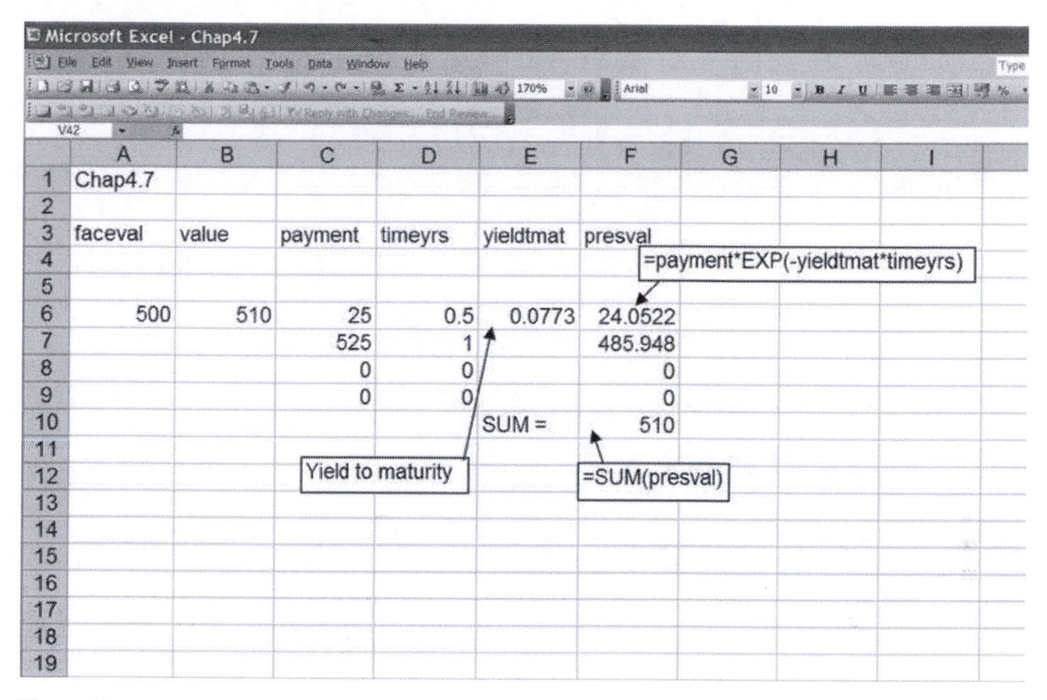

Figure 4.7

Example 11

I am offered three bonds:

Bond	Principal	Maturity	Coupon	Number of coupon payments per year	Today's value
1	500	1	25	2	510
2	100	2	6	2	108
3	1000	5	0	0	670.32

Which bond offers the best value for money?

Solution

The spreadsheet for each bond is shown in Figures 4.7–4.9. Goal Seek is used in each spreadsheet to calculate the yield to maturity.

Bond 1: the yield to maturity is 7.7297%.
Bond 2: the yield to maturity is 7.471%.
Bond 3: the yield to maturity is 8%.

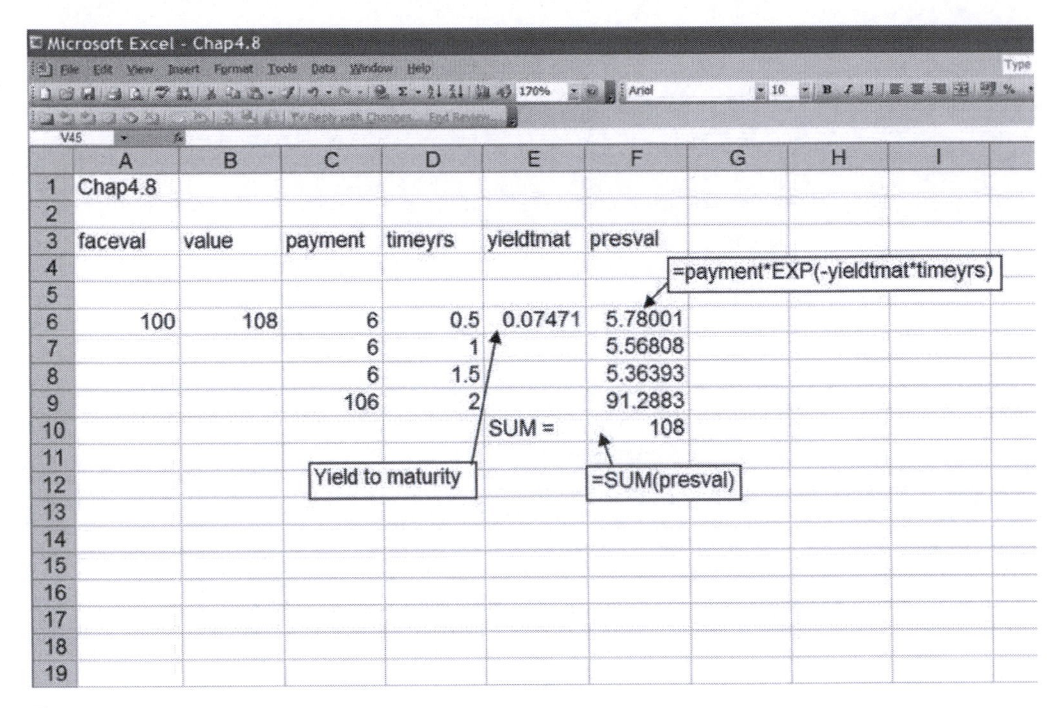

	A	B	C	D	E	F
1	Chap4.8					
2						
3	faceval	value	payment	timeyrs	yieldtmat	presval
4						
5						
6	100	108	6	0.5	0.07471	5.78001
7			6	1		5.56808
8			6	1.5		5.36393
9			106	2		91.2883
10					SUM =	108

Figure 4.8

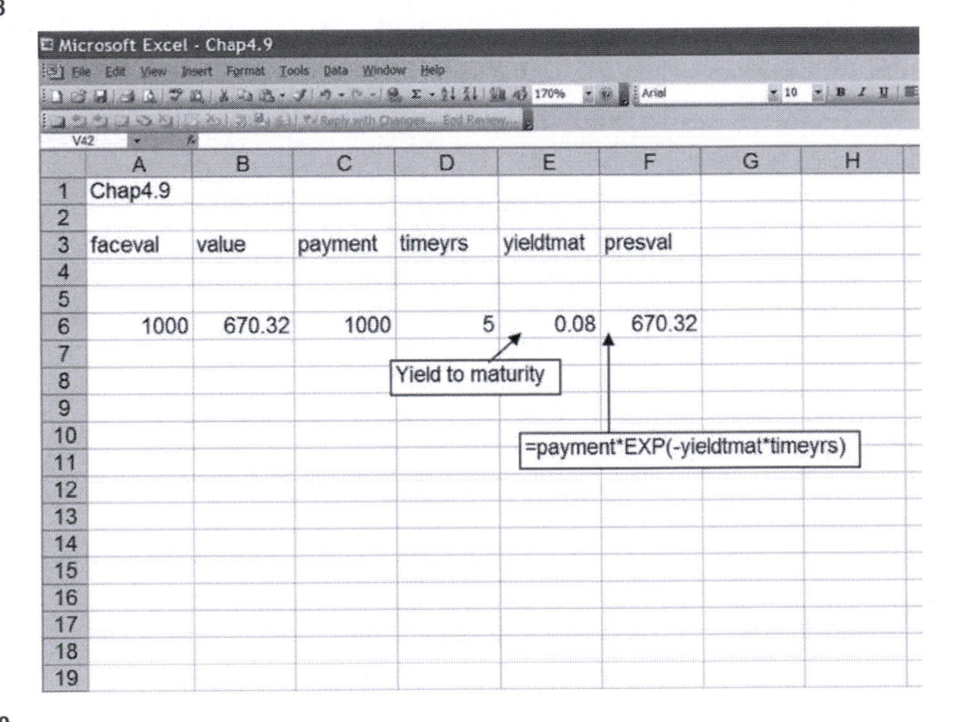

	A	B	C	D	E	F
1	Chap4.9					
2						
3	faceval	value	payment	timeyrs	yieldtmat	presval
4						
5						
6	1000	670.32	1000	5	0.08	670.32

Figure 4.9

Using Figure 4.6a, we can see that the durations of the bonds are:

Bond 1 Duration = 0.9764 years
Bond 2 Duration = 1.8433 years
Bond 3 Duration = 5 years (this is a zero coupon bond)

Bond 3, with the highest yield, represents, in one sense, the best value for money. However, this bond has the longest duration and so carries the greatest risk. A rise in interest rates would see the value of this bond fall significantly. If the bond is chosen on the basis of low duration, bond 1 or bond 2 might be selected. Compare bond 2 with the bond in Example 10 and observe a higher coupon rate (bond 2) leading to lower duration. However, other considerations might come into play. Bond 3 is a zero coupon bond and I might want a regular coupon income. As usual, there is no absolute solution. But bond yield and duration offer calculable and objective measures of the worth of a bond.

4.6 Some names commonly encountered in the bond market

Discount, par, premium

The three yield indicators, coupon rate, current yield and yield to maturity, give different snapshots of the return offered by a bond. These differences are recognised when one of the terms discount, par and premium is used to describe a bond.

A coupon bond is:

par if the current price is equal to the face value (a bond with face value $100 costs $100)

discount if the current price is less than the face value (a bond with face value $100 costs $93)

premium if the current price is greater than the face value (a bond with face value $100 costs $105).

Bonds that sell at a discount do so because the interest rate they offer is below the current market interest rate. (Or, possibly, because the bond attracts high risk.)

A bond is a premium bond if the interest rate it offers is greater than the current market rate.

A useful guide (see Exercise 27 and its spreadsheet bondyields) is

for a par bond (current price = face value)
  current yield = coupon rate (approx) = yield to maturity

for a discount bond (current price < face value)
  coupon rate < current yield < yield to maturity

for a premium bond (current price > face value)
yield to maturity < current yield < coupon rate.

Junk bonds

A junk bond is a bond issued by a company that is considered to be of high credit risk. Junk bonds are high-yield bonds, reflecting the greater risk of default. Bonds are graded to reflect the creditworthiness of the company issuing the bond (see Credit rating agencies in Chapter 8). If a bond is classified 'investment grade', it is thought that the risk of default is acceptable. However, a bond classified as 'speculative' is thought to carry a higher risk of default. Such bonds are more commonly described as junk bonds.

Before the 1980s, junk bonds were created by the decline in creditworthiness of the issuing company. As the name 'junk' implies, it was not thought a good thing if your bonds fell into this category; indeed, these issues were also sometimes described as 'fallen angels'. But more recent research has shown that the risk-adjusted returns for portfolios of junk bonds were quite high. It appeared that the risk attached to these bonds could be compensated for by their higher yields. Studies have suggested that portfolios consisting of high-yield bonds have higher returns than other bond portfolios. This suggests that the higher yields from junk bonds more than compensate for the additional risk attached to these bonds.

A callable bond

This is a bond where the issuer has the right to buy back the bond, at a predetermined price, at certain times in the future. The issuer could recall the bond if the value of the bond rose above a certain level.

For example, suppose that a prosperous (little risk of default) company issued a £100, ten-year, callable bond paying 8% per year in coupons. Interest rates fell and the value of the bond rose sharply. Because this was a callable bond, the condition of sale was that the company had the right to buy back the bond for:

£110 in years 3 and 4
£107.5 in years 5 and 6
£106 in years 7 and 8
£103 in years 9 and 10

If the bond price rises above the call price in the years specified, the company makes a profit.

Callable bonds are usually not called during the first few years of existence. After that, the call price is a decreasing function of time.

Callable bonds tend to have a lower value than ordinary, comparable bonds. One reason for this is that the holder might, at some time in the future, be required to sell the bond at a loss. Another is that the person who has to give up the bond, if required to do so, must then find somewhere else to put their money.

Bonds with call features generally offer higher yields than bonds with no call features.

Convertible bonds

These bonds can be (but do not have to be) converted into stock at certain predetermined times using a predetermined exchange ratio. These bonds are usually callable. They are also more valuable than non-convertible bonds because of this (optional) stock transfer option.

A US Treasury bond futures contract (introduced on the CBOT in 1977)

These are futures contracts (almost) like any other. There is no cost on entry. There is a margin account containing, initially, the initial margin. A maintenance margin will be specified. The contract will have a value at the time it is entered and at the end of each trading day margin accounts will be marked to market. Funds will be withdrawn from your margin account if the market moved against you and funds will be paid into your margin account if the market moved in your favour. Variation margin will have to be found if funds in the margin account fall below the maintenance margin level. Your position can be closed out simply by entering an 'opposite' position on the same asset with the same maturity.

A US Treasury bond futures contract is an agreement to buy or to sell (in an agreed month in the future) US (30-year) Treasury bonds with a face value of $100 000. Initial margin is usually in the region of 10% of $100 000, with maintenance margin being usually at around 75% of the initial margin. Contracts are traded on the CBOT and prices are quoted for delivery months of September, December, March and June. A **long** December 2007 Treasury bond futures contract would be a contract to **buy** US Treasury bonds with a face value of $100 000 in December 2007. A **short** Treasury bond futures contract is a contract to **sell** US Treasury bonds (face value = $100 000) on delivery day.

What interests traders is the underlying interest rate. As we have seen, if the interest rate falls, bond prices rise, and conversely. So anyone wanting to invest in the belief of a falling interest rate could enter a long Treasury bond futures contract. Similarly, to invest in a rising interest rate, enter a short Treasury bond futures contract. We now provide the details.

The value of a US Treasury bond futures contract – the quoted futures price

Treasury bond futures prices are quoted in points and $\frac{1}{32}$ of a point. So 128-20 means $\$128\frac{20}{32}$ or \$128.625. The quoted futures price gives the price per \$100 face value of the bonds. A futures quote of 128-20 would give one contract (bonds with face value of \$100 000) a value of $\$128\frac{20}{32} \times 1000 = \$128\,625$.

Example 12

Today is 28 January 2005. The quoted futures price for a March 2005 US Treasury bond futures contract is 108-12. The futures prices on successive days are 110-02, 107-28, 108-06. The initial margin is 10% of \$100 000 and maintenance margin is set at \$7500. Show the daily gains and losses made by the holder of a short Treasury bond futures contract.

Solution

Date	Quoted price	Contract value	F_1–F_2	Margin account
28 Jan	108-12	108 375		10 000
29 Jan	110-02	110 062.5	−1687.5	8312.5
30 Jan	107-28	107 875	2187.5	10 500
31 Jan	108-06	108 187.5	−312.5	10 187.5

At the close of trading on 29 January, the value of the contract has risen. The investor contracted to sell bonds has made a loss: 1687.5 is withdrawn from their margin account and deposited in the margin account of the holder of the long contract. The following day, the value of the contract falls. The holder of the short contract makes a profit: \$2187.5 is deposited in their margin account. On 31 January, the contract value rises slightly. The holder of a short position makes a loss of \$312.5. Funds in the margin account remain above the level of the maintenance margin. There are no margin calls.

At close of trading on 31 January, the investor closes out her position. The contract value is a little below the value on entry, so the holder of a short contract has made a small profit of 108 375 − 108 187.5 = \$187.5.

Delivery regulations

If the contract goes through to maturity, the party with the short position (the seller) must deliver to the buyer, on any agreed day in the delivery month, Treasury bonds with a face value of \$100 000. But on delivery day, there will be many different Treasury bonds floating around the money markets of the world; there will be bonds with different maturities and different coupon structures. To protect the buyer and to achieve a degree of uniformity that will allow sensible pricing for futures contracts, the exchange will require the seller to hand over Treasury bonds where on the first day of the delivery month:

(i) the bonds have more than 15 years to maturity
(ii) the bonds are not callable for at least 15 years.

The party with the long position (the buyer) pays the seller, on delivery day, a sum of money designed to neutralise the diversity of the bonds being delivered. For each $100 face value of bonds being delivered, the buyer pays:

today's quoted futures price × *conversion factor*

+ *accrued interest since last coupon date from the bond being delivered*

- *Today's quoted futures price* is as quoted by the exchange (see above).
- The *conversion factor* needs some explanation. The conversion factor is a scale factor for each bond, based on the present value of the cash flows from that bond. The conversion factor aims to unify the yields of the deliverable bonds and can be viewed as the price of a deliverable bond (per $1) which gives the bond a yield of 6%. (This last percentage is subject to change: it is 6% as I write; some not very old books use the old figure of 8%.) The CBOT produces extensive tables from which the required conversion factors may be read.
- *The accrued interest since last coupon date from the bond being delivered* is as described in section 4.4.

$$\text{Accrued interest} = \text{coupon payment} \times \frac{\text{number of days since last payment}}{\text{number of days between coupon payments}}$$

The correct day count convention must be used. For Treasury bonds, this is actual/actual.

Note: as described above, the cost of buying a coupon bearing bond is *quoted price of the bond* + *accrued interest since last coupon date.*

Observe that the *quoted price of the bond* and the *quoted futures price* are not necessarily the same.

Example 13

Today is 28 March 2004 and it is delivery day for a Treasury bond futures contract. A 30-year $100 US Treasury bond, which was issued on 15 November 1996, is used in settlement of this futures contract. US Treasury bonds pay their coupon semi-annually. This bond carries a coupon rate of 6.5% per year.

Today, the quoted price of this bond is \$114-11; the quoted futures price is \$105-01.

(i) Calculate what it would cost to buy this bond today.

(ii) Calculate how much a buyer must pay for this bond in settlement of a Treasury bond futures contract.

Solution

(i) The quoted price of the bond is $\$114\frac{11}{32} = \$114.34$.

$$\text{Accrued interest} = \text{coupon payment} \times \frac{\text{number of days since last payment}}{\text{number of days between coupon payments}}$$

The bond pays 6.5% in two equal instalments: each coupon payment is \$3.25.

Using an actual/actual day count, number of days between 15 November 2003 (date of last coupon payment) and 28 March 2004 is 134. Number of days between 15 November 2003 and 15 May 2004 (date of next coupon payment) is 182.

Hence: $$\text{accrued interest} = 3.25 \times \frac{134}{182} = \$2.39$$

The cost of this bond, on 28 March, is $114.34 + 2.39 = \$116.73$.

(ii) The quoted futures price (today) is $\$105\text{-}01 = 105\frac{1}{32} = 105.03125$.

The table gives the conversion factors for a collection of bonds.

Issue date	Coupon rate	Maturity date	Conversion factor
02/16/1993	$7\frac{1}{8}$	02/15/2023	1.1177
08/16/1993	$6\frac{1}{4}$	08/15/2023	1.0265
08/15/1994	$7\frac{1}{2}$	11/15/2024	1.1663
02/15/1995	$7\frac{5}{8}$	02/15/2025	1.1813
08/15/1995	$6\frac{7}{8}$	08/15/2025	1.0990
02/15/1996	6	02/15/2026	0.9999
08/15/1996	$6\frac{3}{4}$	08/15/2026	1.0871
11/15/1996	$6\frac{1}{2}$	11/15/2026	1.0585
02/18/1997	$6\frac{5}{8}$	02/15/2027	1.0735
08/15/1997	$6\frac{3}{8}$	08/15/2027	1.0446
11/17/1997	$6\frac{1}{8}$	11/15/2027	1.0150
08/17/1998	$5\frac{1}{2}$	08/15/2028	0.9389

The conversion factor for this bond is 1.0585.

$$\text{Accrued interest} = 3.25 \times \frac{134}{182} = \$2.39.$$

The price per \$100 for this bond is:

$$105\frac{1}{32} \times 1.0585 + 2.39 = \$113.57.$$

Strategy at maturity

For each contract, the person with the long position (the buyer) hands over the price described above and the person with the short position (the seller) delivers bonds with face value \$100 000. But which bonds should the seller deliver? Subject to the mild conditions described above, any bond can be delivered. So there is an enormous pool of bonds from which the seller can select the deliverable bonds. Is there a strategy for choosing the 'best' bonds to deliver?

The answer is: probably not. But there is an obvious way of selecting, from a given collection of deliverable bonds, the bonds it would be cheapest to deliver.

The cost of buying a bond to deliver is: *quoted price of bond + accrued interest since last coupon date.*

The cash received for delivering this bond at maturity is: *quoted futures price × conversion factor + accrued interest since last coupon date.*

Clearly, the seller wishes to minimise:

$$\begin{aligned}&(\textit{quoted price of bond} + \textit{accrued interest since last coupon date})\\&\quad - (\textit{quoted futures price} \times \textit{conversion factor}\\&\quad + \textit{accrued interest since last coupon date})\\&= \textit{quoted price of bond} - \textit{quoted futures price} \times \textit{conversion factor}.\end{aligned}$$

The method is to work out this quantity for each of the possible deliverable bonds and deliver the bond which produces a minimum. This process is known as selecting the bond which is **cheapest to deliver**.

Example 14

Suppose that on delivery day the quoted futures price for a US Treasury bond futures contract is \$90.53. Suppose also that on delivery day the person holding the short position has to choose between three bonds to deliver:

Bond	Quoted price	Conversion factor
1	115-14	1.2383
2	121-23	1.3325
3	121-11	1.1131

Which of these three bonds is cheapest to deliver?

Solution

Calculate, for each bond,

quoted price − quoted futures price × conversion factor

This gives:

Bond 1: $115\frac{14}{32} - 90.53 \times 1.2383 = 3.3342$

Bond 2: $121\frac{23}{32} - 90.53 \times 1.3325 = 1.0875$

Bond 3: $121\frac{11}{32} - 90.53 \times 1.1131 = 20.5748$

Hence, bond 2 would be selected for delivery.

In general, when bond yields exceed 6%, the above method will tend to favour (for delivery) low-coupon, long-maturity bonds. When bond yields are below 6%, the reverse holds and the system favours high-coupon, short-maturity bonds.

Who enters a long US Treasury bond futures contract?

As shown earlier in the chapter, the value of a bond rises when interest rates fall. So, to profit from a declining interest rate, buy a Treasury bond futures contract (go long).

Who enters a short US Treasury bond futures contract?

The value of a bond will fall as interest rates rise. To profit from a rising interest rate, sell a Treasury bond futures contract (go short).

4.7 The zero curve (introduction)

We have seen that interest rates are a fundamental tool in calculating the price of a bond. Now we reverse this. Every trading day, vast numbers of bonds are bought and sold. The natural process of trading establishes a market price for each bond and the prices of the more important bonds (e.g. US Treasury bonds) are published daily in the financial journals. So the trading price (clean price) of many leading bonds is known. We will use the known bond price to calculate an estimate of the interest rate over the maturity of the bond. This interest rate will be compatible with the known bond price. Using this method, we will calculate an improved zero curve – this is the aim of the next section.

The zero curve (a continuously compounded annual rate)

As mentioned at the beginning of this chapter, US Treasury bonds are backed completely and in full by the US government and so may be regarded as free from risk of default. The prices of US Treasury bonds are published for each trading day. We shall use these prices to calculate the interest rate these prices imply. These interest rates will then be used to construct the zero curve.

We use:

> Bond price = present value of all cash payments (**using the appropriate interest rate**)

The bond price is known. If we include in this equation one interest rate we do not know, we can then solve the equation to reveal the unknown interest rate.

The easiest bonds to use, for this purpose, are zero coupon bonds and we start with these. However, most bonds in the market are coupon bearing bonds, so the second step is to extend the technique to deal with coupon bearing bonds. We will 'start up' the zero curve with interest rates derived from zero coupon bonds and then, when things are up and running, use the more heavily traded coupon bonds.

Zero coupon bonds

Method:

(1) Select zero coupon bonds with a wide range of maturities.
(2) Rank the bonds in ascending order of their maturities.
(3) Calculate the yield to maturity for each bond.
(4) Plot the points representing interest rate against maturity.

Suppose we have the zero coupon bonds (already ranked according to maturity).

Bond	Face value	Value today	Maturity
1	100	99	0.25
2	100	98.04	0.5
3	50	47.8	1
4	500	449.71	2
5	100	74.08	5
6	1000	522.05	10

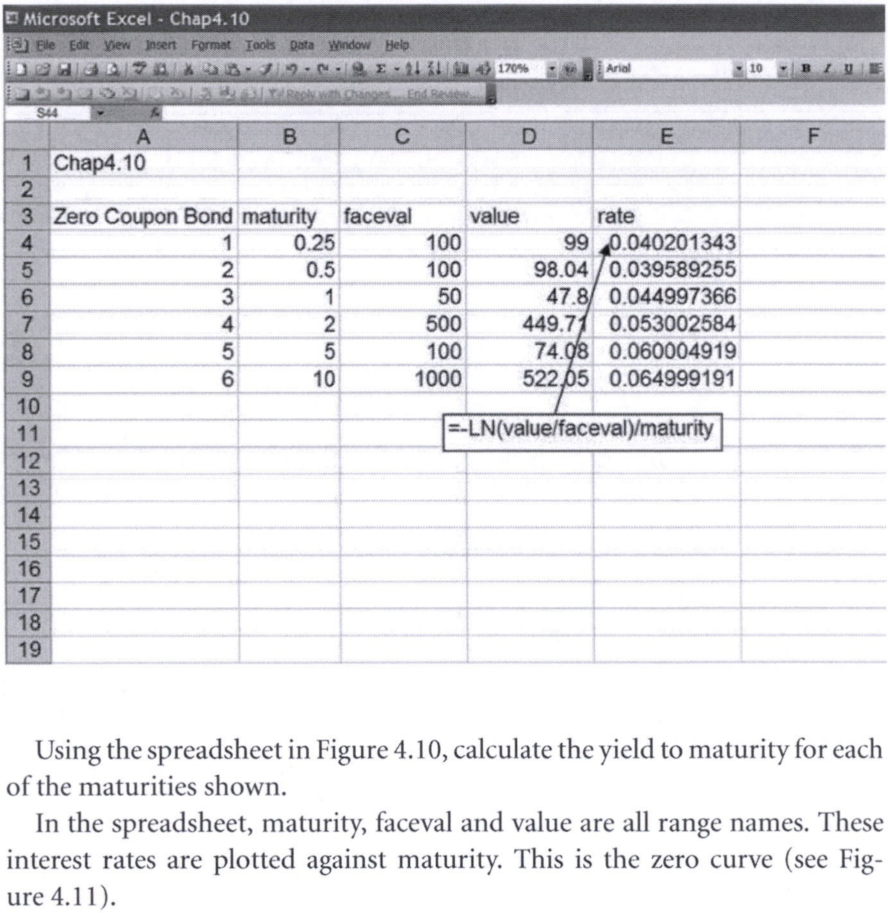

Microsoft Excel - Chap4.10

	A	B	C	D	E	F
1	Chap4.10					
2						
3	Zero Coupon Bond	maturity	faceval	value	rate	
4	1	0.25	100	99	0.040201343	
5	2	0.5	100	98.04	0.039589255	
6	3	1	50	47.8	0.044997366	
7	4	2	500	449.71	0.053002584	
8	5	5	100	74.08	0.060004919	
9	6	10	1000	522.05	0.064999191	

=-LN(value/faceval)/maturity

Figure 4.10

Using the spreadsheet in Figure 4.10, calculate the yield to maturity for each of the maturities shown.

In the spreadsheet, maturity, faceval and value are all range names. These interest rates are plotted against maturity. This is the zero curve (see Figure 4.11).

For a general calculation:

P = face value

T = maturity

B(0, T) = value today

r = implied interest rate (continuously compounded)

Then, as before: $P \times e^{-rT} = B(0, T)$

and $e^{-rT} = B(0, T)/P$

so $-rT = \ln(B(0, T)/P)$

giving $r = \dfrac{-\ln(B(0, T)/P)}{T}$

Coupon bearing bonds

We shall use zero coupon bonds, and the method developed above, to calculate an interest rate appropriate for short maturities (up to one year). We will use coupon bearing bonds to calculate interest rates for longer maturities.

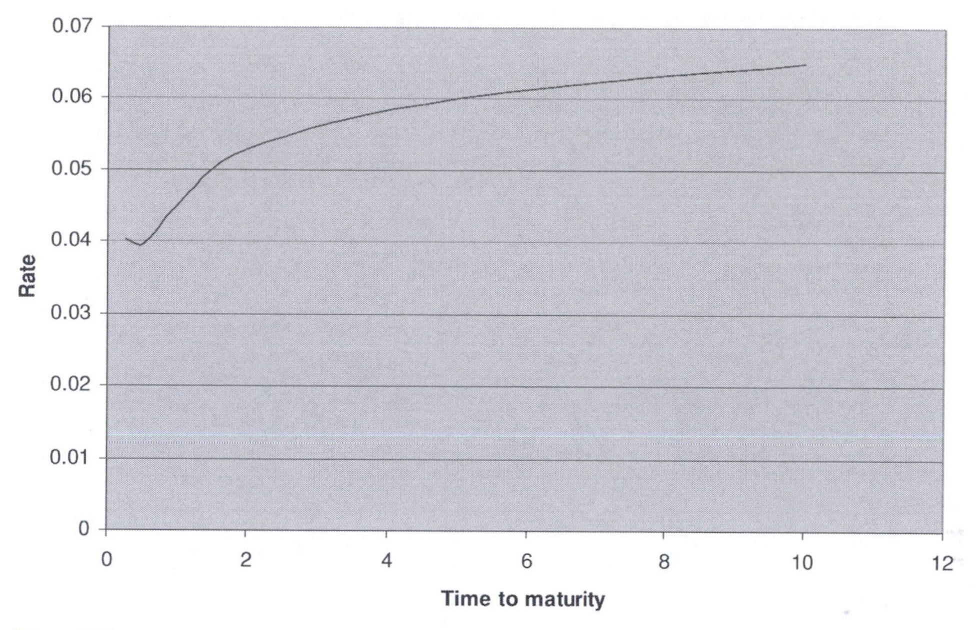

Figure 4.11

Consider the situation where we have five bonds, the first three being zero coupon bonds. The interest rates over 0.25 years, 0.5 years and 1 year are calculated as shown above and are shown in the table.

Bond	Face value	Price today	Maturity	Coupon	Coupon payments per year	Interest rate
1	100	99	0.25	0		0.04020
2	100	98.04	0.5	0		0.03959
3	50	47.8	1	0		0.04500
4	100	101.65	1.5	3	2	
5	500	509.02	2	16	2	

To calculate the interest rate appropriate to a 1.5 year maturity: this will be calculated from the information provided by bond 4. We will find the present value of each payment made by this bond **using the appropriate interest rate.**

Bond 4 makes three payments:

$3 after 0.5 years: the interest rate appropriate for this payment is 0.03959.

$3 after 1 year: the interest rate appropriate for this coupon payment is 0.04500.

$103 after 1.5 years. The interest rate appropriate for this payment is the one we want to find.

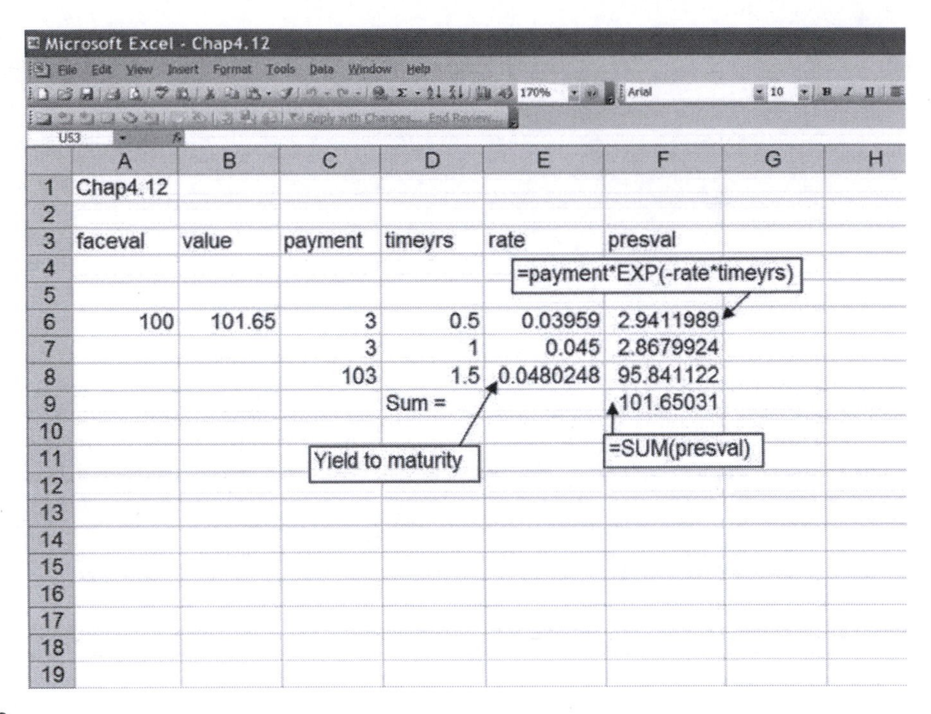

Chap4.12

faceval	value	payment	timeyrs	rate	presval
100	101.65	3	0.5	0.03959	2.9411989
		3	1	0.045	2.8679924
		103	1.5	0.0480248	95.841122
			Sum =		101.65031

Figure 4.12

We present two methods. The first uses Goal Seek, the second provides an analytical solution.

The spreadsheet in Figure 4.12 shows the three payments made by the bond in C6:C8. We give these the range name payment. The times the payments are made have the range name timeyrs. The 0.5 and the 1 year rates are entered in E6 and E7. We will use E8 as the 'changing cell'. (This is reasonable: we want the interest rate to appear here.) Put a value (0.5 say) in E8 and give this column the range name rate. Calculate the entries in column F using the formula shown. Give F6:F8 the range name presval. As above, click Tools, Goal Seek. In 'Set cell' enter F9. In 'To value' enter 101.65. In 'By changing cell' enter E8. Click OK.

This gives an interest rate for a maturity of 1.5 years of 0.04803. Record this in the spreadsheet.

For an analytical solution, the unknown, 1.5-year maturity rate is denoted by r.

> Bond price = present value of all cash payments (**using the appropriate interest rate**)

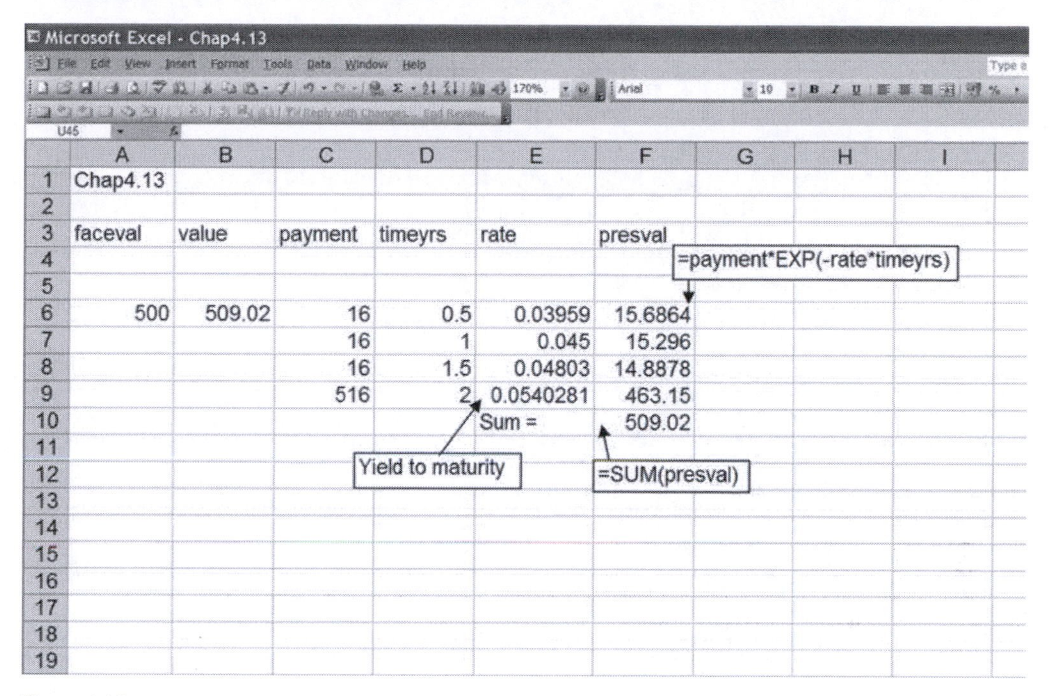

Figure 4.13

This gives:

$$3 \times e^{-0.03959 \times 0.5} + 3 \times e^{-0.04500 \times 1} + 103 \times e^{-r \times 1.5} = 101.65$$

$$\text{So, } 103 \times e^{-r \times 1.5} = 101.65 - 3 \times e^{-0.03959 \times 0.5} - 3 \times e^{-0.04500 \times 1} = 95.84$$

$$e^{-r \times 1.5} = \frac{95.84}{103}$$

$$r = -\ln\left(\frac{95.84}{103}\right) \Big/ 1.5 = 0.04803$$

To calculate the interest rate appropriate to a two-year maturity: we use the information provided by bond 5. Bond 5 makes four payments:

$16 after 0.5 years: the appropriate interest rate is 0.03959.

$16 after 1 year: the appropriate interest rate is 0.04500.

$16 after 1.5 years: the appropriate interest rate is 0.04803.

$516 after 2 years: the appropriate interest rate is the interest rate we want to calculate.

The calculation is illustrated in Figure 4.13.

E9 is the cell chosen to store the required interest rate. (It might be worth entering 0.5, say, in E9 before setting up Goal Seek.) Click Tools, Goal Seek.

In 'Set cell' enter F10.

In 'To value' enter 509.02.
In 'By changing cell' enter E9.
Click OK.
The interest rate for a maturity of two years is 0.05402814.
Analytically, again let r represent the two-year interest rate.

Bond price = present value of all cash payments (**using the appropriate interest rate**)

$$16\times e^{-0.03959\times 0.5}+16\times e^{-0.04500\times 1}+16\times e^{-0.04803\times 1.5}+516\times e^{-r\times 2}=509.02$$

$$\text{So,}\quad 516\times e^{-r\times 2}=509.02-45.870178$$

$$e^{-r\times 2}=\frac{463.1498}{516}$$

$$\text{Giving,}\quad r=\frac{-\ln\left(\frac{463.1498}{516}\right)}{2}=0.05403$$

So we have the completed table:

Bond	Face value	Value today	Maturity	Coupon	Coupon paid per year	Interest rate
1	100	99	0.25	0		0.04020
2	100	98.04	0.5	0		0.03959
3	50	47.8	1	0		0.04500
4	100	101.65	1.5	3	2	0.04803
5	500	509.02	2	16	2	0.05403

Bootstrapping

This method of calculating the interest rate over different maturities using bond prices is called bootstrapping. We will bootstrap again in Chapter 5 when we produce our final version of the zero curve.

Plotting the interest rate against maturity gives our second version of a zero curve. This is illustrated in Figure 4.14.

Interpreting the zero curve

The zero curve normally is a gently increasing curve. Shorter maturities (left-hand end) then carry lower interest rates than the longer maturities (the

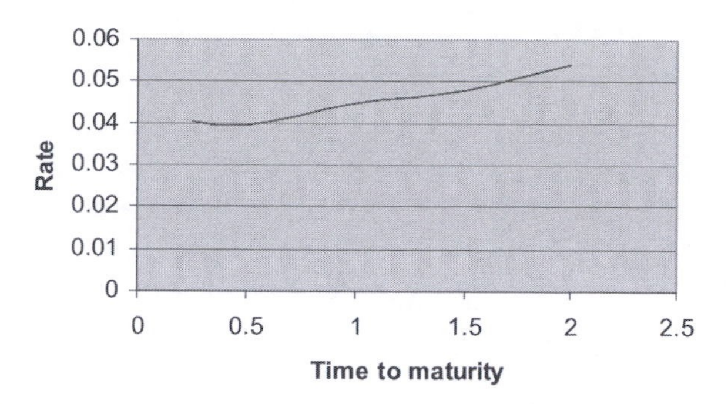

Figure 4.14

right-hand end). This is reasonable. Longer-term investors are compensated by higher interest rates for putting their money at risk for longer periods. If the risk is thought to be increasing, the zero curve will become steeper. Sometimes, though, the graph is flat or shows only a very small increase over the time to maturity. When the zero curve has this shape, interest rates are the same (almost) across all maturities. So then it makes good sense to lend money (buy bonds) over shorter maturities. You will be getting the same interest rate as over longer maturities but you will have the greater security of the short-term loan. The conventional wisdom is that when the zero curve is flat, traders expect interest rates to fall. With this belief, no one would want to borrow money (sell bonds) over the longer term. The main selling activity, in this case, would be at the short end. Occasionally, the zero curve takes an inverted shape, with the shorter maturities carrying higher rates than the longer-term maturities. This type of curve suggests a lot of interest in short-term investment. Curves of this type are thought to be indicators of economic slowdown or even recession. Typically, when the zero curve takes an inverted shape, lower interest rates across the board tend to follow.

One important use of the zero curve is to estimate future interest rates. This will be discussed in Chapter 5.

The website www.bankofengland.co.uk/statistics/yieldcurve contains a vast amount of useful and up-to-date information on yield curves.

Exercise 4

1. A zero coupon bond with face value $100 matures in two years' time. The current interest rate is 6.5% with interest compounded annually. Find the price of this bond today.

2. A £1000 zero coupon bond will mature in 3.5 years. If the interest rate is 5.8%, compounded annually, what would be a fair price for this bond?

3. Aziz is offered a \$100 zero coupon bond with six months to maturity for \$97.36. The interest rate (compounded annually) is 5.4%. What should Aziz do?

4. A £100 bond pays 7.5% per year in two six-monthly coupons. The bond matures in two years. The interest rate is 6.6% per year compounded annually. What is the value of this bond today?

5. A \$1000 bond matures in 12 months' time. The bond pays a coupon of \$22 each quarter. The safe interest rate is 10.3% per year (compounded annually).
   (i) What annual interest is paid by the bond?
   (ii) What is the value of the bond today?
   (iii) Why is the bond so cheap?

6. A \$500 bond pays a coupon of \$18.75 every six months. The bond matures in two years. The interest rate is 5% per year, compounded annually.
   (i) What is the coupon rate of this bond?
   (ii) What is the value of this bond today?
   (iii) Why is this bond expensive?

7. (i) A bond has a value considerably less than its face value. Say something about this bond.
   (ii) A second bond has a value greater than its face value. Say something about this bond.

8. A \$100 bond pays \$5 per year in two, semi-annual coupons and matures in 2.5 years.
   (i) Calculate the value of this bond for each of the interest rates shown in the table.

Interest rate (compounded annually)	3.5	4	4.5	5	5.5	6	6.5
Value of bond							

   (ii) Plot a graph showing bond value against the interest rate. What do you deduce from this?

9. A bond with face value \$100 pays 8% per year in two six-monthly coupons. A coupon was paid on 14 February 2005. The next coupon will be

paid on 14 August 2005. Today is 6 May 2005. Calculate the accrued interest using the day count conventions (i) actual/actual, (ii) actual/360, (iii) 30/360.

10. What is the year fraction 10 December 2004 to 8 July 2005 using the day count convention (i) 30/360, (ii) actual/360?

11. A $1000 bond pays out 6% per year in two six-monthly coupons. The most recent coupon was paid on 16 March 2005 and the next coupon will be paid out on 16 September 2005. Today is 28 July 2005. Calculate the accrued interest using the day count conventions (i) actual/actual, (ii) 30/360.

12. What is the dirty price of a bond? What is the clean price of a bond?

13. A bond with face value $100 pays 6.5% per year in two coupons paid out on 6 March and on 6 September. Today is 18 August 2005 and the bond is selling for $104.
    (i) Find the accrued interest using the day count conventions (a) actual/actual, (b) 30/360.
    (ii) What is the clean price of the bond? Find the dirty price of this bond under both day count conventions.

14. A £100 bond has clean price £110. What does this mean?
    The bond pays a coupon of £4.50 every six months. Today is 13 May 2004. The most recent coupon was paid on 6 February 2004. Write expressions for the dirty price of this bond using the day count conventions (i) actual/actual, (ii) actual/360, (iii) 30/360.

    In the following questions, the spreadsheet in Figure 4.15 might be of use. This spreadsheet calculates the coupon rate (E8), the current yield (F8), the par yield (G8) and the yield to maturity (H8). The face value of the bond is in A8, the price is in B8, the coupon is in C8 and the number of times each year the coupon is paid is in D8. The spreadsheet shows a $100 bond priced at $105 with a coupon of $2.5 paid semi-annually (starting in six months' time), with the payment of the principal and the final coupon payment being made in three years' time. The safe interest rate, (0.06) annually compounded, is given in C12. (If the given interest rate is not annually compounded, then the equivalent annually compounded rate must be calculated and written in C12.)

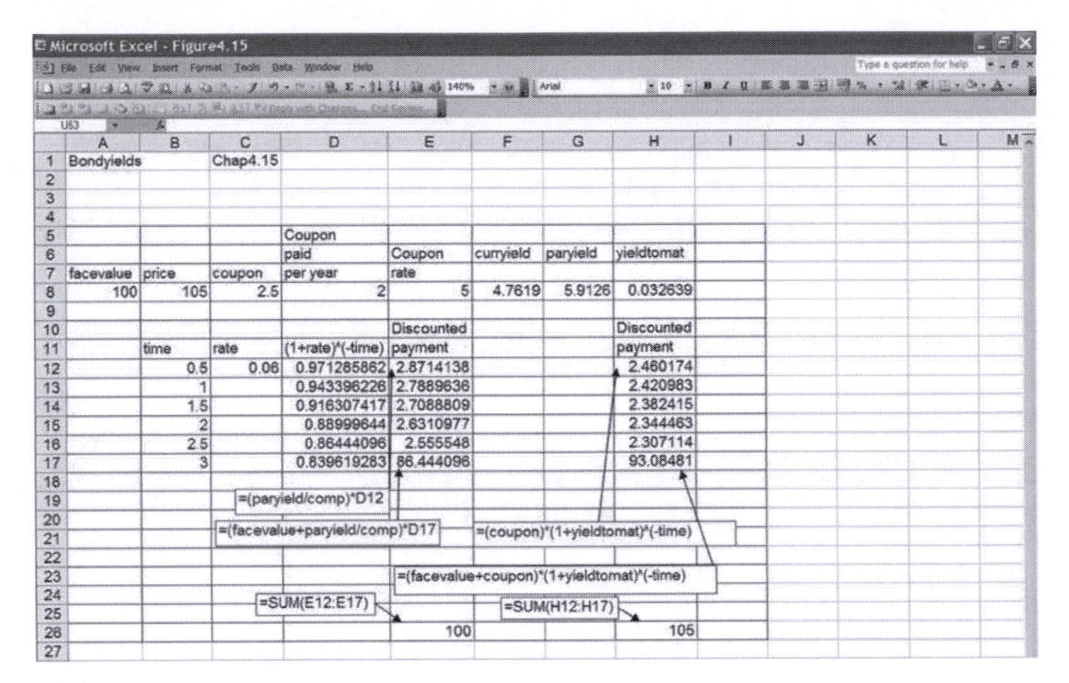

Figure 4.15

The par yield and the yield to maturity are calculated as shown.

For the par yield: enter coupon (2.5) in G8. The discounted payments from the bond (assuming the coupon written in G8) are given in E12:E17. These are summed and the answer stored in E26 (leaving space for bonds with maturity greater than three years). Goal Seek might then be used to calculate the par yield. (Tools, Goal Seek, Set cell (E26), To value (100). By changing cell (G8).) The par yield appears in G8.

For yield to maturity, enter 0.05 (or any number) in H8. The discounted payments from the bond (assuming an interest rate as written in H8) are given in H12:H17. These are summed and the answer stored in H26. Goal Seek will then calculate yield to maturity. (Tools, Goal Seek, Set cell (H26), To value (105), By changing cell (H8).) The yield to maturity appears in H8.

15. A bond has face value \$100 and pays a coupon of \$4 in six months' time and every six months thereafter. The bond has 18 months to maturity and is selling today for \$106. The interest rate is 9% per year compounded annually.

Use a spreadsheet to calculate the coupon rate, the current yield, the par yield and the yield to maturity. Comment on the relationship between coupon rate, current yield, par yield and yield to maturity.

16. The interest rate today is 5.5% per year, annually compounded. A bond has face value $1000 and pays out 5% per year in two coupons. The first coupon is to be paid in six months' time and the bond matures in three years. The value of the bond today is $950. What is (i) the coupon rate, (ii) the current yield, (iii) the par yield and (iv) the yield to maturity of this bond?

17. The interest rate is 6.2% compounded annually. A £100 bond with coupon rate 6.5% makes semi-annual coupon payments and matures in two years' time. The value of the bond today is £107.50 and the first coupon is paid in six months' time. Find the par yield and the yield to maturity of this bond.

18. Today, the interest rate is 4.8%, continuously compounded. A bond with face value £1000 pays 7% per year with semi-annual coupon payments. The first coupon is paid in six months' time and the bond matures in 18 months' time. Today, the bond is selling for £1100. Find the par yield and the yield to maturity of this bond.

19. A bond with face value $500 matures in 18 months' time. The bond pays 6% in quarterly coupon payments (the first coupon is paid in three months' time) and is priced at $501. The current interest rate is 7.4% per year (compounded semi-annually). Find the current yield, the par yield and the yield to maturity.

20. A bond (face value $250, price today = $242) matures in 15 months' time and pays 5.5% annually in two coupons – the next coupon payment is due in three months' time. The interest rate is 5% per year, compounded continuously. (i) What is the par yield? (ii) What is the yield to maturity?

21. (i) What happens to (a) par yield, (b) yield to maturity as a bond increases in value?
    (ii) A bond has face value £100 and pays a coupon of 6% per year semi-annually (the first coupon is paid in six months' time). The bond

matures in two years' time and the safe interest rate is 5.5% compounded annually. Copy and complete the table:

Bond value	90	95	100	105	110	115
Par yield						
Yield to maturity						

(iii) Was your answer to (i) correct? Why has the value of £115 given a strange (impossible) answer?

22. Amend the spreadsheet to accommodate:
    (i) a different interest rate for each time to maturity
    (ii) a continuously compounded interest rate.

23. The interest rates for different maturities are given below.

Maturity (years)	Interest rate (annually compounded)
0.5	0.05
1	0.052
1.5	0.053

A bond (face value = \$100, price = \$104) matures in 18 months. The bond pays 6% per year in two coupons, the first coupon being due in six months' time. Find the yield to maturity and the par yield of this bond.

24. Petra is offered four bonds, described below. With each bond, assume that a coupon has just been paid. The current safe interest rate is 6.2% per year (continuously compounded). Which bond would you advise that she buy?

Bond	Face value	Price	Coupon	Paid/year	Maturity (years)
1	\$100	105	2.5	2	2
2	\$1000	1025	12.5	4	1
3	\$10	9.6377	0	–	1.5
4	\$5000	5080	68	4	0.5

25. Describe the terms par, discount, premium when applied to a bond. Give an example of each.

26. (i) An investor thinks interest rates are likely to fall. Would you advise that she buys (a) a discount bond, (b) a premium bond, (c) a bond at par? She asks: why? What do you answer?
    (ii) An investor thinks interest rates are going to rise. Would he be better off buying (a) a bond at par, (b) a discount bond, (c) a premium bond? Explain your answer.

27. A bond with face value \$100 pays out \$5 per year in coupons in each of the following four years. Let B be the value of the bond today and R an annually compounded interest rate.
    (i) Show that: $\frac{5}{1+R}+\frac{5}{(1+R)^2}+\frac{5}{(1+R)^3}+\frac{5}{(1+R)^4}+\frac{100}{(1+R)^4}=\text{B}$. This makes R the YTM for this bond.
    (ii) Show that if the bond is par (so $\text{B}=100$), then $\frac{5}{100}=\text{R}$. Hence show that with a par bond, coupon rate = current yield = YTM.
    (iii) Show that if the bond is discount (so $\text{B}<100$), then coupon rate < current yield < yield to maturity.
    (iv) Show that if the bond is premium ($\text{B}>100$), then coupon rate > current yield > yield to maturity.
    (v) Use the spreadsheet in Figure 4.15 to investigate the relationship between coupon rate, current yield and yield to maturity with discount and with premium bonds.

28. The interest rates for different maturities are given below.

Maturity (years)	Interest rate (continuously compounded)
0.5	0.045
1	0.049
1.5	0.051

A \$100 bond with two years to maturity pays 6% per year in two coupons, with the first coupon being due in six months' time.
    (i) The cost of the bond today is \$96. What is the interest rate for a two-year maturity?
    (ii) The cost of the bond is \$104. What is the interest rate for a two-year maturity?
    (iii) What do you deduce from this?

29. It is said that 'a decrease in yields raises bond prices more than the same increase lowers bond prices'. (This is known as convexity.) Investigate convexity.

30. Today is 18 March 2004. The quoted price for a December 2005 Treasury bond futures contract is 117-15. Douglas enters two long December 2005 Treasury bond futures contracts. Initial margin is set at $10 000 per contract, with maintenance margin set at $7500 per contract. On successive trading days, the price of a December 2005 Treasury bond futures contract was 117-29, 118-19, 119-16, 121-20, 122-30, 122-06. Calculate gains/losses over these six days.

    At the end of the sixth day, Douglas closed out the contract. How did he do this? What was his gain/loss at the end of the sixth day?

31. If the quoted futures price of a US Treasury bond futures contract changes by $1, by how much will the value of the contract change?

32. Jaymin entered a long Treasury bond futures contract and today, 8 October 2005, is delivery day. One of the bonds being delivered has face value $100 and pays 6% per year in two coupons. The last coupon was paid out on 26 August 2005; the next coupon will be paid on 26 February 2006. The conversion factor is 1.1287 and the quoted futures price is 96-10. Use an actual/actual day count convention and calculate how much Jaymin would pay for this bond.

33. In settlement of a short Treasury bond futures contract, there are three $1000 bonds which could be delivered.

Bond	Quoted price	Conversion factor
1	113-28	1.1732
2	97-18	1.0115
3	101-09	1.0414

    Each bond has a quoted futures price of 95-19. Which bond is cheapest to deliver?

5 The forward rate, forward rate agreements, swaps, caps and floors

International Students is a charity providing reasonably priced housing in London for students from overseas. The charity wants to build three new hostels. It projects that in six months' time, it will need to borrow £5 million and this can be paid back over 20 years from rents and donations, provided that interest rates over the next 20 years do not rise above 7.5%. Is there a way the charity can protect its loan against a rising interest rate?

Structure of the chapter

In the first part of the chapter, we discuss four ways to protect an investment or a loan against an adverse interest rate movement.

In section 5.1, we discuss the **forward rate.** This is the interest rate that current rates imply will be in force during a given future time period. We show how to calculate the forward rate and how it is always possible to obtain the forward rate. We would like to have at our disposal a structure for interest rates similar to a forward contract (described in Chapter 2). This is the **forward rate agreement** and is described in section 5.2. Like forward contracts, forward rate agreements are not traded – they are bought 'over the counter'. It would be useful to have a solution to the problem faced by International Students that involved an asset that was traded. We provide two: in section 5.3 we discuss **swaps** and in 5.4 **caplets and caps and floorlets and floors.**

Earlier (in Chapter 3), we discussed futures contracts on commodities and shares. In section 5.5 we consider futures contracts based on interest rates and finally, in section 5.6, we show how the huge volume of trading in swaps and interest rate futures can be used to produce a more sophisticated zero curve.

The example at the beginning of this chapter is realistic. Unfortunately, real events are usually complex and involve an unacceptably (for our purposes) large amount of computation. To illustrate ideas we shall use the more straightforward example given below.

Example 1

The construction company W. Obble and Sons has won a contract to build a large bridge in Asia. The company is aware that in 12 months' time it will have to take out a loan of £1 000 000 which will be repaid two years later. The financial director is concerned about rising interest rates and would like to know **today** the interest rate that will be applicable in 12 months' time.

5.1 The forward rate

The **forward rate** is the interest rate over a future time period that is compatible with today's zero curve. Suppose the time period is $t = T$ through to $t = S$. We show the dependence of the forward rate on the time period in which it is to operate by writing the forward rate as $f[T, S]$.

The financial director of W. Obble wants to know the interest rate for two-year borrowing that will be in place in one year's time. To know the forward rate $f[1, 3]$ would be useful.

Note: in this section we will use only continuously compounded interest rates.

We will assume that we have a zero curve giving the interest rate (continuously compounded) for maturities up to five years (see Figure 5.1).

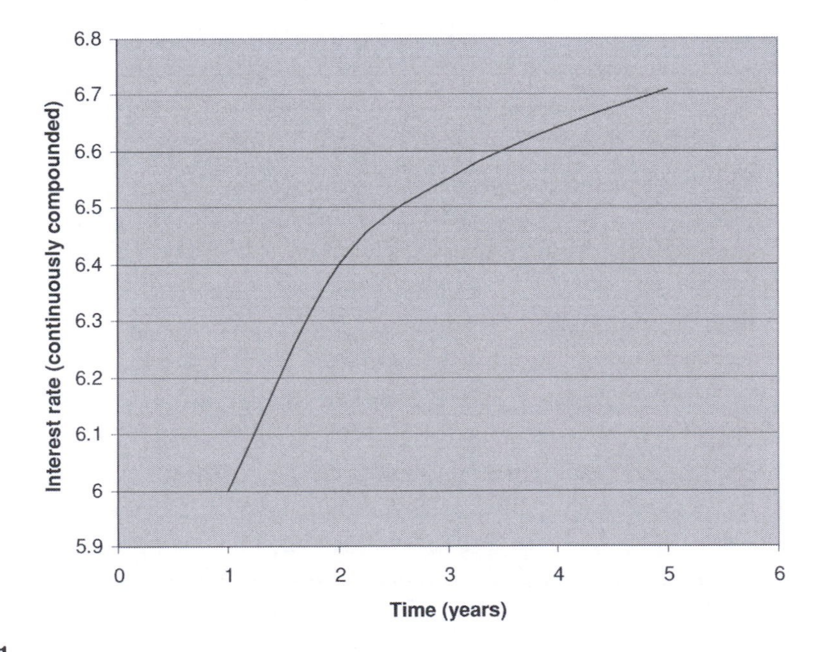

Figure 5.1

Maturity	Interest rate
1 year	6.00
2 years	6.40
3 years	6.55
4 years	6.65
5 years	6.71

To calculate the forward rate f[1, 3]

Write r = f[1, 3] (here, r is a decimal).

From the table, we know that the interest rate for a maturity of one year is 6% and the interest rate for a maturity of three years is 6.55%. This information is illustrated in Figure 5.2.

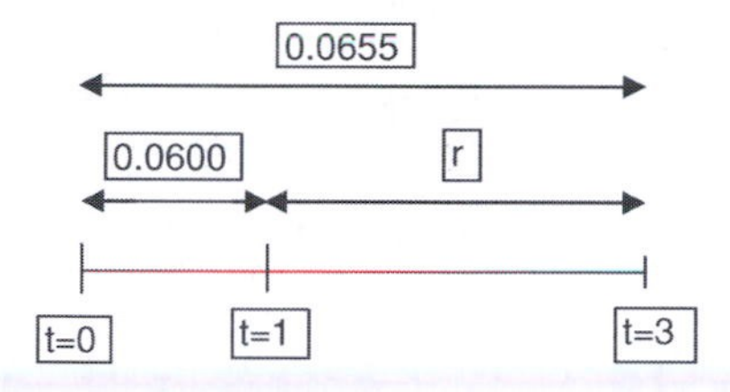

Figure 5.2

Now, consider two schemes:

Scheme 1. Invest £100 for one year at the one-year rate.

In one year's time, re-invest the money for two years, at the two-year rate then prevailing. Call this rate r (r = will be f[1, 3]).

At the end of the three years, the investment will have value $100e^{0.06\times 1} \times e^{r\times 2}$.

Scheme 2. Invest £100 for three years at the three-yearly rate.

At the end of three years, this investment will have value $100e^{0.0655\times 3}$.

At the end of the three years, both schemes must yield the same amount or an arbitrage opportunity would occur.

So $$100e^{0.06\times 1} \times e^{r\times 2} = 100e^{0.0655\times 3}$$

Hence: $$e^{0.06\times 1+r\times 2} = e^{0.0655\times 3}$$

Giving: $$0.06 \times 1 + r \times 2 = 0.0655 \times 3$$

$$r = \frac{0.0655 \times 3 - 0.06 \times 1}{2}$$

$$= 0.06825$$

So the forward rate $f[1, 3] = 0.06825$

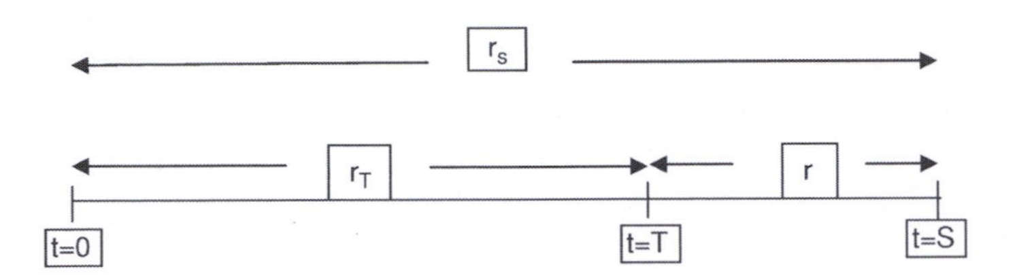

Figure 5.3

Here, and in all cases, the amount of the investment (£100) conveniently cancels. As we might have expected, the forward rate is independent of the amount of the investment. A formula would be useful.

General result: to calculate the forward rate f[T, S]

Let r = f[T, S]:

Let r_T be the interest rate for a maturity of T years and r_S the interest rate for a maturity of S years – see Figure 5.3.

Scheme 1. Invest P for T years at rate r_T. Re-invest immediately for S – T years at rate r.

Value of investment at time S is: $P \times e^{r_T \times T} \times e^{r(S-T)}$

Scheme 2. Invest P at rate r_S for S years.

Value of investment at time S is: $P \times e^{r_S \times S}$

After S years, the investments must be equal (or face arbitrage).

$$P \times e^{r_T \times T} \times e^{r(S-T)} = P \times e^{r_S \times S}$$

Therefore: $$e^{r_T \times T + r(S-T)} = e^{r_S \times S}$$

Giving: $$r_T \times T + r(S-T) = r_S \times S$$

So: $$r = \frac{r_S \times S - r_T \times T}{S - T}$$

An important result is: the forward rate can always be obtained, without cost. We illustrate this result first for borrowing and then for an investment.

A Borrowing at the forward rate

What the financial director should do:

1. Calculate the amount that will grow, in one year, to £1 million.
2. Today, borrow this amount for three years.
3. Invest this amount for one year.

The detail

1. The amount that will grow, in one year's time, to £1 million is $e^{-0.06\times 1} \times 1\,000\,000 = £941\,764.53$.
2. Borrow £941 764.53 for three years at the three-year rate (6.55%).
3. Invest £941 764.53 for one year at 6%.

In one year's time, the company (from 3) will **receive** £1 million. In three years' time, it will repay the loan (set up in 2) and **pay out** $e^{0.0655\times 3} \times 941\,764.53 = £1\,146\,254.88$.

This mirrors a loan of £1 million, taken out in 12 months' time and repaid two years later. What interest rate, r, has been paid on this loan? By studying the two schemes in the General Result, we can see that r must be the forward rate f[1, 3]. A calculation confirms this.

$$e^{r\times 2} \times 1\,000\,000 = 1\,146\,254.88$$

$$e^{r\times 2} = \frac{1\,146\,254.88}{1\,000\,000}$$

$$r = \frac{1}{2} \times \ln\left(\frac{1\,146\,254.88}{1\,000\,000}\right)$$

$$= 0.06825$$

So effectively, in one year's time, £1 million was 'borrowed' at 6.825% per year for two years.

B Investing at the forward rate

Example 2

Matt expects to have $25 000 to invest in six months' time. He would like to invest this money for one year. Matt fears that interest rates might fall. He would like to invest the money at the forward rate f[0.5, 1.5].

(i) Using the interest rates shown in the table, calculate f[0.5, 1.5].

Maturity	Interest rate
1 month	4.72
3 months	4.92
6 months	5.09
1 year	5.34
1.5 years	5.61
2 years	5.87

(ii) Explain how Matt could, today, lock in a one-year investment at the forward rate r = f[0.5, 1.5].

Solution

(i) The six-monthly rate is 0.0509 and the 1.5-year rate is 0.0561.
$f[0.5, 1.5] = \frac{0.0561 \times 1.5 - 0.0509 \times 0.5}{1.5 - 0.5} = 0.0587$
So the forward rate Matt would like to use is 5.87%.

(ii) The scheme:
(a) Calculate the amount that will grow in six months to \$25 000.
(b) Today, borrow this amount for six months at 5.09%.
(c) Invest this amount for 1.5 years at 5.61%.

The detail

1. The amount that will grow, in six months' time, to \$25 000 is $e^{-0.0509 \times 0.5} \times 25\,000 = \$24\,371.78$.
2. Borrow \$24 371.78 for six months at 5.09%.
3. Invest \$24 371.78 for 1.5 years at 5.61%.

In six months' time, Matt will pay out, in settlement of the loan, \$25 000. In 1.5 years' time, he will receive (from the investment in (3)), $e^{0.0561 \times 1.5} \times 24\,371.78 = 26\,511.43$. So an investment of \$25 000 in six months' time has paid out \$26 511.43 one year later. What rate of interest does this represent?

$$e^{r \times 1} \times 25\,000 = 26\,511.43$$
$$e^{r \times 1} = \frac{26\,511.43}{25\,000}$$
$$r = \ln\left(\frac{26\,511.43}{25\,000}\right)$$
$$= 0.0587 \quad \text{as expected.}$$

Effectively, a one-year investment of \$25 000, starting in six months' time, has attracted an annual rate of 5.87%.

Note: the method, but not the formula, holds if the interest rates are not continuously compounded. To illustrate, suppose the interest rates in the table below are annually compounded. Use these rates to calculate f[1, 1.5].

Maturity	Interest rate (annually compounded)
over night	4.89
1 month	4.91
3 months	5.09
6 months	5.2
1 year	5.29
2 years	5.39

From the table, we will take the 1.5-year rate to be 5.34%.

As before:

Scheme 1. Invest £100 for one year at 5.29%. Then, re-invest for 0.5 years at the forward rate 100r%.

Scheme 2. Invest £100 for 1.5 years at 5.34%.

These investments must (or create an arbitrage opportunity) yield the same amount after 1.5 years.

$$100(1+0.0529)^{1} \times (1+r)^{0.5} = 100(1+0.0534)^{1.5}$$

Hence: $1.0529^{1} \times (1+r)^{0.5} = 1.0534^{1.5}$

$$(1+r)^{0.5} = \frac{1.0534^{1.5}}{1.0529} = 1.0268402$$

Square both sides: $1+r = 1.0268402^{2} = 1.0544008$

$$r = 0.0544008$$

giving a forward rate percentage of 5.44%.

The interest rates in the calculations have different compounding periods

It might happen that the 'best' interest rates available are not all either continuously or annually compounded. Indeed, the interest rates might have differing compounding periods and in this case the process remains as shown above, but the calculations reflect the increasing complexity. One way of meeting this is to calculate, for each of the interest rates, the equivalent continuously compounded rate. Then use the formula established earlier to calculate the forward (continuously compounded) rate. And finally (if necessary), calculate the equivalent discretely compounded rate. This is shown in the spreadsheet in Figure 5.4.

The interest rates with maturities T and S are shown in B8 and B9 and have the cell names rateDT and rateDS. Their compounding periods appear in C8 and C9 and have the range name comp. The times to T and to S appear in D8 and D9 and have cell names timeT and timeS. The equivalent continuously compounded rates (rateCT and rateCS) appear in E8 and E9. The T – S forward rate (continuously compounded) lies in E17: the equivalent discretely compounded rate (having for.comp compounding periods per year: C17) lies in B17.

Finding, and using, a forward rate by calculating the rate consistent with the zero curve over the required time period is, as we have shown, always possible. But every event has to be structured from first principles. It would

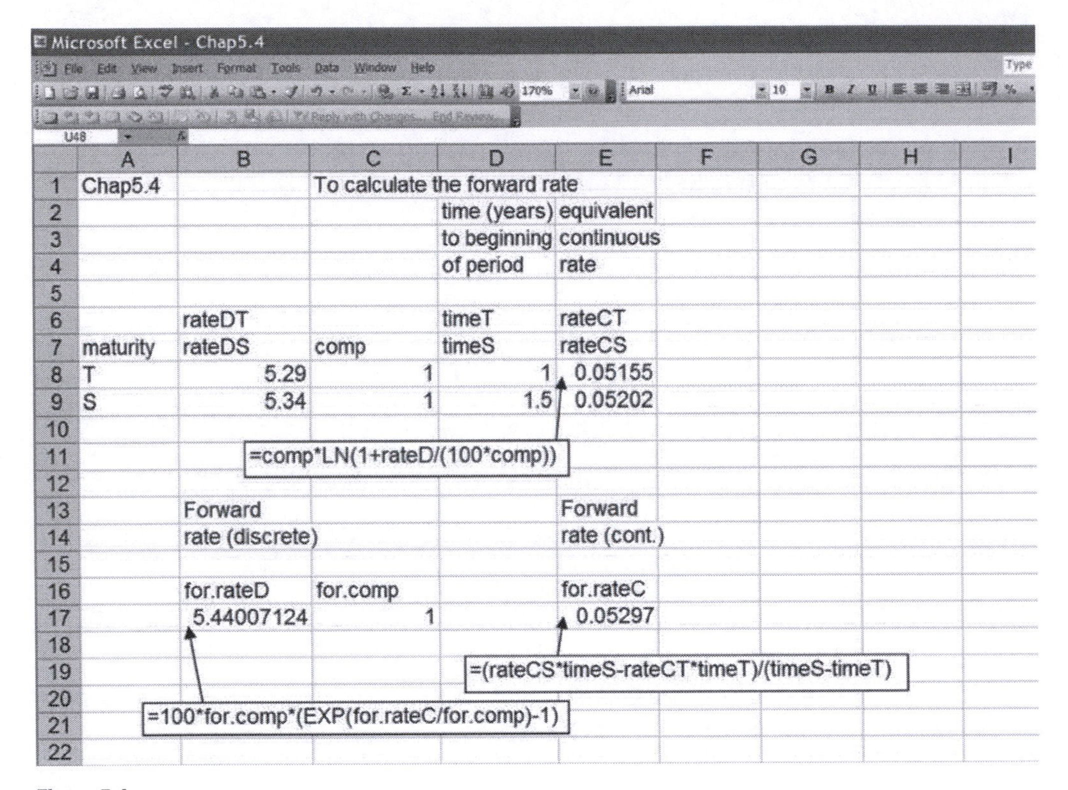

Figure 5.4

be useful to have an existing product that could be bought or sold as a package to satisfy particular requirements. Ideally, this product could offer protection against a rising interest rate (or a falling interest rate, if we wanted to protect an investment) in the same way that a forward contract offers protection against a rising commodity price. A forward rate agreement is such a product.

5.2 Forward rate agreements (FRAs)

A sum of money is nominated. An interval of time is agreed upon. Two interest rates are proposed. Were the money to be invested over this period of time at each of the proposed interest rates, two interest payments would accrue. Put very simply, in a forward rate agreement, two parties agree to exchange these interest payments.

But an FRA is a financial contract. For mathematical and for legal reasons, a tighter definition is required.

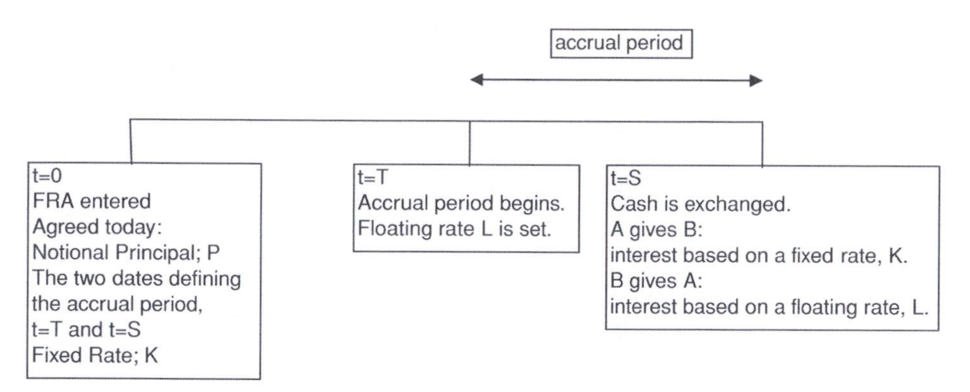

Figure 5.5

A forward rate agreement could be structured as follows. Today is 15 May. Two parties, A and B, agree three things.

1. An amount of money. This is usually a large sum. It is called the **notional principal**. Suppose the notional principal is $5 000 000.
2. Two future dates. The first date is called the **reset date**, the second date is called the **payment date**. The time between the two dates is called the **accrual period** (or sometimes, the **tenor**).

   Suppose the dates are 15 June (the reset date) and 15 September (the payment date). So the accrual period (the tenor) is three months.
3. Two interest rates. One of these interest rates will be agreed today. This will be called the **fixed rate.** The other interest rate will be set on the reset date. This rate – not known when the FRA is established – will be called the **floating rate**.

Suppose the fixed rate (agreed today) is 5.5%. Suppose that on 15 June the interest rate for three-monthly borrowing is set at 5.32%. Then the floating rate will be 5.32%.

In an FRA, on payment day, A gives B the interest generated from the notional principal over the accrual period by the floating rate. B gives A the interest generated from the notional principal over the accrual period by the fixed rate (see Figure 5.5).

In practice, the floating rate is almost always a LIBOR rate – see Chapter 1 for discussion of this important rate. We mention, as a reminder, that LIBOR is a **simply compounded** rate. This means that if $P is invested for α years at the simply compounded rate L (for LIBOR), the interest that accrues is αLP and the amount of the investment at the end of the T years will be $P(1+\alpha L)$. Here, α is calculated using the actual/360 day count convention

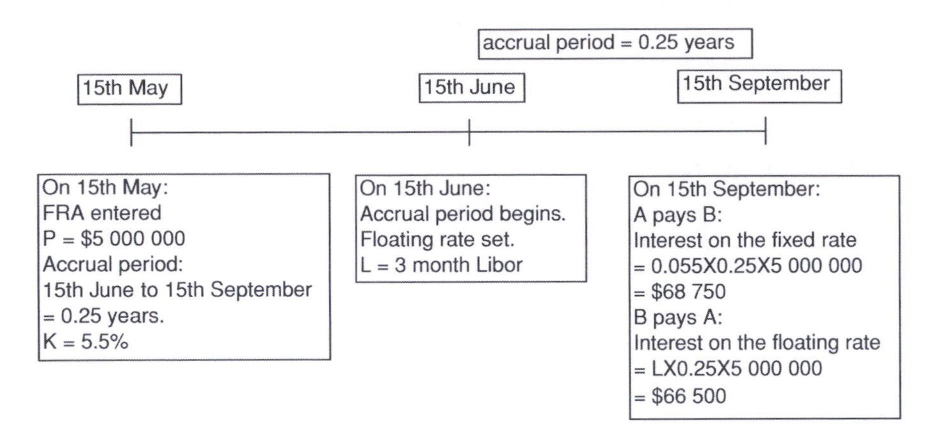

Figure 5.6

(Chapter 4 – section 4). However, to keep calculations as straightforward as possible, we will usually give α a simple fractional value.

Since the floating rate in a forward rate agreement will be a LIBOR rate, we will take both interest rates (the fixed rate and the floating rate) to be simply compounded. However, we shall be using the zero curve to provide interest rates of different maturities and we shall use these continuously compounded rates for discounting purposes.

It might be useful to complete the calculations started above in an example.

Example 3

It is 15 May. A and B enter a forward rate agreement on a notional principal of \$5 000 000 with the fixed and floating rates and the accrual period as given above. Calculate the amount A gives to B and the amount B gives to A on the payment date.

Solution

A agrees to pay a fixed rate of 5.5% (per year, simply compounded): B agrees to pay the three-month floating rate set on 15 June – see Figure 5.6.

Come 15 June, the LIBOR rate for the ensuing three months is set at 5.32%. On 15 September, A gives B $\$0.25 \times 0.055 \times 5\,000\,000 = \$68\,750$ and B gives A $\$0.25 \times 0.0532 \times 5\,000\,000 = \$66\,500$.

We can show the two interest payments for this example on a diagram.

Convention

Dotted lines will represent floating rate payments; solid lines will represent fixed rate payments. Lines pointing upwards will indicate cash received; lines pointing downwards will indicate cash paid out (see Figure 5.7).

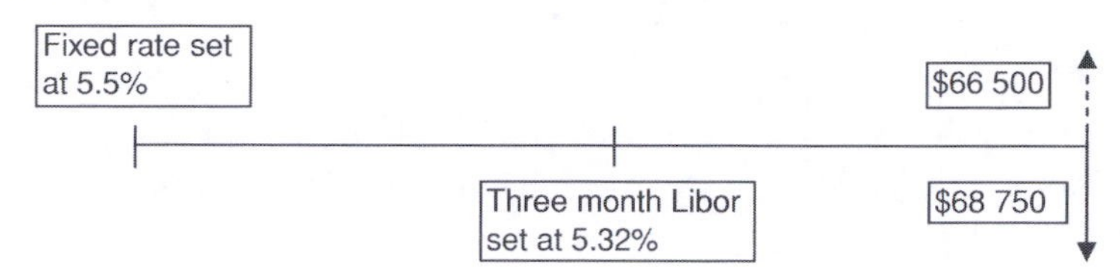

Figure 5.7

It is time to put this all together.

Definition A forward rate agreement is an agreement, made today, that counterparties A and B will exchange cash payments on a specified date in the future. Associated with an FRA there is:

(1) a notional principal, P
(2) two dates: the reset date, T
    the payment date, S
(3) a fixed interest rate, K.

The dates will be chosen so that the period from T to S will be the accrual period for a standard interest rate, starting on date T. Usually, the period T to S is three months or six months. Usually, the time up to T is a whole number of months extending out to 24 months.

An FRA is named according to the fixed interest rate. In a **payers** FRA, the fixed rate is paid out and the floating rate received. In a **receivers** FRA, the fixed rate is received and the floating rate paid out.

Let α represent the accrual period: so α is the time T to S calculated according to an agreed day count convention (actual/360 for LIBOR).

Under a payers FRA, on the payment date,

A pays B αKP
B pays A αLP

where L is the LIBOR rate set at T and appropriate to the period from T to S.

There are three obvious questions.

(1) In practice, how is the fixed rate determined?
(2) How are FRAs valued?
(3) How is an FRA used?

It will turn out that (2) is used to answer (1) and (3) is the lead into the next section, but before we answer these questions, we establish three useful results that will be used again in section 5.3.

Result 1

The value today ($t = 0$) of a zero coupon bond paying out \$1 at $t = T$ is written as $B(0, T)$. If the interest rate in the interval $t = 0$ through to $t = T$ is constant and equal to r (continuously compounded), then $B(0, T) = e^{-rT}$.

Proof

Today, invest $\$e^{-rT} \times 1$ at rate r for T years. At time T, the investment is worth $\$e^{-rT} \times 1 \times e^{rT} = \$1$.

Today, buy one zero coupon bond which pays out \$1 at time T.

Since both investments pay out \$1 at time T, the investments must (or face an arbitrage opportunity) have the same value today.

Hence $B(0, T) = \$e^{-rT}$.

Example 4

The interest rate (continuously compounded) is 6.2% per year. A zero coupon bond paying \$1 in six months' time is worth, today,
$B(0, 0.5) = e^{-0.062 \times 0.5} \times 1 = \$0.9695$.

Result 2

If a zero coupon bond pays out \$N at time T, then the value of this bond at time $t = 0$ is $N \times B(0, T)$.

Proof

Buy a zero coupon bond paying out \$N at time T.

Buy N zero coupon bonds, each paying out \$1 at time T.

Each investment pays out \$N at time T. To avoid arbitrage, the value of the investments at $t = 0$ must be identical.

Hence, value (at $t = 0$) of a zero coupon bond paying out \$N at time T is $N \times B(0, T)$.

Example 5

The interest rate (continuously compounded) is 5.25% per year. A zero coupon bond pays out \$100 in three months' time. The value of this bond, today, is $100 \times B(0, 0.25) = 100 \times e^{-0.0525 \times 0.25} = \$986.96$.

Result 3

The floating rate payment in an FRA is equivalent to two zero coupon bonds. Each bond pays out \$P. One bond matures at time T, the other at time S – see Figure 5.8.

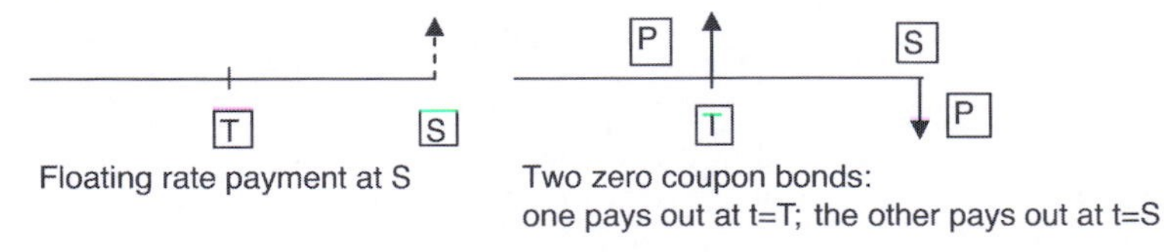

Figure 5.8

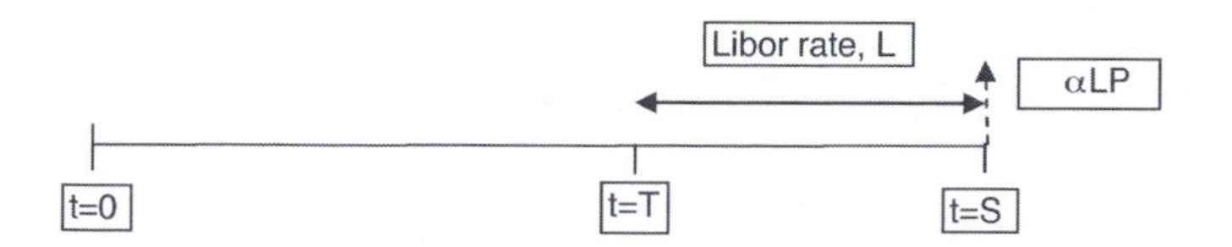

Figure 5.9

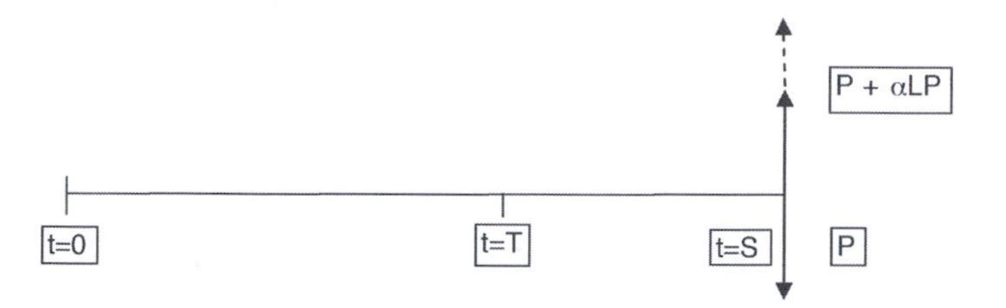

Figure 5.10

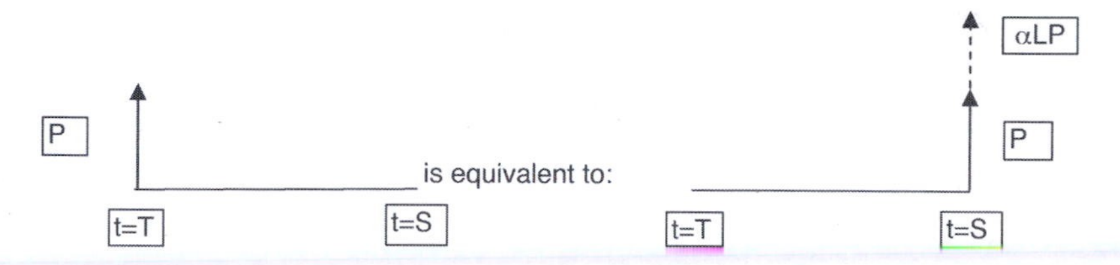

Figure 5.11

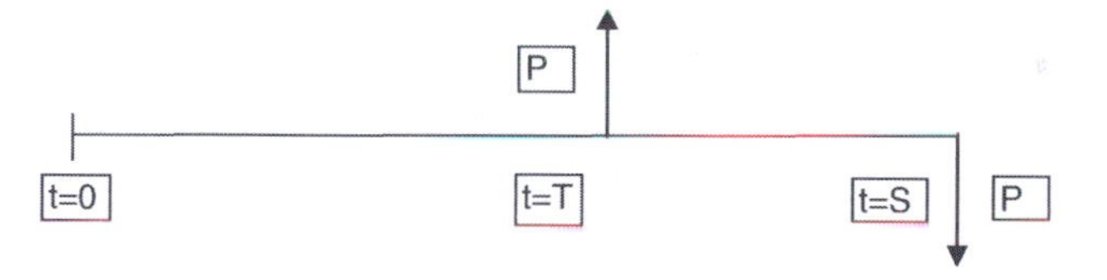

Figure 5.12

Proof

The floating rate payment is αLP (Figure 5.9).

At time S, receive and pay out the notional principal, P (Figure 5.10).

Clearly, these payments at S are equivalent to that shown in Figure 5.9.

By the definition of the LIBOR rate, P at time T grows to $P(1 + \alpha L) = P + \alpha L \times P$ at time S (Figure 5.11).

Replacing the payment $P + \alpha LP$ at S by the equivalent payment of P at time T gives Figure 5.12.

This shows that the single floating rate payment αLP made at time S is equivalent to two zero coupon \$P bonds, one maturing at time T, the other maturing at time S.

These results are now used to prove the following.

(Question 2) To find the value, at t = 0, of a (payers) FRA

There are two cash payments in an FRA – see Figure 5.13.

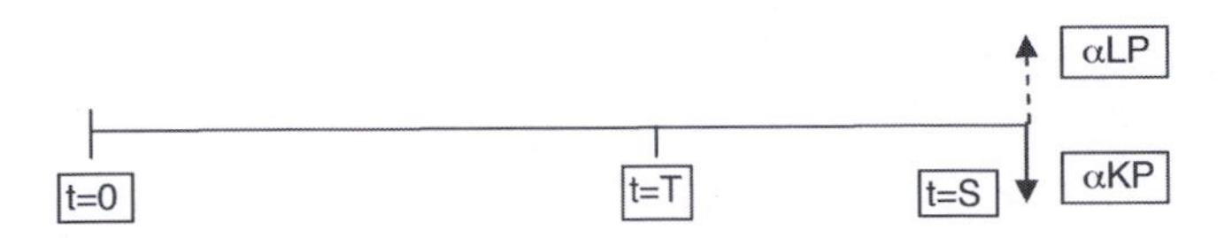

Figure 5.13

We find the discounted value of each payment at t = 0. Then:

Value (at t = 0) of (payers) FRA

= value (at t = 0) of floating rate payment – value (at t = 0) of fixed rate payment.

(1) Floating rate payment

As shown in Result 3, a floating rate payment αLP at t = S (Figure 5.9) is equivalent to two zero coupon \$P bonds (Figure 5.12).

The value at t = 0 of a zero coupon bond paying out \$P at time T is: P × B(0, T). Similarly the value at t = 0 of a zero coupon bond paying out \$P at time S is P × B(0, S)

Hence: Value at t = 0 of the floating rate payment is

P × B(0, T) –P× B(0, S)

(2) Fixed rate payment

A single payment of αKP at time S can be thought of as a zero coupon bond paying out αKP at time S (see Figure 5.13a).

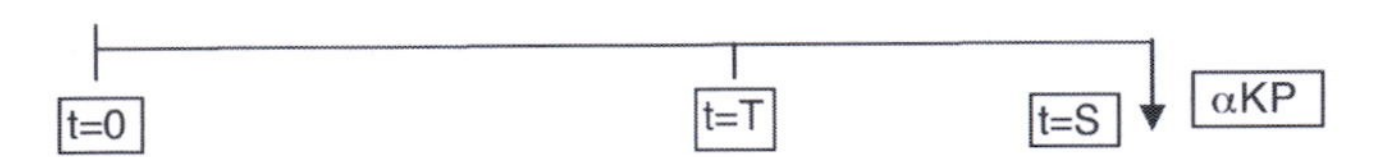

Figure 5.13a

By result 2,

Value at t = 0 of the fixed rate payment is αKP × B(0, S).

Finally:

Value (at t = 0) of FRA is P[B(0, T) – B(0, S) – αK × B(0, S)]

In a receivers FRA, the payments at time S are as shown in Figure 5.14.

It may easily be shown that the value of a receivers FRA is also P[B(0, T) – B(0, S) – αK × B(0, S)].

We use these results to answer Question 1.

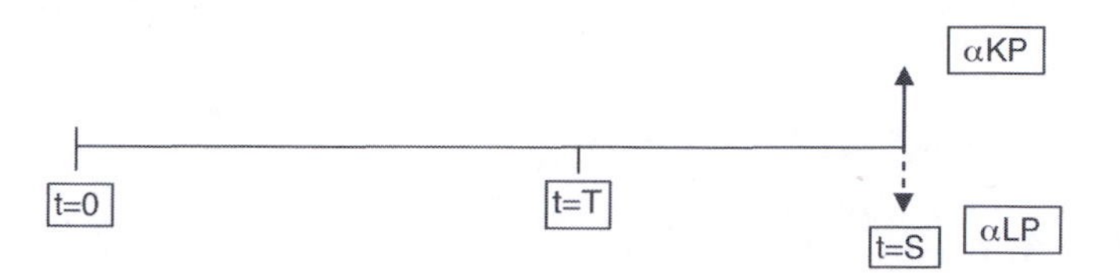

Figure 5.14

(Question 1) To determine the fixed rate K

We would like forward rate agreements to be the interest rate equivalents of forward contracts. We would like to be able to use an FRA to fix, today, the interest rate that will be paid (received) on a future loan (investment). With a forward contract, we declared that the value of the contract, on entry, was zero. This condition was then used to calculate the delivery price. We now repeat this line of thinking with the FRA.

The cost of entry (the value at $t = 0$) of an FRA is zero.

This gives: $P[B(0, T) - B(0, S) - \alpha K \times B(0, S)] = 0$

Dividing through by P gives:

$B(0, T) - B(0, S) = \alpha K \times B(0, S)$

And $$K = \frac{B(0, T) - B(0, S)}{\alpha \times B(0, S)}$$

This is the fixed rate K that gives the FRA an initial value of zero. And this is the fixed rate offered as part of a payers or a receivers FRA.

Example 6

In five months' time, Joe will borrow £500 000 for three months at the LIBOR rate current on the day the loan is taken out. (In practice, Joe would borrow at LIBOR plus a number of basis points. The method can be adapted to cope with this.) The interest rate today (continuously compounded) for a five-month maturity is 5.43%; the interest rate for an eight-month maturity is 5.6%. Joe is concerned that interest rates are on the rise and he would like to fix, today, a constant rate for the loan.

(i) Find the constant rate Joe would pay in a payers FRA.
(ii) Show how Joe can use an FRA to obtain, today, a fixed rate for his loan.

Solution

(i) The fixed rate, K, in the FRA is given by: $K = \frac{B(0,T) - B(0,S)}{\alpha \times B(0,S)}$
(see Figure 5.15).

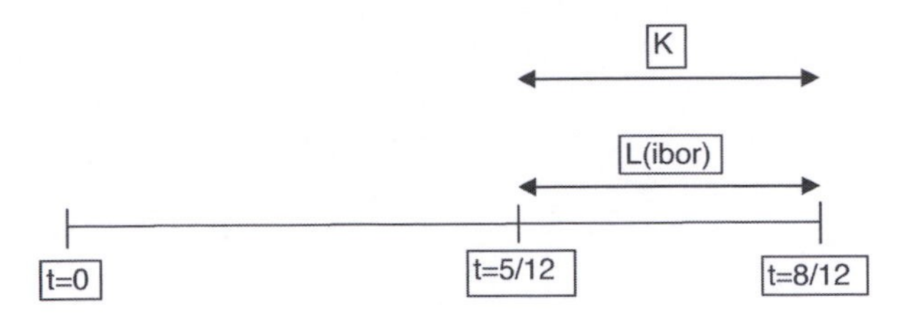

Figure 5.15

$$B(0, T) = e^{-rT} \times 1 \quad \text{(Result 1)}$$

when $t = \frac{5}{12}$, r=5.43%. This gives $B\left(0, \frac{5}{12}\right) = e^{-0.0543 \times \frac{5}{12}} \times 1 = 0.97763$

when $t = \frac{8}{12}$, r=5.6%. This gives $B\left(0, \frac{8}{12}\right) = e^{-0.056 \times \frac{8}{12}} \times 1 = 0.96335$

$$\alpha = \frac{3}{12}$$

$$\text{So} \quad K = \frac{0.97763 - 0.96335}{(\frac{3}{12}) \times 0.96335} = 0.05929$$

Or, $K = 5.93$

(ii) **Today,** Joe enters a payers FRA (notional principal = £500 000; $T = \frac{5}{12}$; $S = \frac{8}{12}$; K = 5.93%).

So he will pay the fixed rate (K = 5.93%) and receive the floating (LIBOR) rate. Entering an FRA costs Joe nothing.

In five months' time, Joe borrows £500 000 for three months at the current three month LIBOR rate, L.

In eight months' time, Joe pays back £500 000 plus interest of £$\frac{3}{12} \times L \times 500\,000$. Under the terms of the FRA, Joe receives £$\frac{3}{12} \times L \times 500\,000$ and pays £$\frac{3}{12} \times 0.0593 \times 500\,000 =$ £7412.5.

The net effect of all this is that Joe pays interest on the loan of £$\frac{3}{12} \times 0.0593 \times 500\,000$. Joe has used the FRA to transform an unknown floating rate into a known fixed rate. Joe knows, today, the rate he will pay on his loan.

The example provides a partial answer to Question 3. Forward rate agreements can be used to reduce the uncertainty surrounding interest rate movements.

(Question 3) Uses of an FRA

(1) A loan is to be taken out on a date in the future. The loan will involve a currently unknown (floating) interest rate, which, if you think interest rates are about to rise, can be worrying. An FRA can be used to determine today the interest that will be paid on the loan.

Today: Enter a payers FRA.

Reset date = date you take out the loan. Payment date = date you pay off the loan.

On the reset date: Take out the loan at the floating rate. Agree to pay off the loan on the payment date.

On the payment date: repay the amount of the loan. Pay the (floating rate) interest.

Under the FRA, receive the floating rate interest. Pay the fixed rate interest.

The overall effect is that you have paid interest on the loan calculated at the fixed rate. So the FRA has transformed a floating rate loan into a fixed rate loan.

(2) A large amount of money is to be invested on a future date. The money will be invested at a currently unknown, floating rate. You are concerned that interest rates might fall.

Today: Enter a receivers FRA.

Reset date = date you invest the money. Payment date = date you close out the investment.

On the reset date: invest the money at the floating rate for the accrual period.

On the payment date: withdraw the money. Receive the (floating rate) interest on the investment.

Under the FRA, pay the floating rate interest. Receive the fixed rate interest.

Overall, you have received interest calculated at the fixed rate on the investment. The FRA has transformed a floating rate investment into a fixed rate investment.

Forward LIBOR rate

The above result, which calculates the fixed rate in an FRA, is important. This result determines the fixed rate and so completes the specification of an FRA. But more importantly, this result defines, **today**, a rate that in the time period T through to S will be compared with the **presently unknown** LIBOR rate setting at time T. The value of K, as determined above, is, for this reason, called a **forward LIBOR rate.**

Definition The 3×6 **forward LIBOR rate** is the fixed rate in an FRA that has the reset date in three months' time and the payment date three months later. In general, the $\mathbf{n \times (n + m)}$ **forward LIBOR rate** is the fixed rate in an FRA having the reset date in n months' time and an accrual period of m months. Forward LIBOR is, essentially, an estimate, made today, of a future LIBOR rate. Because LIBOR is used most often as a short-term interest rate, the defining parameters n and m are given in months.

Example 7

Suppose that the 2×8 forward rate is 4.87%. Louise believes that in two months' time, the six-month LIBOR rate will be less than 4.87%. How could Louise back her hunch financially?

Solution

Louise could enter a 2×8 receivers FRA with a fixed rate of 4.87%.

Suppose she is right and in two months' time the six-monthly rate is 4.71%. On payment day, Louise will receive interest calculated at 4.87% and pay out interest calculated at 4.71%.

Clearly, FRAs can be used for speculation. But an FRA does not solve International Students' problem (at the beginning of the chapter). From the time the loan is entered through to maturity is 20 years. This does not fall into an FRA framework. A neat solution would be to have several FRAs operating back to back through the 20 years. Such a package is called a swap and swaps are the subject of the next section.

5.3 Swaps

An interest rate swap is a sequence of back-to-back forward rate agreements. Or, in greater (much greater) detail, an **interest rate swap** is an agreement by two parties to exchange amounts of cash on specified dates in the future. A sequence of dates, agreed at the outset, is a fundamental part of a swap agreement. The dates are an equal time period apart. This time period (called the **accrual period**) is designed to agree with a standard LIBOR rate (usually three months or six months).

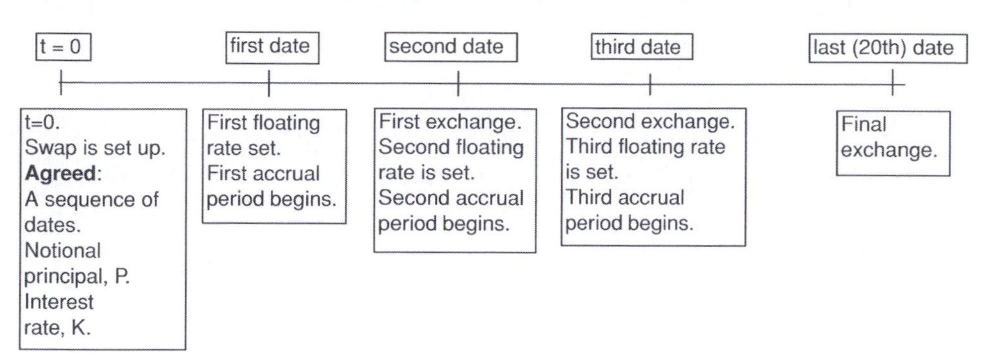

Figure 5.16

There are two interest rates. One interest rate is fixed at the outset (**the fixed rate**), the other is the LIBOR rate set at the beginning of each accrual period (**the floating rate**).

The cash exchanged is the interest that would accrue if an agreed amount of money, **the notional principal**, was invested at each of the interest rates over the accrual period.

On the first date in the sequence, the first LIBOR rate is set. On the second date (at the end of the first accrual period), the first exchange takes place and the second LIBOR rate is set and so on until, on the last date, the last exchange takes place. The time between the first date and the last date is known as the **tenor** of the swap.

A 20-year swap is illustrated in Figure 5.16.

Notation The set of fixed rate payments is called the **fixed leg** of the swap. Similarly, the set of floating rate payments is called the **floating leg** of the swap.

Swaps are named after the fixed payments. If I enter a **payers swap**, I will pay the fixed rate and receive the floating rate. If I entered a **receivers swap**, I would receive the fixed rate and pay the floating rate.

Again, in diagrams, an up arrow will represent cash received, a down arrow will represent cash paid out. A solid line indicates a fixed rate payment, a dotted line indicates a floating rate payment.

Example 8

An interest rate swap is designed to start on 10 August 2005. The first exchange of cash will take place on 10 February 2006 and the last exchange will take place on 10 August 2015. The notional principal is fixed at £1 000 000 and the fixed rate is 4.8%.

A receivers swap

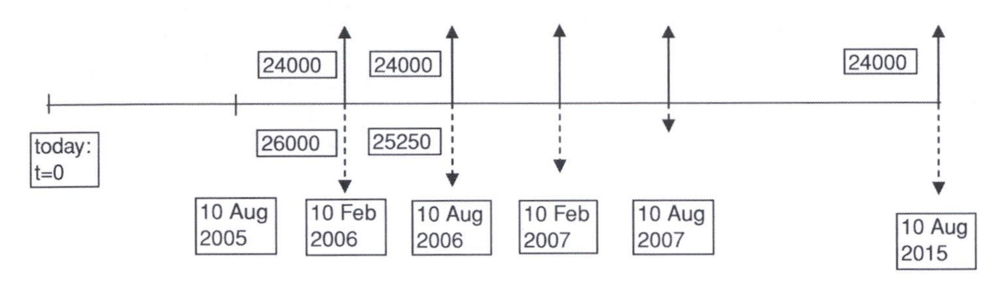

Figure 5.17

(i) What is the accrual period of the swap? What is the tenor of the swap?
(ii) If the LIBOR rates set on 10 August 2005 and on 10 February 2006 are 5.2% and 5.05% respectively, describe the first two exchanges.

Solution

(i) The time between the first LIBOR rate being set (10 August 2005) and the first exchange (10 February 2006) is six months. The accrual period is six months. The tenor is the time between the first date (10 August 2005) and the last date (10 August 2015). The tenor is ten years.
(ii) On 10 February 2006: the fixed rate interest payment is $0.5 \times 0.048 \times 1\,000\,000 = 24\,000$.

The floating rate set on 10 August 2005 is 5.2%. The floating rate payment is $0.5 \times 0.052 \times 1\,000\,000 = 26\,000$.

Hence, on 10 February 2006 a party who entered a payers swap would pay out £24 000 and receive £26 000.

On 10 August 2006: the fixed rate interest payment is $0.5 \times 0.048 \times 1\,000\,000 = 24\,000$.

The floating rate set on 10 February 2006 is 5.05%. The floating rate payment is $0.5 \times 0.0505 \times 1\,000\,000 = 25\,250$.

Hence, on 10 August 2006 a party who entered a receivers swap would receive £24 000 and pay out £25 250.

The payments for a receivers swap are as shown in Figure 5.17.

The remainder of this section will follow the structure of section 5.2.

(1) To find the value (at t = 0) of a payers swap

There is more algebra in this section. Anyone wishing to escape can use the spreadsheet in Figure 5.24 which follows this section.

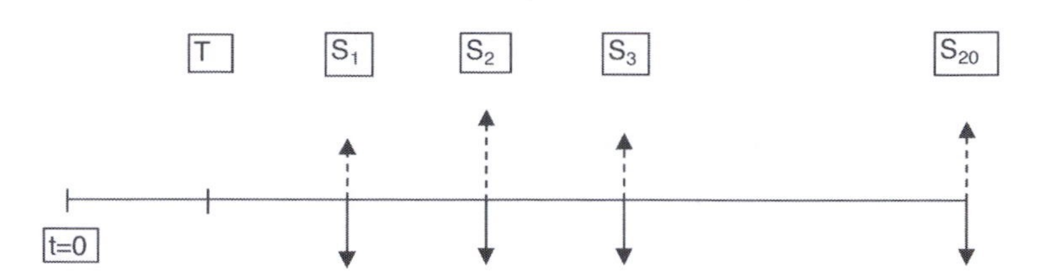

Figure 5.18

Let the dates associated with the swap be T, S_1, S_2, ... S_{20}.

Figure 5.18 illustrates a payers swap.

The value of a swap at t = 0 is the sum of the present values (at t = 0) of all cash payments made by the swap. We consider the floating rate payments and the fixed rate payments separately.

(a) The floating rate payments

Consider Figure 5.19. Recall Result 1 of section 5.2 (see Figure 5.20).

Replace each floating rate payment with the equivalent pair of zero coupon P bonds (Figure 5.21).

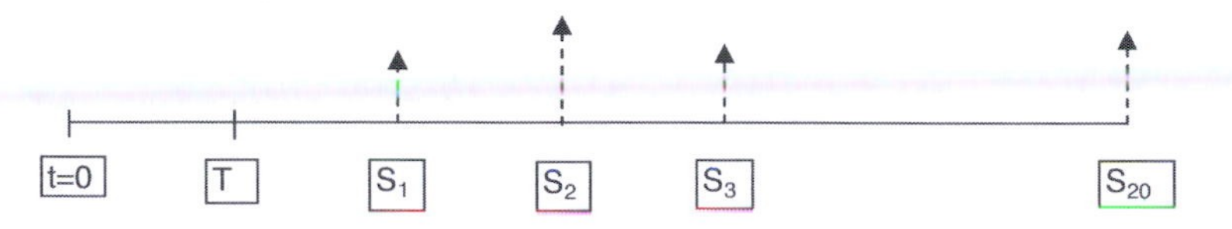

Figure 5.19

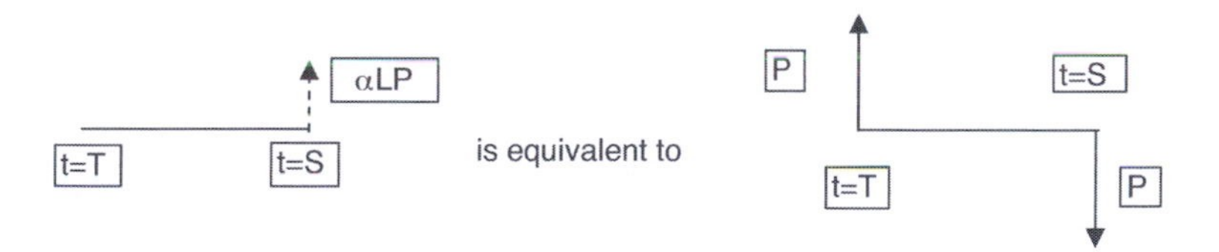

Figure 5.20

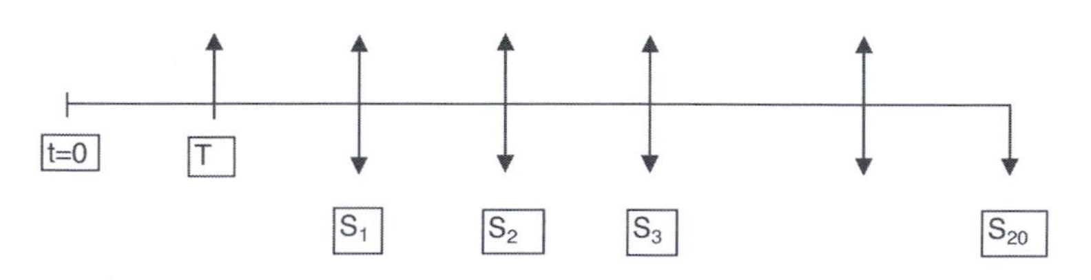

Figure 5.21

So, remarkably, the 20 floating rate payments are equivalent to two zero coupon P bonds, one paying out at time T, the other paying out at time S_{20} (Figure 5.22).

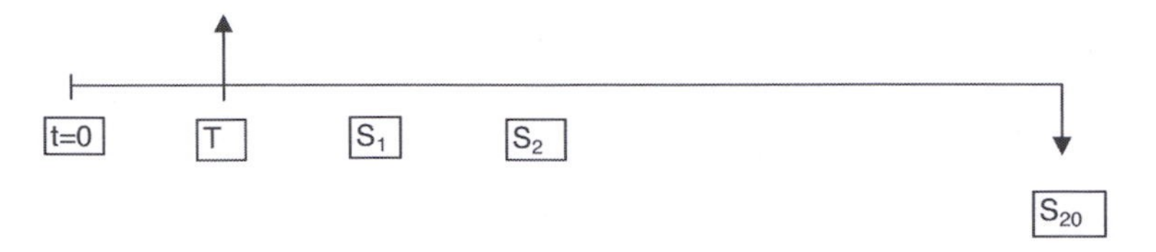

Figure 5.22

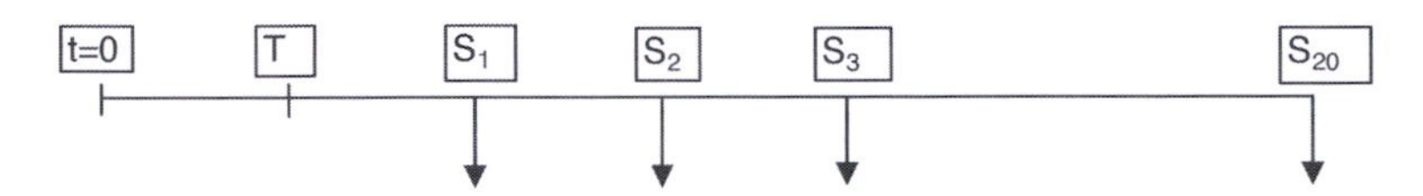

Figure 5.23

The present value (t = 0) of these two payments is:
$P \times B(0, T) - P \times B(0, S_{20})$ (see Result 2 in section 5.2).

We will write this as $PV(\text{floating}) = P \times B(0, T) - P \times B(0, S_{20})$.

(b) The fixed rate payments

Consider Figure 5.23. Each of these payments is αKP. So each can be considered as a zero coupon bond paying αKP at its maturity. The present value of the bond with maturity S_1 is (by Result 3, section 5.2) $\alpha KP \times B(0, S_1)$. Each of the 20 fixed rate payments will have a similar present value $\alpha KP \times B(0, S_i)$. The present value of the 20 fixed payments is:
$\alpha KP \times B(0, S_1) + \cdots + \alpha KP \times B(0, S_{20})$.

We will write this as $PV(\text{fixed}) = \alpha KP \times B(0, S_1) + \cdots + \alpha KP \times B(0, S_{20})$.

Hence, the value of the payers swap at t = 0
= present value (t = 0) of floating payments
− present value (t = 0) of the fixed rate payments.

$$\text{Value}(t = 0) = PV(\text{floating}) - PV(\text{fixed}).$$

This is an important result in its own right. And, of course, the value today (t = 0) of a receivers swap is given by:

$$\text{Value}(t = 0) = PV(\text{fixed}) - PV(\text{floating}).$$

Now we put this result to use.

(2) To determine the fixed rate in a payers swap

As with an FRA, we shall select the fixed rate so as to give the swap an initial value of zero.

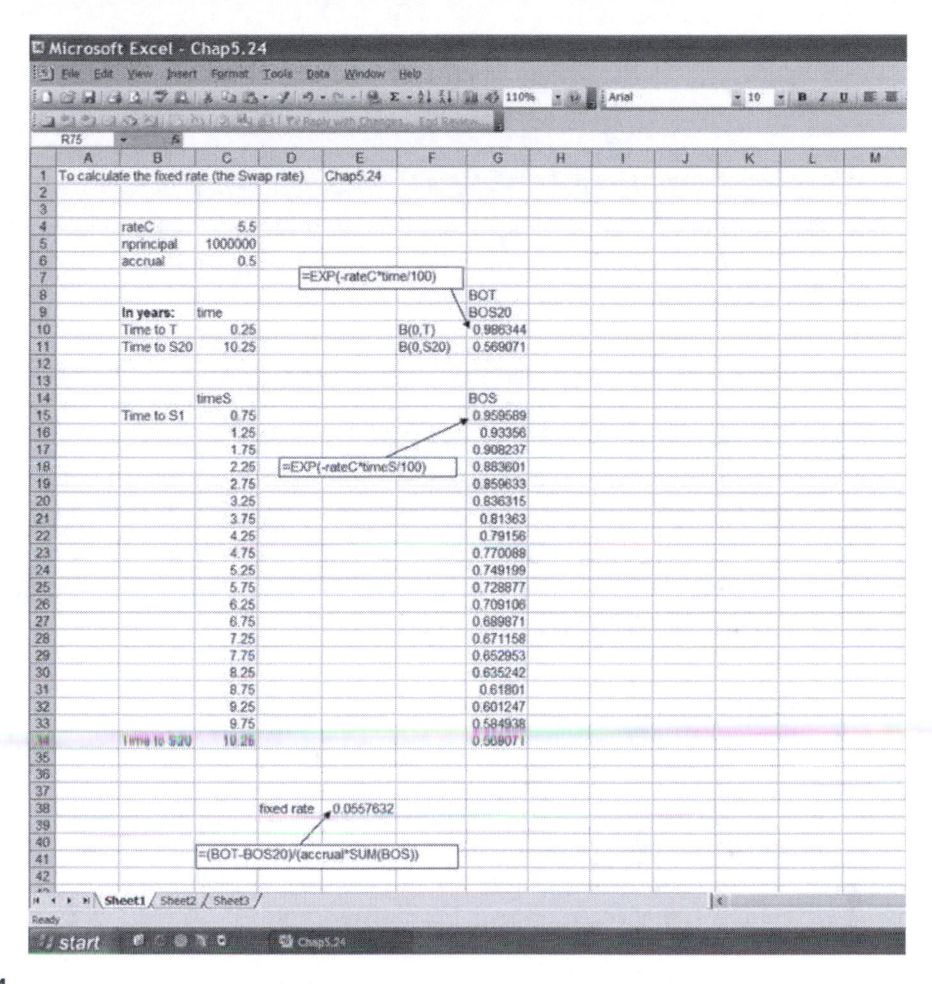

Figure 5.24

Simply: put Value $(t = 0) = 0$.

So PV(floating) = PV(fixed).

$$P \times B(0, T) - P \times B(0, S_{20}) = \alpha KP \times B(0, S_1) + \cdots + \alpha KP \times B(0, S_{20})$$

Divide through by P.

$$B(0, T) - B(0, S_{20}) = \alpha K \times [B(0, S_1) + \cdots + B(0, S_{20})]$$

Giving: $$K = \frac{B(0, T) - B(0, S_{20})}{\alpha(B(0, S_1) + \cdots + B(0, S_{20}))}$$

This calculation is performed in a spreadsheet in Figure 5.24.

The interest rate (continuously compounded and assumed constant throughout the period of the swap) is 5.5% – this lies in C4 and has the cell name rateC.

The notional principal (£1 000 000) lies in C5; the accrual period (with cell name accrual) appears in C6. The time to T and the time to S20 enter with the range name time. The sequence of dates of the swap appears in C15:C34 with the range name timeS. The tenor of the swap is ten years.

$B(0, T)$ and $B(0, S_{20})$ appear in G10 and in G11 with cell names BOT and BOS20, respectively.

$B(0, S_1), B(0, S_2), \ldots B(0, S_{20})$ lie in G15:G34 with the range name BOS.

The fixed rate of the swap appears in E38.

The fixed rate in a swap is called the **(forward) swap rate**. This rate (and not the value of the swap) is quoted in the financial press. We will use the forward swap rate later in the chapter to construct a more sophisticated zero curve.

Observe that it costs nothing to enter a swap when the fixed rate is the forward swap rate. This is because the forward swap rate is constructed from a zero value for the swap at time $t = 0$.

Example 9

ZZZ Finance is aware that in three months' time it will be taking out a loan of £1 000 000 which will be repaid 18 months later. There will be three interest rate payments, each based on the six-month floating LIBOR rate set six months before the interest payment is to be paid. But the financial director is worried. He feels that interest rates are about to rise. He enters a payers swap with notional principal £1 000 000, starting in three months' time, ending eighteen months later and with accrual period six months.

The zero curve (rates continuously compounded) is as shown in Figure 5.25.

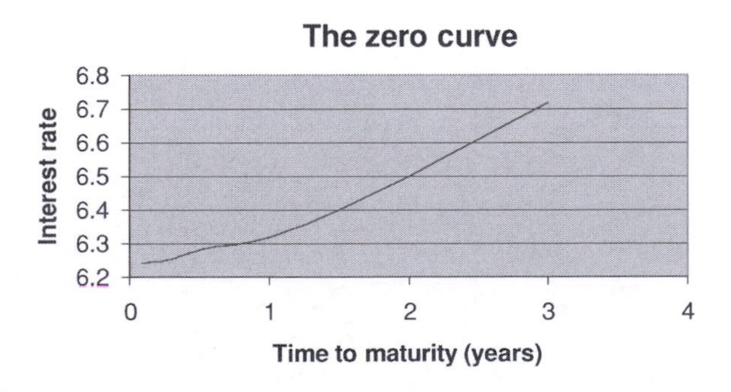

Figure 5.25

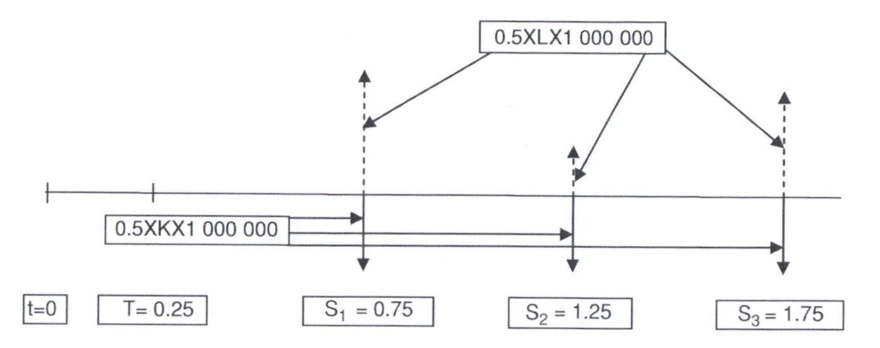

Figure 5.26

(i) Find the fixed rate for this swap.
(ii) Show that the swap can be used to transform the company's loan from a floating rate loan to a fixed rate loan. What fixed rate will the company pay?

Solution

(i) The payments from the swap are as shown in Figure 5.26.
We use the zero curve to calculate the interest rate appropriate for each payment.

Time to maturity	Rate
0.25	6.25
0.75	6.30
1.25	6.36
1.75	6.45

The present value (t = 0) of the floating rate payments is
$P \times B(0, 0.25) - P \times B(0, 1.75)$.

$$\begin{aligned} PV(\text{floating}) &= e^{-0.0625\times 0.25} \times 1\,000\,000 - e^{-0.0645\times 1.75} \times 1\,000\,000 \\ &= 91\,234.13 \end{aligned}$$

And the fixed rate payments have a present value of:

$$\begin{aligned} &PV(\text{fixed}) \\ &\quad = 0.5KP \times B(0, 0.75) + 0.5KP \times B(0, 1.25) + 0.5KP \times B(0, 1.75) \\ &\quad = 0.5K \times 1\,000\,000 \times (e^{-0.063\times 0.75} + e^{-0.0636\times 1.25} + e^{-0.0645\times 1.75}) \\ &\quad = 1\,385\,344.61822K \end{aligned}$$

$$\begin{aligned} \text{The value of the swap at } t = 0 \text{ is: } & PV(\text{floating}) - PV(\text{fixed}) \\ &= 91\,234.13 - 1\,385\,344.61822K \end{aligned}$$

$$\text{Putting this equal to zero gives: } K = \frac{91\,234.13}{1\,385\,344.61822}$$
$$= 0.065856631483$$
$$\text{Or, } K = 6.59\%$$

(ii) **Today:** the financial director takes out a payers swap with notional principal £1 000 000. The dates of the swap are: $t = 0.25$, $S_1 = 0.75$, $S_2 = 1.25$ and $S_3 = 1.75$. The accrual period is 0.5 years, the tenor is 1.5 years and the fixed rate is 6.59%.

At t = 0.25: he takes out a loan of £1 000 000 over 1.5 years. There will be three interest payments, each calculated at the six-month LIBOR rate set six months before the interest payment is to be made.

At t = 0.75: make the first interest payment on the loan.

Pay £$0.5 \times L \times 1\,000\,000$ where L is the LIBOR rate set at $t = 0.25$.

Make the first fixed rate payment of the swap. Pay £$0.5 \times 0.0659 \times 1\,000\,000$.

Receive the first floating rate payment of the swap. Receive £$0.5 \times L \times 1\,000\,000$.

The net effect is a single fixed rate payment of £$0.5 \times 0.0659 \times 1\,000\,000$.

At t = 1.25: make the second floating rate payment of the loan, £$0.5 \times L \times 1\,000\,000$.

Make the second fixed rate payment of the swap, £$0.5 \times 0.0659 \times 1\,000\,000$.

Receive the second floating rate payment of the swap, £$0.5 \times L \times 1\,000\,000$.

As above, the net effect is a single fixed rate payment of £$0.5 \times 0.0659 \times 1\,000\,000$.

And similarly at t = 1.75.

Hence, by taking out a payers swap (and receiving the floating rate), a floating rate loan has been transformed into a fixed rate loan.

The fixed rate of the loan was $K = 6.59\%$.

(3) Uses of a swap

There are many. We describe two.

A. Use a swap to convert a sequence of floating rate payments into a sequence of fixed rate payments. Use a swap to convert a sequence of fixed rate payments into a sequence of floating rate payments.

(1) A loan is to be taken out on a future date. The loan will involve a series of currently unknown (floating) interest rates. If it is thought that interest rates might rise, then:

Today: enter a payers swap with notional principal equal to the value of the loan and the payment dates of the swap coinciding with the payment dates of the loan.

At time T: take out the loan.

On each payment day: on the loan, make the floating rate interest payment. On the swap, make the fixed rate interest payment and receive the floating rate interest payment.

Overall effect: pay the fixed rate interest payment.

(2) A large sum of money is to be invested on a date in the future. The interest received will be calculated at the floating rate and the investor fears that interest rates might fall.

Today: enter a receivers swap with notional principal equal to the value of the investment and the payment dates of the swap coinciding with the payment dates of the investment.

At time T: invest the money.

On each payment day: on the investment, receive the floating rate interest payment. On the swap, receive the fixed rate interest payment and make the floating rate interest payment.

Overall effect: receive the fixed rate interest payment.

Generally: the procedure for changing the type of interest paid or received is set out in the table below.

Loan	*Enter*
Paying floating rate	Payers swap [pay fixed, receive floating]
Paying fixed rate	Receivers swap [receive fixed, pay floating]
Investment	*Enter*
Receiving floating rate	Receivers swap [receive fixed, pay floating]
Receiving fixed rate	Payers swap [pay fixed, receive floating]

The example given above is not entirely realistic. As mentioned above, LIBOR is the rate at which one (respectable) bank will lend money to another. Loans made to organisations less financially secure will carry an interest rate of LIBOR plus an additional percentage. So a floating rate loan might pay interest at LIBOR plus 1.5%. This is usually written in terms of basis points. One basis point is $\frac{1}{100}th$ of 1%. So LIBOR + 1.5% would be described as LIBOR + 150 basis points.

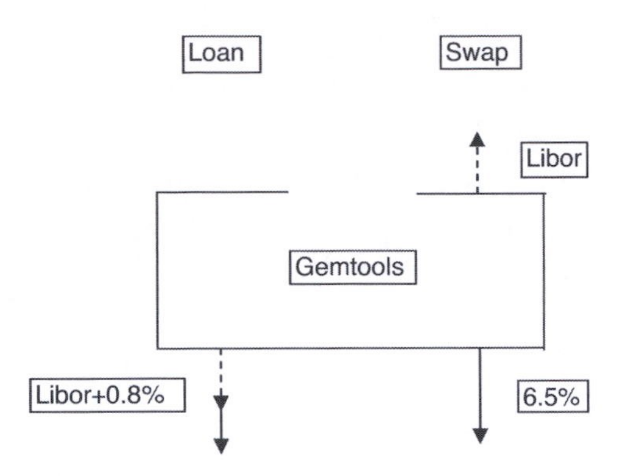

Figure 5.27

Notation The aim is to show how swaps can be used to achieve a particular objective. To avoid unnecessary detail, in the few examples that follow we present annual cash flows. So in the diagrams, LIBOR + 0.8% will represent the annual return from a floating rate of LIBOR + 0.8%.

Example 10

Gemtools has arranged a floating rate loan. The company will borrow $10 million and make interest payments every three months at the three-monthly LIBOR rate plus 0.8%. (This would be described as LIBOR + 80 basis points.) The directors are concerned about a rise in interest rates and would prefer to have a fixed rate for the repayments. Illustrate how a swap could be used to transform this floating rate into a fixed rate and determine this fixed rate.

Solution

A payers swap is arranged. The floating rate is three-month LIBOR: the fixed rate is 6.5% per year. This leads to the diagram in Figure 5.27, which illustrates what is received (up arrow) and what is paid out (down arrow).

	Gemtools
Loan	pay: LIBOR + 0.8
Swap	pay: 6.5
	receive: LIBOR
Overall	pay: 6.5 + 0.8 = 7.3

The net effect is: the floating rate loan has been transformed into a loan paying a fixed rate of 7.3%.

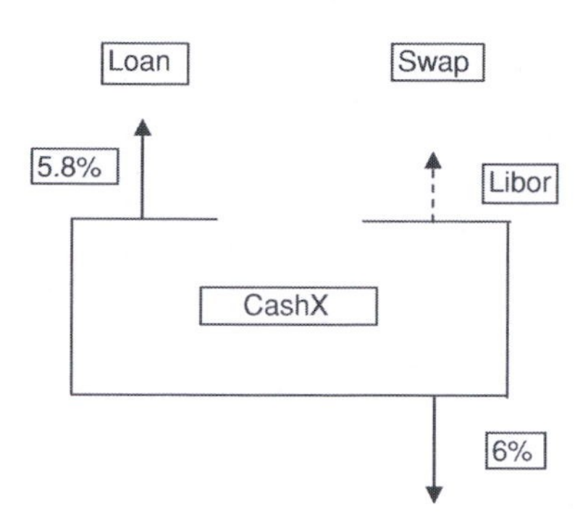

Figure 5.28

Example 11

The chairman of CashX woke up with the feeling that interest rates were due to rise. He was aware that CashX had loaned $1 million to DebtsY at a **fixed** rate of 5.8% per year. Explain how CashX could convert this loan into a potentially more profitable floating rate loan.

Solution

That morning, CashX entered a payers swap – the fixed rate was 6%, the floating rate was six-month LIBOR (Figure 5.28).

	CashX
Loan	receive: 5.8%
Swap	pay: 6.0%
	receive: LIBOR
Overall	receive: LIBOR – 0.2%

With the loan and the payers swap, CashX receives LIBOR – 20 basis points. If interest rates do rise, so will the interest payments received by CashX.

The examples so far have ignored the mechanics of setting up a swap.

How would a company enter a swap agreement?

Finding a company to be the partner in a swap agreement is not easy. First, the companies must agree on the size of the notional principal. Then, they must each desire the type of interest payments the swap will provide. Finally, they must have compatible creditworthiness to ensure that a meaningful swap can be constructed. It would be difficult for two companies to do this for

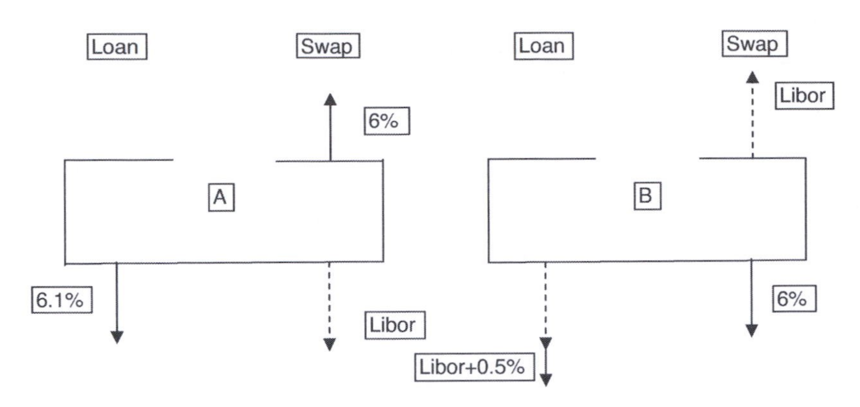

Figure 5.29

themselves. Usually, companies intending to become involved in a loan will contact a financial institution (a bank) that offers specialist skills in this area. The financial institution will arrange the swap.

The two companies involved in a swap generally will not know the identity of the other. All payments will be made to and through the financial institution. Of course, the financial institution will levy a charge for providing expert advice, for setting up the swap and for handling the administration of the swap. The usual charge is three or four basis points of the notional principal per year (0.03% or 0.04%). So on a notional principal of $10 million, the financial institution would charge, typically, 0.03% of $10 million or $3000 for each year the swap was in operation. This amount is spread equally between the partners to the swap.

Example 12

Companies A and B each borrow $100 million. A borrows at a fixed rate of 6.1% per year and B borrows at the floating rate of six-monthly LIBOR + 50 basis points (LIBOR + 0.5%), with interest payments made twice a year.

A bank sets up a swap agreement between A and B. Under the terms of the swap, A pays six-monthly LIBOR and B pays 6% per year (Figure 5.29).

	A		B
Loan	Pays: 6.1%	Loan	Pays: LIBOR + 0.5%
Swap	Pays: LIBOR	Swap	Pays: 6%
	Receives: 6%		Receives: LIBOR
Overall	Pays: LIBOR + 0.1%	Overall	Pays 6.5%

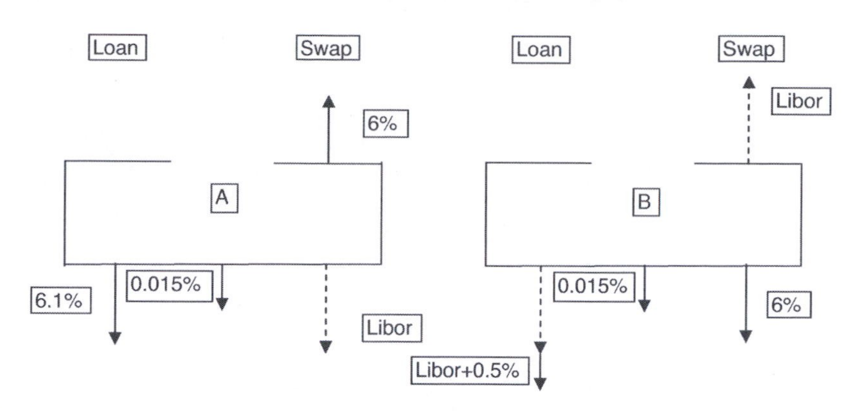

Figure 5.30

Now add in the financial institution. The financial institution charges 0.03% per year. A and B will each pay 0.015% per year to the bank (Figure 5.30).

	A		B
Loan	Pays: 6.1%	Loan	Pays: LIBOR + 0.5%
Swap	Pays: LIBOR + 0.015%	Swap	Pays: 6% + 0.015%
	Receives: 6%		Receives: LIBOR
Overall	Pays: LIBOR + 0.115%	Overall	Pays 6.515%

B. The second use of a swap that we describe concerns comparative advantage.

Comparative advantage

It might be possible for an alert swap specialist to observe two companies with different, but complementary, credit ratings.

Ibank and Jbank each want to borrow $100 million for three years. Ibank is demonstrably sound and will generally be offered lower borrowing rates than Jbank, which may, or may not – no one is very sure – have a problem with some outstanding loans. Ibank wants to borrow at a floating rate while Jbank, which might suddenly find itself vulnerable to credit scrutiny, is keen to borrow at a fixed rate.

The rates the banks have been offered are:

	Floating	Fixed
Ibank	LIBOR + 0.4%	8%
Jbank	LIBOR + 1.5%	10%

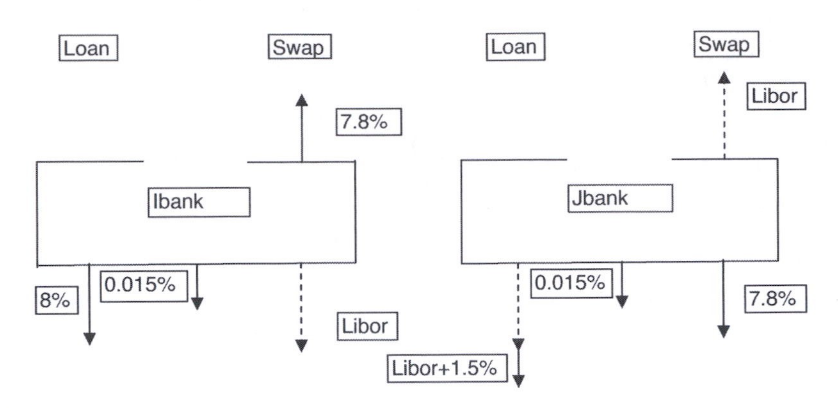

Figure 5.31

What is interesting here is that although Ibank has been offered more attractive rates than Jbank for both floating and fixed interest rates, the **difference** between the rates they have been offered is less for the floating rate (1.1%) than for the fixed rate (2%). This suggests that Jbank might have a slight advantage with floating rate (which it does not want) while Ibank might have a slight advantage with fixed rate borrowing (which it does not want either). An interest rate swap might be the answer.

So: Ibank takes out a loan of $100 million for three years at a **fixed** rate of 8% per year. Jbank takes out a loan of $100 million for three years at a **floating** rate of LIBOR + 1.5%. A swap is arranged. Ibank pays LIBOR (floating) to Jbank. Jbank pays 7.8% (fixed) to Ibank. Both banks pay 0.015% to the institution that arranged the swap (Figure 5.31).

The effect of this is:

	Ibank		Jbank
Loan	Pays: 8%	Loan	Pays: LIBOR + 1.5%
Swap	Pays: LIBOR + 0.015%	Swap	Pays: 7.8% + 0.015%
	Receives: 7.8%		Receives: LIBOR
Overall	Pays: LIBOR + 0.215%	Overall	Pays: 9.315%

So both banks, after the swap, are making interest payments that are smaller than they would have been had the swap not been arranged. This is truly a remarkable phenomenon. The name given to such an arrangement is **comparative advantage**.

There are questions about whether, in an arbitrage-free world, comparative advantage opportunities exist. One problem with the above is the assumption that the floating rate of LIBOR + 1.5% will operate throughout the period of the swap. In the floating rate market, the company lending the money usually has the opportunity to review the floating rate every six months. So in practice, if the creditworthiness of Jbank declined, the lender could increase the spread (1.5%) over LIBOR to produce a new floating rate. If this happened, the above structure might not look as attractive. Indeed, in extreme cases, the lender might refuse to roll over the loan for a further six months and in this case, the swap, as described above, would collapse. However, in less extreme circumstances, swaps can be used, as shown above, to obtain loans or to make investments at more attractive rates.

How swap rates are presented

In the financial pages, swap rates might be presented as shown in the table below. We see two rates for swaps of duration two through to five years. The swaps are against six-month LIBOR (so the time interval between exchanges is six months).

Maturity	Bid (%)	Ask (%)
2	3.16	3.19
3	3.62	3.66
4	3.96	3.99
5	4.23	4.27

Meaning of bid and ask:

1. If a party is entering a payers swap (pay fixed, receive floating), the **bid** rate is the fixed rate they would pay.

   If a party is entering a receivers swap (receive fixed, pay floating), the **ask** rate is the fixed rate they would receive.
2. It is the convention to take the swap rate for a maturity that is a whole number of years to be the average of the bid and the ask rate. So the swap rate for a maturity of two years will be $\frac{3.16+3.19}{2} = 3.175\%$. The swap rate for a maturity of three years will be $\frac{3.62+3.66}{2} = 3.64\%$.

   For a maturity of 2.5 years, the swap rate will be taken to be the average of the swap rate for two years and the swap rate for three years. So the swap rate for a maturity of 2.5 years will be $\frac{3.175+3.64}{2} = 3.4075$.

Maturity	Bid (%)	Ask (%)	Swap rate
2	3.16	3.19	3.175
2.5			3.4075
3	3.62	3.66	3.64
3.5			3.8075
4	3.96	3.99	3.975
4.5			4.1125
5	4.23	4.27	4.25

3. The rates given in the table are percentages per year using an actual/365 day count convention with payments exchanged semi-annually. When using 'real' data, care should be taken to discover the day count convention used and the time interval between exchanges.
4. The swaps on which these rates are based are entered on the first date of the swap. (This is at time T, the date on which the first LIBOR rate is set.) For a swap with a maturity of three years, the final exchange of cash takes place three years after this date, i.e. the swap has a tenor of three years.

One option for International Students would be to enter a payers interest rate swap at a fixed rate that would be acceptable to its financial situation. This would transform its uncertain floating rate interest payments into fixed rate payments and so determine at the outset the interest it would pay.

However, possibly the best solution for International Students would be to purchase a cap.

Caplets and caps

International Students wants to borrow £10 000 000 at a variable interest rate with interest payments made half yearly. It does not want the floating rate to rise above 8% per year. Hence, the most it can afford to pay, each half year, is £$0.5 \times 0.08 \times 10\,000\,000 =$ £400 000.

Suppose that for one particular interest payment, International Students has an agreement under which it will be paid the excess by which the interest payment exceeds £400 000. So if, for this particular payment, the floating rate is 8.5% per year, and International Students is required to make an interest payment of £$0.5 \times 0.085 \times 10\,000\,000 =$ £425 000, then, under the terms of the agreement, it would receive £25 000. But if the floating rate was 7.8% (making an interest payment of £390 000), it would receive nothing. International Students would make the interest payment in the usual way. Then, under the terms of the agreement, it would receive either the excess over £400 000 (if the interest payment was over £400 000) or nothing at all (if the interest payment was at or below £400 000). In this way, International Students would not pay more than £400 000 on this interest payment. Such an agreement is called a **caplet**.

So a caplet is an insurance on one interest payment against high interest rates. Suppose we have a caplet that protects us against the floating (LIBOR) rate L rising above an agreed rate (called the **strike rate**) K. In the above, $K = 8\%$. If the period between interest payments is 0.5 years and the loan is for £P, then on the day the interest payment is to be made, the caplet pays out

$0.5 \times L \times P - 0.5 \times K \times P$ if $L > K$

0 otherwise.

A **cap** is a sequence of caplets, one in place for each interest payment of the loan. So a cap provides, for the duration of the loan, an insurance on each payment against high interest rates. On each payment date, a cap pays out:

$\alpha \times L \times P - \alpha \times K \times P$ if $L > K$

0 otherwise.

Here, α is the interval between interest payments.

If it bought a cap, then on **every** payment date International Students would receive the excess of the interest payment over £400 000 (if this is positive) and nothing if the interest payment was less than or equal to £400 000. This agreement would ensure it would never have to pay more than £400 000.

Alternatively, a cap is a payers swap where each exchange payment is executed only if it has positive value.

A cap, offering insurance, has a value. A cap is more difficult to price than any of the products considered so far. We will indicate a method for pricing a cap in Chapter 7.

Floorlets and floors

You have made an investment (£100 000) and you are using the interest payments for some specific purpose – university fees, medical insurance. It would be inconvenient if a particular interest payment fell below the amount needed. A **floorlet** provides insurance against a single payment falling below the **strike rate** of (say) 6.5%. On payment day, you would hope to receive at least £0.5 × 0.065 × 100 000 = £3250. If, on this day, the floating rate lies below the strike rate, a floorlet will pay out the amount the interest payment lies below that calculated from the strike rate; if the floating rate is greater than or equal to the strike rate, a floorlet will pay out nothing. So if the floating rate was 6.2%, you would receive an interest payment of £0.5 × 0.062 × 100 000 = £3100 and the floorlet would pay you £150. If the floating rate was 6.5%, the floorlet would pay you nothing. A floorlet ensures you will receive at least £3250 on this payment.

A **floor** is a sequence of floorlets, one in place for each interest payment of the investment. A floor provides, for the duration of the investment, an insurance on each interest payment and ensures that you will receive at least a sum calculated on the strike rate. On each payment date, a floor pays out:

$$\alpha \times K \times P - \alpha \times L \times P \quad \text{if} \quad K > L$$

$$0 \quad \text{otherwise.}$$

Here, α is the interval between interest payments.

Alternatively, a floor is a receivers swap where each exchange payment is executed only if it has positive value.

Floors are priced in the same way as caps – the method is indicated in Chapter 7.

A cap with strike rate 8% (per year) is probably the best answer to International Students' dilemma.

We now introduce a second interest rate futures contract (the first was the US Treasury bond futures contract in Chapter 4, section 4.6). This is the Eurodollar futures contract. Our immediate purpose is the construction of the zero curve in section 5.6. However, we use information provided by Eurodollar futures contracts in the zero curve precisely because of the huge volume of trading in these contracts. It has been estimated that in excess of 1 200 000 Eurodollar futures contracts are traded daily on the Chicago Merchantile Exchange. Clearly, Eurodollar futures contracts are of enormous importance in the financial world.

5.4 Eurodollar futures contracts (introduced on the CME in 1981)

First, we describe Eurodollars.

Eurodollars and the Eurodollar interest rate

A **Eurodollar** is a dollar deposited in a commercial bank outside the United States (and so not subject to US banking regulations). The bank could be in Singapore or Calcutta, so the title Eurodollar is a little misleading. **The three-month (90-day) Eurodollar interest rate** is the rate of interest earned when one bank deposits Eurodollars for 90 days in another bank. This interest rate is compounded quarterly and uses an actual/360 day count convention. The Eurodollar interest rate is essentially the same as the three-month LIBOR rate.

A Eurodollar futures contract

A three-month Eurodollar futures contract is a futures contract based on the three-month Eurodollar interest rate. Prices are quoted for delivery months of March, June, September and December and for up to ten years in the future. (Additionally, the CME trades short maturity contracts for some other months.)

Suppose you buy/sell a September 2010 three-month Eurodollar futures contract. You are contracting, nominally, to buy/sell Eurodollars on the agreed delivery date in September 2010. The size of the contract (the number of Eurodollars you are contracting to buy or sell) is based on $1 000 000 and the three-month Eurodollar rate R that is declared on delivery day in September 2010. The contract size is $1 000 000 minus the interest that would accrue if one million Eurodollars were invested at rate R for three months. We will say more about this in 'The settlement procedure', below. As usual, a **long** Eurodollar futures contract is an agreement to **buy** Eurodollars; a **short** Eurodollar futures contract is a contract to **sell** Eurodollars.

Note: Money is not actually bought or sold on the delivery date. This is a nominal principal. What is of interest to those in the market is the changing interest rate affecting such a transaction. Just as with a swap, where the nominal principal is not exchanged at the maturity of the swap, so in a Eurodollar futures contract Eurodollars are not bought or sold on the delivery date.

This is a futures contract. There is no cost on entry, but you will have a margin account containing, initially, the initial margin. A maintenance margin level will be set. The contract will have a value at the time it is entered and at the end of each trading day, margin accounts will be marked to market. If the value of the contract has risen, money will be paid into the margin account of the holder of the long contract and withdrawn from the margin account of the holder of the short contract. If the value has fallen, the direction of the money will be reversed. With the size of one contract based on $1 000 000, the initial margin in each contract will be a percentage (usually around 10%) of $1 000 000. Maintenance margin is often in the region of 75% of the initial margin.

Eventually, one of the following must happen:

(i) The contract is closed out. (The holder of a long contract will enter an otherwise identical short contract; the holder of a short contract will enter an otherwise identical long contract.)

(ii) The contract is held on delivery day in September 2010. On delivery day, the final marking to market takes place and the contract is settled in cash.

Now for the details.

The value of a Eurodollar futures contract

The quoted futures price

For each Eurodollar futures contract, there will be a quoted futures price. See for example page 230. Suppose the futures price for a September 2010 contract is 96.35.

Value of contract

For a quoted futures price q, the value of one futures contract is $10\,000[100 - \frac{1}{4}(100 - q)]$.

So with a price of 96.35 being quoted for a September 2010 contract, the value of one September 2010 Eurodollar futures contract is:

$$10\,000\left[100 - \frac{1}{4}(100 - 96.35)\right] = \$990\,875.$$

Note: this method of pricing a Eurodollar futures contract was originally intended to make the contract price behave in a similar manner to the value of a bond in that an increase in price would correspond to a decrease in the interest rate.

Example 13

Al buys a Eurodollar futures contract. Initial margin is set at \$100 000; the maintenance margin is \$75 000. The quoted price (or the settlement price, on that day) at the end of each of five successive trading days is shown in the table.

	Quoted price (q)	Contract value (V)	$V_1 - V_2$	Margin account
End of 1st day	93.48	983 700		100 000
End of 2nd day	92.31	980 775	2925	97 075
End of 3rd day	94.62	986 550	−5775	102 850
End of 4th day	95.85	989 625	−3075	105 925
End of 5th day	94.79	986 975	2650	103 275

The value of the contract over successive days is shown in column 3. Column 4 gives successive differences. In column 4, we see the amounts that would be deducted from Al's margin account and paid to the exchange (which would then credit this amount to the margin account of the party with the short contract). A negative figure indicates that this sum was paid into Al's margin account.

At the end of the 5th day, Al closed out his position (by selling an identical Eurodollar futures contract). There were no margin calls and Al paid the exchange, overall, $V_1 - V_5 = 983\,700 - 986\,975$
$= -3275.$

So Al made a profit, over the five days' trading, of \$3275.

The settlement procedure

Delivery day: this is the third Wednesday of the delivery month. So for a September 2010 three-month Eurodollar futures contract, delivery day would be the third Wednesday of September 2010.

Settlement value: suppose the contract runs through to maturity. If the three-month Eurodollar interest rate on delivery day is R% (R is compounded quarterly and uses an actual/360 day count convention), take $q = 100 - R$. The contract value on delivery day is
$10\,000[100 - \frac{1}{4}(100 - q)] = 10\,000[100 - \frac{1}{4}R]$.

So if the three-month Eurodollar rate on the third Wednesday of September 2010 was 5.28%, the value of the contract for the final marking to market would be $10\,000[100 - \frac{1}{4} \times 5.28] = \$986\,800$. The final marking to market settles the contract.

Pointer to the future

If q is a Eurodollar futures quote, then (100 – q)% is the value the market places today on the three-month Eurodollar interest rate starting on delivery day. So today's quote for a September 2010 Eurodollar futures contract of 96.35 indicates that the market estimates the three-month rate on the third Wednesday of September 2010 will be 3.65%. In this way, a Eurodollar futures quote can be used to obtain an estimate of a future three-month interest rate (Figure 5.32). We will use this in section 5.5 to construct a more sophisticated version of the zero curve.

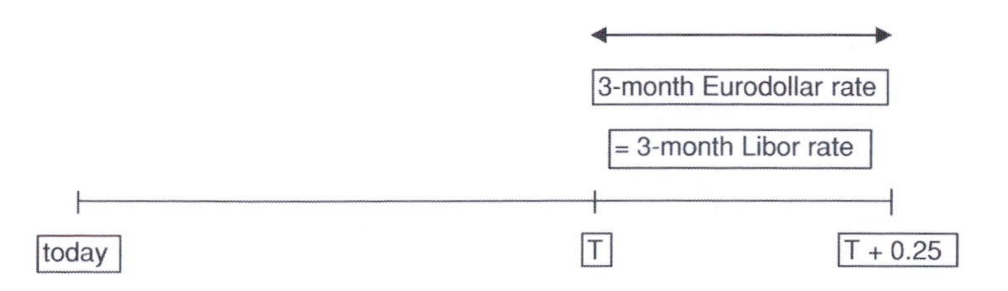

Figure 5.32

Notes:

1. If $r = 100 - q$ is the value the market places today on the three-month Eurodollar interest rate starting on delivery day, then an increase in the quoted price (q) will correspond to a decrease in the interest rate (r). And conversely.

   $r = 5.6\%$ Contract value = 983 750

   $r = 5\%$ Contract value = 987 500

   So the value of a Eurodollar futures contract does behave in a similar way to the value of a bond.

2. $$\begin{aligned} 10\,000[100 - \tfrac{1}{4}R] &= 1\,000\,000 - 10\,000 \times \tfrac{1}{4}R \\ &= 1\,000\,000 - 1\,000\,000 \times \tfrac{1}{4} \times \tfrac{R}{100} \end{aligned}$$

Hence, as mentioned earlier, the contract value at maturity is \$1 000 000 *reduced* by the interest that would accrue if one million Eurodollars were invested for three months at the three-month Eurodollar rate declared on the delivery date.

Who buys a Eurodollar futures contract?

As observed above, an investor who has bought a Eurodollar futures contract makes a profit if the contract increases in value. But the contract increases in value if the Eurodollar rate falls.

Buy a Eurodollar futures contract if you think the interest rate is likely to fall (go long).

Who sells a Eurodollar futures contract?

If you sell a Eurodollar futures contract, you make a profit if the value of the contract falls. The contract falls in value if the interest rate rises.

Sell a Eurodollar futures contract if you think the interest rate is going to rise (go short).

5.5 The zero curve

Our purpose is to construct a graph which will illustrate interest rates for maturities up to eight years. These rates will be determined by today's market conditions. We will use LIBOR rates for short-term maturities. Among the most widely traded financial instruments are Eurodollar futures contracts, swaps and US Treasury bond futures contracts. Precisely because these instruments are so fluid (widely traded) we can have confidence that their prices will accurately reflect market conditions today.

We will construct our zero curve (or, to give it its correct name, the LIBOR zero curve) from LIBOR rates (out to one year), Eurodollar futures contracts (one year out to two years), Swaps (two years out to five years) and US Treasury bonds (out to eight years). We will use the following notation in this section.

Notation All interest rates represented in this zero curve will be **continuously compounded** rates.

The rates used to form the zero curve will use an actual/365 day count convention. However, to ease calculations, whenever it is reasonable to do so, we shall write three months $= \frac{1}{4}$ year and six months $= \frac{1}{2}$ year. In the real world, three months might appear as $\frac{91}{365}$ years and six months as $\frac{181}{365}$ years.

Because the letters T and S are used as swap dates, we will use t and s to represent the maturities of interest rates.

We will need four intermediate results, two of which are of interest in their own right.

(1) **The US$ LIBOR rate, L, is simply compounded and uses an actual/360 day count convention. To calculate the equivalent continuously compounded rate operating with actual/365 day count convention.**

We have: L uses an actual/360 day count convention.

So $\widehat{L} = \text{L} \times \frac{365}{360}$ uses actual/365 day count convention $[\frac{91}{360} \times \text{L} = \frac{91}{365} \times \widehat{L}]$

Both L and $\widehat{L}$ are simply compounded.

Let R be the equivalent continuously compounded rate.

$e^{Rt} = 1 + t \times \widehat{L}$ where t is calculated using an actual/365 day count convention.

Take the ln of both sides.

$\text{R}t = \ln(1 + \text{t} \times \widehat{L})$.

$$\text{Giving R} = \frac{1}{t} \times \ln(1 + \text{t} \times \widehat{L}).$$

(2) **To convert a futures rate into the corresponding continuously compounded forward rate.**

The three-month Eurodollar futures interest rate F is compounded quarterly and uses an actual/360 day count convention. The first step is to convert this rate into a continuously compounded rate, R, using an actual/365 day count convention.

As in (1), $\widehat{F} = \mathrm{F} \times \frac{365}{360}$ uses an actual/365 day count convention.
Let R be the equivalent continuously compounded rate.
Then $\mathrm{e}^{Rt} = (1 + \frac{\widehat{F}}{4})^{4t}$
Take the *t*th root of both sides.

$$\mathrm{e}^{R} = \left(1 + \frac{\widehat{F}}{4}\right)^{4}$$

Take the ln of both sides:

$$R = \ln\left(1 + \frac{\widehat{F}}{4}\right)^{4} = 4 \times \ln\left(1 + \frac{\widehat{F}}{4}\right)$$

Within the first year, we can take the forward rate to be the same as the corresponding futures interest rate. But when we look at the second and subsequent years, there is a problem. Marking to market introduces a distortion and to calculate the forward rate corresponding to each time period, a correction term, known as a convexity adjustment, must be used.

We use: Forward rate = futures rate $- \frac{1}{2}\sigma^{2}\mathrm{ts}$ (5.1)

where

(i) the forward rate and the futures rate are continuously compounded rates.
(ii) σ is the standard deviation of the change in the short-term rate in one year. A typical value of σ is 0.012 (this represents a standard deviation of 1.2%).
(iii) t is the time to the maturity of the futures contract and s is the time to the maturity of the interest rate underlying the futures contract. So with a three-month Eurodollar futures contract, $\mathrm{s} = \mathrm{t} + \frac{1}{4}$.

Example 14

It is March 2005. The quoted price for a March 2006 three-month Eurodollar futures contract is 97.32. Taking $\sigma = 0.012$, calculate the forward rate for the three-month period starting in March 2006.

Solution

The required futures rate (March 2006 to June 2006) is 100 − 97.32 = 2.68%.

This rate is compounded quarterly and uses an actual/360 day count convention.

Step 1. Express this rate using actual/365 and in continuously compounded form:

(i) $2.68\times\frac{365}{360} = 2.7172\%$ is compounded quarterly and uses an actual/365 day count convention.

(ii) The equivalent continuously compounded form is:

$$R = 4 \times \ln\left(1 + \frac{0.027172}{4}\right)$$
$$= 0.027080$$

The continuously compounded futures rate is 2.708%.

Step 2. Apply equation 5.1 with $\sigma = 0.012$, $t = 1$ and $s = 1.25$.

$$\text{Forward rate} = 0.027080 - \frac{1}{2} \times 0.012^2 \times 1 \times 1.25$$
$$= 0.02699$$

The continuously compounded forward LIBOR rate March 2006–June 2006 is 2.699%.

(3) **Let K be the fixed rate in a receivers swap. The swap has notional principal \$P, an accrual period of six months and is set up at time T, the first of the swap dates and the date the first six-month LIBOR rate is set. Payments are exchanged every six months. Let B be a coupon bond paying out \$P at maturity and whose coupon payments match exactly the fixed leg of the swap. Hence, each coupon payment is \$0.5 × K × P. Then the value of the bond at time T is \$P. (This makes K the par yield of the bond.)**

Proof

The receivers swap makes payments as shown in Figure 5.33.

Let each party make a payment of \$P at maturity (Figure 5.34).

This will not change the value of this swap at time T.

Hence: value of swap at time T = value fixed payments + P − (value floating payments + P).

As we have seen, the value of the swap at the time it is set up (at T) is zero.

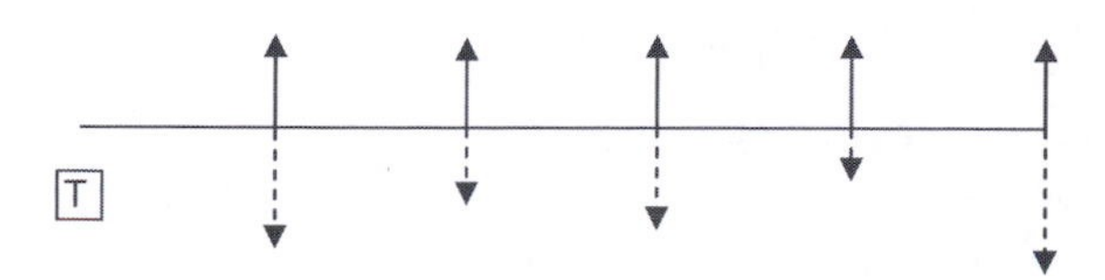

Figure 5.33

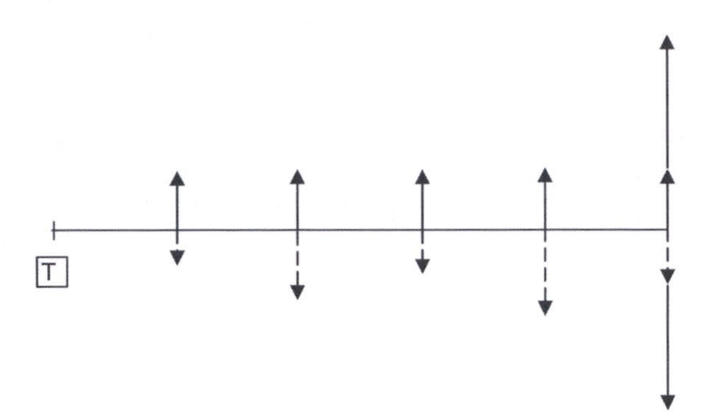

Figure 5.34

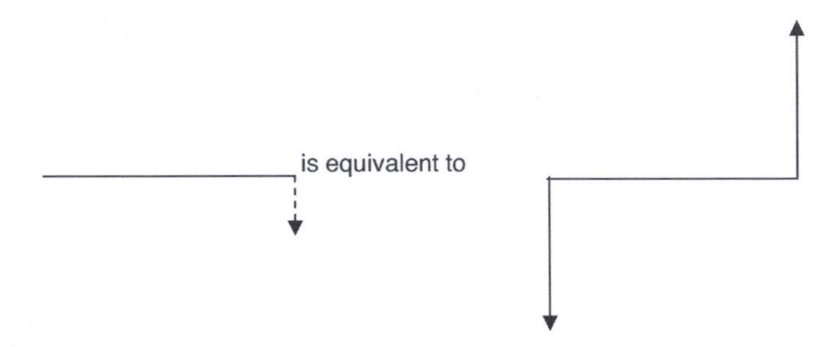

Figure 5.35

Therefore: value fixed payments + P = value floating payments + P.

Consider each side of this equation separately:

The set of fixed payments + P matches exactly the payments from the bond.

This gives: value (time T) of the fixed payments + P = value of bond at time T.

For the floating payments, we use the old trick of replacing each floating rate payment by the payment (six months earlier) and receipt (today) of $P (Figure 5.35).

Then, we see that the floating rate payments + P are equivalent to a single payment of $P at time T (Figure 5.36).

Putting the two sides together, we have: value of bond at time T = $P.

Since the value of the coupon bond at time T is precisely the notional principal P, this makes K the par yield of this bond.

(4) **Bootstrapping (a reminder of the method)**

Suppose we know the interest rates for all maturities up to two years. We want to know the interest rate for a maturity of 2.5 years. The method is: find a coupon-paying bond making semi-annual coupon payments (the first

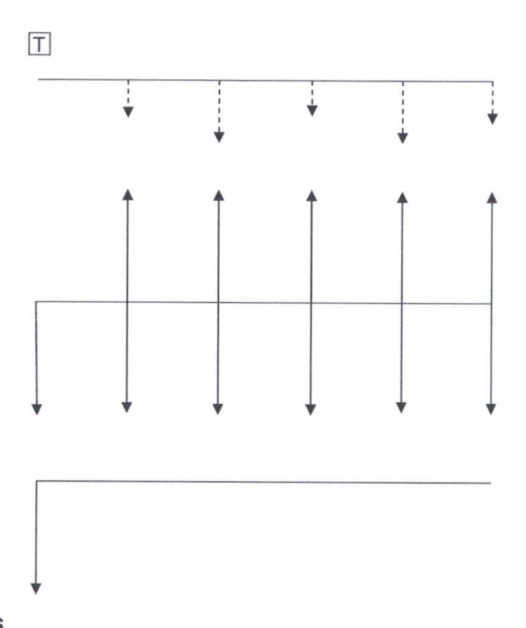

Figure 5.36

payment is made in six months' time) and having a maturity of 2.5 years. The value of this bond is known. Calculate the value today of all payments from the bond, using known interest rates for payments up to two years ahead and the unknown interest rate R for the payment made after 2.5 years. The sum of all such present values must be (or create arbitrage) today's value of the bond. Solve the resulting equation for R.

Construction of the zero curve

Maturity	Rate used	What must be done
Up to one year	LIBOR	Write simply compounded rates in continuously compounded form
One year up to two years	Eurodollar futures rate	Transform (continuously compounded) futures rates into forward rates. Find the interest rates compatible with these forward rates.
Two years up to five years	Swap rates	Use swap rates as par yields of suitable bonds. Bootstrap.
More than five years	US Treasury bond yields	Bootstrap

To illustrate, we construct the LIBOR zero curve for today, 21 March 2005. We will calculate interest rates with maturity up to eight years.

Maturities out to one year

LIBOR rates are quoted for each trading day in the press. The LIBOR rates for 21 March 2005 are shown below.

US$ LIBOR	
Overnight	2.72750
1 month	2.85
3 months	3.05
6 months	3.3
1 year	3.6925

LIBOR rates are simply compounded. The US$ LIBOR rate uses an actual/360 day count convention. As in (1), calculate the equivalent rate using an actual/365 day count convention, then calculate the equivalent continuously compounded rate.

To illustrate, the three-month US$ LIBOR rate is 3.05% per year.

$$
\begin{aligned}
\mathrm{L} &= 0.0305 \\
\widehat{L} &= 0.0305 \times \frac{365}{360} = 0.03092 \\
\mathrm{R} &= \frac{1}{t} \times \ln(1 + t \times \widehat{L}) \\
&= \frac{1}{0.25} \times \ln(1 + 0.25 \times 0.03092) = 0.03080
\end{aligned}
$$

The continuously compounded three-month rate is 3.080%.

These calculations are very straightforward in Excel. In Table 5.1, we show the interest rates for other maturities and how the calculations might be carried out.

Note that maturity, LIBOR and LIBOR365 are range names.

Maturities one year out to two years

We use Eurodollar futures contracts. On 21 March 2005, these were as shown below.

Eurodollar 3m futures	
Jun	96.51
Sept	96.12
Dec	95.86
Mar	95.60
Jun	95.50
Sept	95.42
Dec	95.35
Mar	95.30

Table 5.1

Microsoft Excel - Table5.1

File Edit View Insert Format Tools Data Window Help

Arial 10

Reply with Changes... End Review...

Text Box 1

	A	B	C	D	E	F
1	Table5.1				for 21st March, 2005	
2						
3	US$ Libor					
4						
5	Maturity	maturity	Libor	Libor365	rateC	
6						
7						
8	Over night	0.0027	2.7275	2.765381944	0.027652787	
9	1 month	0.0833	2.85	2.889583333	0.028861113	
10	3 months	0.25	3.05	3.092361111	0.03080469	
11	6 months	0.5	3.3	3.345833333	0.033181551	
12	12 months	1	3.6925	3.743784722	0.036754065	
13						
14			=Libor*365/360		=LN(1+maturity*Libor365/100)/maturity	
15						
16						
17						

To illustrate the method, we will look at a Eurodollar futures contract with one year to maturity and use the quoted price of this contract to calculate the three-month forward rate March 2006 through to June 2006. This forward rate will then be used to calculate the interest rate for a maturity of 1.25 years.

(i) Observe a three-month Eurodollar futures contract which matures in 12 months. From the table, the quoted futures price is 95.60. So the three-month Eurodollar futures rate March 2006–June 2006 is 4.4%.

(ii) Use (2) above to calculate the equivalent continuously compounded rate.

$$F = 4.4 \quad \widehat{F} = 4.4 \times \frac{365}{360} = 4.4611 \text{ (}\widehat{F}\text{ uses an actual/365 day count)}$$

$$R = 4 \times \ln\left(1 + \frac{0.044611}{4}\right)$$
$$= 0.04436$$

(iii) Use (2) above to calculate the corresponding forward rate.

$$\text{Forward rate} = \text{futures rate} - \frac{1}{2}\sigma^2 1 \times 1.25$$
$$= 0.04436 - \frac{1}{2} \times 0.012^2 \times 1 \times 1.25$$
$$= 0.04427$$

(iv) In section 5.1 we showed that the forward rate r (continuously compounded) is given by:

$$r = \frac{r_s \times s - r_t \times t}{s - t}$$

where r_t is the rate with maturity t and r_s is the rate with maturity s.
But $r = 0.04427$, $t = 1$, $s = 1.25$ and, from Table 5.1, $r_t = 0.03675$.
We know everything in the equation except r_s.

Rearranging:

$$r_s = \frac{r(s - t) + r_t \times t}{s}$$

$$= \frac{0.04427 \times 0.25 + 0.03675 \times 1}{1.25}$$

$$= 0.03825$$

The continuously compounded rate for a maturity of 1.25 years is 3.825%. Now we have the continuously compounded rate for a maturity 1.25 years, we can start the entire process again and calculate the rate with maturity 1.5 years and so on through to two years. These rates (and a method for calculating them) are shown in Table 5.2.

The entry in G9 was copied in from the 12-month maturity interest rate in Table 5.1. Note that timeyrs, quotedprice, futrate, futrateC and fwdrateC are all range names.

Maturities greater than two years and up to five years

US$ swap rates are used. Swap rates for 21 March 2005 are as shown below.

Interest rate swaps (US$)	Bid	Ask
1 year	3.68	3.71
2 years	4.08	4.11
3 years	4.29	4.33
4 years	4.44	4.47
5 years	4.54	4.58
6 years	4.63	4.66
7 years	4.70	4.74
8 years	4.78	4.80

Method:

(i) Calculate (as shown in section 5.3) swap rates associated with 2.5 years, 3 years, 3.5 years, and so on out to 5 years.

Table 5.2

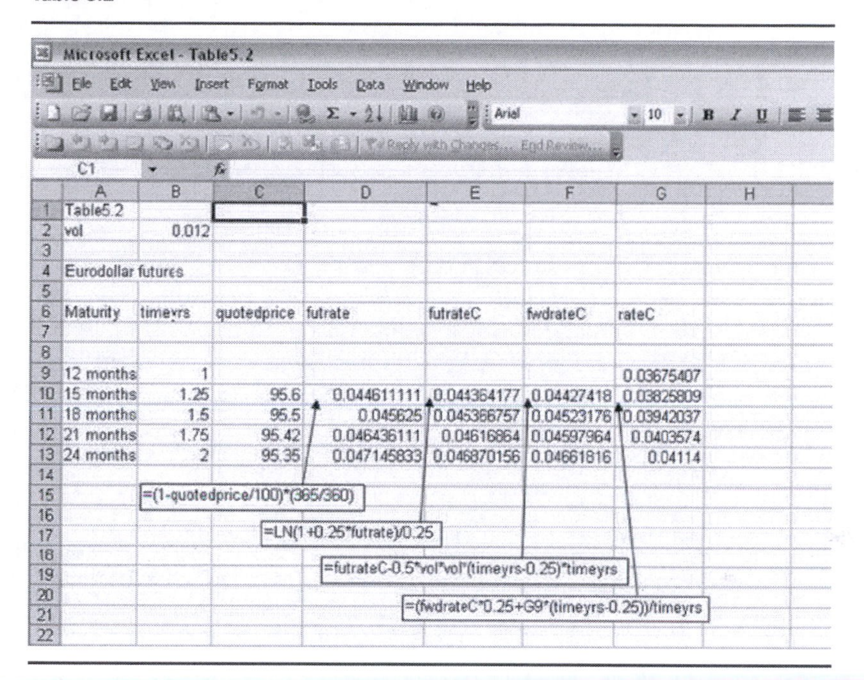

	A	B	C	D	E	F	G
1	Table5.2						
2	vol	0.012					
3							
4	Eurodollar futures						
5							
6	Maturity	timeyrs	quotedprice	futrate	futrateC	fwdrateC	rateC
7							
8							
9	12 months	1					0.03675407
10	15 months	1.25	95.6	0.044611111	0.044364177	0.04427418	0.03825809
11	18 months	1.5	95.5	0.045625	0.045366757	0.04523176	0.03942037
12	21 months	1.75	95.42	0.046436111	0.04616864	0.04597964	0.0403574
13	24 months	2	95.35	0.047145833	0.046870156	0.04661816	0.04114

=(1-quotedprice/100)*(365/360)

=LN(1+0.25*futrate)/0.25

=futrateC-0.5*vol*vol*(timeyrs-0.25)*timeyrs

=(fwdrateC*0.25+G9*(timeyrs-0.25))/timeyrs

(ii) Consider the swap rate for 2.5 years. Now consider a receivers swap having this percentage as the fixed rate. The accrual period of the swap is six months, the first exchange takes place in six months' time and the swap has a tenor of 2.5 years.

(iii) By (3) above, there is a bond (face value = \$100) whose coupon payments match the fixed leg of the swap and whose value, today, is the face value of the bond (\$100).

(iv) By (4) above, we can use a bootstrapping technique to find the interest rate associated with a maturity of 2.5 years.

(i) The table giving swap rates for two years out to five years is shown below.

Interest rate swaps (US$)	Bid	Ask	Swap rate
2 years	4.08	4.11	4.095 (average of bid, ask)
2.5 years			4.2025 (average of 2y, 3y)
3 years	4.29	4.33	4.31
3.5 years			4.3825
4 years	4.44	4.47	4.455
4.5 years			4.5075
5 years	4.54	4.58	4.56

(ii) and (iii) The 2.5-year swap rate is 4.2025%. Consider a bond (face value $100) paying a semi-annual coupon of 4.2025% per year. The first coupon ($2.10125) is paid out in six months' time; the final coupon (with the principal) is paid out two years later. By (3) above, the value of this bond, today, is $100.

The table below shows the cash flows from the bond and the interest rates pertinent to these maturities.

Maturity	Cash payment	Interest rate (cont. comp.)
0.5	2.10125	0.03318
1	2.10125	0.03675
1.5	2.10125	0.03942
2	2.10125	0.04114
2.5	102.10125	R

(iv) The present value of all cash payments is 100. Hence:

$$2.10125 \times e^{-0.03318\times 0.5} + 2.10125 \times e^{-0.03675\times 1} + 2.10125 \times e^{-0.03942\times 1.5} + 2.10125 \times e^{-0.04114\times 2} + 102.10125 \times e^{-R\times 2.5} = 100$$

We can write this as (this bit of algebra explains the Excel spreadsheet in Table 5.3):

$$2.10125 \times (e^{-0.03318\times 0.5} + e^{-0.03675\times 1} + e^{-0.03942\times 1.5} + e^{-0.04114\times 2}) + 102.10125 \times e^{-R\times 2.5} = 100$$

The terms in the brackets are the discount factors for maturities 0.5 years, 1 year, 1.5 years and 2 years.

$$2.10125 \times (\text{sum discount factors}) + 102.10125 \times e^{-R\times 2.5} = 100$$

$$e^{-R\times 2.5} = [100 - 2.10125 \times (\text{sum discount factors})]/102.10125^{*}$$

ln both sides:

$$-R \times 2.5 = \ln(\text{RightHandSideoflineabove})$$

$$R = -\frac{\ln(\mathit{RightHandSideoflineabove})}{2.5}$$

$$= 0.04171$$

This gives the interest rate for a maturity of 2.5 years.

Now we know interest rates for all maturities through to 2.5 years. The process starts again and calculates the interest rate for a maturity of three

Table 5.3

Microsoft Excel - Table5.3

File Edit View Insert Format Tools Data Window Help

D90

	A	B	C	D	E	F	G	H
1	Table5.3							
2	US$ swap rates							
3								
4								
5	maturity	swaprate	val	rateC	EXP(-rateC*maturity)			
6	0							
7	0.5			0.03318	0.9835189			
8	1			0.03676	0.9639171			
9	1.5			0.03942	0.9425862			
10	2			0.04114	0.921014			
11	2.5	4.2025	100	0.041705316	0.900989			
12	3	4.31		0.042799795	0.879592			
13	3.5	4.3825		0.043537874	0.8586597			
14	4	4.455		0.044284973	0.8376626			
15	4.5	4.5075		0.044825245	0.817329			
16	5	4.56		0.045372819	0.7970251			
17								
18								
19								
20								
21								
22								
23								

=-LN((val-0.5*swaprate*SUM($E$7:$E10))/(val+0.5*swaprate))/maturity

years and so on out to five years. This is best performed on a computer and the results are shown in Table 5.3.

Here, the interest rates for maturities out to two years (D7:D10) are copied from Table 5.2. Maturity (colA), swaprate (colB), rateC (colD) are range names. Column E contains the discount factors $e^{-rateC \times maturity}$. We can write equation * as:

$$e^{-R \times 2.5} = [100 - 2.10125 \times (\mathrm{SUM}(E7 : E10))]/102.10125$$

ln both sides. Then:

$$-R \times 2.5 = \ln([100 - 2.10125 \times (\mathrm{SUM}(E7 : E10))]/102.10125)$$

$$R = -\ln([100 - 2.10125 \times (\mathrm{SUM}(E7 : E10))]/102.10125)/2.5$$

This explains the Excel formula for column D in Table 5.3.

Maturities greater than five years and out to eight years

Use US Treasury bonds. Interest rates out to five years are known. Select a US Treasury bond which pays its first coupon in six months' time and matures in 5.5 years. Use this bond (and bootstrapping) to calculate the interest rate pertinent to a maturity of 5.5 years.

Now, interest rates out to 5.5 years are known. Select a US Treasury bond which pays its first coupon in six months' time and matures in six years. Calculate the interest rate for a maturity of six years, and so on. We illustrate the calculation for the 5.5-year maturity.

The bonds:

US Treasury bonds	Coupon rate	Price today
5.5 years	5.02	102
6 years	5.5	104.1
6.5 years	6.3	108.4
7 years	5.5	103.7
7.5 years	4.98	99.8
8 years	5.96	106

The 5.5-year bond pays a semi-annual coupon of \$2.51. The value of this bond, today, is \$102. The present value of all the cash payments from the bond must be \$102. Let the interest rate with a 5.5-year maturity be R.

Hence:

$$2.51 \times e^{-0.03318\times 0.5} + 2.51 \times e^{-0.03675\times 1} + \cdots + 2.51 \times e^{-0.04537\times 5}$$
$$+ 102.51 \times e^{-R\times 5.5} = 102$$

Again, on the Left Hand Side, the coupon is multiplied by a succession of discount factors. We can write:

$$2.51 \times (\text{sum of discount factors}) + 102.51 \times e^{-R\times 5.5} = 102$$
$$102.51 \times e^{-R\times 5.5} = 102 - 2.51 \times (\text{sum discount factors})$$
$$e^{-R\times 5.5} = \frac{102 - 2.51 \times (sumdiscountfactors)}{102.51}$$

ln both sides:

$$-R \times 5.5 = \ln(\text{RightHandSide})$$
$$R = -\frac{ln(RightHandSide)}{5.5}$$
$$= 0.04586 \text{ or } 4.586\%.$$

Table 5.4

Microsoft Excel - Table5.4

File Edit View Insert Format Tools Data Window Help

Arial

Reply with Changes... End Review...

E18 fx

	A	B	C	D	E	F	G	H
1								
2	Table5.4							
3	US Treasury Bonds				=SUM($E$7:$E$16) in Table5.3			
4								
5	maturity	couponrate	bondval	rateC	8.902233			
6	5.5	5.02	102	0.045864	0.77705	=EXP(-rateC*maturity)		
7	6	5.5	104.1	0.047042	0.754082			
8	6.5	6.3	108.4	0.047937	0.732282			
9	7	5.5	103.7	0.048845	0.710408			
10	7.5	4.98	99.8	0.050401	0.685224			
11	8	5.96	106	0.05084	0.665832			
12								
13	=-LN((bondval-0.5*couponrate*SUM($E$5:E5))/(100+0.5*couponrate))/maturity							
14								
15								
16								

The reader will now be very sure that these calculations are best carried out by computer. A spreadsheet showing the remaining calculations is shown in Table 5.4.

In the spreadsheet, maturity (colA), couponrate (colB), bondval (colC) and rateC (colD) are all range names.

The sum of the discount factors up to five years (SUM(E7:E16)) is written in E23. The calculation in D24 is as illustrated above (and very similar to that shown in Table 5.3).

The zero curve plots interest rates against their maturities. In Figure 5.37, we have allowed Excel to plot the graph. Some feel that the calculated points should be joined by a sequence of straight lines (linear interpolation), others take the view that cubic splines should be used. Useful and interesting references can be found on the Bank of England's website: www.bankofengland.co.uk/statistics/yieldcurve. The bank also offers an email address for comments and queries: yieldcurve@bankofengland.co.uk.

The Excel version of our LIBOR zero curve is shown in Figure 5.37.

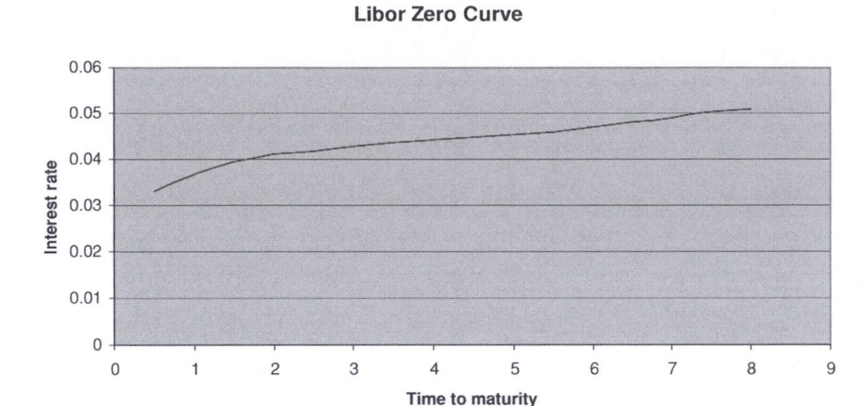

Figure 5.37

Exercise 5

1. The interest rate for a one-year loan is 5.5%; for a two-year loan the interest rate is 6.0%, both rates being continuously compounded. What will be the one-year rate set in one year's time? (Find f[1, 2].)

2. Today is 4 May 2005. Interest rates with maturities one year out to five years are as shown below.

Maturity (years)	Interest rate % (continuously compounded)
1	4.5
2	4.9
3	5.2
4	5.4
5	5.6

Calculate (i) the forward rate for two-year borrowing on 4 May 2006.
(ii) the forward rate for two-year borrowing on 4 May 2007.
(iii) the rate we might expect for a three-year loan taken out on 4 May 2007.

3. The interest rate for two-yearly borrowing is 5.8%, compounded annually. The rate for three-year borrowing is 6.4%, compounded annually. Find the one-year forward rate (annually compounded) for the third year.

4. Money can be borrowed at 3.8% (compounded semi-annually) for 2.5 years and at 4.2% (compounded quarterly) for three years. What is the six-months forward rate starting in 2.5 years' time?

5. The interest rate table gives interest rates with maturities out to two years. The interest rates are continuously compounded.

Maturity (years)	Interest rate (continuously compounded)
0.5	5.1
1	5.2
1.5	5.3
2	5.35

   (i) Describe carefully how today you could arrange to invest money in six months' time with an 18-month maturity.
   (ii) Calculate the one-year forward rate which will begin in one year's time. How would you arrange to borrow $25 000 in one year's time, for one year, at the one-year forward rate? Check that the interest rate paid is indeed the one-year forward rate.
   (iii) Describe how, in six months' time, you could invest $100 000 for 18 months at a rate known today. What is this rate?

6. The interest rate with a three-year maturity is 6.2%, compounded annually. The interest rate with a four-year maturity is 6.5% (compounded annually).
   (i) What is the one-year forward rate (compounded annually) for the period starting at the end of year three and going through to the end of year four? Describe carefully how today money could be invested from the beginning of the fourth year for one year at this rate.
   (ii) Describe carefully the arrangements to be made today that would lead to a loan of £10 000 at the beginning of the fourth year, for one year, at the rate f[3, 4].

7. What is a forward rate agreement? Why does a forward rate agreement need to specify two dates? What happens on the first date and what is this first date called? What is the second date called? Why might a day count convention be important in a forward rate agreement? What is the notional principal? What is (i) a payers FRA, (ii) a receivers FRA?

8. A forward rate agreement is set up today. The safe rate at which money can be borrowed or invested is 5% (continuously compounded). The notional principal is £1 000 000. The reset date is in three months' time, with the payment date six months later. The fixed rate is 3.5% (simply compounded). What is the value of this FRA today?

9. An FRA is set up today. What rule or principle, other than the absence of arbitrage, is used to determine the fixed rate K?

10. An FRA has reset date T, payment date S and fixed rate K. The time period between the reset date and the payment date is α. Show that the value of the FRA at time t ($t < T$) is given by: value $= B(0, T) - (1 + \alpha K)B(0, S)$.

11. An FRA initially has zero value. Why does the value of an FRA change as time progresses?

12. Why might anyone want to enter an FRA?

13. In three months' time, Eza will take out a loan of £5 000 000 for six months at the six-month floating rate in force in three months' time. He would prefer the loan to be a fixed rate loan.
    (i) How, by entering an FRA, can Eza convert the floating rate loan into a fixed rate loan?
    (ii) If the current interest rate is 6% per year, compounded continuously, what will be the fixed rate in the FRA?
    (iii) How would the fixed rate change if the notional principal was £10 000 000.

14. (i) One year from now, Walter will invest £1 000 000 for six months at a fixed rate of interest. This does not please him. He would prefer a floating rate. How could Walter change the fixed rate loan into a floating rate loan?
    (ii) If the current interest rates are as shown in the table, calculate the fixed rate Walter should try to achieve.

Maturity (years)	Interest rate (compounded annually)
0.5	5.5
1	5.55
1.5	5.6
2	5.64

(iii) In fact, he is offered a fixed rate of 6%. What would be the value of this FRA today?

15. What is a swap? In your answer, explain carefully the payments made and describe when these payments are made.

16. A swap is arranged. The notional principal is £10 000 000 and the first date is three months hence. The second date is six months later and each succeeding date is six months after its predecessor. The final date in the swap is ten years after the first date. The fixed rate is 5% per year (simply compounded).
   (i) Describe what happens on each of these dates.
   (ii) What is the tenor of the swap?
   (iii) What is (a) a payers swap, (b) a receivers swap?
   (iv) What is the accrual period of the swap?

17. A payers swap is arranged. The notional principal is $5 000 000. The first date of the swap is in six months' time. The remaining two dates follow at six-monthly intervals. The current (safe) interest rate is 5% per year (continuously compounded).
   (i) Calculate the fixed rate in this swap.
   (ii) A swap having the same notional principal and the same dates has a fixed rate of 4.5%. Find the value of this swap (a) today, and (b) in three months' time.

18. The reset date in a receivers swap is in six months' time. The notional principal is £10 000 000. The first of the four payment dates in the swap follows three months later; the remaining payment days follow at three-monthly intervals. The interest rate is 5.5%, compounded annually.
   (i) Draw a diagram to illustrate the payments made by the swap.
   (ii) Find the fixed rate in the swap.
   (iii) An otherwise identical swap has a fixed rate of 5%. Find the value of this swap today.
   (iv) If the fixed rate of the swap was 4%, what would be the value of this swap in three months' time?

19. Mita agrees to borrow $1 000 000 in six months' time at 6.5% per year (she will make an interest payment of $32 500 every six months). The loan is to be repaid two years later. The first interest payment is made six months after the loan was made; the remaining three interest payments

are made at six-monthly intervals. However, what Mita really wants is a loan involving floating rate payments. She has been told that by entering a swap, she can transform her fixed rate payments into floating rate payments.

(i) How precisely does she do this?

(ii) The bank arranging the swap charges, in total, 2% of the notional principal, with the payments spread equally over the four payments and split equally between the two parties to the swap. Draw a diagram indicating clearly what Mita will pay out and what she will receive on each payment date.

20. The safe interest rate is 5% per year (continuously compounded). Alven is interested in entering a payers swap where the notional principal is \$10 000 000, the reset date is in one year's time and there are four payment dates, with an accrual period of three months. The cost of the swap is \$20 000. What is the fixed rate of the swap?

21. Two companies, AASureties and BBDoubtfuls, want to borrow \$15 million for five years. They have been offered the rates shown in the table.

Company	Fixed rate (annual)	Floating rate
AA	9.0	LIBOR + 0.2%
BB	10.3	LIBOR + 1%

AA wants to borrow at a floating rate and BB wants to borrow at a fixed rate. Both want to make six-monthly interest payments. Clearly, BB has been offered poorer rates than AA.

(i) Describe carefully how both companies, by entering a swap with fixed rate 8.9%, can achieve the type of loan they desire, at a reduced interest rate. Draw diagrams to illustrate the payments made by each company. What is this application of a swap called?

(ii) Let x = the difference between the fixed rate interest rates. Let y = the difference between the floating rate rates. Show that the total apparent gain achieved by entering the swap is x − y. Is this always true? Create examples to test this formula.

(iii) Suppose the swap is arranged through a bank which charges for its services 0.03% per year of the \$15 million. This cost is shared equally between AA and BB. Draw new diagrams to show what each company will now pay. What interest rate will AA pay? What interest rate will BB pay?

22. FandC Fast Foods borrows £100 000 000 (interest paid six monthly) in the knowledge that each six months it can pay interest of $3 750 000. What can the company do to ensure that it never has to make an interest payment of more than this amount?

23. A relationship that must always hold between caplets, floorlets and FRAs is:

    $V_t(\text{caplet}) - V_t(\text{floorlet}) = 0.5(L_t - K) \times B(t, S)$

    where the caplet and the floorlet are activated (or not) by the interest rate in the period T through to S and S is six months ahead of T. L_t is the six-month LIBOR rate set at time T.
    (i) Show that $\frac{V_t(caplet) - V_t(floorlet)}{B(t,S)}$ = pay-off from a payers FRA.
    (ii) The values of caplets and floorlets are quoted in the market. Describe how these quotes could be used to calculate an estimate, at time t, for the forward LIBOR rate.

24. Buy the *Financial Times* (or click onto FT.com, Bloomberg or Reuters) and produce a LIBOR zero curve.

25. If a Eurodollar futures contract quote changes by one basis point (0.01), what will happen to the value of the Eurodollar futures contract?

26. What is a swap rate? Use the definition of the swap rate to prove that the swap rate is the par yield of a certain coupon bearing bond.

27. (i) A payers swap resets at time T and has payment dates at S_1, S_2, $S_3, \ldots S_n$. The fixed rate is K. Show that the value of the swap at time zero can be written as:
    $B(0, T) - B(0, S_n) - K\sum \alpha_i \times B(0, S_i)$ where α_i represents the accrual period between S_{i-1} and S_i.
    (ii) Let y_0 be the swap rate at $t = 0$. Show that the value of a swap can be written $\sum \alpha_i B(0, S_i)(y_0 - K)$.

28. Companies P and Q each want to borrow $10 million for five years (interest paid semi-annually). The rates they have been offered are:

	Fixed	Floating
P	8.0%	LIBOR + 0.1%
Q	8.8%	LIBOR + 0.5%

P wants to borrow at a fixed rate, Q wants to borrow at a floating rate.

Design a swap that will appear equally attractive to both P and Q and which will pay the institution that arranges the swap 0.02% per annum.

6 Options

Profit and **pay-off** diagrams will be used a great deal in this chapter.

A profit diagram shows the profit at maturity calculated from a range of asset values (Figure 6.1).

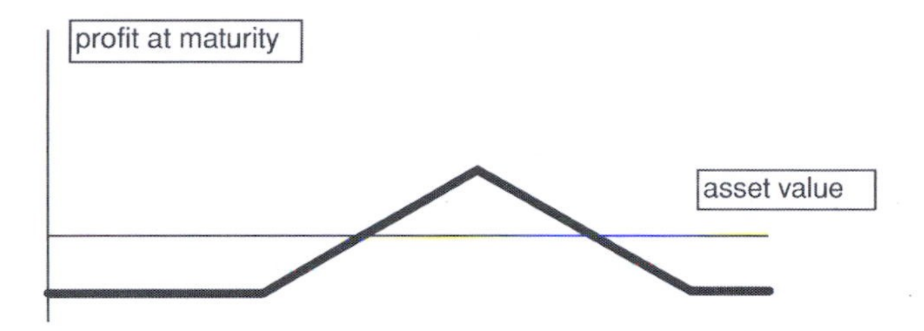

Figure 6.1

A pay-off diagram illustrates the pay-off at maturity (what a contract pays out at maturity) for a range of asset values (Figure 6.2).

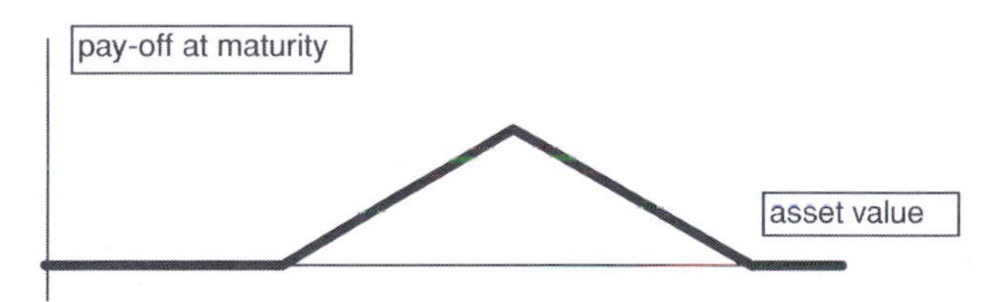

Figure 6.2

Introduction

A trader hears that VIY telecom company is undertaking research into a new design of mobile telephone. The price today of a VIY share is £2.45 and on the basis of what he hears, the trader expects the share price to rise. The delivery price for a six-month forward contract on a VIY share is £2.52, but the dealer expects the share price to rise by more than 7p. The trader enters a six-month forward contract on 100 000 VIY shares.

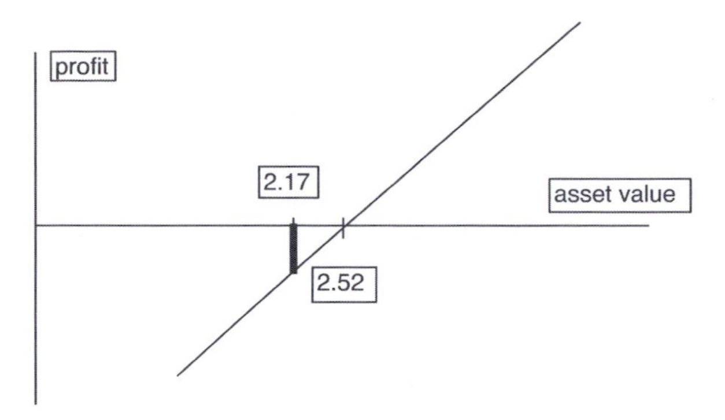

Figure 6.3

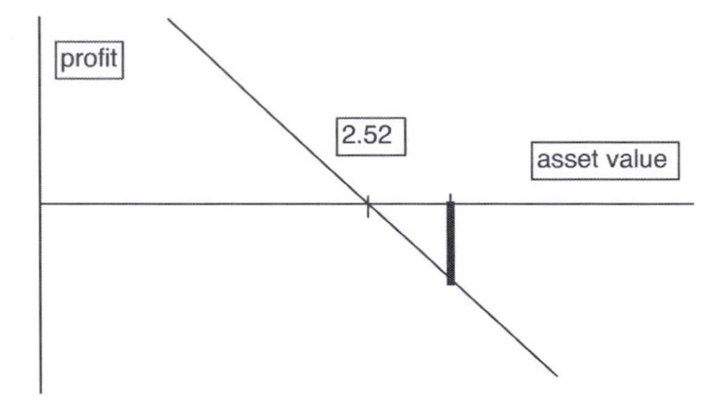

Figure 6.4

Unfortunately, the research was unsuccessful and six months later the company, having invested heavily in the project, declares a profits warning. The share price drops to £2.17. On delivery day, the dealer pays £252 000 to buy shares whose value is £217 000. Not a good deal. The situation is illustrated by a profit diagram (Figure 6.3).

In the same sort of way, if the trader had entered a forward contract to sell shares and by delivery day the price of the shares had risen above the delivery price, the trader would be in the position of having to sell shares at below their present value. This would not be a good deal either and the profit diagram in such a situation might look like Figure 6.4.

We might conclude (see Chapter 2) that forward contracts are extremely useful for reducing uncertainty (they can be used to fix today a price for the future) and if market movements are predicted correctly, a forward contract will make a handsome profit. However, if you get it wrong, you can lose a lot of money. Losses from a forward contract are potentially unlimited, as the profit diagrams Figure 6.3 and Figure 6.4 show.

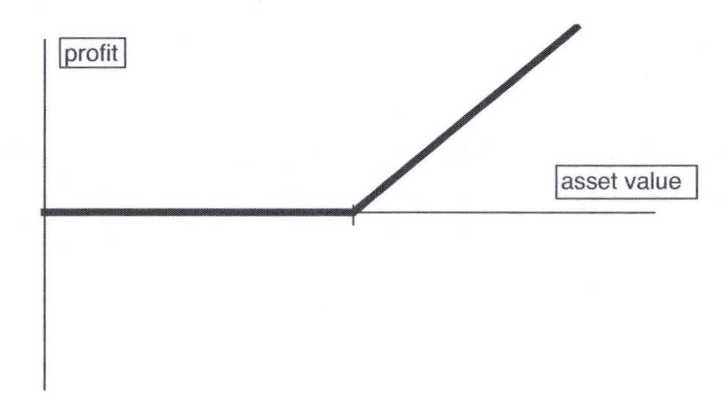

Figure 6.5

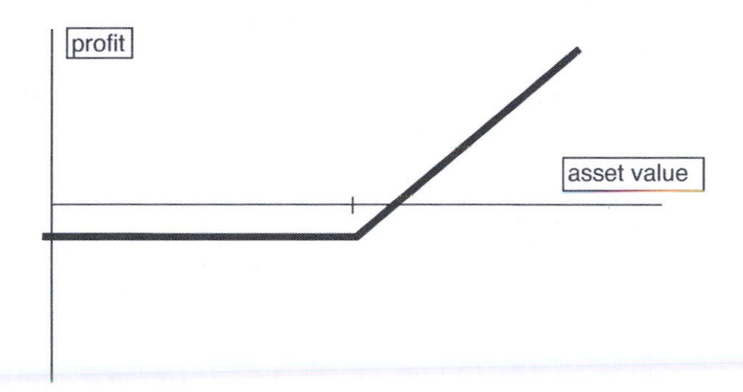

Figure 6.6

With forward contracts carrying so many desirable features, the possibility of potentially unlimited losses is unfortunate. Can these contracts be modified in some way to reduce this unpleasant feature?

Ideally, we would like to see a profit diagram that looked like Figure 6.5.

But for such a contract, under no circumstances would the owner of the contract lose money. In fact, the owner would, with positive probability, make money. This is clearly an arbitrage opportunity and under our 'no arbitrage opportunities assumption' we can assume that no such contract will exist.

However, by making a small but important modification to this profit diagram, as in Figure 6.6, we produce the profit diagram of a contract that can be priced and traded. Such a contract is called a **call option** and this is the type of option we look at first.

6.1 Call options

A **call option** on an asset is a contract which gives the holder the **right**, but not an obligation, to **buy** the asset by a certain date and for a certain price. The date in the contract is called the **maturity** of the contract; the price is called the **strike price**, or the **strike.**

What is important here is the word **right**.

- With a (long) forward contract, the holder of the contract has an obligation to buy the asset on the delivery date, at the delivery price.
- With a call option, the holder has the right to buy the asset at maturity at the strike price. So if market conditions move against his interests, the holder of a call option **does not have to proceed with the purchase**.

Example 1

On 1 March, a commodities trader takes out a call option to buy 10 000 bushels of wheat on 1 September for $3.1 per bushel.

On 1 September, if the spot price of wheat is $3.21 per bushel, the trader buys the wheat for $3.1 per bushel under the terms of the call option and immediately sells the wheat in open market for $3.21 per bushel. It is in the trader's interests to proceed with the contract.

If the spot price is $3.02 per bushel, the trader does not want to buy at $3.1 a commodity that is worth only $3.02. The trader exercises his right NOT to proceed with the contract. The purchase does not take place.

Having an option that allows you to walk away from a contract that is unfavourable to you seems, at first sight, to be every businessman's dream. Certainly, the holder of a call option has a clear advantage over the holder of a forward contract with the same delivery date and the same price. It costs nothing to enter a forward contract. So arguably, the holder of a call option should have to pay something to gain the advantage he holds over the owner of an otherwise identical forward contract. There should be a cost, let us call it C, to enter a call option.

But how can this cost be calculated? At first sight, this is a huge problem. A call option seems to be a very loose contract. The holder can honour the contract, or walk away, as he sees fit.

A solution to the problem first appeared in 1973. Fisher Black and Myron Scholes, in a paper that appeared in the May/June issue of the *Journal of Political Economy*, produced a formula that gives the value of C. This work was fundamental to modern financial mathematics. Black died in 1995, but in 1997, Scholes, jointly with Robert Merton, another pioneer of financial mathematics, was awarded a Nobel Prize in Economics. The formula produced by Black and Scholes has become extremely famous (infamous, some have said). This formula will be given and described in Chapter 7. Also in Chapter 7 we describe a method for calculating the value of different types of options. But to fix ideas and to show how options can be used in practice, **we will assume that the value of a call option is known**. In practice, this is not unduly restrictive; prices of call options are available to traders.

General principle

It will always be assumed that the holder of an option behaves so as to maximise their profit and minimise their loss. This principle will be used to establish trading strategies.

Example 2

It is 1 March. A call option on 10 000 bushels of wheat has strike price = \$3.1 per bushel with maturity on 1 September. The call option is valued at \$0.54 per bushel. A trader buys ten call options.

(i) How much does the trader pay for the ten call options?
(ii) What is the trader's profit (per bushel) if the price of wheat (per bushel) on 1 September is (a) \$3.75, (b) \$3.64, (c) \$3.20, (d) \$3.05?

Solution

(i) For ten call options, the trader pays $\$10 \times 10\,000 \times 0.54 = \$54\,000$.
(ii) On 1 September (all prices are per bushel)

(a) The price of wheat is \$3.75. The trader buys at \$3.1 under the terms of the call option and sells at \$3.75 in the open market.

He pays out $3.1 + 0.54$
He receives 3.75
Profit $= 3.75 - 3.1 - 0.54 = 0.11$

(b) The price of wheat is \$3.64. The trader buys at \$3.1 and sells at \$3.64.

He pays out $3.1 + 0.54$
He receives 3.64
Profit $= 3.64 - 3.1 - 0.54 = 0$

(c) The price of wheat is \$3.20. The trader buys at \$3.1 and sells at \$3.20.

He pays out $3.1 + 0.54$
He receives 3.20
Profit $= 3.20 - 3.1 - 0.54 = -0.44$

(d) The price of wheat is \$3.05. The trader does not want to buy at 3.1 a commodity that can be bought in the open market for 3.05. The trader chooses not to exercise the option.

The trader's profit $= -0.54$

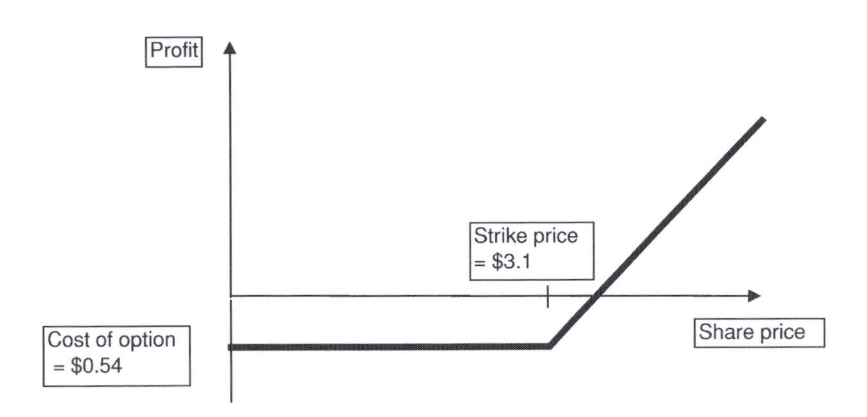

Figure 6.7

Note: in (c), although the trader makes a loss by exercising the option, his loss is not as great as it would have been if he had not exercised the option. See (d). By the General Principle, the trader exercises the option.

What happens at maturity: a profit diagram for a call option

In Figure 6.7 the profit is calculated from a range of possible asset values at maturity. The graph shows the profit diagram for a call option.

Observe: at maturity:
- if asset value $\leq$ strike price
  - the option is not exercised
  - the holder loses the cost of the option
- if asset value $>$ strike price
  - the option is exercised
  - profit $=$ asset value $-$ strike price $-$ cost of option

Note: in this chapter we shall ignore the time value of the cost of an option and treat this sum simply as a cash outflow to be set against later possible profits.

What happens at maturity: a pay-off diagram for a call option

It is important to observe what an option pays out at maturity. This amount is called the pay-off and this is the value of the option at maturity. In Chapter 7 we will describe a method for calculating the value of an option prior to maturity. The pay-off will be the starting point in this calculation.

Pay-off from a call option

$$= \text{asset value} - \text{strike price} \qquad \text{if asset value} > \text{strike price}$$
$$0 \qquad \text{if asset value} \leq \text{strike price}$$

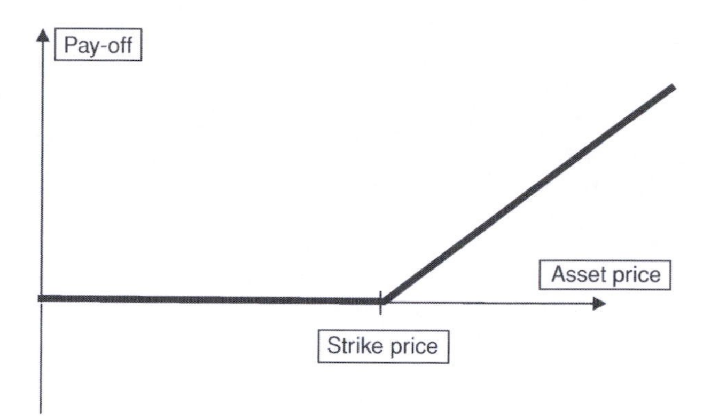

Figure 6.8

The graph of a pay-off function for a call option is shown in Figure 6.8.

In Example 2, the pay-off from the call option for the four asset values is given in the table below:

Asset value	Pay-off
3.75	$3.75 - 3.1 = 0.65$
3.64	$3.64 - 3.1 = 0.54$
3.20	$3.20 - 3.1 = 0.10$
3.05	0

Who buys a call option?

Generally, an investor will buy a call option if they believe that the value of the underlying asset will rise. They expect that, at maturity, the value of the asset will exceed the strike price plus the cost of the option. This can be seen from Figure 6.7. The investor is prepared to make an initial outlay (the cost of the option) to avoid the possibility of a potentially unbounded loss.

Who sells a call option?

If someone sells a call option, they are obligated to sell the asset at maturity to the buyer of the option for the strike price if the buyer wishes to execute the contract. The seller of a call option does not have the right to walk away if market conditions are unfavourable.

The seller of a call option makes a profit when the buyer makes a loss and vice versa. So the profit diagram for the seller of a call option will be the reflection (in the horizontal axis) of the profit diagram for the buyer – Figure 6.9.

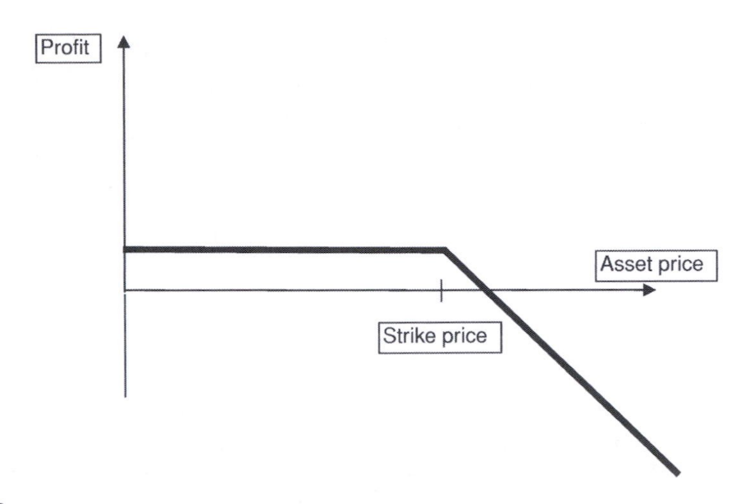

Figure 6.9

Example 3

A three-month call option on XXX shares with strike price £21.78 costs £2.34. A company sells 10 000 such call options. In three months' time, the XXX share price is £30.53. Calculate the pay-off from the option and the company's profit/loss.

Solution

In three months' time, the holder(s) of the call options have the right to buy at £21.78 shares worth £30.53. Of course, they exercise these options.

The company buys shares at £30.53 (in the open market) and sells them (under the terms of the call option) at £21.78.

The company's profit per share is: $21.78 + 2.34 - 30.53 = -6.41$

Overall, the company loses $10\,000 \times 6.41 =$ £64 000.

The seller of a call option is hoping that the option will not be exercised. She expects that, at maturity, the value of the asset will be less than the strike price. The profit for the seller is, at most, the cost C of the call option.

But, seller beware! The asset could, in theory, rise in value without limit and, as mentioned, the seller of a call option must, if required to do so, sell the asset to the holder at the strike price. Someone selling a call option is exposing themselves to a potentially unlimited loss. We describe some ways of dealing with this problem in section 6.4.

Call options are used, in practice, for speculation and for hedging. We give an example to demonstrate the considerable speculative power of a call option. Examples of how a call option might be used for hedging (to reduce risk) are given in section 6.4.

Example 4

Sang plans to invest \$500 000. A1B shares have been suggested as likely to rise in value. The cost of one A1B share, today, is \$14.50. The cost of a six-month call option on A1B shares with strike \$15.00 is \$1.76.

Consider two investment strategies. One strategy invests all the money in A1B shares; the other invests the money in call options on A1B shares. Calculate the profits of the strategies if the market value of A1B shares in six months' time is (a) \$18.75, (b) \$14.68.

Solution

Today:

Portfolio 1. Buy 34 482 shares ($\frac{500\,000}{14.50} = 34\,482.76$)

Portfolio 2. Buy 284 090 call options on A1B shares. Strike = \$15; maturity = 0.5 years.

$$\left(\frac{500\,000}{1.76} = 284\,090.91\right)$$

In six months' time:

(a) A1B shares are selling at \$18.75.

Portfolio 1. Each share has increased in value by \$4.25.

Profit $= 34\,482 \times 4.25 = \$146\,548.50$

Amount invested $= 34\,482 \times 14.50 = \$499\,989$

Percentage profit $= \frac{146\,548.50}{499\,989} \times 100 = 29.31\%$

Portfolio 2. The call options are exercised. By buying shares at \$15 (under the terms of the call options) and selling at \$18.75, each option has a pay-off of \$3.75.

Profit $= 284\,090 \times 3.75 = \$1\,065\,337.50$

Amount invested $= 284\,090 \times 1.76 = \$499\,998.40$

Percentage profit $= \frac{1\,065\,337.5}{499\,998.4} \times 100 = 213.07\%$

The percentage profit from the portfolio consisting of call options is more than 700% greater than the percentage profit on the portfolio consisting only of shares. Not bad. But see (b).

(b) A1B shares are selling at $14.68.

Portfolio 1. Each share has increased in value by $0.18.

Profit $= 34\,482 \times 0.18 = \$6206.76$

Percentage profit $= \frac{6206.76}{499\,989} \times 100 = 1.24\%$

Value of portfolio $= \$506\,195.76$

Portfolio 2. None of the calls is exercised. Each has zero value at maturity.

Value of portfolio $= 0$.

The roles are now reversed. The share portfolio (even with a small profit) is the clear winner. The call option portfolio, being without value, is looking less impressive.

Clearly, using call options in a speculative investment can be massively profitable. The downside is that an adverse movement of the market can result in an investor losing everything. Buying shares might produce smaller profits but in the end the investor still has the shares, whatever their worth. Huge profits are usually accompanied by heavy risk.

What would be useful here would be a device for an investor who believes the value of the asset is likely to fall but does not want the risk involved in selling a call option. Such a device is the put option.

But first, some terminology.

Definition (Writing an option, expiring worthless, naked and covered options)

A person who **sells** an option is said to **write** the option.

If, at maturity, an option is not exercised, it is said that the option **expires worthless.**

An option is **covered** if the writer of the option owns the asset. An option is **naked** when the writer does not own the asset. If the option is covered, then at maturity the worst that can happen is that the writer hands over the asset (which she owns) and pockets the strike price and the cost of the option. But if the option is naked, the writer must first purchase the asset, then sell it at the strike price, which could, in a hostile market, be well below the purchase price. Writing a naked option is regarded as one of the most risky activities in finance. Most option writers who sleep at nights hedge their risk. We describe ways of doing this later in the chapter.

6.2 The put option

The holder of a **put** option has the right, but not an obligation, to **sell** the asset by a certain date (maturity) for a certain price (the strike price). As with a call option, a put option has an initial value, P, and this is the amount it will cost to acquire a put option.

Example 5

It is 3 May. The value today of a BBB1 share is £16.38. A four-month put option on BBB1 shares with strike price £17.50 costs £2.44. Jenny buys 5000 put options.

(i) What would Jenny pay for the 5000 put options?
(ii) What would be Jenny's profit if the price of a BBB1 share on 3 September was (a) £14.28, (b) £16.81, (c) £17.94?

Solution

(i) Jenny would pay $5000 \times 2.44 = £12\,200$.
(ii) It is now 3 September.
  (a) The share price is £14.28. Jenny buys a share (in the open market) for £14.28 and sells it (under the terms of the put option) for £17.50.
    She pays out (per share) $14.28 + 2.44$
    She receives (per share) 17.50
    Profit $= 17.50 - 14.28 - 2.44 = 0.78$
    Total profit $= 5000 \times 0.78 = £3\,900$.
  (b) The share price is £16.81. Jenny buys a share at £16.81 and sells it at £17.50
    She pays out (per share) $16.81 + 2.44$
    She receives (per share) 17.50
    Profit $= 17.50 - 16.81 - 2.44 = -1.75$
    Total profit $= 5000 \times (-1.75) = -£8\,750$
  (c) The share price is £17.94. Jenny does not want to sell for £17.50 a share that could be sold in the open market for £17.94. She does not exercise the option (the option expires worthless).
    Profit (per share) $= -£2.44$
    Total profit $= 5000 \times (-2.44) = -£12\,200$.
  Again, in (b), although Jenny makes a loss by exercising the option, her loss is less than that incurred by not exercising the option

What happens at maturity: profit and pay-off diagrams for a put option

Profit diagram for a put option

This is shown in Figure 6.10.

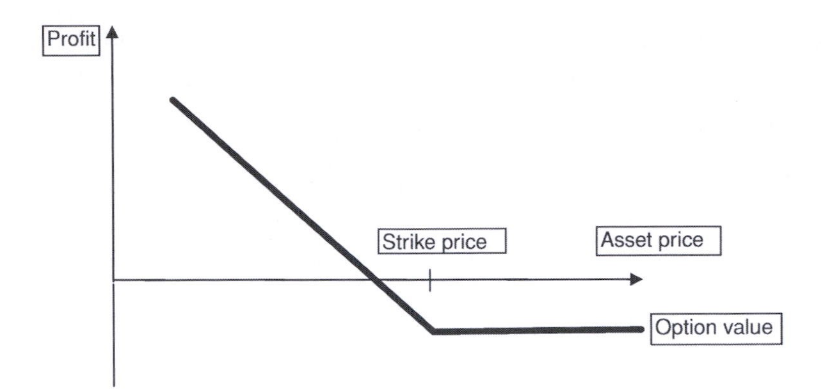

Figure 6.10

Observe: at maturity:
if asset value ≥ strike price
the option is not exercised (expires worthless)
the holder loses the cost of the option
if asset value < strike price
the option is exercised
profit = strike price − asset value − cost of option

Pay-off from a put option

The amount an option pays out at maturity is known as the pay-off. The pay-off is the value of the option at maturity.

Pay-off from a put option

= strike price − asset value	if asset value < strike price
0	if asset value ≥ strike price

See Figure 6.11.

In Example 5, the pay-off for the three values of the share price is given in the table below:

Asset value	Pay-off
14.28	17.50 − 14.28 = 3.22
16.81	17.50 − 16.81 = 0.69
17.94	0

Put options, also, have the power to rachet up profits.

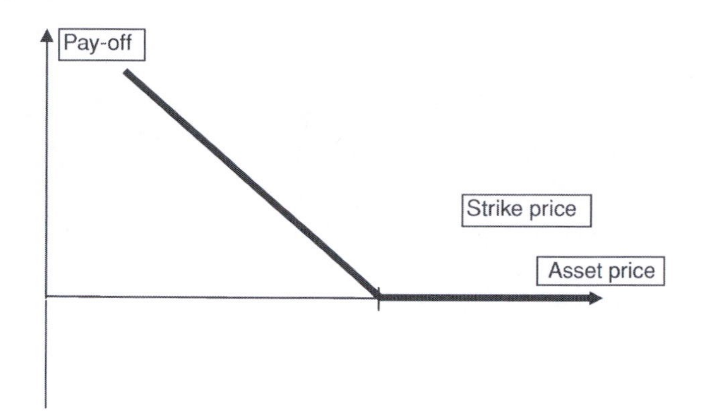

Figure 6.11

Example 6

Gemma is investing £10 000 for a client. Today is 7 July. PQR Avionics is looking a little shaky and Gemma suspects the share price will fall over the next three months. Yet she is not completely sure. The value of a PQR Avionics share today is £4.57. Gemma decides to spend one third of the money buying PQR Avionics shares and two thirds buying three-month put options on these shares. The cost of each put option (strike price = £4.50) is 21p.

Calculate the value of this portfolio on 7 October if the value of a PQR Avionics share on that day is (i) £3.68, (ii) £4.55.

Solution

Gemma spends £3333.33 on shares and £6666.67 on three-month put options.

She buys 729 shares ($\frac{3333.33}{4.57} = 729.4$) and 31 746 put options ($\frac{6666.67}{0.21} = 31\,746.04$).

(i) On 7 October, the share price is £3.68.

The portfolio has 729 shares – these are worth $729 \times 3.68 = 2682.72$; and 31 746 put options – for each put option, Gemma could buy a share for 3.68 and then sell it for 4.50. So each put option is worth $4.50 - 3.68 = 0.82$.

Value of put options is: $31\,746 \times 0.82 = £26\,031.72$.

Total value of portfolio $= 2682.72 + 26\,031.72 = £28\,714.44$.

Note: in practice, an investor would use the 729 shares to exercise 729 put options. They would buy a further $31\,746 - 729 = 31\,017$ shares, at 3.68 per share, then sell these shares (under the terms of the put option) at 4.50 each. Value of portfolio $= 729 \times 4.50 + 31\,017 \times 0.82 = £28\,714.44$.

So on 7 October the portfolio is worth £28 714.44 and we observe the awesome speculative power of put options.

(ii) On 7 October, the share price is £4.55.

The put options are not exercised and expire worthless. The shares (and the portfolio) are worth $729 \times 4.55 = £3316.95$.

In this case, Gemma's investor has taken a bad loss. But by broadening the portfolio, Gemma has ensured that the whole of the investment has not been lost. We will pursue this idea further in section 6.4.

Who buys a put option?

A put option is bought by an investor who believes the value of the asset will fall. She expects that, at maturity, the value of the asset will be less than the strike price reduced by the cost of the option. The purchaser of a put option is prepared to make an initial outlay to escape the possibility of unlimited loss.

Who sells (writes) a put option?

An investor writes a put option if she believes that the option will not be exercised. She believes that, at maturity, the value of the asset will be greater than (or equal to) the strike price. A profit graph for the writer of a put option is shown in Figure 6.12.

Writing a put option is an extremely risky business. All written put options are naked options. The writer of a put option will, if the option is exercised, buy the asset at the strike price and if the value of the asset has fallen well below the strike, the writer of a put option will make a heavy loss. Without a sound

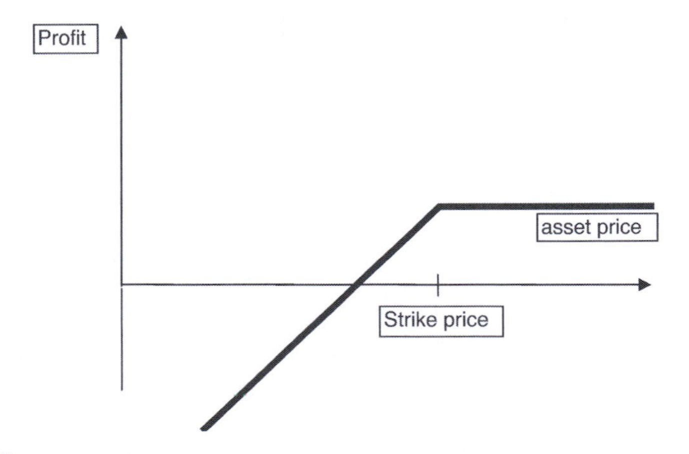

Figure 6.12

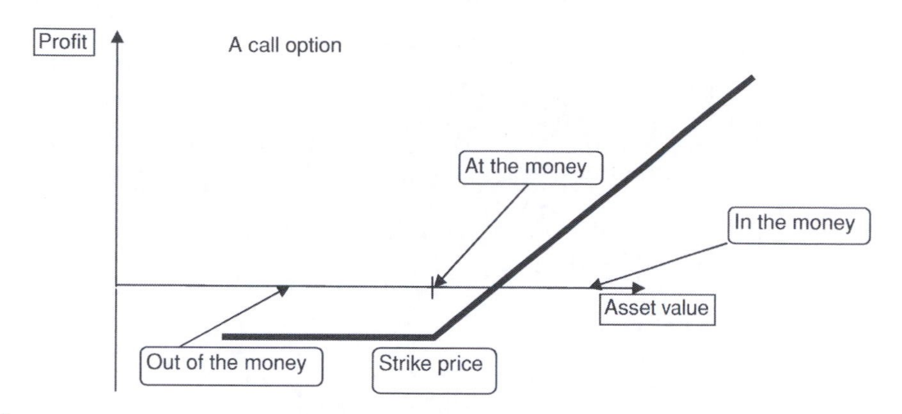

Figure 6.13

hedging strategy, the writer of a put option faces potentially unlimited losses. We show some ways in which written puts can be hedged later in the chapter.

Definition (In the money, at the money and out of the money)

An option that would deliver to its owner a positive amount of money if exercised today is said to be **in the money**. So a call option is in the money if today the value of the asset exceeds the strike price (S_t > strike). A put option is in the money if today the value of the asset is less than the strike price (S_t < strike).

An option that would give its owner a zero amount of money if exercised today is said to be **at the money**. So a call or a put option is at the money if today the value of the asset equals the strike price (S_t = strike).

An option that would give its owner a negative amount of money if exercised today is said to be **out of the money**. So a call option is out of the money if today the value of the asset is less than the strike price (S_t < strike). A put option is out of the money if today the value of the asset exceeds the strike price (S_t > strike) – see Figure 6.13.

Two stories

Just one of the stories that surfaced in the wake of September 11th 2001 is that several days before the attack on the World Trade Center, someone bought a large number of put options on American airlines' shares. The value of airlines' stock fell sharply after September 11th, making such put options very valuable. These options, apparently, were never exercised.

In 1987, many investors were advised to write put options with a low strike price on reasonably highly priced shares. The shares were well regarded, the reasoning went, and unlikely to fall very much in value. So the options would expire worthless

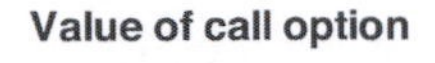

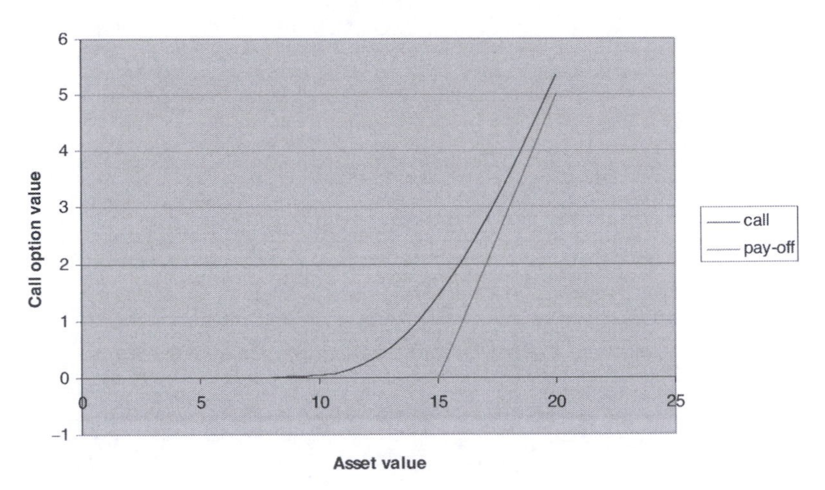

Figure 6.14

and the writer would keep the premiums. Because of this, the options were cheap and investors had to write a large number of the options to make a reasonable amount of money. Alas, the market crashed in 1987, share prices fell sharply and many of the put options were exercised. A large number of investors who had not hedged their risk were ruined.

We have illustrated the profits that can be obtained from a call option and from a put option. Now we ask an important question. How do the values of a call option and a put option depend on the underlying share price?

A brief discussion (in advance of Chapter 7) of the values of call and put options

To illustrate how the values of a call option and a put option react to a changing share price, consider a call and a put option on BBB2 shares. The strike price = £15, time to maturity = three months. The values of such a call option for a range of share values are as shown in Figure 6.14.

(These values were calculated using the Black–Scholes formula, described in Chapter 7.)

The values of the corresponding put option and a graph illustrating these values are given in Figure 6.15.

In Figure 7.33 in Chapter 7, we give a spreadsheet from which values of call and put options can be calculated and similar graphs drawn. We recommend that the reader uses this spreadsheet to see what happens to the values of call and put options as the time to maturity shrinks to zero.

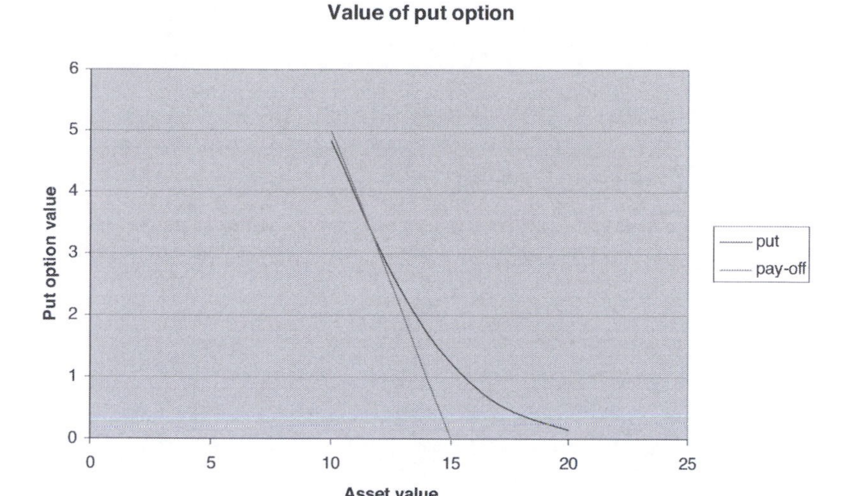

Figure 6.15

Useful observations

Assuming all other market factors remain constant:

A call option becomes more valuable as the asset price rises and less valuable as the asset price falls.

A put option becomes less valuable as the asset price rises and more valuable as the asset price falls.

In terms of the strike price:

With a call option, the higher the strike price, the cheaper the option.

With higher strike prices, it becomes more likely that at maturity $S_T < K$. So it becomes more likely that the option will expire worthless. The option becomes less attractive and the price falls.

With a put option, the higher the strike price, the more expensive the option.

With higher strike prices, it becomes more likely that at maturity $S_T < K$. It becomes more likely that the option will be exercised: the option becomes more attractive and the price rises.

Trading options

Options have the potential to become more valuable. Hence they are traded. The principal trading venue in England is Liffe (London International Financial Futures and Options Exchange). In the US, two of the big players in option trading are the Chicago Board Option Exchange and the Philadelphia Stock Exchange. Useful websites are:

www.liffe.com	(Liffe)
www.cbot.com	(Chicago Board of Trade)
www.PHLX.com	(Philadelphia Stock Exchange)

The profit diagrams for call and put options suggest that there ought to be a simple relationship linking the price of a call option and a put option on the same asset, with the same maturity and strike price. This relationship is known as put–call parity and this we now establish.

6.3 Put–call parity

Notation:

S_0 = asset price today
K = strike price
r = rate (continuously compounded)
T = time to maturity
C = price of call option today
P = price of put option today

Then $\boxed{C + K \times e^{-rT} = P + S_0}$

We illustrate this result.

It is 4 April. The price of one CrashBang Insurance share is £9.54, the interest rate (continuously compounded) is 7.2% and the strike price for a three-month call option is £9.27. Let the price of a call option on one share be C; let P represent the price of the corresponding put option.

Today: set up two portfolios:

Portfolio A:

Buy one call option and invest £9.27 × $e^{-0.072\times\frac{3}{12}}$ at 7.2% per year, continuously compounded, for three months. This is not a randomly chosen amount of cash. Interest rate growth will ensure that in three months' time, this cash investment will grow to the strike price, £9.27.

The value of portfolio A, today, is $C + 9.27 \times e^{-0.072\times\frac{3}{12}}$

Portfolio B:

Buy one put option and one share.

The value of portfolio B, today, is P + 9.54.

At maturity:

Portfolio A:

The cash investment has grown to
$(£9.27 \times e^{-0.072\times\frac{3}{12}}) \times e^{0.072\times\frac{3}{12}} = £9.27$.

The value of the share will also have changed. Either the share value is greater than the strike price or the share value is less than, or equal to, the strike price. Let S_T represent the share value at maturity and consider each of these possibilities in turn.

(1) $S_T > £9.27$

The call option is in the money and is exercised. Under the terms of the call option, a share is bought for £9.27. This share could then be sold for S_T. The pay-off from the call option is $S_T - 9.27$.

Portfolio A is worth $S_T - 9.27 + 9.27 = S_T$.

(2) $S_T \leq £9.27$

The call option expires worthless.

Portfolio A is worth £9.27.

This tells us that portfolio A is worth the greater of $(S_T, 9.27)$. We write this as: $\max(S_T, 9.27)$.

Portfolio B:

Again, there are two possibilities.

(1) $S_T \geq £9.27$

The put option expires worthless.

Portfolio B is worth S_T.

(2) $S_T < £9.27$

The put option is exercised. The holder of the put buys a share for S_T and under the terms of the put, sells a share for £9.27. Pay-off from the put option is $9.27 - S_T$.

Portfolio B is worth $9.27 - S_T + S_T = 9.27$.

Portfolio B is worth the greater of $(S_T, 9.27) = \max(S_T, 9.27)$.

The two portfolios have identical values at maturity. To avoid arbitrage, they must have identical values throughout their lives. In particular, they must have identical values today. So

$$C + 9.27 \times e^{-0.072\times\frac{3}{12}} = P + 9.54.$$

This establishes the put–call parity formula.

We can use put–call parity to calculate the value of a put when the value of the corresponding call option is known. Similarly, when the put price is known, we can calculate the value of the corresponding call. This is illustrated in Example 7.

If the values of both call and put options are known, they should satisfy the put–call parity equation. If they do not, there is an arbitrage opportunity. We show how to deal with this in Example 8.

Example 7

A call option on one troy oz of silver (today's price is $4.69) with six-month maturity and strike price $6.28 costs, today, 50 cents. The interest rate (continuously compounded) is 11.3%. Find the price of the put option on the same asset with the same maturity and strike price.

Solution

$$\begin{aligned} C + K \times e^{-rT} &= P + S_0 \\ 0.5 + 6.28 \times e^{-0.113 \times \frac{1}{2}} &= P + 4.69 \\ P &= 0.5 + 6.28 \times e^{-0.113 \times \frac{1}{2}} - 4.69 \\ &= 1.745 \end{aligned}$$

The value of the corresponding put option is $1.75.

Example 8

Jack has been looking at the share price of a German brewery. Today the price of a share in the brewery is £14.50 and the rate at which Jack can borrow and invest money is 6.5% per year (continuously compounded). A call option on one share with maturity one month and strike price £14.00 costs £1.50. A put option with the same maturity and strike price costs £0.91.

$$\begin{aligned} C + K \times e^{-rT} &= 1.5 + 14 \times e^{-0.065 \times \frac{1}{12}} \\ &= 15.4244 \\ P + S_0 &= 0.91 + 14.50 \\ &= 15.41 \end{aligned}$$

Grand, Jack thought, there is something wrong here. What should Jack do?

Solution

We know that $P + S_0 < C + K \times e^{-rT}$

So $P + S_0 - C < K \times e^{-rT}$

And $(P + S_0 - C)e^{rT} < K$

The aim:

At maturity: pay out $(P + S_0 - C)e^{rT}$
receive K

This will generate a positive cash flow.

Strategy today $(t = 0)$

Borrow $P + S_0 - C$ at 6.5% per year (continuously compounded) for one month. Use the money to:

buy one put, buy one share and write one call option

(So borrow $0.91 + 14.5 - 1.5 = 13.91$ to be repaid at 6.5% [continuously compounded] after one month. Buy one put and one share and write one call: $0.91 + 14.5 - 1.5 = 13.91$)

At maturity $(t = \frac{1}{12})$

Repay the loan: pay out $(P + S_0 - C)e^{rT}$

So pay out: $13.91 \times e^{0.065 \times \frac{1}{12}} = 13.9856$

(Observe: as expected, the pay-out is less than the strike price $K = 14$.)

Today, we do not know what will be the value of the share at maturity. But we do know that exactly one of the following must occur.

(1) The share price at maturity is less than the strike price. So: $S_T < K$.

The call option is out of the money and expires worthless. The put option is in the money. Under the terms of the put, Jack hands over the share and receives the strike price, K.

Receive K = £14.

(2) $S_T > K$

Now, the put option is out of the money and expires worthless. The call option is in the money. The holder of the call will want to buy the share for the strike price. Jack exchanges the share and receives the strike price, K.

Receive K = £14.

(3) $S_T = K$

Neither the call nor the put are in the money. Sell the share for its market value.

Receive K = £14.

So *whatever the value of the share*, the structure of the portfolio ensures that at maturity, £13.9856 is paid out and the strike price of £14 is received.

The aim has been achieved. This is an arbitrage opportunity. If the strategy is replicated 700 000 times, the profit is approximately £10 000.

There is another situation to consider. What should Jack do if, instead, $C + K \times e^{-rT} < P + S_0$?

Suppose that, in the example:

$S_0 = 14.50,\ C = 1.50,\ K = 14.00,\quad r = 0.065,\ T = \frac{1}{12},\ P = 0.98$

Now, $C + K \times e^{-rT} = 1.5 + 14 \times e^{-0.065 \times \frac{1}{12}} = 15.4244$

$P + S_0 = 0.98 + 14.50 = 15.48$

So $P + S_0 > C + K \times e^{-rT}$

This gives us: $P + S_0 - C > Ke^{-rT}$

and $(P + S_0 - C)e^{rT} > K$.

The aim:

At maturity: pay out K

receive $(P + S_0 - C)e^{rT}$

This will generate a positive cash flow.

Strategy:

Today ($t = 0$)

Borrow one share (S_0). Write one put option; sell the share; buy one call option. (Selling a share you do not own is known as 'short selling'. See the Introduction for a brief description of what is involved.)

This gives a cash inflow of $P + S_0 - C$.

Invest this cash ($P + S_0 - C$) at 6.5% (continuously compounded) for one month.

(So invest $0.98 + 14.5 - 1.5 = 13.98$ at 6.5% for one month.)

At maturity ($t = \frac{1}{12}$)

Receive, from the investment, $(P + S_0 - C)e^{rT}$

$$= 13.98 \times e^{0.065 \times \frac{1}{12}}$$

$$= 14.0559$$

(Observe: the amount received from the portfolio is greater than the strike price, K.)

Consider again the three possibilities for the share price at maturity.

(1) $S_T < K$

The call option expires worthless. The put option is in the money: the holder will want to sell one share for the strike price. Hand over K (= £14) and receive one share. Return the borrowed share.

Pay out £14.

(2) $S_T > K$
The put expires worthless. Under the terms of the call option, hand over $K = £14.00$ and receive one share. Return the borrowed share.
Pay out £14.

(3) $S_T = K$
The put and the call are both out of the money. Buy one share for £14.00. Return the share.
Pay out £14.

Hence, whatever the value of the share, the portfolio ensures that, at maturity, £14.0559 is received and £14 is paid out. The share that was borrowed is returned. There is a profit of £0.0559 and this represents an arbitrage opportunity. If 100 000 such contracts were made, a risk-free profit of £5590 would be made.

This example shows that call and put options can be used to great advantage in conjunction with cash and a share. There are other ways that calls and puts can be combined to produce significantly altered profit diagrams with very useful properties. This leads us to consider spreads, straddles, straps and strips and these are explained fully in the following sections.

6.4 Strategies involving multiple calls and puts (spreads, straddles, strips and straps)

We started this chapter with a discussion on how the disadvantage of a forward contract – a potential for an unlimited loss – could be mitigated by buying, instead, a call option. However, to buy a call option, there must be someone prepared to sell the option. As we have seen, the writer of a call option (and a put option) also faces potentially unlimited loses. In this section, we show how investors selling call and put options can limit their losses. We demonstrate different strategies involving the purchase and sale of call and put options and show how these strategies may be used to achieve desired financial goals.

We begin with one of the simplest such strategies, a spread.

Spreads

A spread is a collection of two or more call options or of two or more put options. One very popular spread is the bull spread.

Bull spread

Buy a call option. On the same asset and with the same maturity, sell a call option with a **higher** strike price.

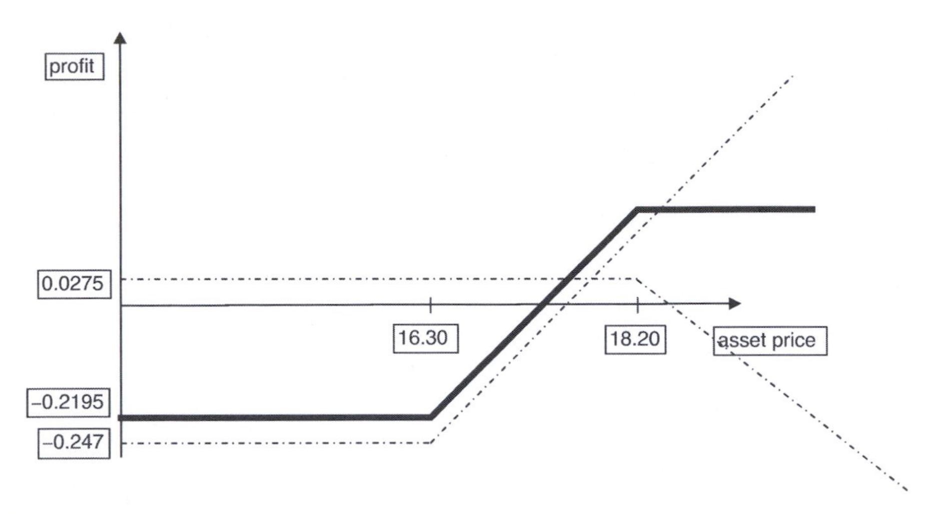

Figure 6.16a

Example 9

A bull spread is created by buying a call option (strike price = $16.30, maturity = three months, cost = $0.2470) and selling a call option (strike price = $18.20, maturity = three months, cost = $0.0275).

Recall: with a call option, the higher the strike price, the cheaper the option.

The call you sell has a higher strike price than the call you buy. So the call you sell will be less expensive than the call you buy. When setting up a bull spread using call options, you receive less than you pay out. There is a cost attached to setting up a call bull spread. (In this case, the cost of setting up the bull spread is 0.2470 – 0.0275 = 0.2195.) A profit diagram for this bull spread is shown in Figure 6.16a.

Notes:

- From the profit graph, we see that the person setting up a bull spread believes the value of the asset will **rise** (hence the name, **bull** spread). Profits and losses will be limited.
- Compare the bull spread to the call option the investor buys to set up the bull spread. For an initial outlay, the buyer of a call option glimpses a potential for unlimited profit. By then selling a call option to create a bull spread, the possibility of an unlimited profit is removed. Compensation is provided by a reduced initial outflow of cash. So essentially, the creator of a bull spread has surrendered the possibility of a large pay-off against a reduced initial outlay.

- The seller of a call option, as mentioned previously, faces potentially unlimited losses if the value of the asset increases above the strike price. So if the seller of a call option buys a call option (same asset, same maturity) with a lower strike price, then they own a bull spread on which, as the profit diagram shows, losses are limited. In this way, the writer of a call option can hedge their risk. In fact, the writer of a call option, by entering a bull spread in this way, has engineered a profit from a rising asset value and a loss from a falling asset value.
- Bull spreads can also be created from put options (buy a put option; on the same asset and with the same maturity, sell a put option with a **higher** strike price). See Exercise 12. Observe that if the writer of a put option creates a bull spread by buying a put option with a lower strike price, she makes a (reduced) profit if the asset value rises and a (limited!) loss if the asset value falls. By setting up a bull spread in this way, the writer of a put option is accepting a reduced profit in exchange for removing the possibility of a very large loss. She has hedged her risk.

Example 10

Today, the value of a TexO share is £4.68. Uma sets up a three-month bull spread on TexO shares by buying a three-month call option on TexO shares with strike price £12.50 (cost = £0.27) and selling a three-month call option on TexO shares with strike price £14.30 (cost = \$0.21).

(i) What does it cost to set up this bull spread?
(ii) Describe the pay-off and the profit at maturity.
(iii) Describe Uma's thinking in setting up the bull spread.

Solution

(i) Since the share price today is so far below the two strike prices, Uma expects both calls to be cheap. The initial outlay is £0.06.
(ii) What happens at maturity? It all depends on the share price in three months' time (S_T) and there are three possibilities.
  (a) $S_T \leq 12.50$
  The probability of this event is high. With the share price today standing at 4.68, it is likely that at maturity the share price will be less than 12.50.
  In this case, both options expire worthless   pay-off = 0   profit = −0.06

(b) $12.50 < S_T \leq 14.30$

The probability of this event is low. It is unlikely that the share price will surge to a level of above 12.50 at maturity.

The call that was bought expires in the money	pay-off $= +(S_T - 12.50)$
The call that was sold expires worthless	pay-off $= 0$ Total pay-off $= S_T - 12.50$ Profit $= S_T - 12.50 - 0.06$ $= S_T - 12.56$

(c) $14.30 < S_T$

The probability of this event is very low.

The long call expires in the money	pay-off $= +(S_T - 12.50)$
The short call expires in the money	pay-off $= -(S_T - 14.30)$ Total pay-off $= S_T - 12.50 - (S_T - 14.30)$ $= 14.30 - 12.50$ $= 1.80$ Profit $= 1.80 - 0.06 = 1.74$

The reasoning is: initially, a small amount of cash (£0.06 per share) will be put up and with high probability, this money will be lost. With small probability, there will be a modest profit and there is a very small probability that there will be a big profit. Not so very different to buying a lottery ticket.

A profit diagram for this bull spread is shown in Figure 6.16b.

A bull spread can also be created from two put options (see Exercise 12). Equally popular, but for a very different market, is the bear spread.

Bear spread

Buy a call option. On the same asset and with the same maturity, sell a call option with a **lower** strike price.

The call option with the higher strike price is cheapest. So the option you buy has lower cost than the option you sell. There is more cash coming in than is being paid out. This means that setting up a bear spread involves a cash inflow.

Example 11

Loui buys a three-month call option on A1A shares (strike price = \$10.00) for \$0.4681 and sells a three-month call option on A1A shares (strike price = \$7.50) for \$2.6027. Loui has set up a bear spread and received, initially,

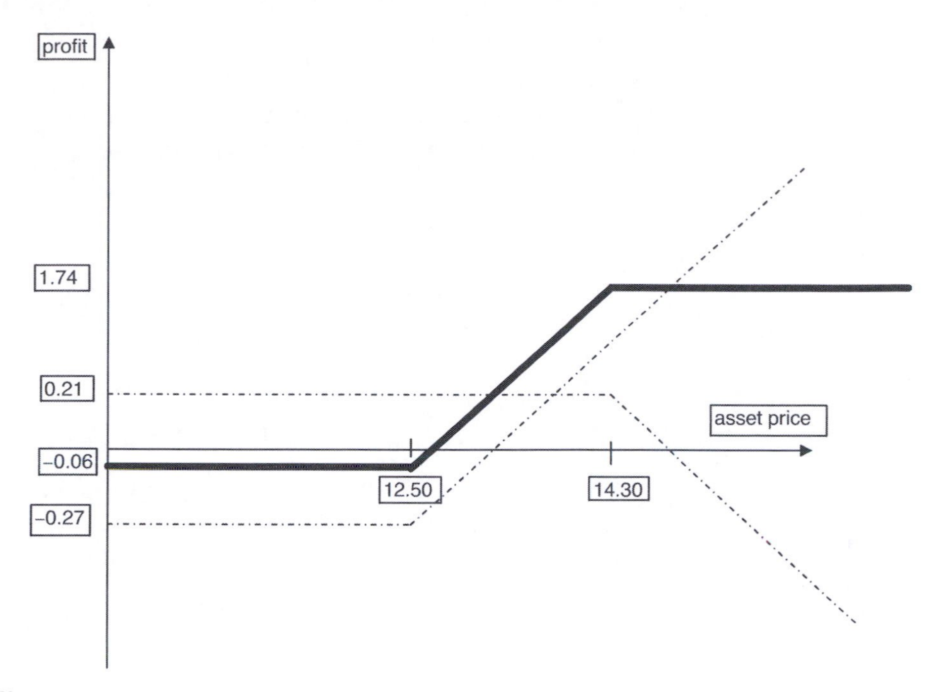

Figure 6.16b

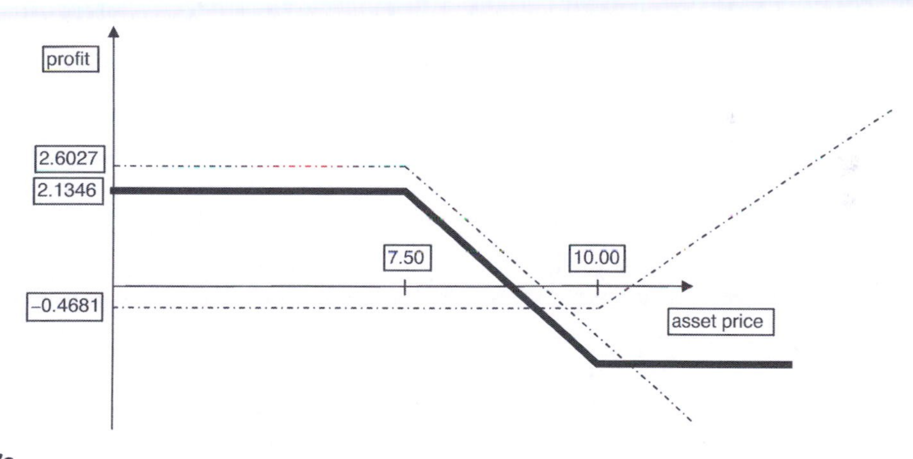

Figure 6.17a

\$2.6027 – \$0.4681 = \$2.1346. The profit diagram for this bear spread appears in Figure 6.17a.

Notes:

- From the profit diagram, an investor setting up a bear spread believes the value of the asset will fall (hence the name, **bear** spread).

- The writer of a call option believes the price of the asset will fall. By buying a call option with higher strike price (otherwise identical) he has reduced the profit he will make if the option is not exercised. But against this he has eliminated the potential for large losses. He has hedged his risk.

Example 12

Today, a share in SpeedyE is selling for \$5.58. Jake buys a one-month call option with strike price \$6.00 for \$0.0196 and sells a one-month call option with strike price \$5.30 for \$0.3318.

(i) Calculate the initial cost of this bull spread.
(ii) Calculate the pay-off and the profit from the option for all possible values of the asset at maturity.

Solution

(i) Initially Jake receives \$0.3318 and pays out \$0.0196. He receives \$0.3122 when he sets up the bull spread.
(ii) At maturity, the share price must lie in one of three bands:
  (a) $S_T \leq 5.30$
  Both options expire worthless — pay-off $= 0$
  profit $=$ \$0.3122.
  (b) $5.30 < S_T \leq 6.00$
  The call with strike 6.00 expires worthless — pay-off $= 0$
  The call with strike 5.30 expires in the money — pay-off $= -(S_T - 5.30)$
  Total pay-off $= -S_T + 5.30$
  Profit $= -S_T + 5.30 + 0.3122$
  $= -S_T + 5.6122$
  (c) $6.00 < S_T$
  Both options expire in the money — Pay-off $= +(S_T - 6.00)$
  Pay-off $= -(S_T - 5.30)$
  Total pay-off $= -6.00 + 5.30$
  $= -0.70$
  Profit $= -0.70 + 0.3122$
  $= -0.3878$

Diagrams for the pay-off and the profit are shown in Figure 6.17b.
A bear spread can also be created from put options. See Exercise 15.

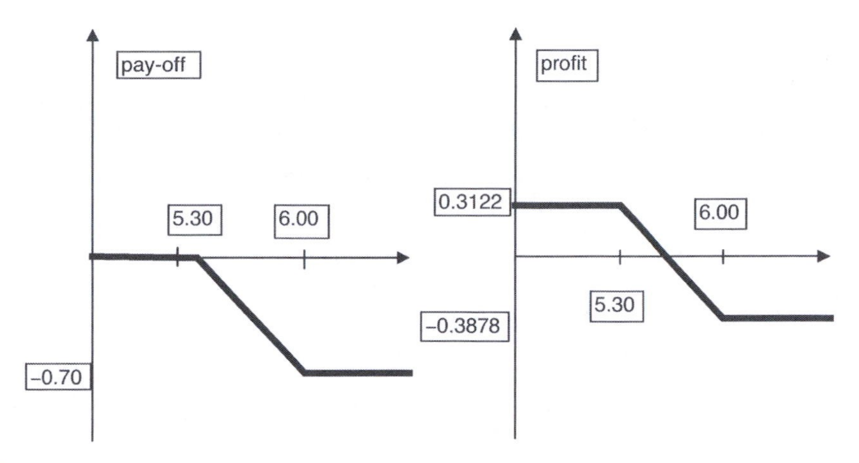

Figure 6.17b

Butterfly spread

An investor believes that over the next month or so, there will be no large movement in the FastEasy2 share price. She believes that over the next month, the price will remain in the region of the present value, £4.25.

She could:

Buy a one-month call option on FastEasy2 shares with low strike price £3.80.

Buy a one-month call option on FastEasy2 shares with high strike price £4.70.

Write two one-month call options on FastEasy2 shares with strike price £4.25.

These 'low' and 'high' strike prices were not chosen randomly. These two strikes are chosen so that their average is close to the 'stable' price of £4.25. In fact, $\frac{3.80+4.70}{2} = 4.25$.

To create a butterfly spread

On the same asset and with the same maturity:

Buy a call option with low strike price.

Buy a call option with high strike price.

Sell two call options with strike price approximately the average of the low and high strikes (this average will be approximately the expected 'stable' price of the asset).

Example 13

Consider one-month call options on FastEasy2 shares.

Call option	Strike price	Cost
	3.80	0.4739
	4.70	0.0054
	4.25	0.1104

(i) Set up a butterfly spread.
(ii) Investigate what happens at maturity.
(iii) How would you sell (write) a butterfly spread? Why might you want to sell a butterfly spread?

Solution

(i) On FastEasy2 shares:
Buy a one-month call option with strike price 3.80.
Buy a one-month call option with strike price 4.70.
Sell two one-month call options with strike price 4.25.
Today the investor receives: $2 \times 0.1104 - 0.4739 - 0.0054 = -0.2585$
It would cost the investor 0.2585 to set up a butterfly spread.

(ii) At maturity, the share price S_T will lie in one of the bands shown below:

(a) $S_T \leq 3.80$
All the options expire worthless — pay-off $= 0$
Total pay-off $= 0$

(b) $3.80 < S_T \leq 4.25$
The option with strike price 3.80 expires in the money — pay-off $= +(S_T - 3.80)$
All other options expire worthless — pay-off $= 0$
Total pay-off $= S_T - 3.80 > 0$

(c) $4.25 < S_T \leq 4.70$
The option with strike price 3.80 expires in the money — pay-off $= +(S_T - 3.80)$
The options with strike price 4.25 expire in the money — pay-off $= -2(S_T - 4.25)$
The option with strike price 4.70 expires worthless — pay-off $= 0$
Total pay-off
$= S_T - 3.80 - 2S_T + 2 \times 4.25$
$= 4.70 - S_T \geq 0$

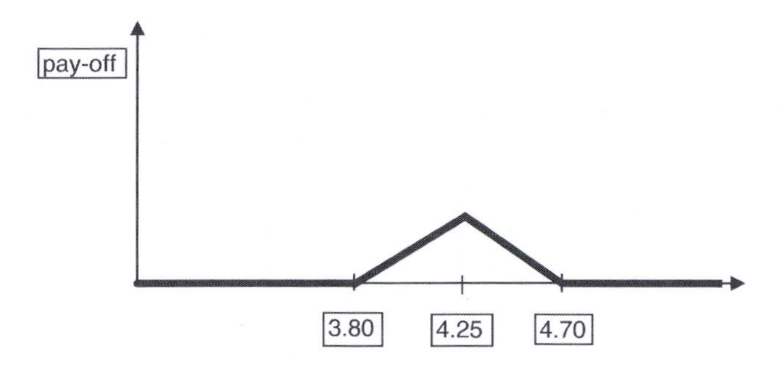

Figure 6.18

(d) $4.70 < S_T$

All options expire in the money. Total pay-off

$$= (S_T - 3.80) - 2(S_T - 4.25) + (S_T - 4.70)$$
$$= 2 \times 4.25 - 3.80 - 4.70$$
$$= 0$$

(The butterfly spread was created with 'average of high and low strikes = middle strike'. This is why. The pay-off when the value of the asset exceeds the high strike is to be zero.)

Putting this together,

At maturity:

If the asset value lies below the low strike or above the high strike, the pay-off is zero.

If the asset value lies between the two strike prices there is a positive pay-off.

The pay-off is: $S_T - 3.80$ if $3.80 < S_T \leq 4.25$

$4.70 - S_T$ if $4.25 < S_T \leq 4.70$

A pay-off diagram for a butterfly spread is shown in Figure 6.18.

A profit diagram is shown in Figure 6.19.

(iii) A butterfly spread is sold by taking steps opposite to those involved in buying a butterfly spread.

On the same asset and with the same maturity:

Sell two call options: one with a high strike price and one with a low strike price.

Buy two call options each with a strike price approximately the average of the high and low strikes.

Pay-off and profit diagrams for a written butterfly spread are shown in Figures 6.20 and 6.21.

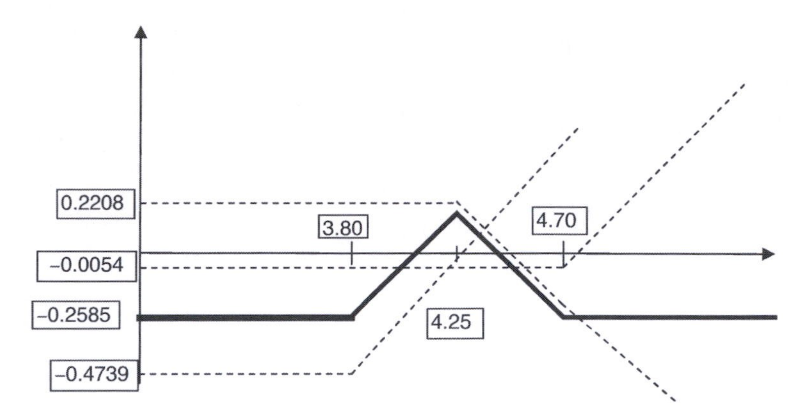

Figure 6.19

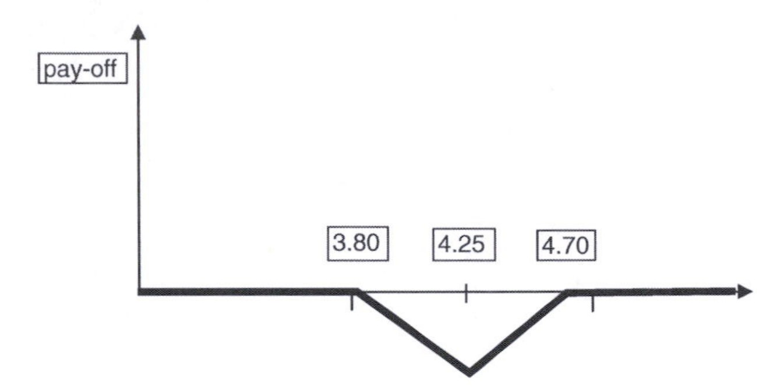

Figure 6.20

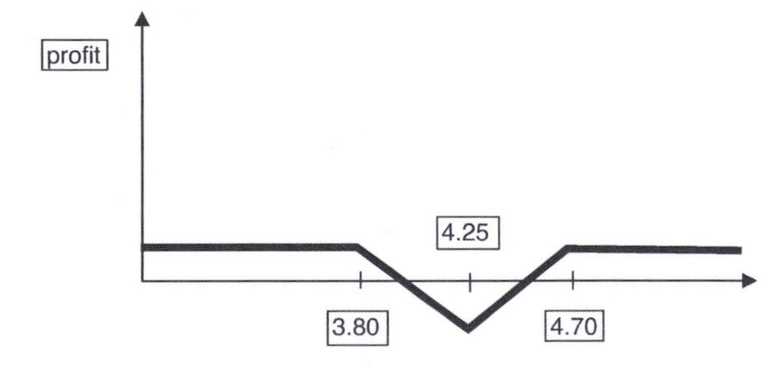

Figure 6.21

You might write (sell) a butterfly spread if you felt there would be, before maturity, a large movement in the asset value. You might not know (or care) whether the movement is upwards or downwards: writing a butterfly spread produces a modest profit if there is a large movement in the share price.

Notes:

- A small initial investment is needed to buy a butterfly spread.

- An investor might buy a butterfly spread if they believe that, before maturity, a large movement in the asset value, in either direction, is unlikely.
- An investor might sell a butterfly spread if they believe that, before maturity, a large movement in the asset value, in either direction, is highly likely.
- Butterfly spreads do not involve big risk. Losses and profits are modest. These are, relatively speaking, safe options.

Note also that butterfly spreads can be created from put options. See Exercise 17.

Combinations

A combination is a trading strategy involving both calls and puts. We consider three such strategies: straddles, strips and straps.

Straddle

CandS Chemicals has invested vast sums of money in a research programme to find a cure for lung cancer. Tom has examined the company's finances carefully. If the research programme is successful, the company will make enormous profits and the share price will increase sharply. But Tom has found that this is an all or nothing project for CandS Chemicals. A very large percentage of the company's assets have been invested in this project and if the programme should fail, it is Tom's belief that the future for CandS Chemicals would be bleak indeed and the share price, almost certainly, would fall sharply. So Tom is confident that over the next six months a large movement in the share price will occur, but he is not sure whether this movement will be upwards or downwards.

Tom could: buy a call option and a put option on CandS Chemicals shares, both options having the same strike price and the same maturity. By doing this, Tom has created a straddle.

On the same underlying asset and with the same maturity: buy a call option and a put option with the same strike price.

Example 14

The present value of CandS shares is \$22.5. Tom buys 2000 call and 2000 put options on these shares, each with strike price \$23 and maturity six months. Each call option costs \$1.41 and each put option costs \$1.12.

(i) Calculate the cost of setting up a straddle on CandS shares.
(ii) Illustrate the profit at maturity.

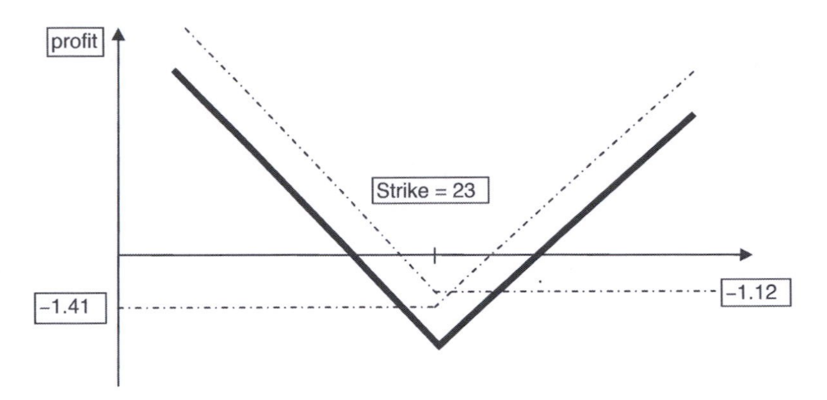

Figure 6.22

(iii) What is the greatest loss that Tom could make?
(iv) If the share price in six months' time is \$30, what profit will Tom make?

Solution

Today:

(i) It will cost $1.41 + 1.12 = \$2.53$ to set up a single straddle.
Tom's cash flow is $2000 \times (-2.53) = -5060$.
It will cost \$5060 to set up the 2000 straddles.

(ii) **At maturity:**
The pay-off for each call and put option at maturity will depend on the share price (S_T) at maturity. We argue, as usual, that this (presently unknown) share price must lie in one of the following bands.

Share price	Pay-off (call)	Pay-off (put)	Total pay-off	Profit
$S_T < 23$	0	$23 - S_T$	$23 - S_T$	$23 - S_T - 2.53 = -S_T + 20.47$
$S_T \geq 23$	$S_T - 23$	0	$S_T - 23$	$S_T - 23 - 2.53 = S_T - 25.53$

This leads to a profit diagram – see Figure 6.22.

(iii) Tom's maximum loss is the initial cost of entry: \$5060.

(iv) If the share price at maturity is \$30, Tom's profit per straddle is:

$$30 - 23 - 2.53 = 4.47$$

Tom's profit from 2000 straddles is $2000 \times 4.47 = \$8940$.

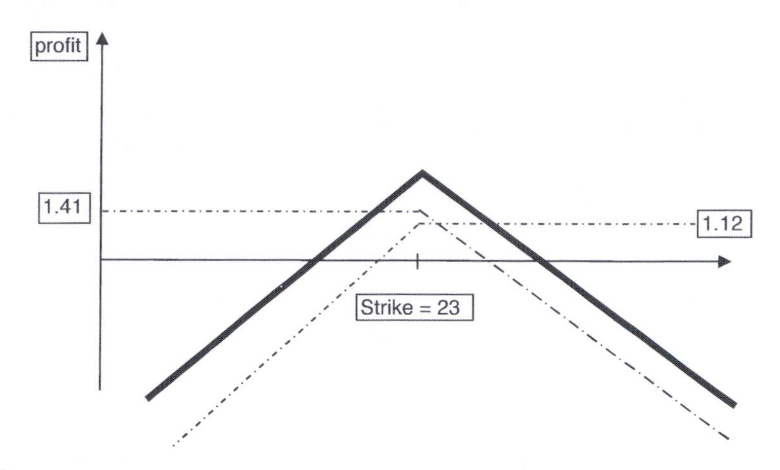

Figure 6.23

Notes:

- There is a positive charge attached to entering a straddle.
- A straddle is a sensible strategy for an investor who believes that a share value is about to undergo a large change but is not clear on whether this change will be an increase in value or a decrease. For his initial outlay, the investor gains the potential for a large profit. If the share price does not undergo a large change, the investor makes a limited loss.

A straddle is sold by taking the opposite steps. On the same underlying asset and with the same maturity: sell a call option and a put option with the same strike price.

The profit diagram for the investor who sold Tom the straddle is shown in Figure 6.23.

Observe that the seller of a straddle makes a limited profit if the share price stays close to the strike price. However, anyone selling a straddle is exposed, potentially, to unlimited losses. This is not just theoretical nonsense. See Exercise 20, which describes a famous straddle sold by Nick Leeson in Singapore in 1995. Extreme caution needs to be exercised when selling a straddle.

Strips and straps

In the previous example, from studying CandS Chemicals, Tom formed the impression the company was throwing money at the project in a manner that suggested a measure of desperation. On balance, Tom felt the research was not going well and a downward movement in the share price was more likely than an upward movement. In this case, Tom would set up a strip.

A strip

On the same asset and with the same maturity: buy **one** call option and **two** put options with the same strike price.

Example 15

With the above data Tom buys 2000 strips.

Value of CandS shares today = \$22.5. A six-month call option with strike price \$23 will cost \$1.41 and a six-month put option with strike price \$23 will cost \$1.12.

Today:

To buy one call option and two put options will cost $1.41 + 2 \times 1.12 = 3.65$. It will cost \$3.65 to set up one strip.

To buy 2000 strips will cost: $2000 \times (3.65) = \$7300$.

At maturity:

Again, the share price will lie in one of two bands:

Share price	Pay-off (call)	Pay-off (put)	Total pay-off	Profit (per strip)
$S_T < 23$	0	$23 - S_T$	$2(23 - S_T)$	$2(23 - S_T) - 3.65 = -2S_T + 42.35$
$S_T \geq 23$	$S_T - 23$	0	$S_T - 23$	$S_T - 23 - 3.65 = S_T - 26.65$

A profit diagram is shown in Figure 6.24.

Notes:

- There is a positive charge attached to entering a strip.

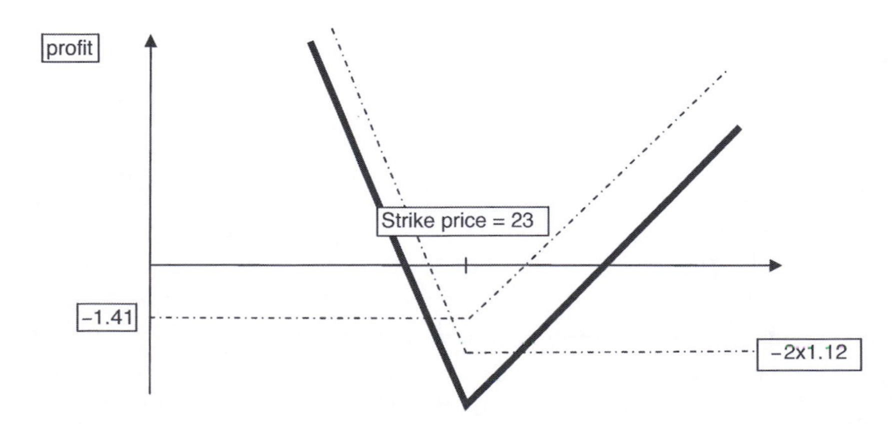

Figure 6.24

- The graph is generated by the profits associated with one call option and two put options. The downward line, calculated from asset values less than the strike price, illustrates the profit from two (in the money) put options and one (out of the money) call option. The upward line, calculated from asset values greater than the strike price, illustrates the profit from one (in the money) call option and two (out of the money) put options. Hence the downward line will be steeper than the upward line. Observe that the gradient of the downward line is -2 while the gradient of the upward line is $+1$.
- A strip is appropriate for an investor who expects a large shift in the value of the share price, is not certain whether the shift will be an upward shift or a downward shift, but on balance believes that a downward shift is the more likely.

A strap

A colleague looked at Tom's data on CandS Chemicals. 'I think they are chasing a result here,' he thought. 'It looks to me as though they are nailing down a product. They might just do it.'

Tom's colleague thought it more likely that CandS shares would rise. He bought a strap.

On the same asset and with the same maturity: buy **two** call options and **one** put option with the same strike price.

Example 16

With the above data, value of CandS shares today = \$22.5. A six-month call option with strike price \$23 will cost \$1.41; a six-month put option with strike price \$23 will cost \$1.12.

Today:

To buy two call options and one put option will cost $2 \times 1.41 + 1.12 = 3.94$. It will cost \$3.94 to set up one strap.

At maturity:

Share price	Pay-off (call)	Pay-off (put)	Total pay-off	Profit (per strip)
$S_T < 23$	0	$23 - S_T$	$23 - S_T$	$23 - S_T - 3.94 = -S_T + 19.06$
$S_T \geq 23$	$S_T - 23$	0	$2(S_T - 23)$	$2(S_T - 23) - 3.94 = 2S_T - 49.94$

A profit diagram for the strip is shown in Figure 6.25.

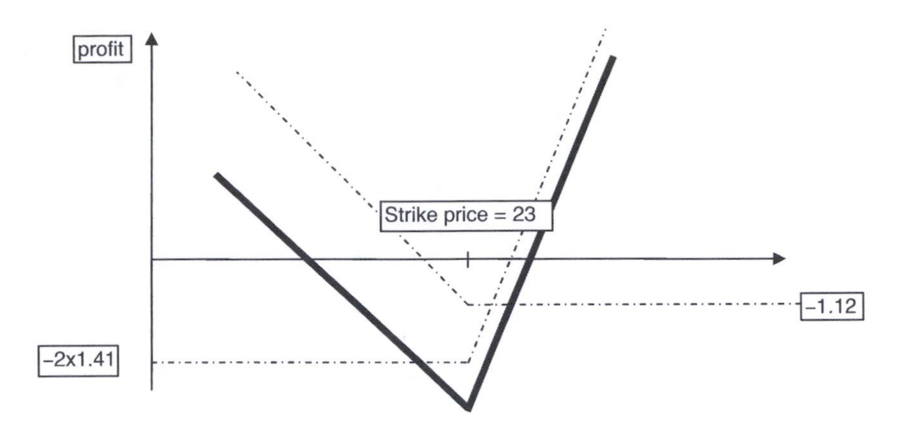

Figure 6.25

Notes:

- There is a positive charge attached to entering a strap.
- The graph is generated from the profits of two call options and one put option. The upward line (calculated from asset values exceeding the strike price) shows the profits from two (in the money) call options and one (out of the money) put option. The downward line shows the profits from one (in the money) put option and two (out of the money) call options. Hence the upward line will be steeper than the downward line. Note that the gradient of the upward line is $+2$ while the gradient of the downward line is -1.
- A strip is appropriate for an investor who expects a large shift in the value of the share price, is not certain whether the shift will be an upward shift or a downward shift, but believes that an upward shift is more likely than a downward shift.

We have described a variety of options based on call and put options. There are many more. Very many more. The reader will find some in the exercises, but it is time to see how call and put options, and some options based on call and put options, are priced. We introduce this topic in Chapter 7.

Exercise 6

1. What is a call option?

   Draw diagrams to illustrate (i) the pay-off, (ii) the profit from a call option.

   A call option on A2Z shares has a strike price of \$20 and costs \$1.50. Describe the range of values of A2Z shares at maturity that would lead to the holder of the option making a loss.

2. Joe will receive $1 000 000 in three months' time in settlement of an account. He is concerned that the pound might strengthen in value against the dollar (more dollars to the pound) over the next three months. Today, £1 = $1.8017. Joe could enter a forward contract or he could enter a call option (to buy pounds for dollars – a price agreed today). Describe carefully the advantages and disadvantages of entering a forward contract and a call option.

3. Jenny buys a call option on ABC shares. Maturity is in one month and the strike price is K = $18.00. The cost of the call option is $1.20. Draw diagrams to illustrate both the pay-off and the profit from the call option. Find (i) the pay-off, (ii) the profit if in one month's time the value of an ABC share is (a) $20.70, (b) $ 19.20, (c) $17.98.

4. What is a three-month put option? Draw pay-off and profit diagrams for a put option. Why might someone enter a put option?

5. Charlie buys a three-month put option (strike price = £25.00) for £2.00. Calculate (i) the pay-off, (ii) the profit if in three months' time the value of the asset is (a) £28.20, (b) £24.00, (c) £22.99. Draw a pay-off diagram and a profit diagram for this put option.

6. Draw graphs illustrating the pay-off for (i) a long call option, (ii) a short call option, (iii) a long put option, (iv) a short put option.

7. Teik has £100 000 to invest. PureSaving shares are doing quite well and he expects their value to continue to rise. Today, the price of a PureSaving share is £18.50. The cost of a three-month call option (strike price = £20.00) on PureSaving shares is £0.3066. The cost of a three-month put option (strike price = £21.00) is £2.3169. If Teik expects the share price to rise, he could:
   (i) buy PureSaving shares
   (ii) buy call options on PureSaving shares
   (iii) sell put options on PureSaving shares.

   Describe how Teik would set up a portfolio.

   Find the value of Teik's portfolio in three months' time if PureSaving shares then had a value of (i) £23.80, (ii) £19.50.

8. Sarah has $500 000 to invest. Cole S Troll and Co. makes monster meat pies and right now its shares are not doing well. The price of one share

is \$7.50. A one-month put option (strike price = \$7.50) on these shares is valued at \$0.1542. A one-month call option (strike price = \$7.50) is priced at \$0.1916.

Devise a strategy for Sarah.

Calculate the value of Sarah's portfolio in one month's time if the share price is then (i) \$5.20, (ii) \$7.90.

9. Chantal can buy a six-month call option (strike price = £10.00) for £1.457. The shares are selling today for £11.00 and the interest rate is 6.5%, annually compounded. A six-month put option (strike price = £10.00) is quoted at £0.16.
   (i) Use put–call parity to decide whether these prices are arbitrage free.
   (ii) Describe a profitable strategy you could follow.
   (iii) What is your profit from a single application of this strategy? How many times must you repeat this strategy to make a profit of £1000?

10. What is a bull spread? Draw a profit diagram for a bull spread. Describe three uses of a bull spread.

11. Ben buys a call option (strike price = \$16.5) for \$0.87 and sells a call option (strike price = \$20.00) for \$0.37. Both options expire in two months' time. Draw a profit diagram for the bull spread created from these call options. Calculate the profit/loss from the bull spread if, in two months' time, the underlying asset is valued at (i) \$25, (ii) \$18.00, (iii) \$15.

12. Describe carefully how to create a bull spread using two put options. Draw a profit diagram for the bear spread you create.

13. What is a bear spread? Draw a pay-off diagram for a bear spread. Describe three uses of a bear spread.

14. Chien buys a call option (strike price = £60.00) for £5.00 and sells a call option (strike price = £50.00) for £8.50. Draw a pay-off diagram to illustrate the pay-off at maturity. Why is this portfolio called a bear spread? Calculate the profit/loss from the bear spread if at maturity the underlying asset is valued at (i) £85.00, (ii) £54.50, (iii) £45.00.

15. Describe how to buy a bear spread using two put options.

16. Petra buys a call option (strike price = £35.00) for £1.50. She buys a call option with strike price £25.00 for £2.20 and sells two call options with a strike price of £30.00 for £1.80. All the options have the same expiry.
    (i) Draw a profit diagram for Petra's portfolio.
    (ii) Calculate the pay-off if the asset value at maturity is (a) £40, (b) £31, (c) £27.
    (iii) Why might someone buy such a portfolio?
    (iv) What is the name given to such a portfolio?

17. How would you buy a butterfly spread with put options? Draw a pay-off diagram for a butterfly spread created from put options. How does the cost of a butterfly spread created from call options differ from the cost of a butterfly spread created from put options?

18. Henry bought a three-month call option (strike price = $18.00) for $2.00 and a three-month put option (strike price = $18.00) for $1.50. Calculate the profit from this portfolio if the value of the asset at maturity was (i) $22, (ii) $18.00, (iii) $14.00. Draw a diagram to illustrate the profit from this portfolio at maturity. What might cause an investor to set up such a portfolio? What is the name given to such a portfolio?

19. What is a strip? What is a strap?
    K9Inc publishes books about dogs and it is not doing well. I buy a six-month call option (strike price = $15, cost = $1) and two six-month put options (strike price = $15, cost = $2) on K9Inc shares. Draw a profit diagram for this portfolio. What is my profit when the value of a K9Inc share at maturity is (i) $20, (ii) $14, (iii) $10? Describe my thinking when I bought this portfolio. Describe a situation that might have caused me to modify my portfolio to meet a different expectation.

20. (i) A call option with a strike price of $100 costs $8. A put option with the same strike price and maturity costs $12. I sell such a call and put option (and by doing so, I write a 'top saddle'). Construct a table showing the profit from this top saddle for different values of the asset. Draw a profit diagram for a top saddle. For which range of values does the top saddle described above reward the holder with a profit? Who would write a top saddle?
    (ii) In November and December 1994, in Singapore, a trader sold 37 925 straddles on the Nikkei 225 index. The strike price for each straddle

was in the region of 19 000 to 20 000 and each had a March maturity. Each straddle had a pay-off, at maturity, of \$5(S − K) where: S = value of Nikkei 225 at maturity and K = strike price.

As long as the Nikkei 225 lay within the range 19 000 to 20 000, the straddles remained broadly profitable.

On 17 January 1995, the Nikkei 225 was at 19 350, but during the day there was an earthquake at Kobe and the Nikkei 225 began to fall. By the end of the week, the Nikkei 225 lay at 18 950 and on 23 January it had fallen to 17 950.

Assume, for simplicity, that each straddle had a strike price of 19 500. Estimate the nominal worth of the 37 925 straddles on 23 January 1995.

On 27 February, Barings Bank, on whose behalf the trader had bought the straddles (and also other financial products), filed for bankruptcy with debts of around £850 million.

21. Show how a forward contract with three-month maturity can be created from a call option and a put option with strike price K and a three-month maturity.

22. A trader buys a call and a put with the same expiration date and different strike prices. The strike price for the call option (K_1) is greater than the strike price for the put option (K_2).

    (i) Copy and complete the table:

S = asset value at maturity	Pay-off (call)	Pay-off (put)	Pay-off
$S \leq K_2$			
$K_2 < S < K_1$			
$S \geq K_1$			

    (ii) Draw a pay-off diagram for this portfolio (called a strangle).
    (iii) Who might (a) buy (b) sell a strangle?

23. Let K_1, K_2 be real numbers with $0 < K_1 < K_2$. A collar option has pay-off $= \min[\max(S_T, K_1), K_2]$. Draw a pay-off diagram for a collar option for all values of the asset S_T at maturity.

24. The value of a share today is S_0. A call option on the share (strike price = K, maturity T years hence) has value C. The risk-free interest

rate is R (continuously compounded). Show that (i) $C \leq S_0$, (ii) $C \geq S_0 - Ke^{-RT}$.

Are there similar bounds for a put option? If so, what are they?

25. Buy a bull spread with call options having strike prices K_1 and K_2 ($K_2 > K_1$) and maturity at time T. Buy a bear spread using put options with strike prices K_1 and K_2 and maturity at time T. (i) Describe the characteristics of such a portfolio (called a box spread). (ii) What is the value of the box spread today (at time $t = 0$)? (iii) How can put–call parity help with the analysis?

7 Option pricing

A supermarket chain was experiencing cash problems. One of the principal share holders is uncomfortably aware that a large fall in the share price would hit her investment hard.

She talked to the chairman. 'Yes, we are having a few problems at the moment, but these are purely short term. The share price will bounce back and may even rise when the market realises this.'

The share holder was reassured. Almost. She rang her financial advisor. 'I would like to know the price of an option that will show a profit if the share price rises. But also, I would like to know the cost of an option that will pay me money when the share price rises and also when the share price falls.'

There was a short silence. 'I'll get back to you.'

In this chapter we describe a method for calculating the value today and at future times of a wide range of options. The value of an option will be dependent on the pay-off from the option and hence on the values of the underlying asset. So we will need to find a model for prices of the underlying asset. Maturity is the time the option value is known. At maturity, option value = pay-off from the option. So it would be sensible to to 'start' option pricing at maturity and then work back through time to today. To do this, we divide the time to maturity into a number of equal time intervals. Within each time interval, we will set up a portfolio consisting of some units of the asset and an amount of cash. Each portfolio, over its time interval, will match exactly (replicate) the option value, so the value of the portfolio will be the value of the option. In particular, the portfolio set up today will provide the value of the option today. Also, by observing a sequence of portfolios, we will see how the option changes value. Each of these stages is now described in greater detail.

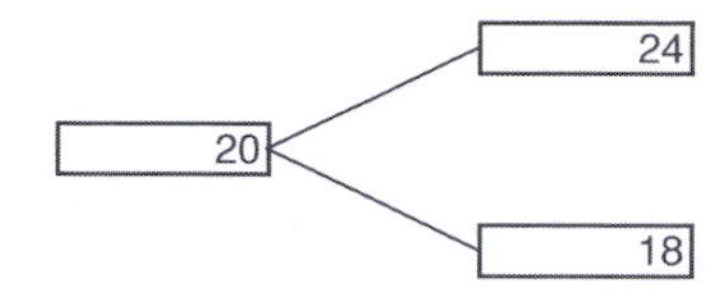

Figure 7.1

7.1 Introduction

We will illustrate the ideas numerically using a very simple example.

Example 1

Today PQ shares are priced at \$20. A call option on PQ shares with strike price \$21 has three months to maturity. To keep the calculations simple, assume the interest rate is 2% per quarter. (Since $1.02^4 = 1.0824$, the annual rate is 8.24%.) What is the value of this option today?

First, we set up a model for the share price. There are many ways of doing this, some elementary and some far from elementary. We will begin elementarily and extend the ideas until we have an effective and efficient model for the asset price.

1. To model the share price (a one-stage model)

We will assume that after three months, either the share price has risen to \$24 or it has fallen to \$18 (Figure 7.1).

This is a very simple model for the movement of a share price. This model allows just one change and is known as a one-stage model. Later, with straightforward extensions, we will consider models where, in the time to maturity, the share changes value more than once (multi-stage models).

2. To calculate the pay-off of the option at maturity

The strike price is \$21.

At maturity: if the share price is \$24, the pay-off $= 24 - 21 = 3$
if the share price is \$18, the pay-off $= 0$ (Figure 7.2).

3. To set up a replicating portfolio

The aim is to calculate the value of the option today. To do this, we will set up a portfolio consisting of PQ shares and cash. The idea is that at maturity, **under**

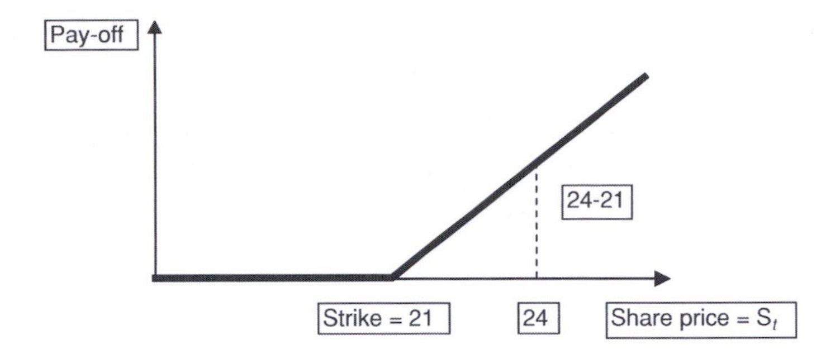

Figure 7.2

all possible movements of the market, the portfolio will match, **exactly**, the pay-off made by the option. In this way, the portfolio will replicate the option. When we know the value of one, we know the value of the other. But we will know, today, the value of the portfolio; hence we will know, today, the value of the option.

Today ($t = 0$)
Set up a portfolio consisting of:

a PQ shares: $b in cash.

$$\text{Value of portfolio today} = a \times 20 + b$$

At maturity ($t = 0.25$)
The share price is either $24 or $18. But there is no doubt about what has happened to the cash. In three months, $b has increased in value to $b \times 1.02$.

Value of portfolio $= a \times 24 + b \times 1.02$ if the share price has increased to $24

$= a \times 18 + b \times 1.02$ if the share price has decreased to $18

But the portfolio is required to match the option pay-off:

So
$$a \times 24 + b \times 1.02 = 3$$
$$a \times 18 + b \times 1.02 = 0$$

This is just a set of simultaneous equations in a and b. To solve these equations:

Subtract: $a \times (24 - 18) = 3$

So
$$a = \frac{3}{24 - 18} = \frac{1}{2}$$

Substituting in the first equation:

$$b \times 1.02 = 3 - \frac{1}{2} \times 24$$

$$b = \left[3 - \frac{1}{2} \times 24\right] \times 1.02^{-1}$$

$$b = \frac{-9}{1.02}$$

$$= -8.824$$

Now we have a portfolio that replicates the option pay-off. We have $\frac{1}{2}$ of one share and we owe (we have borrowed) $8.824.

4. To calculate the value of the option today

The portfolio matches the pay-off and the pay-off is the value of the option at maturity. Hence, value of portfolio = value of option (or introduce an arbitrage opportunity).

This gives: value of option today $= a \times 20 + b$

$$= \frac{1}{2} \times 20 - 8.824$$

$$= 1.18$$

The option is yours for $1.18.

To understand what is happening with this portfolio and to perform the calculations in Excel, an algebraic treatment is needed.

7.2 Repeat (algebraically)

The share price today is known. Call this S. We shall write the future values as $S \times u$ and $S \times d$ where u and d are known, uncontroversially, as the 'up' and the 'down' factors (Figure 7.3).

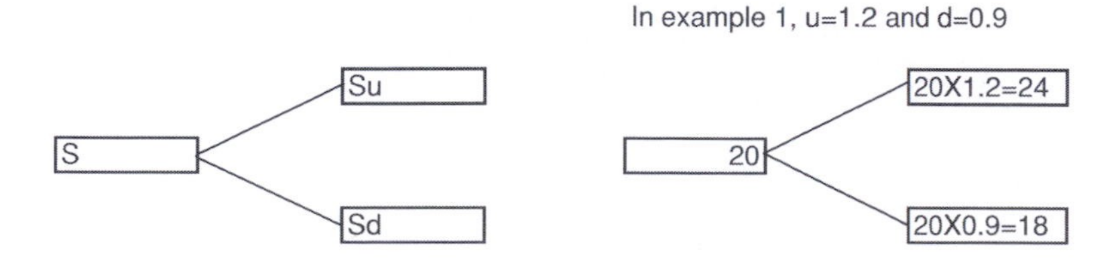

Figure 7.3

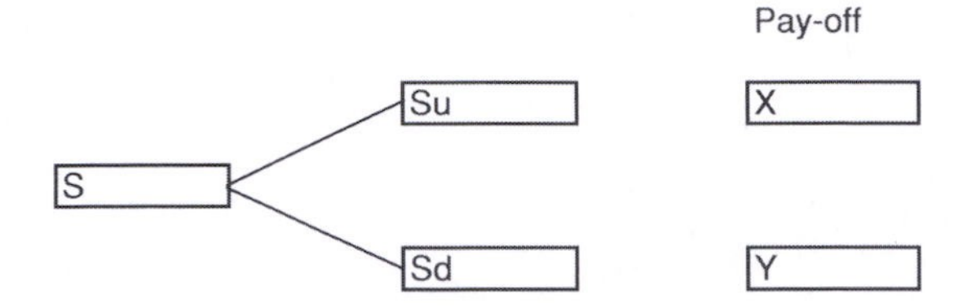

Figure 7.4

We shall write the pay-off for the option as:
X (the pay-off after an up move)
Y (the pay-off after a down move) (Figure 7.4).
Now we do the calculation again. Let the portfolio consist of:

a units of the share   b units of cash.

To ease the notation, we will let the interest rate **over the period to maturity** be r. So if $b is invested today at this rate, the amount of the investment, at maturity, will be $b(1 + r)$.

Today $(t = 0)$
Portfolio value $= aS + b$
At maturity $(t = T)$

Portfolio value $= aSu + b(1 + r)$ after an up move
$= aSd + b(1 + r)$ after a down move

For the portfolio to replicate the pay-off:

$$aSu + b(1 + r) = X$$
$$aSd + b(1 + r) = Y \qquad ****$$

Solving the simultaneous equations, by first subtracting:

$$a(Su - Sd) = X - Y$$
$$a = \frac{X - Y}{S(u - d)}$$

and then substituting:

$$\begin{aligned} b(1 + r) &= X - aSu \\ &= X - \frac{X - Y}{S(u - d)}Su \\ &= X - \frac{(X - Y)u}{u - d} \end{aligned}$$

Take a common denominator of u − d:

$$= \frac{X(u-d) - (X-Y)u}{u-d}$$

Collect X and Y terms in the numerator:

$$= \frac{X(u-d-u) + Yu}{u-d}$$

$$= \frac{X(-d) + Yu}{u-d}$$

This gives: $$b = \frac{X(-d) + Yu}{(u-d)(1+r)}$$

So we have:

Value of portfolio today = aS + b

$$= \frac{X-Y}{S(u-d)} \times S + \frac{X(-d) + Yu}{(u-d)(1+r)}$$

So long as the simultaneous equations **** have a solution (the equations do not represent parallel lines), these equations can be used to value an option. We have, so far, thought only about call options. But this method can be used to value a put option or indeed any other option, simply by using the appropriate pay-off function to calculate values for X and Y.

We illustrate the method in Excel for a call option and a put option. Observe that the pay-off functions for these options (the strike price is K) are:

Call option (Figure 7.5)

$$\text{Pay-off} = \begin{cases} S_t - K & S_t > K \\ 0 & S_t \le K \end{cases} = \max(S_t - K, 0)$$

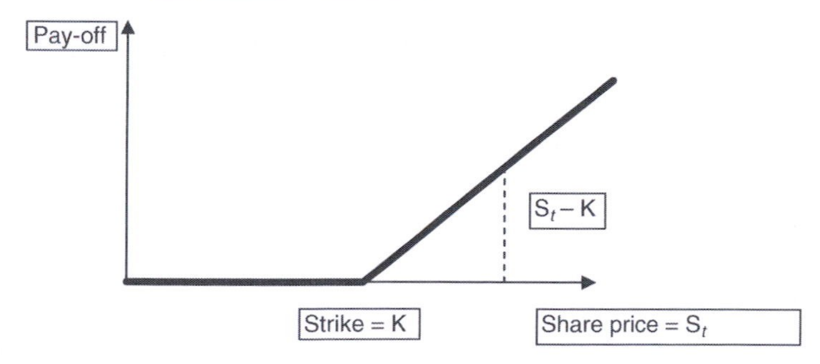

Figure 7.5

Put option (Figure 7.6)

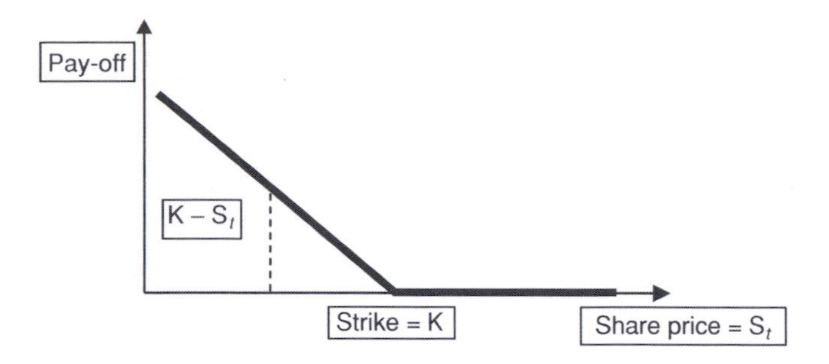

Figure 7.6

$$\text{Pay-off} = \begin{array}{|ll|} \hline K - S_t & S_t < K \\ \hline 0 & S_t \geq K \\ \hline \end{array} = \max(K - S_t, 0)$$

Example 2

The value of one HHX share, today, is £7.50. Take u = 1.2, d = 0.9. The interest rate is 6.09% per year (compounded annually). What is the value, today, of a call option with strike price £6.90 and maturity six months? What is the value of the corresponding put option? Verify the put–call parity relationship.

Solution

Call option:

In the spreadsheet in Figure 7.7, in B10, we see that the multiplying factor for six-monthly borrowing is $1.0609^{0.5} = 1.03$. The pay-off function is $\max(S_T - K, 0)$. This is given for an up move in B12 and for a down move in B13. The portfolio is given in B15 and B17. The option value ($aS + b$) is given in B19. The value of the call option is C = £0.8835.

Put option:

In Figure 7.8, the pay-off function is $\max(K - S_T, 0)$ and this appears in B12 (up move) and B13 (down move). The option value appears in B19. The value of the put option is P = £0.0825.

Put–call parity demands

$$C + K(1 + r)^{-1} = P + S$$

(Observe that since the interest rate is now an annually compounded rate, the discounting factor is $(1 + r)^{-1}$ ($=1.03^{-1}$). In the put–call parity equation

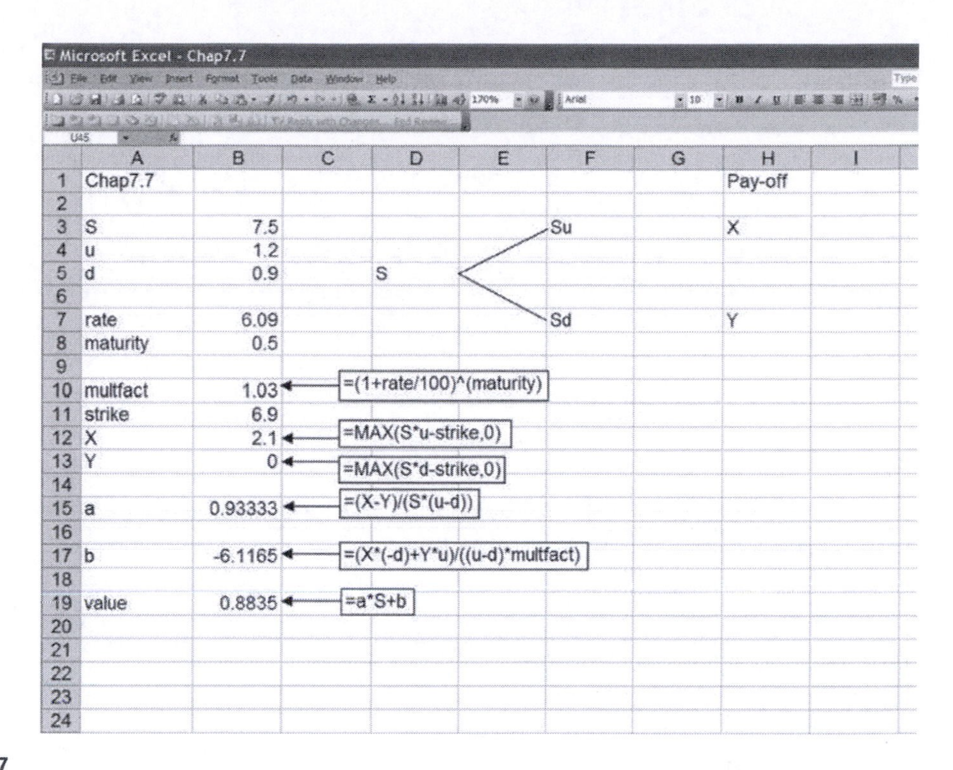

Figure 7.7

Microsoft Excel - Chap7.8

	A	B	C	D	E	F	G	H
1	Chap7.8							Pay-off
2								
3	S	7.5				Su		X
4	u	1.2						
5	d	0.9		S				
6								
7	rate	6.09				Sd		Y
8	maturity	0.5						
9								
10	multfact	1.03	=(1+rate/100)^maturity					
11	strike	6.9						
12	X	0	=MAX(strike-S*u,0)					
13	Y	0.15	=MAX(strike-S*d,0)					
14								
15	a	-0.06667	=(X-Y)/(S*(u-d))					
16								
17	b	0.58252	=(X*(-d)+Y*u)/((u-d)*multfact)					
18								
19	value	0.08252	=a*S+b					
20								
21								
22								
23								

Figure 7.8

in Chapter 6, section 6.3, the interest rate r was continuously compounded and the discounting factor was e^{-rt}.)

$$C + K(1 + r)^{-1} = 0.8835 + 6.90 \times 1.03^{-1} = £7.5825$$
$$P + S = 0.0825 + 7.5 = £7.5825$$

Put–call parity is verified.

Comment: We might have expected that the call option would be more expensive than the put. Today, the share price at £7.50 is higher than the strike price at £6.90. The call option is in the money while the put option is out of the money.

7.3 Risk neutral probabilities

There is a deeper result hidden within the calculations shown above. This result shows us a most attractive way of thinking about option pricing as well as revealing how to create a world free of risk. We look again at the value, today, of an option. But rather than just calculate the numerical value of the option, we shall take the expression giving the value of the option and manipulate this expression into a form that reveals something surprising. The calculations, initially, are intricate, but the result is worth the effort. We perform these calculations, as before, first arithmetically and then algebraically.

Today

Value of call option = a × 20 + b.

We know expressions for a and b. We shall write a and b using the up and down factor notation with 24 = 20 × 1.2 and 18 = 20 × 0.9. We use the three-monthly multiplying factor, 1.02^{-1}

From above we have:

$$a = \frac{3 - 0}{20(1.2 - 0.9)} \text{ and } b = \left[\frac{3 \times (-0.9) + 0 \times 1.2}{1.2 - 0.9}\right] \times 1.02^{-1}$$

This gives:

$$\text{Value of call option} = \frac{3 - 0}{20(1.2 - 0.9)} \times 20 + \left[\frac{3 \times (-0.9) + 0 \times 1.2}{1.2 - 0.9}\right] \times 1.02^{-1}$$

To observe the result we seek, we keep the two possible pay-offs 3 and 0 prominent in the calculation.

First step: cancel the 20 in the first term. Write 1.2 – 0.9 = 0.3.

$$\text{Value of call option} = \frac{3-0}{0.3} + \left[\frac{3 \times (-0.9) + 0 \times 1.2}{0.3}\right] \times 1.02^{-1}.$$

We want 1.02^{-1} to be a factor of the whole expression and not just the second term.

$$\text{Value of call option} = 1.02^{-1}\left[\frac{3-0}{0.3} \times 1.02 + \frac{3 \times (-0.9) + 0 \times 1.2}{0.3}\right].$$

Write the expression in [ ] as a single fraction (and multiply out (3 – 0) × 1.02).

$$\text{Value of option} = 1.02^{-1}\left[\frac{3 \times 1.02 - 0 \times 1.02 + 3 \times (-0.9) + 0 \times 1.2}{0.3}\right].$$

Collect together the pay-off amounts 3 and 0.

$$\text{Value of call option} = 1.02^{-1}\left[\frac{3 \times (1.02 - 0.9) + 0 \times (-1.02 + 1.2)}{0.3}\right].$$

Write the expression in [ ] as the sum of a multiple of 3 and a multiple of 0.

$$\text{Value of call option} = 1.02^{-1}\left[3 \times \frac{1.02 - 0.9}{0.3} + 0 \times \frac{1.2 - 1.02}{0.3}\right]. \quad \text{Eqn 7.1}$$

The numbers multiplying the pay-off amounts 3 and 0 are:

$$\frac{1.02 - 0.9}{0.3} = 0.4 \quad \text{and} \quad \frac{1.2 - 1.02}{0.3} = 0.6$$

These numbers lie between 0 and 1 and they add to 1. They behave like probabilities. Could they be probabilities? 0.4 multiplies the pay-off 3 (the result of an up movement in the asset) and 0.6 multiplies 0 (the result of a down movement). We could interpret 0.4 and 0.6 as the probabilities of up and down movements respectively. This would give the result shown in Figure 7.9.

Remarkably, we appear to have found the probability associated with movements of the share price. If true, that would be astonishing and potentially

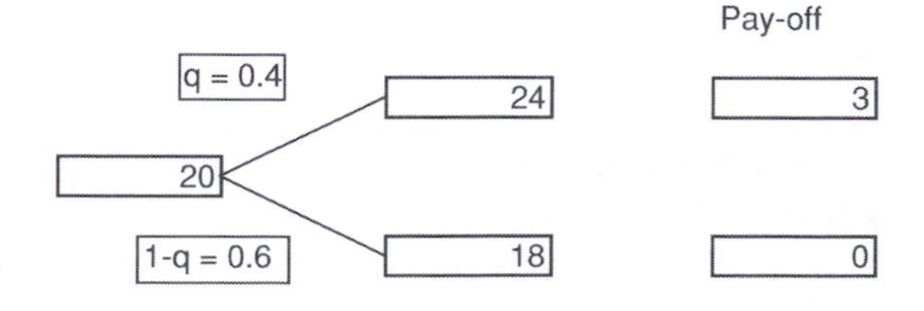

Figure 7.9

enormously profitable. However, these probabilities are not 'real world' probabilities. These probabilities operate in (and define) a world that is 'fair'. They measure the likelihood of up and down moves in a model that contains no arbitrage opportunities. So a price obtained by the use of these probabilities is a 'fair' price; there is no possible movement of the share price that will ensure a certain profit. Because the world governed by these probabilities is a fair world, these are known as **risk neutral probabilities.** In Chapter 1 (section 1.6), we saw how the bookie could calculate probabilities (odds) that removed his risk and so create for himself a risk-free world. Now we have done exactly that in relation to share prices and option values.

Eqn 7.1 is important. We state this result in a more general setting.

Write q for 0.4 and $1 - q$ for 0.6.

Then:

$$\text{Value of call option} = 1.02^{-1}[3 \times q + 0 \times (1 - q)]. \qquad \text{Eqn 7.2}$$

Or:

$$\begin{aligned}\text{Value of call option} &= 1.02^{-1}[q \times \text{pay-off after an up move} \\ &\qquad + (1 - q) \times \text{pay-off after a down move}] \\ &= 1.02^{-1}[qX + (1 - q)Y]. \qquad \text{Eqn 7.3}\end{aligned}$$

The expression in [ ] is familiar. In statistical terms, this is the expected value of the pay-off under the probability distribution $\{q, 1 - q\}$.

We write this E^Q[pay-off] to emphasise the dependence on the probability distribution $\{q, 1 - q\}$.

This gives:

$$\text{Value of option} = 1.02^{-1}E^Q[\text{pay-off from option}].$$

We can go one step further. The pay-off from an option is the cash received or paid out, in settlement, at maturity. So this must be the value of the option at maturity.

This gives the extremely important result:

$$\text{Value of option} = 1.02^{-1}E^Q[\text{value of option at maturity}].$$

As can be seen from this result, risk neutral probabilities are extremely important in our world – that is, in the world of financial mathematics. In [1] and [2] below, we glimpse the way the subject is developed in a more advanced treatment. However, in this book we will not pursue this development and these two sections could easily be skipped on a first reading.

1. Risk neutral probabilities and asset values

Recall Figure 7.9. Suppose we calculate an expression for the asset value that corresponds to Eqn 7.2.

$$\begin{aligned} 1.02^{-1} \times [q \times 24 + (1 - q) \times 18] &= 1.02^{-1} \times [0.4 \times 24 + 0.6 \times 18] \\ &= 1.02^{-1} \times 20.4 \\ &= 20 \end{aligned}$$

This suggests that $S = 1.02^{-1}[q \times Su + (1 - q) \times Sd]$ (you are asked to prove this in Exercise 9).

Again, the expression in [ ] is familiar. This can be written:

q × asset value after up move + (1 − q) × asset value after down move.

This is E[new asset value] under the probability distribution $\{q, 1 - q\}$.

We write this E^Q[new asset value] again to emphasise the dependence on the probability distribution $\{q, 1 - q\}$.

We have:

initial asset value (S) = $1.02^{-1} \times E^Q$[new asset value].

This important equation tells us two things:

(a) initial asset value × 1.02 = E^Q [new asset value].

So the growth of the (initial) asset value under the risk-free rate (the left-hand side) is the expected value, under $\{q, 1 - q\}$, of the new asset values. From this it is reasonable to believe there is no arbitrage in this set-up (although this does need proving).

(b) $$\text{initial asset value (S)} = E^Q\left[\frac{\text{new asset value}}{1.02}\right] = \left[q \times \frac{Su}{1.02} + (1 - q) \times \frac{Sd}{1.02}\right]. \qquad \text{Eqn 7.4}$$

But $\frac{Su}{1.02}$ and $\frac{Sd}{1.02}$ are the new asset values discounted back to $t = 0$. The initial asset value, S, is trivially discounted back to $t = 0$.

Write S_0 = discounted initial asset value

and S_1 = discounted new asset values

then Eqn 7.4 gives: $S_0 = E^Q[S_1]$.

This is a wonderfully neat and concise description of the growth of the asset under a risk neutral probability. In more advanced work, this is often taken as the starting point and is used to define a risk neutral probability distribution.

2. Risk neutral probabilities and option values

We saw in Eqn 7.3:

Value of option $= 1.02^{-1}[qX + (1 - q)Y]$

Guided by **1**(b), we consider:

$$\text{Value of option} = q \times \frac{X}{1.02} + (1 - q) \times \frac{Y}{1.02}. \qquad \text{Eqn 7.5}$$

Again: $\frac{X}{1.02}$ and $\frac{Y}{1.02}$ are the pay-off values (= values of the option at maturity) discounted back to $t = 0$.

Hence the right-hand side is E^Q[discounted option values at maturity].

Let V_1 = discounted option value at maturity.

Trivially, the initial option value is already discounted back to $t = 0$. Write this as V_0.

Then Eqn 7.5 gives: $V_0 = E^Q[V_1]$.

That the asset values and the option values based on that asset satisfy simple equations of identical form is truly remarkable. In more advanced work, these equations would be leading us towards martingales, a vital topic in this subject, but we are not going down that road. This marks the end of [2]. Back to the main text.

Given that the option value is written in terms of risk neutral probabilities, it is in our interest to find out how these probabilities are calculated. From Eqn 7.1 we might make a reasonable guess that

$$q = \frac{1.02 - 0.9}{1.2 - 0.9} = \frac{(1+r) - d}{u - d} \quad \text{and} \quad 1 - q = \frac{1.2 - 1.02}{1.2 - 0.9} = \frac{u - (1+r)}{u - d}$$

We state some important results as a theorem.

Theorem

The price of an asset, today, is S. After a time t, the asset takes one of the values Su or Sd.

An option has pay-off: X if the asset takes the value Su

Y if the asset takes the value Sd.

The interest rate over the period to time t has multiplying factor $1 + r$ (Figure 7.10).

Then:

(a) The risk neutral probabilities $\{q, 1 - q\}$ are given by:

$$q = \frac{(1+r) - d}{u - d} \qquad 1 - q = \frac{u - (1+r)}{u - d}$$

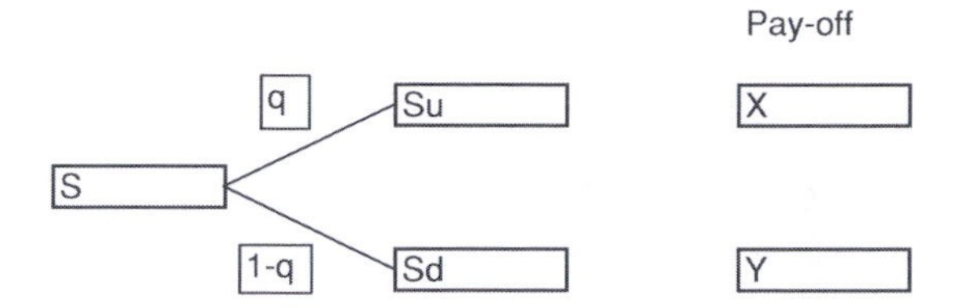

Figure 7.10

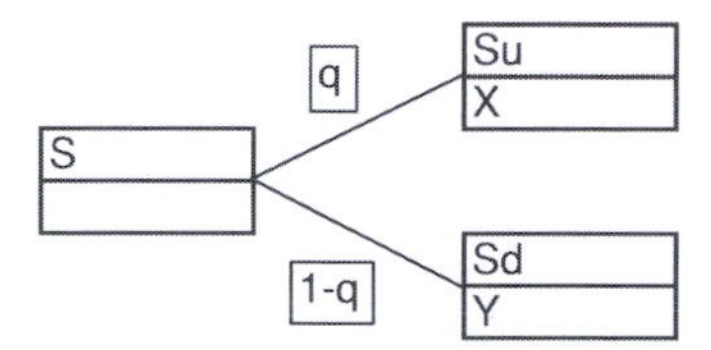

Figure 7.11

(b) $S = (1 + r)^{-1}[qSu + (1 - q)Sd]$
$\quad = (1 + r)^{-1}E^{Q}[\text{new asset value}]$

(c) Value of option initially $= (1 + r)^{-1}[qX + (1 - q)Y]$
$\quad = (1 + r)^{-1}E^{Q}[\text{pay-off}]$
$\quad = (1 + r)^{-1}E^{Q}[\text{option value at maturity}]$

where E^{Q} denotes the expected value under the risk neutral probabilities $\{q, 1 - q\}$.

(c) is proved in Appendix 1. The proofs for (a) and (b) are Exercises 8 and 9.

Notation

We can think of $\{q, 1 - q\}$ as moving the asset forward to its future values. We can also think of $\{q, 1 - q\}$ as taking the pay-off back (via discounting) to the present value of the option. Since the probability distribution is used with both the asset and the pay-off, we shall write the asset, the pay-off and, where appropriate, the risk neutral probabilities together (Figure 7.11).

Example 3

The price of one share in BeefUp Fitness Centres is £15.50. The up and down factors are $u = 1.1$, $d = 0.95$. Find the price of a three-month put option with a strike price of £15 on BeefUp Fitness Centres shares. (Assume that £1 today will be worth £1.015 in three months' time.)

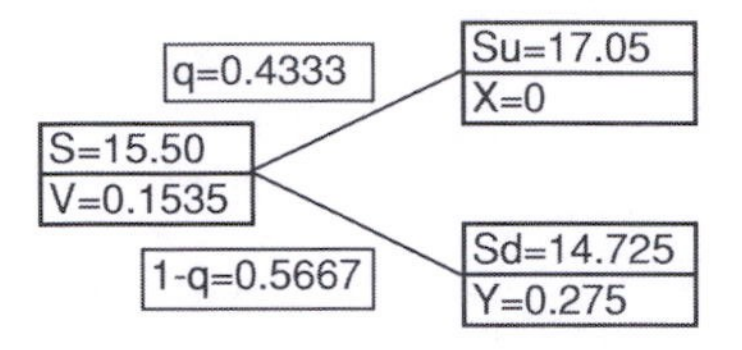

Figure 7.12

Solution

$S = 15.50$
$u = 1.1$ giving $Su = 17.05$
$d = 0.95$ giving $Sd = 14.725$
$1 + r = 1.015$
Strike price $= 15$
$X = \max(15 - 17.05, 0) = 0$
$Y = \max(15 - 14.725, 0) = 0.275$

$$q = \frac{1 + r - d}{u - d} = \frac{1.015 - 0.95}{1.1 - 0.95} = 0.4333$$

$1 - q = 1 - 0.4333 = 0.5667$

$$\text{Value} = 1.015^{-1}[0.4333 \times 0 + 0.5667 \times 0.275]$$
$$= £0.1535. \text{ Or } £0.15.$$

See Figure 7.12.

Notes:

1. We have used $(1 + r)^{-1}$ to discount the expected pay-off. This was to ease the notation through a difficult patch. It is common, however, to consider a continuously compounded interest rate, r. In this case, the discounting factor is e^{-rt} where t is the time (in years) to the up/down move in the share price.

   But the discounting factor occurred also in the expression giving the risk neutral probabilities. We re-state the relevant results using a continuously compounded interest rate r and a time of t years to the up/down move in the share value.

   Risk neutral probabilities: $q = \frac{e^{rt} - d}{u - d}$ $\quad 1 - q = \frac{u - e^{rt}}{u - d}$

   Value of option $= e^{-rt}[qX + (1 - q)Y]$
   $= e^{-rt}E^Q[\text{pay-off}]$

   where E^Q denotes the expected value under the risk neutral probabilities $\{q, 1 - q\}$.

2. There needs to be a sensible way of choosing the up, down factors, u and d. Some thoughts might be useful.
   (i) The model we have used allows just one change in the asset value before maturity. The time to this change is measured as t years. But realistically, models should allow the share price to change several times before maturity. (We do this in section 7.4.) We might set up a model, for example, where the share price changes daily. In this case, $t = \frac{1}{365}$. It might be expected that if the change in asset price occurs in (say) three months, the up/down factors would be more extreme than those in a model where the change occurs in one day. So it would be sensible to expect the up and down factors to be sensitive to the time period t between changes in the share price.
   (ii) We would expect u and d to be responsive to market volatility. Volatility is a measure of uncertainty over movement in the value of the stock. In a highly volatile market (large movements in share values over short periods of time) there will be more uncertainty than in a market of low volatility. We will let σ represent market volatility. In a 'normal' market, volatility is around 25% and we would take $\sigma = 0.25$. But in a more volatile market, we might have $\sigma = 0.6$ (volatility of 60%). In a flat market, σ might be 0.1 (10%) or even 0.05 (5%) (becalmed!).

   We will decide when setting up the model the period of time after which the share price will alter (one day, one week, one month, etc.) and this will give a value for t. But volatility has to be estimated (usually from past data). One way of doing this is described in Appendix 2. For the present, we will assume that volatility over the period to the next change in the share value is known.

When a continuously compounded interest rate r is used, a method suggested by Cox-Ross-Rubinstein in an important paper in 1979 is to take:

$$u = e^{\sigma\sqrt{t}} \qquad d = e^{-\sigma\sqrt{t}}$$

where:
t is the time, in years, to the creation of the new share prices (Su and Sd) and σ is the volatility of the share price.

[If the interest rate is not given in continuously compounded form, then a conversion equation should be used. Suppose, for example, that the given interest rate is 6.5% per year, compounded twice yearly. Let r be the equivalent continuously compounded rate. Then, over one year:

$$e^{r\times 1} = \left(1 + \frac{0.065}{2}\right)^{2\times 1} = 1.0661 \quad \text{and } r = \ln(1.0661) = 0.0640].$$

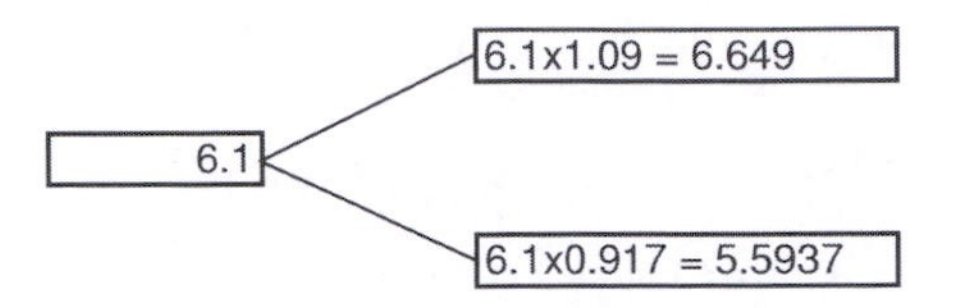

Figure 7.13

Note: the Cox-Ross-Rubinstein choice of u and d has intuitive appeal: u and d are both positive, u > 1, d < 1 and u and d can reflect different time periods and more (or less) volatility in the market. However, we note here that when the strike price differs from the value of the asset, there can be convergence problems with this choice of u and d and the use of Leisen parameters is recommended. These are described at the end of section 7.4.

Example 4

The share price of Batty Electronics, today, is $6.10. The current interest rate (compounded annually) is 5% and the volatility over the next month has been estimated at 0.3.

Calculate (i) the up and down factors, u and d, for movement in the share price over the next month, (ii) the value of a one-month put option on Batty shares with strike price $6.20.

Solution

(i) $\sigma = 0.3 \qquad t = \dfrac{1}{12}$

$$u = e^{\sigma\sqrt{t}} = e^{0.3\times\sqrt{\frac{1}{12}}} = 1.09$$

$$d = e^{-\sigma\sqrt{t}} = e^{-0.3\times\sqrt{\frac{1}{12}}} = 0.917$$

See Figure 7.13.

We know: value of put option $= e^{-rt}[qX + (1-q)Y]$

(ii) We need to calculate e^{rt} where r is the equivalent continuously compounded rate and t is the time to change in value of the share value.

$$e^{r\times 1} = 1.05^1$$

$$e^{r\times\frac{1}{12}} = 1.05^{\frac{1}{12}} = 1.0041$$

(iii) We need the risk neutral probabilities $\{q, 1-q\}$.

$$q = \frac{e^{rt}-d}{u-d} = \frac{1.0041-0.917}{1.09-0.917} = 0.5035$$

$$1-q = 1-0.5035 = 0.4965$$

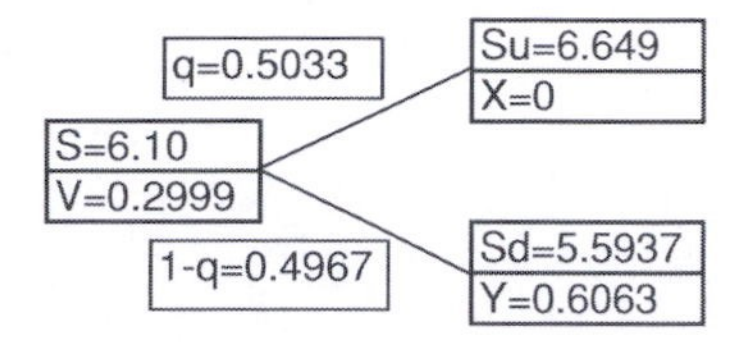

Figure 7.14

(iv) We need the pay-off values, X and Y.

$$\begin{aligned} X &= \text{pay-off from the put option after an up move} \\ &= \max(6.20 - 6.649, 0) = 0 \\ Y &= \text{pay-off from a put option after a down move} \\ &= \max(6.20 - 5.5937, 0) = 0.6063 \end{aligned}$$

Hence:

$$\begin{aligned} \text{value of put option} &= 1.0041^{-1} \times [0.5035 \times 0 + 0.4965 \times 0.6063] \\ &= 0.2998. \quad \text{Or} \quad \$0.30. \end{aligned}$$

See Figure 7.14 – there are slight rounding errors.

The model we have constructed is called a **one-stage binomial tree**. The model is straightforward and allows us to achieve with ease the twin objectives of replicating the pay-off and pricing the option. However, one-stage binomial trees have an obvious flaw. In real life the asset will change value frequently and to inject realism into the model we must allow for frequent changes in the asset value. The model we set up in section 7.4 allows for more than one change in the asset value but is not so complex as to make option pricing difficult.

7.4 Multi-stage binomial trees

To model the asset value

We will set up a model where up and down movements in the asset value occur in sequence. There will be a time period (an hour, a day, a month) during which the asset value makes one change. During this period, the asset value behaves like a one-stage binomial tree. But each one-stage tree in the process branches into two others (Figure 7.15).

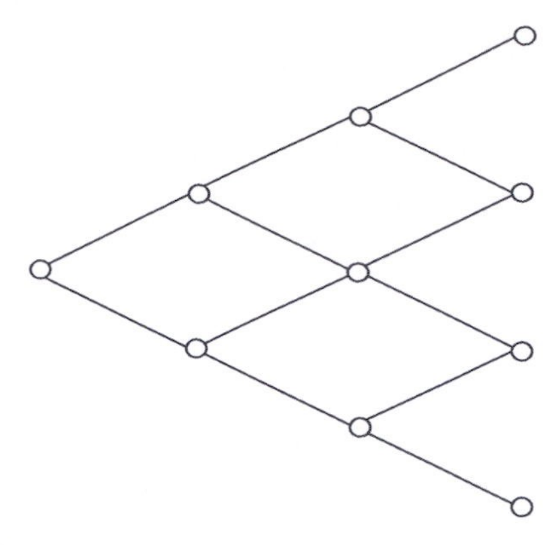

Figure 7.15

In each time period (in each one-stage tree):

either the asset increases in value and moves to the new value:

(present value) × u

or the asset decreases in value and takes the value:

(present value) × d.

Example 5

Today, an asset is priced at \$5. It is thought the up–down factors per month are given by:

$u = 1.1 \qquad d = 0.95.$

Construct a three-stage tree to model the growth of the asset over a three-month period.

Solution

Consider Figure 7.16. Observe:

(1) We could use different u and d values in each time period. In this way, we could model changing market conditions. However, in this book we will keep the same u, d values throughout the tree.

(2) In this model, an up move followed by a down move gives the same asset value as a down move followed by an up move. When this happens, we have what is known as a recombining tree. The recombining property is more for computational efficiency than for realistic asset modelling.

Example 6

Today, the asset is priced at \$10. Let $u = 1.03$, $d = 0.99$. Suppose that, in the real world, up and down moves are equally likely. So prob(up) = 0.5,

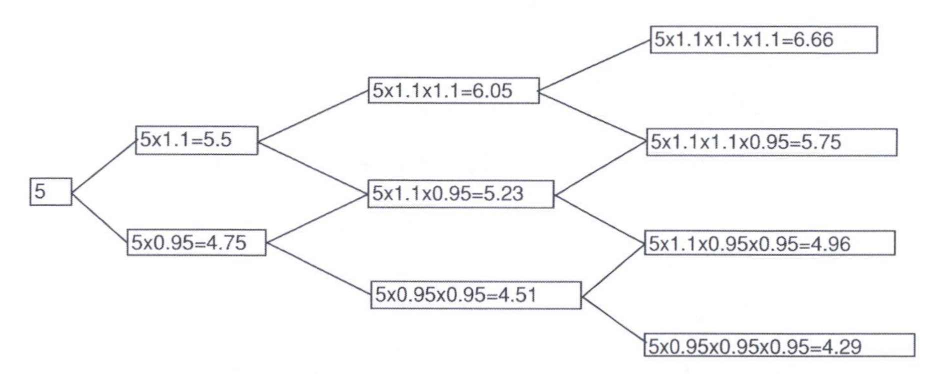

Figure 7.16

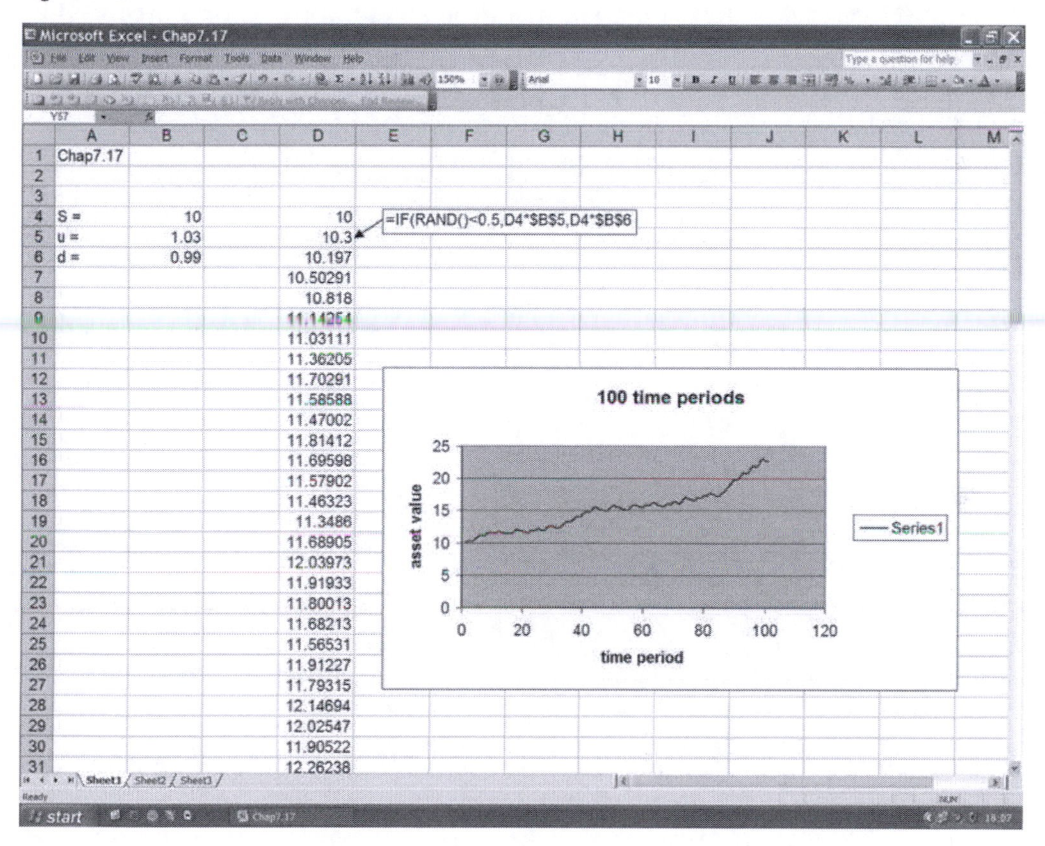

Figure 7.17

prob(down) = 0.5. Consider a model with 100 time periods. We simulate one possible route through the multi-stage tree. In Figure 7.17 we show the Excel spreadsheet and the graph of the simulated asset values.

This is beginning to look like the history of a share price. By varying u and d, the reader could generate different asset price histories.

To calculate option values from a multi-stage tree

The method is an extension of that described above.

Procedure

(1) Decide how many time periods (changes in asset value) are to occur before maturity.

(2) Starting with today's value for the asset, sweep out a tree with the number of time periods agreed in (1).

For example: three periods will give the tree in Figure 7.18.

In this way, we sweep forward from today through to maturity, calculating, at each vertex, a value of the asset.

(3) Calculate the interest rate multiplying factor for each time period. This will be of the form $1 + r$ for discrete compounding and e^{Rt} (where R is the annual rate and t is the time period) for continuous compounding.

(4) Use the interest rate multiplying factor together with u and d to calculate, for each one-stage tree, the risk neutral probabilities $\{q, 1 - q\}$.

(5) At maturity, calculate the pay-off from the option for each possible final value of the asset. The pay-off is the value of the option at that vertex of the tree.

(6) Let V be a vertex one time period back from maturity. Originating from V is a one-stage tree terminating at maturity. Use the known option values at maturity (X, Y), the risk neutral probabilities and the interest rate multiplying factor for this tree to calculate the value of the option at V (Figure 7.19).

Repeat for all vertices one time period back from maturity. Now, we know the value of the option both at maturity and one time period back from maturity.

(7) Let V be a vertex two time periods back from maturity. Originating at V is a one-stage tree where, at both end points, the option value (X and Y) is known. The interest rate multiplying factor and the risk neutral probabilities are known. Use Figure 7.19 to calculate the option value at V. In this way, calculate the option value at all vertices two time periods back from maturity.

(8) Repeat this method, working backwards through the tree, moving back one time period at each stage, until the option value for the first vertex (today) has been calculated.

Each vertex of the tree will now have both an asset value and an option value. The option value today is the price we require.

Now we illustrate the method. We proceed as before, first numerically and then, to find out what is actually happening in the process, algebraically.

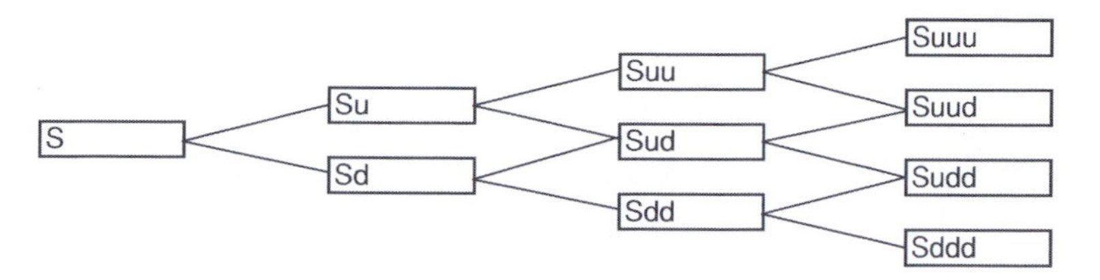

Figure 7.18

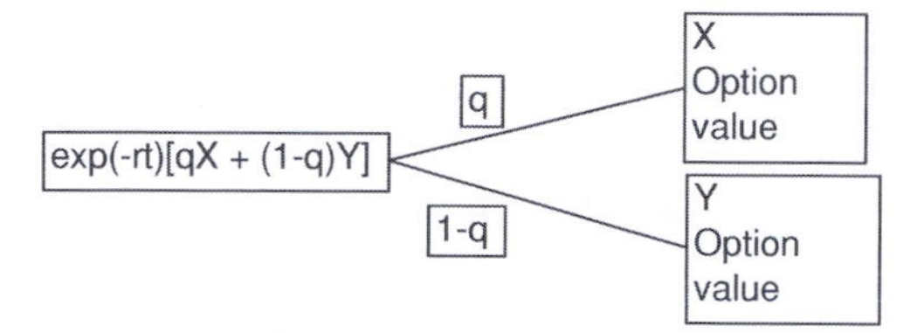

Figure 7.19

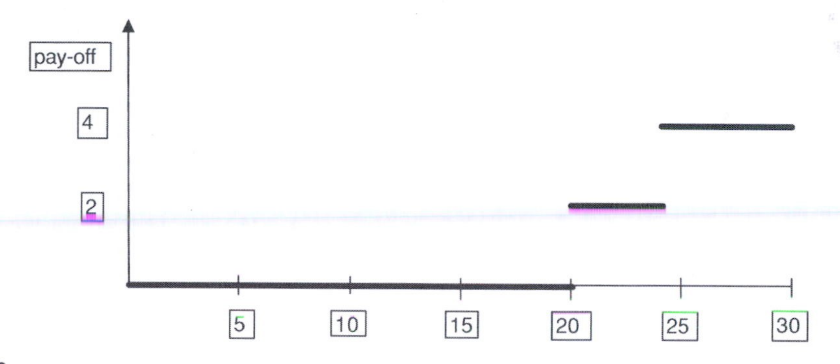

Figure 7.20

Example 7

A share is valued today at \$20. The up and down factors over a three-month period are $u = 1.1$, $d = 0.95$.

At maturity, in six months' time, the option will pay out:

\$4 if the share price exceeds \$24

\$2 if the share price is greater than \$20 but less than or equal to \$24

0 otherwise (Figure 7.20).

The interest rate is 8% per year, compounded continuously. How much would it cost, today, to buy such an option?

Solution

(1) The time to maturity is six months. We know how the share price changes over three months. Each time period is 0.25 years. Set up a two-stage binomial tree.

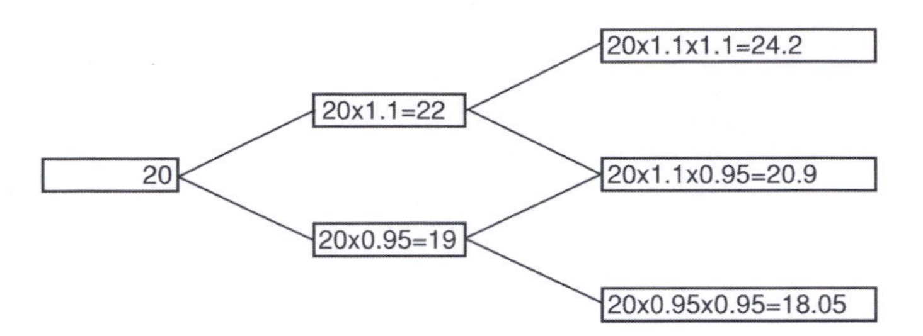

Figure 7.21

(2) Sweep out a two-stage tree using u = 1.1, d = 0.95 (Figure 7.21).

(3) The interest rate multiplying factor for the period between asset value changes is $e^{0.08\times 0.25} = 1.0202$.

(4) Calculate the risk neutral probabilities {q, 1 − q}.

Because u, d and r hold over both three-month periods, the risk neutral probabilities will be identical over the two stages.

$$
\begin{aligned}
q &= \frac{e^{rt} - d}{u - d} \\
&= \frac{e^{0.08\times\frac{3}{12}} - 0.95}{1.1 - 0.95} \\
&= 0.468
\end{aligned}
$$

$$1 - q = 0.532$$

(5) Calculate the pay-off at maturity for each possible value of the asset.

This gives the option value at the three maturity vertices. It will be convenient to write the option value under the asset value (as in Figure 7.22).

(6) Look at the vertices one time period back from maturity. These two vertices are the starting points for two one-stage trees, A and B. The trees and the associated option values are illustrated in Figure 7.23.

The calculations are:

$$\text{At A:}\quad e^{-0.08\times\frac{3}{12}}[0.468 \times 4 + 0.532 \times 2] = 2.8779$$

$$\text{At B:}\quad e^{-0.08\times\frac{3}{12}}[0.468 \times 2 + 0.532 \times 0] = 0.9175.$$

(7) Look at the vertices two stages back from maturity. There is just one vertex. This is the starting point for tree C. This tree (with associated option values) is shown in Figure 7.24.

The calculation is:

$$e^{-0.08\times\frac{3}{12}}[0.468 \times 2.8779 + 0.532 \times 0.9175] = 1.7986.$$

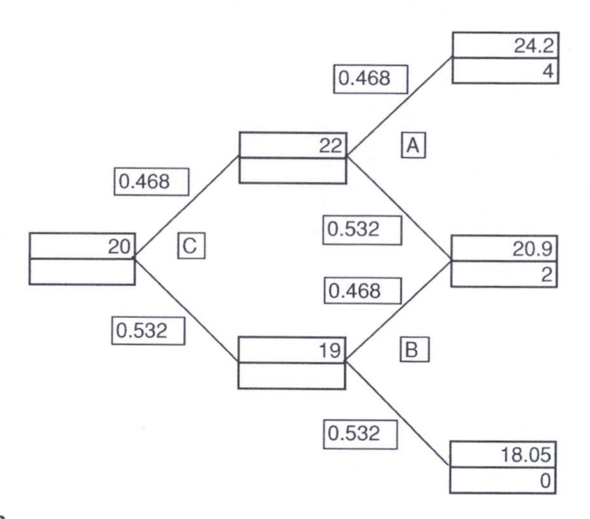

Figure 7.22

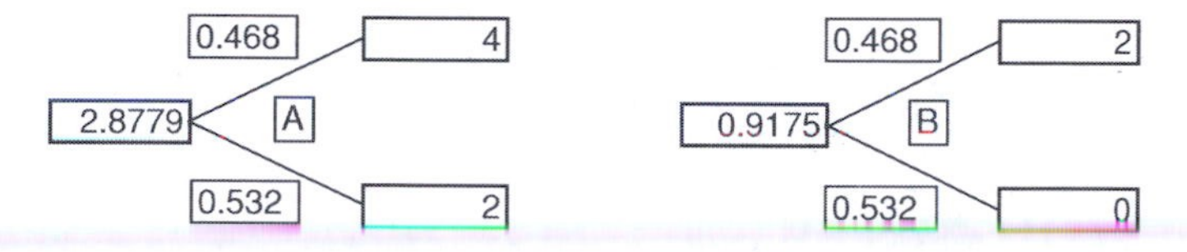

Figure 7.23

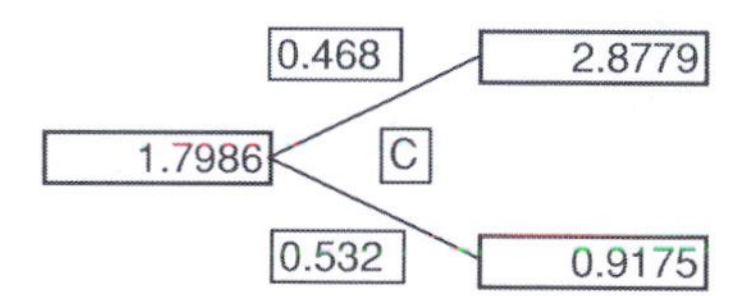

Figure 7.24

(8) All vertices now have both an asset value and an option value. The value of the option today is the value underneath today's share price.

Putting all this together, we get Figure 7.25.

Hence, today you would pay $1.7986 to buy this option. Or $1.80.

This illustrates the process arithmetically. An algebraic treatment reveals that a result established previously holds more widely than might have been expected. We assume, as before, that the up, down factors, u and d, and the risk neutral probabilities are constant throughout the model (Figure 7.26). (Although a slight extension of the algebra shows that this does not have to be so.)

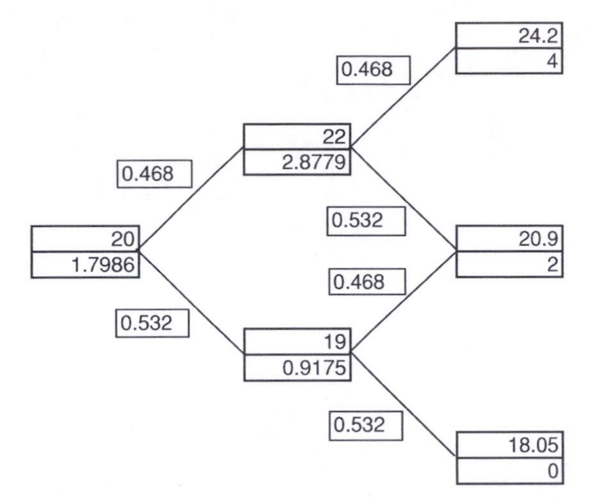

Figure 7.25

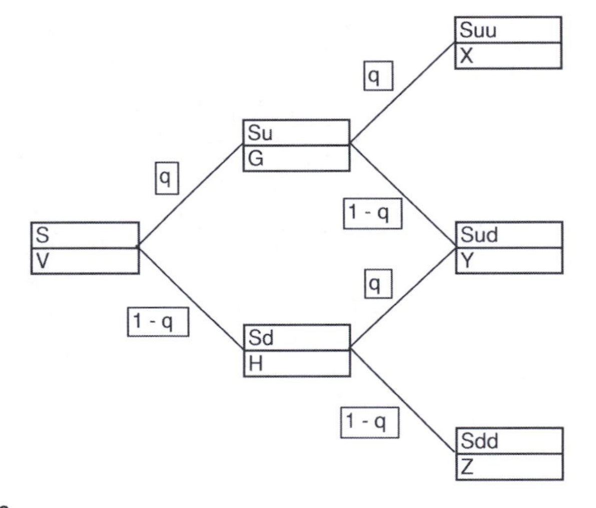

Figure 7.26

From the two one-stage trees terminating at maturity:

$$G = e^{-rt}(qX + (1 - q)Y)$$
$$H = e^{-rt}(qY + (1 - q)Z)$$

And from the one-stage tree terminating at the intermediate vertices:

$$V = e^{-rt}[qG + (1 - q)H]$$

Substituting values for G and H:

$$V = e^{-rt}[q \times e^{-rt}(qX + (1 - q)Y) + (1 - q) \times e^{-rt}(qY + (1 - q)Z)]$$
$$= e^{-2rt}[q(qX + (1 - q)Y) + (1 - q)(qY + (1 - q)Z)]$$
$$= e^{-2rt}[q^2X + q(1 - q)Y + (1 - q)qY + (1 - q)^2Z]$$

The expression in [ ] is:

prob(reaching a pay-off) $\times$ pay-off   summed for all routes through to maturity.

This is, E^Q[pay-off] Hence:

$$V = e^{-2rt} \times E^Q[\text{pay-off}].$$

In a two-stage tree, e^{-2rt} is the discounting factor from maturity back through to today. Hence, as before:

V = discounted value of expected pay-off under Q.

An identical result holds for trees with three or more stages.

This shows that the risk neutral probabilities behave exactly as we might have hoped. We have here a probability tree adorned with the values of the asset and the option.

The above calculations show how to work out the value of an option using a multi-stage binomial tree. This is hugely important. However, in the one-stage tree model, we demonstrated a portfolio that replicated the option. This portfolio told us how to arrive at the pay-off holding exactly what would be needed to settle the contract. By holding such a portfolio we were making sure we would not be exposed to adverse movements in the market.

We would like to set up a similar strategy with multi-stage trees and remarkably, the method established for a one-stage tree goes through unchanged to a multi-stage tree.

In section 7.1 we formed a portfolio:

a: units of the asset,   \$b in cash.

We showed that

$$a = \frac{X - Y}{Su - Sd} \quad b = \frac{X(-d) + Yu}{u - d} e^{-rt}$$ assuming a continuously compounded interest rate.

$$b = \frac{X(-d) + Yu}{u - d}(1 + r)^{-1}$$ if (1 + r) is the multiplying factor for the period between changes in the asset value.

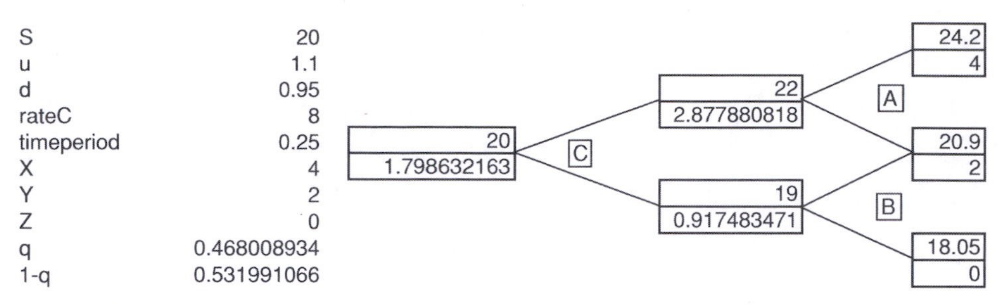

Figure 7.27

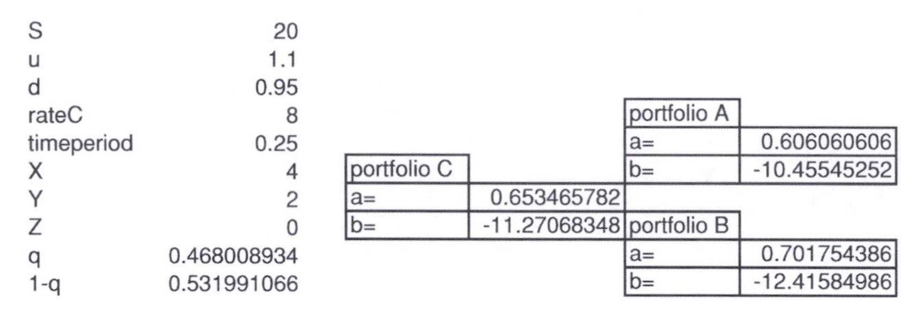

Figure 7.28

Looking again at Example 7, we calculate the a, b portfolio for each of the one-stage trees A, B and C (Figure 7.27).

For A:

$$a = \frac{4-2}{24.2-20.9} = 0.6061$$

$$b = \frac{4(-0.95) + 2 \times 1.1}{1.1 - 0.95} e^{-0.08 \times \frac{1}{4}}$$

$$= -10.4555$$

For B:

$$a = \frac{2-0}{20.9-18.05} = 0.70175$$

$$b = \frac{2(-0.95) + 0 \times (1.1)}{1.1 - 0.95} \times e^{-0.08 \times \frac{1}{4}}$$

$$= -12.41585$$

The portfolio for C is calculated in the same way.

The three portfolios are shown in Figure 7.28.

Of course, we could have used these three portfolios to calculate the option values at the two intermediate vertices and then at the initial vertex. But observe something remarkable. In Figure 7.29, we show the value of each portfolio at the time it was set up and again at the end of the life of the portfolio. The interesting feature here is that the value of the first portfolio at the end of its life (2.8779 after an up move, 0.9175 after a down move) is exactly the same as the value of the succeeding portfolio at the beginning of its life.

But of course, these values had to be equal. Otherwise, an arbitrage opportunity would appear. Yet after the reassurance of zero arbitrage, we can appreciate an important fact. This is that the first portfolio, at the end of its life, can be

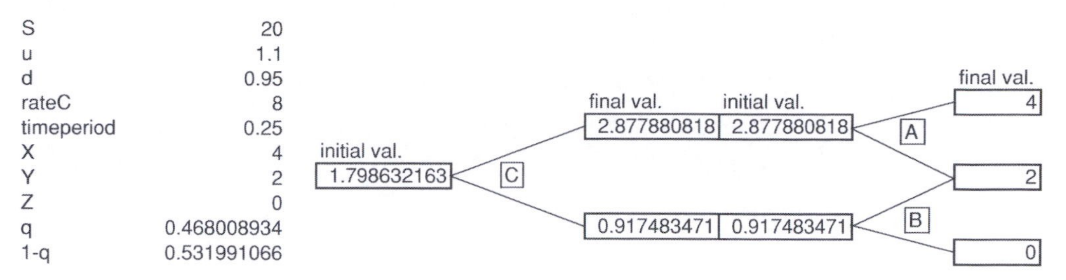

Figure 7.29

replaced by the second portfolio **at no additional cost.** At any vertex, we can determine the portfolio emanating from that vertex, but we do not know which portfolio will replace it at the end of its life. This will depend on whether an up move or a down move occurs. But we do know that when the time arrives to replace that portfolio, we will be able to buy the replacement portfolio from the funds made available from the sale of its predecessor. This is extremely neat. We can replace the first portfolio by the second, the second by the third, the third by the fourth and so on in a sequence of costless transactions. So we know, initially, that each movement in the value of the option will be matched (costlessly) by the purchase of a new portfolio. In this way, we know that we will be able to ride the twists and turns of the share price and replicate the value of the option. By following the strategy of successively buying and selling portfolios, we can arrive at maturity with precisely what will be needed to settle our obligations. This is replication and this strategy eliminates risk.

This concludes the discussion. To illustrate the ideas, we have a (rather long) example. The solution to each section is given after the statement of the question.

Example 8

Peter believes that RX1 shares are going to change in value, substantially, over the next three months, but he is not sure whether the change will be an increase in value or a decrease. RX1 shares are priced today at £8.

He buys an option that rewards him if the share price does undergo a large change in value. The pay-off of the option, where S_T is the share price in three months' time, is given by:

$$\text{Pay-off} = \begin{array}{l} 2 \text{ if } 10 < S_T \\ 1 \text{ if } 9 < S_T \leq 10 \\ 1 \text{ if } 6 \leq S_T < 7 \\ 2 \text{ if } S_T < 6 \\ 0 \text{ otherwise} \end{array}$$

The interest rate is 8% per year, compounded annually.

(i) Construct a three-stage binomial tree to model the RX1 share price over the coming three months. Take u = 1.1, d = 0.93. Calculate also the risk neutral probabilities {q, 1 − q}.

Solution

This achieved most comfortably in Excel.

The time (in years) over a single stage of the tree is $\frac{0.25}{3} = 0.083333$. The interest rate multiplying factor over one stage is $(1 + 0.08)^{0.083333} = 1.006434$.

The risk neutral probabilities are given by:

$$
\begin{aligned}
q &= \frac{1 + r - d}{u - d} \\
&= \frac{1.006434 - 0.93}{1.1 - 0.93} \\
&= 0.449612
\end{aligned}
$$

$$1 - q = 0.550388$$

The calculations are shown in Figure 7.30.

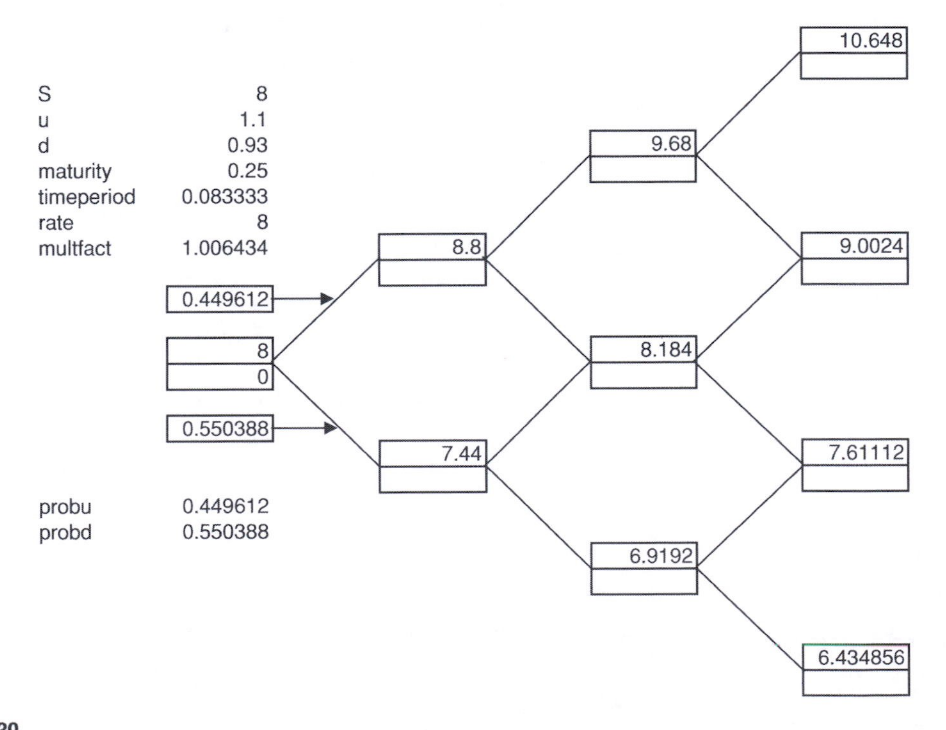

Figure 7.30

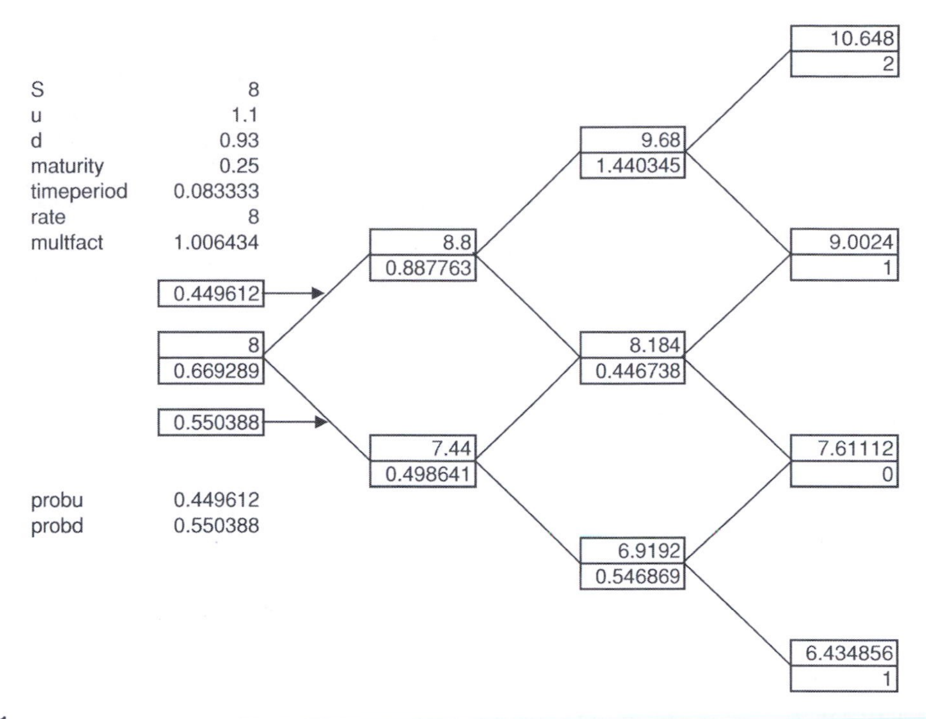

Figure 7.31

(ii) Enter the pay-off at maturity. Work back through the tree to calculate the option value at each vertex. Find the value of the option today.

Solution

The pay-off at maturity, per option, is:

£2	if $S_T > 10$	or $S_T < 6$
£1	if $9 < S_T \leq 10$	or $6 \leq S_T < 7$
0	otherwise	

To calculate the option values at vertices before maturity, use:

$$\text{option value} = 1.006434^{-1} \times (q \times optionv(u) + (1 - q) \times optionv(d)).$$

So the option value corresponding to the share price £9.68 will be:

$$\begin{aligned}\text{option value} &= 1.006434^{-1} \times (0.449612 \times 2 + 0.550388 \times 1)\\ &= 1.440345.\end{aligned}$$

This is illustrated in Figure 7.31. The value of the option today is £0.6693. Or £0.67.

(iii) Knowing the option values at the intermediate vertices, we can calculate the (a,b) portfolios.

Calculate the first portfolio. Show that the value of this portfolio is the value of the option today. Find the value of this portfolio at **its** maturity.

Solution

$$a = \frac{X - Y}{Su - Sd} \qquad b = \frac{X(-d) + Yu}{u - d}(1 + r)^{-1}$$

So for the first portfolio,

$$a = \frac{0.887763 - 0.498641}{8.8 - 7.44} = 0.28612$$

$$b = \frac{0.887763(-0.93) + 0.498641 \times 1.1}{1.1 - 0.93} \times 1.006434^{-1} = -1.619668.$$

So the plan is to buy 0.28612 of one share and borrow £1.619668.

Initially, this portfolio has the value $0.28612 \times 8 + (-1.619668) =$ £0.669289 (as we had hoped). At maturity, the portfolio has value:

$$0.28612 \times 8.8 + (-1.619668) \times 1.006434 = 0.887763 \text{ (after an up move)}$$

$$0.28612 \times 7.44 + (-1.619668) \times 1.006434 = 0.498641 \text{ (after a down move).}$$

So the first portfolio does replicate the option value over the first stage of the tree.

(iv) Knowing the option value at each intermediate stage, we can calculate (a,b) portfolios for each one-stage binomial tree in the model. At the end of the first stage, we will know whether an up move or a down move has occurred. At this moment, we will need a new portfolio, based on the move that has, in fact, occurred. We calculate this new portfolio. As can be checked, the initial value will be the option value at the vertex we have reached and the value of the portfolio at **its** maturity will match exactly the two possible option values.

Suppose that, in fact, the share price follows a udd progression and has the value £7.61112 at maturity. Show that the portfolios track the option values and so replicate the option.

Solution

The calculations are best carried out in Excel (Figure 7.32).

The three portfolios that will accompany a udd progression of the share price will be:

F D B

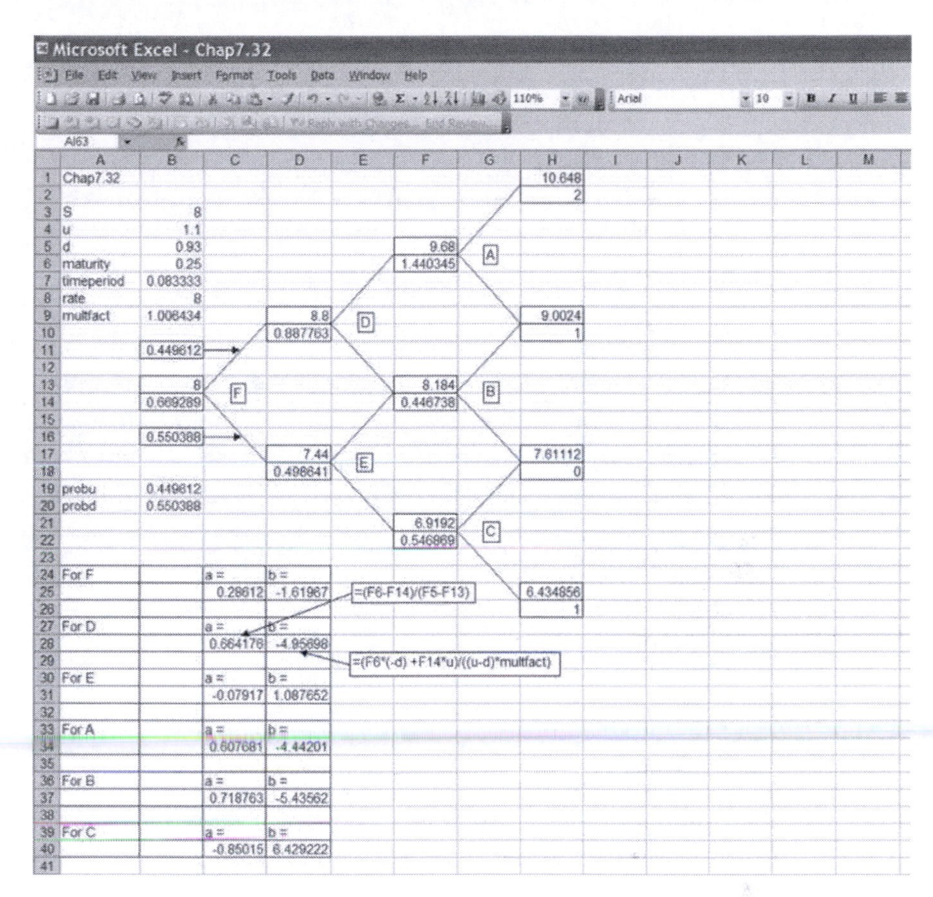

Figure 7.32

The initial and final values of these portfolios are given by:

F	initial value	0.669289
	final value (up move)	0.887763
	final value (down move)	0.498641
D	initial value	$0.664176 \times 8.8 + (-4.956984) = 0.887763$
	final value (up move)	$0.664176 \times 9.68 + (-4.956984) \times 1.006434 = 1.440345$
	final value (down move)	$0.664176 \times 8.184 + (-4.956984) \times 1.006434 = 0.446738$
B	initial value	$0.718763 \times 8.184 + (-5.435615) = 0.446738$
	final value (up move)	$0.718763 \times 9.0024 + (-5.435615) \times 1.006434 = 1$
	final value (down move)	$0.718763 \times 7.61112 + (-5.435615) \times 1.006434 = 0$

As expected, the D, B portfolios can be set up with the money created by their predecessors and B terminates with the pay-off values from the option. One portfolio has made way for its successor costlessly and the final portfolio in the chain has terminated with the pay-off values. The option has been costlessly replicated.

Accuracy

As the number of stages in the tree becomes large (and the time between changes in the asset value small), the accuracy of the calculated value of the option should improve. But more stages mean more calculation and a lot of work has been done to find choices for u and d that will give a high level of accuracy with fewer stages (and less calculation). The Cox-Ross-Rubinstein equations (section 7.3, just before Example 4) can produce an unsatisfactory convergence pattern when the strike price differs from the initial asset price. One choice for u and d that extends the Cox-Ross-Rubinstein equations is:

$$u = e^{\sigma\sqrt{\delta t} + \frac{1}{n}\ln(\frac{K}{S})} \qquad d = e^{-\sigma\sqrt{\delta t} + \frac{1}{n}\ln(\frac{K}{S})}$$

where δt is the time of each stage in the tree
n is the number of stages used
$K =$ strike price and $S =$ spot price.

These are known as the Leisen parameters.

For the Leisen parameters, 30 stages should provide satisfactory accuracy (with other forms for u and d more stages may be necessary). With a process involving four or more stages, a higher-level programming language (C++ or VBA) is needed.

Under suitable conditions, which we do not describe here (see Baxter and Rennie for an excellent treatment of this topic), as t becomes very small ($t \to 0$) and n, the number of stages, becomes very large ($n \to \infty$) with suitable u and d, the tree merges into a continuous process. On this stage there is a big player: the hugely famous Black–Scholes formula.

7.5 Black–Scholes formula

Black–Scholes formula (for a call or a put option)

Take, as above:
$S_0 =$ spot price of the underlying share
$K =$ strike price

r = rate (continuously compounded) at which money can be safely loaned or borrowed

σ = volatility. This is sometimes given as a percentage (15%). It is entered in the Black–Scholes formula as a decimal (0.15)

T = time to maturity.

The value today of a call option is:

$$C = S_0 \times N(d_1) - K \times N(d_2) \times e^{-rT}$$

where:

$$d_1 = \frac{\ln\left(\frac{S_0}{K}\right) + \left(r + \frac{1}{2}\sigma^2\right)T}{\sigma\sqrt{T}}$$

$$d_2 = \frac{\ln\left(\frac{S_0}{K}\right) + \left(r - \frac{1}{2}\sigma^2\right)T}{\sigma\sqrt{T}}$$

and $N(d) = \text{Prob}(X \leq d)$ where X is distributed normally with mean zero and variance one. In other words, N is the cumulative distribution function of the standard normal distribution.

The value today of a put option is:

$$P = K \times N(-d_2) \times e^{-rT} - S_0 \times N(-d_1)$$

Example 9

The price today of an ElectroMax share is £5.50.

(a) Calculate the value of

(i) a three-month call option (strike price = £5.20),

(ii) a three-month put option (strike price = £5.20) on ElectroMax shares. Assume the interest rate is 6% (compounded continuously) and volatility is estimated at 20%.

(b) Arnold has the idea that ElectroMax shares will fall in value. He has £10 000 to invest. Consider two investment schemes:

(i) Borrow 1818 ElectroMax shares ($\frac{10\,000}{5.5} = 1818.2$). Sell these shares at £5.50 each. (This is known as short selling. See Introduction.)

(ii) Spend all the £10 000 buying three-month put options on ElectroMax shares.

In three months' time, the value of an ElectroMax share was £5.10. Calculate the profit Arnold would have made from each of these schemes.

Solution

(a) $S_0 = 5.50,\ K = 5.20,\ r = 0.06,\ \sigma = 0.20,\ T = 0.25$
We can calculate d_1 and d_2

$$d_1 = \frac{\ln\left(\frac{S_0}{K}\right) + \left(r + \frac{1}{2}\sigma^2\right)T}{\sigma\sqrt{T}}$$

$$= \frac{\ln\left(\frac{5.50}{5.20}\right) + (0.06 + 0.5 \times 0.2^2) \times 0.25}{0.2 \times \sqrt{0.25}} = 0.7608947$$

$$d_2 = \frac{\ln\left(\frac{S_0}{K}\right) + \left(r - \frac{1}{2}\sigma^2\right)T}{\sigma\sqrt{T}}$$

$$= \frac{\ln\left(\frac{5.50}{5.20}\right) + (0.06 - 0.5 \times 0.2^2) \times 0.25}{0.2 \times \sqrt{0.25}} = 0.6608947$$

From tables, $N(d_1) = N(0.7609) = 0.7764$
and $N(d_2) = N(0.6609) = 0.7454$

$$N(-d_1) = 1 - N(d_1) = 1 - 0.7764 = 0.2236$$
$$N(-d_2) = 1 - N(d_2) = 1 - 0.7454 = 0.2546$$

(i) The value of a call option is:

$$V = S_0 \times N(d_1) - K \times N(d_2) \times e^{-rT}$$
$$= 5.5 \times 0.7764 - 5.20 \times 0.7454 \times e^{-0.06 \times 0.25}$$
$$= 0.4518$$

(ii) The value of a put option is:

$$V = K \times N(-d_2) \times e^{-rT} - S_0 \times N(-d_1)$$
$$= 5.20 \times 0.2546 \times e^{-0.06 \times 0.25} - 5.50 \times 0.2236$$
$$= 0.0744$$

The calculation is shown in Excel in Figure 7.33.

Note that N(d) is calculated in Excel as NORMSDIST(d) (NORMalStandardDISTribution). All the quantities appearing in the formula have cell names. The value of the call option appears in E5, the value of the put option in E7. Put–call parity is verified in E9.

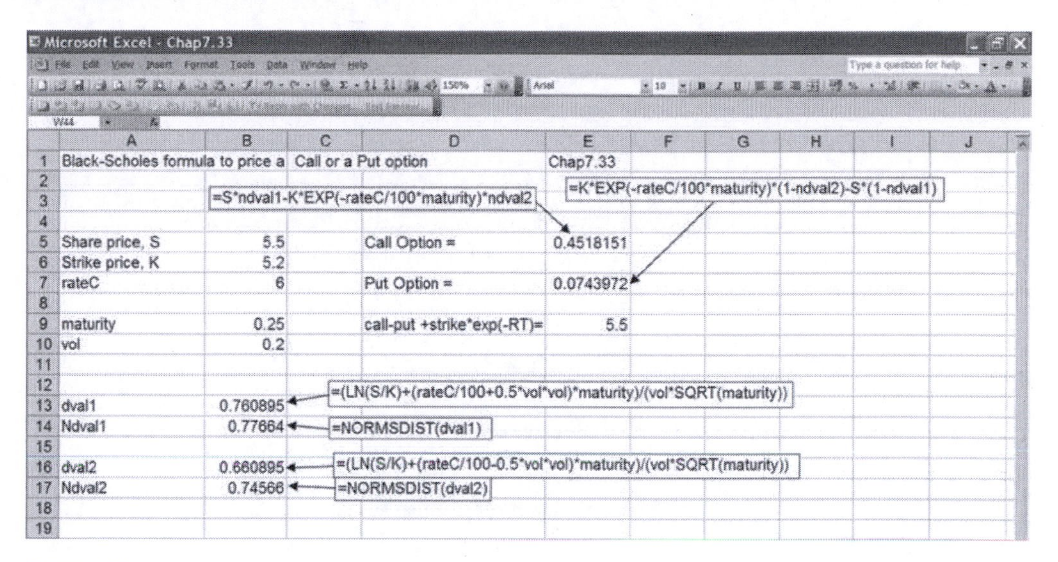

Figure 7.33

(b) (i) If, in three months' time, Arnold bought 1818 ElectroMax shares at £5.10 each (and returned the shares he had borrowed), he would have made a profit of £0.40 per share, or $1818 \times 0.40 = £727.2$ in total.

(ii) With a put option costing £0.0744, Arnold could buy 134 408 put options. In three months' time these options would be in the money. Arnold could buy 134 408 ElectoMax shares in the market for £5.10 each and sell them under the terms of the put options for the strike price of £5.20. This would give Arnold a pay-off of $134\,408 \times 0.1 = £13\,440.8$ (and a profit of £3440.8).

This example demonstrates again the awesome power of options to ratchet up the profits.

7.6 Further options

We are almost at the end. But there is one further class of options we should consider. These are, in practice, the most widely traded options and they incorporate one new feature. This involves the time at which the contract is exercised. A contract is 'exercised' when the pay-off is made. Until now, all the options have been (and could only be) exercised on the stated date of maturity. The new feature allows an option to be exercised at any time before maturity. To be clear about the type of option being considered, we need a definition.

An option that can be exercised only on the date of maturity is called a **European option**. All the options described so far have been European options.

An option that can be exercised at any moment of the holder's choosing, up to and including the date of maturity, is called an **American option**.

An option that can be exercised early but only on certain prearranged dates is called a **Bermudan option.** These are similar to American options. For example, early exercise would be possible only on the first trading day of each month.

American options

With a multi-stage binomial tree, an American option can be exercised at any vertex. The holder of the option could elect to exercise the option at that moment and receive the pay-off as calculated at that vertex. To enable the holder to make an informed decision on whether or not to exercise, we need, at each vertex:

(i) the asset value

(ii) the option value (calculated from a backward trawl through the tree as described in section 7.4)

(iii) the pay-off the holder would receive if they choose to exercise at this vertex. The pay-off that would be made to the holder if the option was exercised at this vertex is called the **intrinsic value** of the option.

With an American option, at each vertex, three boxes are displayed.

Box 1: Asset value

Box 2: Value of option. As calculated in section 7.4.

Box 3: Pay-off from immediate exercise. The intrinsic value.

We illustrate this.

Example 10

An EPUX share costs £18. Peter is convinced the price is about to fall. He buys an American put option on EPUX shares with strike price £18 and maturity in one month's time. The interest rate is 6.5% (compounded annually) and the volatility of the share price is 25%. Using a three-stage binary tree model, calculate the value of the put option.

Solution

$S = 18, \; K = 18.$

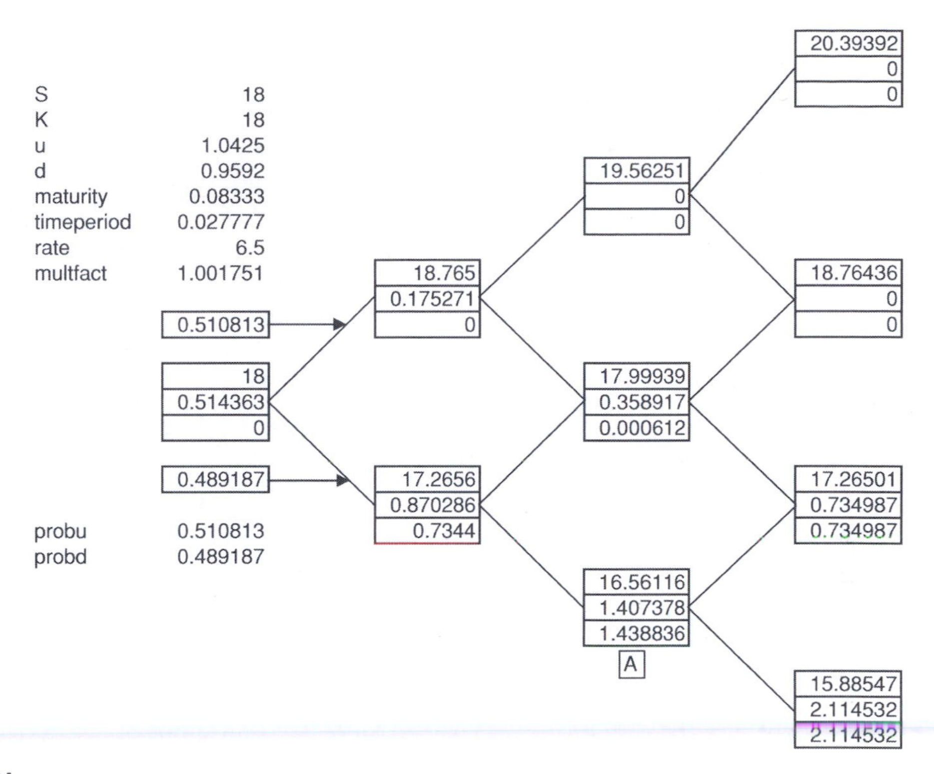

Figure 7.34

Time to maturity is $\frac{1}{12} = 0.083333$. The time between changes in the share price in a three-stage model is $\frac{1}{3} \times 0.083333 = 0.027778$.

With volatility $\sigma = 0.25$ and $t = 0.027778$,

$$u = e^{\sigma\sqrt{t}} = e^{0.25\times\sqrt{0.027778}} = 1.0425$$
$$d = e^{-\sigma\sqrt{t}} = \frac{1}{u} = 0.9592$$

(Note: since S = K, the Leisen parameters exactly match the Cox-Ross-Rubinstein u, d values.)

The three-stage tree is shown in Figure 7.34.

The asset value is displayed in box 1.

The interest rate is 6.5% per year, compounded annually. With this form of u and d, we should convert the interest rate to the equivalent continuously compounded form. The multiplying factor for a continuously compounded rate is:

$$e^{r\times 0.027778} = (1 + 0.065)^{0.027778} = 1.001751.$$

Risk neutral probabilities are calculated from
$q = \frac{e^{rt}-d}{u-d} = \frac{1.001751-0.9592}{1.0425-0.9592} = 0.510813.$

The pay-off at maturity and the option values (as calculated in section 7.4) are shown in box 2.

The intrinsic values appear in box 3. For a put option, the intrinsic value is: max(strike − asset value, 0) This is: max(18 − box 1, 0).

The value of the option, according to Figure 7.34, is £0.5144. Or, £0.51.

But there is something wrong here. At A, the intrinsic value of the option (what the holder of the option will receive if the option is exercised at that moment) appears to exceed the option value. This cannot be right. What you receive for an asset must be, or face arbitrage, the value of the asset. So the value of the asset at A must be £1.438836.

What we are saying here is that with an American option, at any vertex, if the intrinsic value (box 3) exceeds the option value (box 2), we must replace the calculated option value (box 2) by the intrinsic value (box 3). This means that with an American option, we must put in box 2 the maximum of box 2 and box 3. If box 2 and box 3 share the same value, then box 2 continues to keep its value.

With an American option, the instruction for box 2 becomes:

$$\text{option value} = \max(\text{discounted value } (q \times optionv(u) + (1-q) \times optionv(d)), \text{intrinsic value})$$

Making this change at A will, of course, cause changes further back down the tree. Using the new option value at A will cause changes at the vertex leading to A, and so on, back through the tree to the initial vertex. So the value of the option will also change.

Figure 7.35 shows the process with this new instruction to box 2. The value of the option is now given as £0.5219. The first answer, £0.5144, is the value today of a European put option. The second is the value of an American put option.

We see that the value of the American put is greater than that of its European counterpart. This is to be expected. An American option offers the holder more opportunities to make a profit. The buyer must expect to pay more for these additional privileges.

When to exercise an American option

When the pay-off formula is known, all the vertices of a binary tree can be completed, as shown in Figure 7.35. *It can be shown that the option should be*

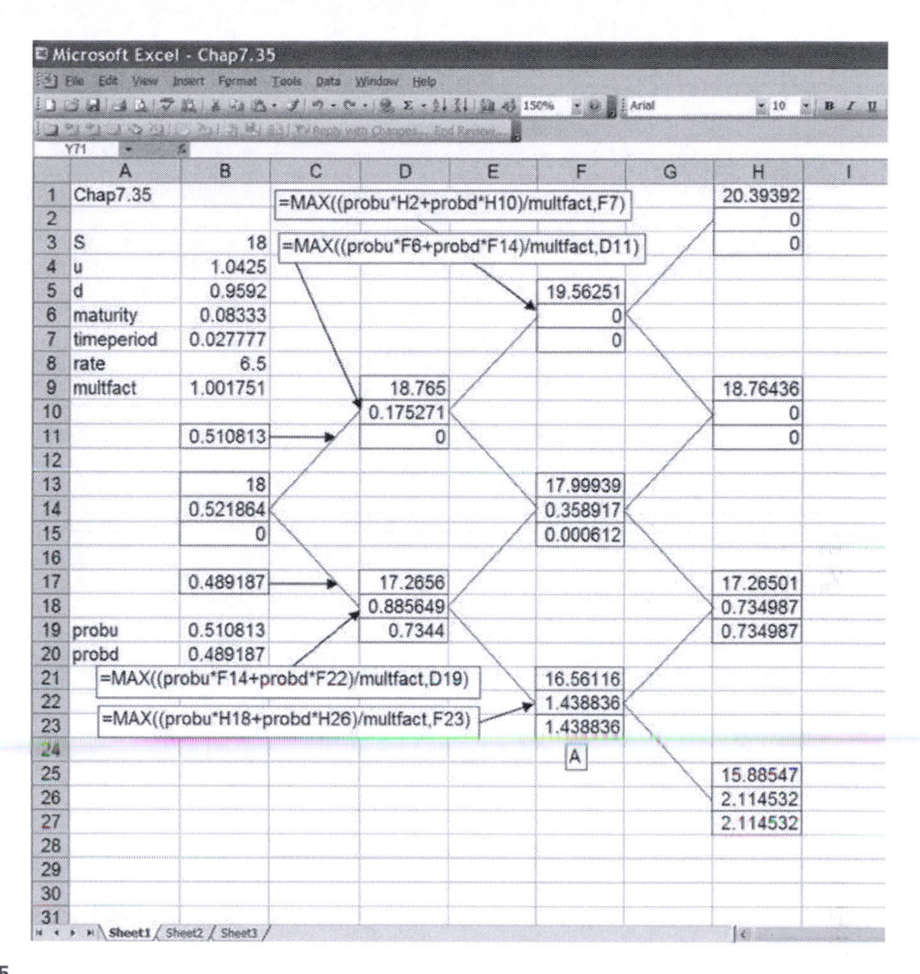

Figure 7.35

exercised on the first occasion the intrinsic value equals or exceeds the option value (Box 3 $\geq$ Box 2). If the intrinsic value exceeds the option value, this advice is reasonably obvious. (If you are offered more than the worth of an asset, accept.) If the intrinsic value equals the option value, the situation is more subtle. These two quantities will be equal at maturity, but a general rule says that 'cash now is better than cash in the future'. If the option value and the intrinsic values are equal, this could be rephrased as 'getting value for money today is better than getting value for money in the future'. This result can be proved, but the proof lies beyond the scope of this book.

Three points need to be made:

- Put–call parity does not hold if either option is American.
- There is, at the moment, no closed formula (such as the Black–Scholes formula) for valuing an American call or put option.

- An American call option should not be exercised early. Or, to put this another way, there is no financial advantage in exercising an American call option before maturity. This, effectively, says that all call options are priced as European options. A proof of this is given in Appendix 3.

The method we have demonstrated is valid for any option that can be replicated. (An a,b portfolio can be found for each one-stage tree in the model.) So whether the aim is to value an American put option, or something more exotic, so long as the pay-off formula is well defined and can be evaluated at each vertex, the procedure described above can be used to price the option. In practice, as mentioned earlier, 30 or more steps are needed to ensure reasonable accuracy.

Example 11

Janet has inherited £10 000. She wants to invest the money in the stock market.

Ewan, her advisor, suggests a balanced portfolio of shares, but Janet reads the financial pages and fancies a bit of risk. 'I have read that GF supermarkets are experiencing some cash problems and their share price has fallen,' she said. 'Well, I shop there. They are good shops. Their shares are £20 each at the moment but I think that with a bit of reorganisation, their value could rise quite a bit. I would like to buy GF supermarket shares.'

Ewan maintained that a balanced portfolio was essential and he presented Janet with three options for the risky part of her portfolio.

1. Buy one-month call options on GF shares with strike price £21.
2. Buy one-month binary options. A binary option pays out a fixed amount if the share price, at expiry, exceeds an agreed price. Otherwise, the option pays out nothing.

   The pay-off function for this binary option is:
   $$\begin{cases} £2 & \text{if } S \geq 21 \\ 0 & \text{otherwise} \end{cases}$$
3. Buy one-month options that pay out fixed but differing amounts depending on the final value of the share price.

   The pay-off function for this option is:
   $$\begin{cases} £2 & \text{if } S \geq 23 \\ £1 & \text{if } 21 \leq S < 23 \\ 0 & \text{if } 19 < S < 21 \\ £1 & \text{if } 17 < S \leq 19 \\ £2 & \text{if } S \leq 17 \end{cases}$$

   (a) Explain why Ewan suggested each of these possibilities.
   (b) What would be the cost of each of these options?

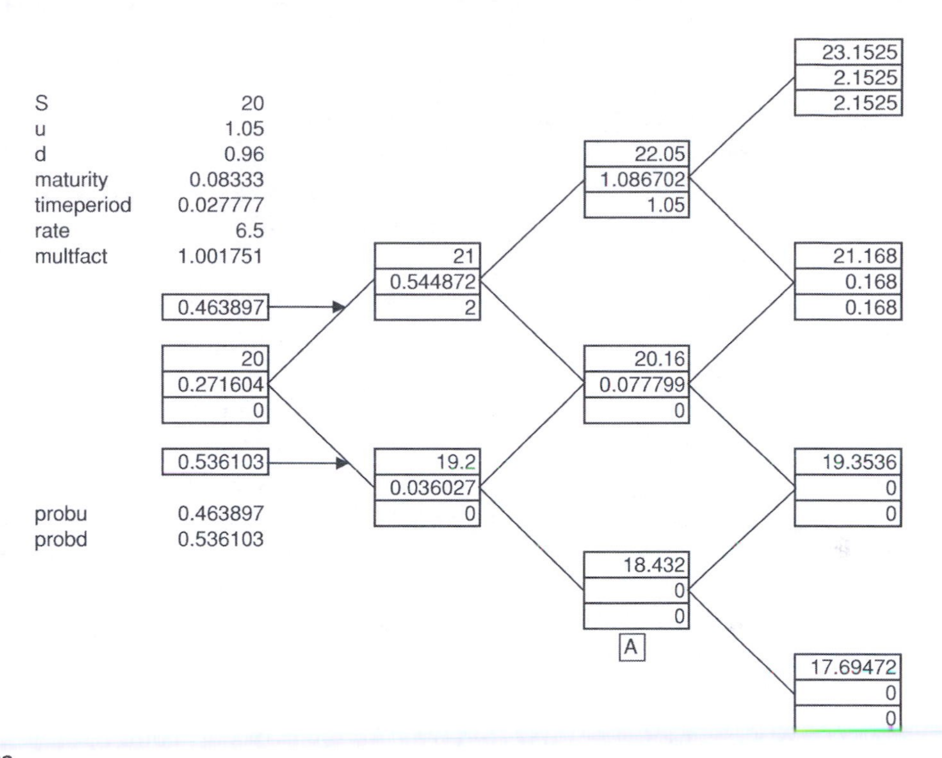

Figure 7.36

Solution

Banks try to match their financial products to their customers' needs.

1. If Janet is right and the shares increase in value (above £21 + cost of the option), her investment will show a profit. Because call options cost less than the share price, Janet can buy more call options than she could buy shares. So there is potential here for greater profit. But if the share price does not rise above £21, Janet loses her investment in call options.

   Above, we show a three-stage binomial tree for this call option.

   Note that the intrinsic value (box 3) remains less than the calculated value (box 2). The option is not exercised early, illustrating the comment described just before this example. The value of one call option is £0.2716.

2. Janet's reward, if the share price rises above £21, is limited to £2. The potential for unlimited profit offered by a call option has gone. However, if the share value at expiry lies in the range £21 through to £23, a binary option offers a greater reward than a call option. So a binary option would be the preferred choice if a small rise in the share value was expected. The cost of increased benefit from a small rise in the share value will be reduced slightly

in view of the smaller benefit Janet would receive from a large increase in the share value.

A three-stage tree for this option is shown in Figure 7.37E and in Figure 7.37A.

Above is the European option; the American option is shown below. The cost of the European option is £0.8872. The cost of the American option is £1.1557.

An American option should be exercised the first time (in the American option calculations) box 2 = box 3. If, initially, an up move occurred, Janet would exercise the American option.

3. Changes in the GF supermarket share value might well be on the way, but will they be for the better or for the worse? Ewan is backing it both ways with this option. Janet wins if the price rises above £21, or falls below £19. If the share price rises to £23 or falls below £17, she wins even more. But these are fixed amounts, so the option will be cheaper than, say, a butterfly spread (in which the profits are, potentially, without limit). However, if the share price stays within the £19 to £21 range, Janet loses her investment in this option.

   Three-stage binomial trees, illustrating both a European option and an American option, are shown in Figure 7.38E and Figure 7.38A.

   The cost of the European option is £0.6962; the cost of the corresponding American option is £0.8643.

   With an American option, Janet would exercise the option the first time box 2 = box 3. If she hits A by exercising early Janet will receive a pay-off of £1 for an option valued at £0.9246. The phrase in current use might be 'Go for it, girl.' If she hits B, she will receive £1 for an option valued at £0.5352.

Observe again that an American option, with its greater advantages for profit, costs more than a European option.

These options might well be those recommended to the share holder in the situation described at the beginning of the chapter.

In a last example, we illustrate what happens if the holder of an American option fails to exercise that option when it is optional to do so.

Example 12

Jarndyce & Co is a rather bleak finance house specialising in protracted wills. The value of a Jarndyce share today is £60. An American put option (strike price = £58) on Jarndyce shares is sold. A two-stage binomial tree for the share price is as shown in Figure 7.39. The risk neutral probabilities are

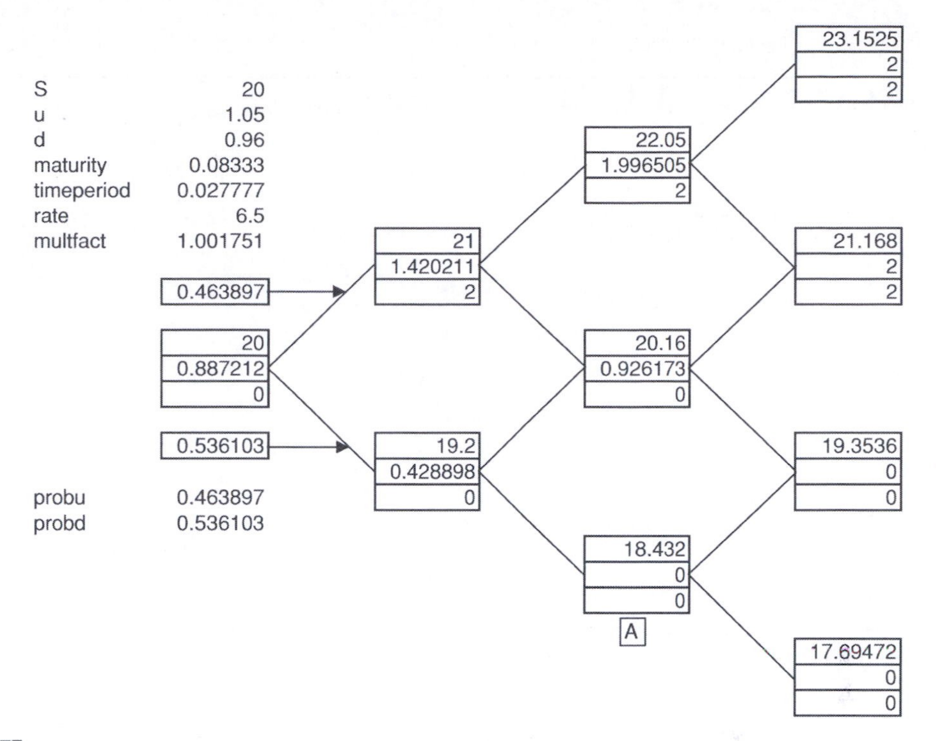

Figure 7.37E

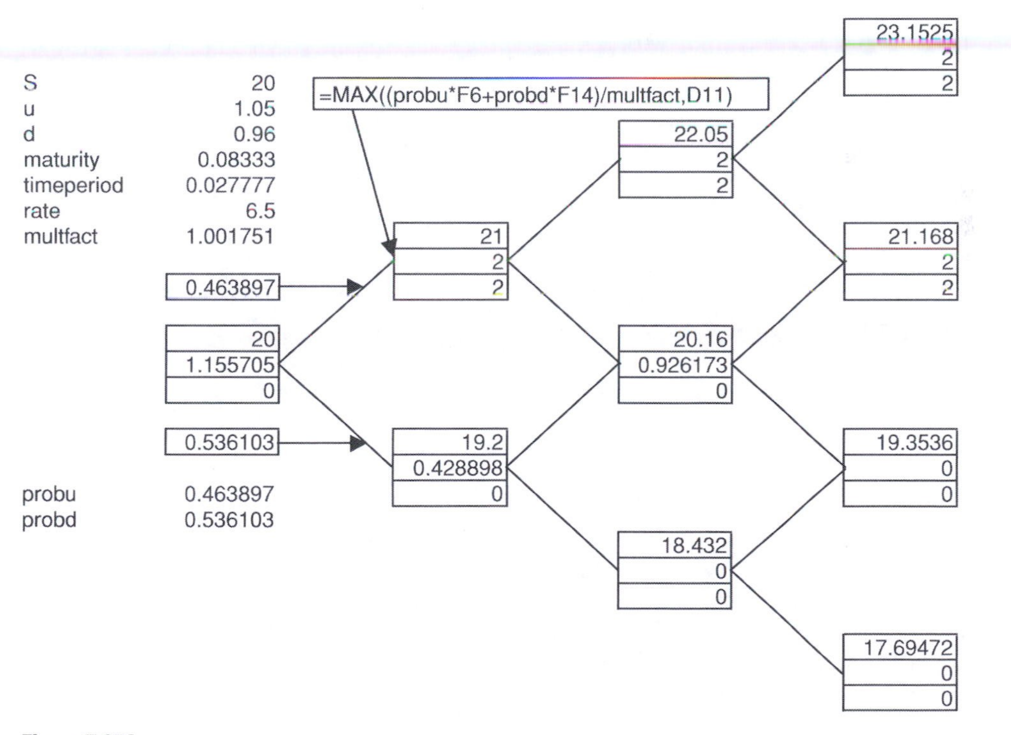

Figure 7.37A

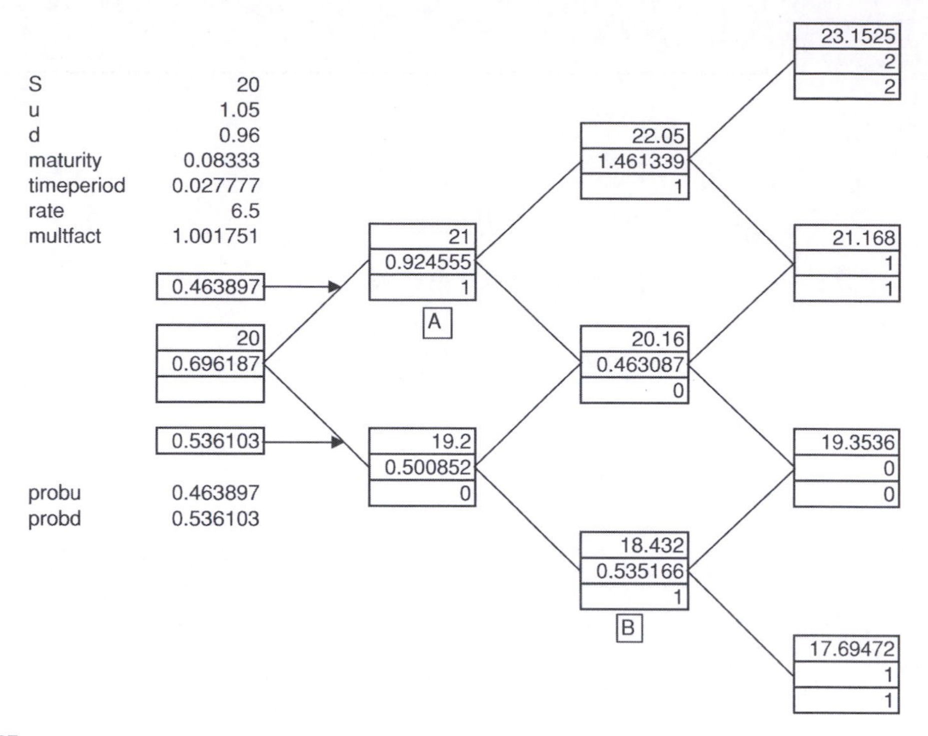

Figure 7.38E

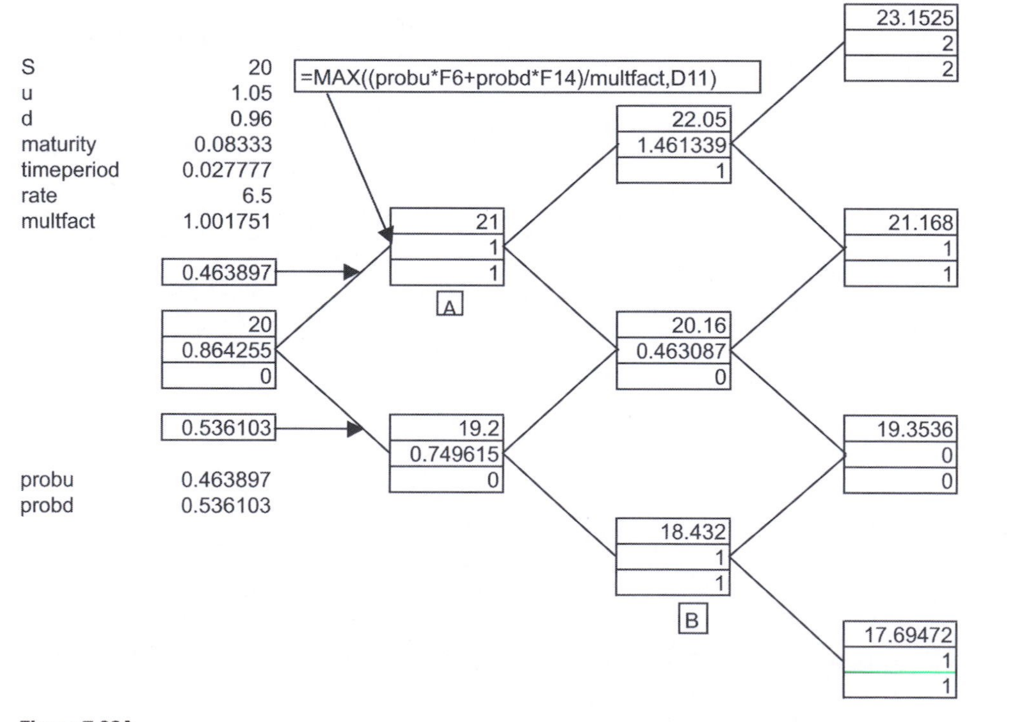

Figure 7.38A

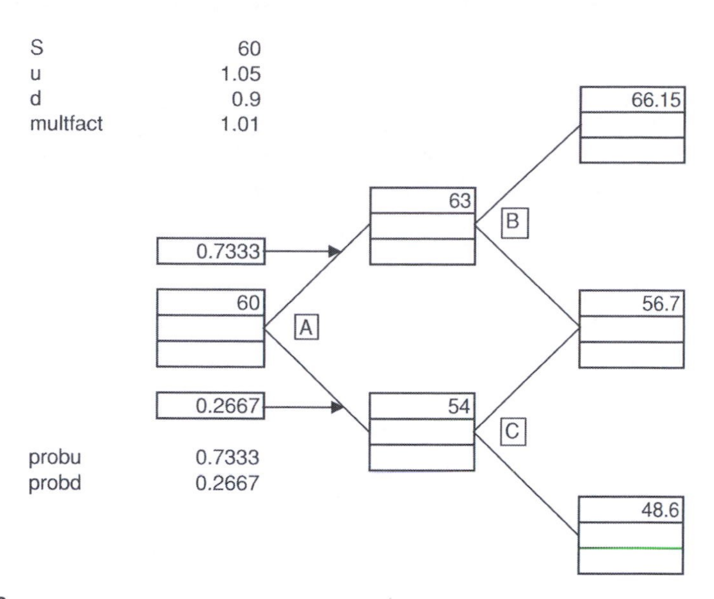

Figure 7.39

prob(up move) = 0.7333, prob(down move) = 0.2667 and the interest rate multiplying factor for each stage of the tree is 1.01.

(i) At each vertex write the calculated value of the option in box 2 and the intrinsic value in box 3.
(ii) At which vertex is it optional to exercise this put option?
(iii) Explain carefully what will happen if the option is not exercised when it is optimal to do so.

Solution

(i) The values of the share price, together with entries in boxes 2 and 3, are given in Figure 7.40.
(ii) The option should be exercised at vertex C.
(iii) Suppose that initially the asset moves (down) to £54. The calculated value of the option is £3.4260, while the intrinsic value is £4. We are agreed: the option should be exercised, the value of the option (at C) is £4.0000 and after being exercised, the option terminates.

However, suppose the holder does *not* exercise the option. Then the game is not over and we move forward into the second stage of the tree. To see clearly what happens next, we set up a portfolio at A and to follow it, a portfolio at C.

Recall: $a = \dfrac{X - Y}{Su - Sd}$ $\qquad b = \dfrac{1}{1 + r} \times (X - aSu).$

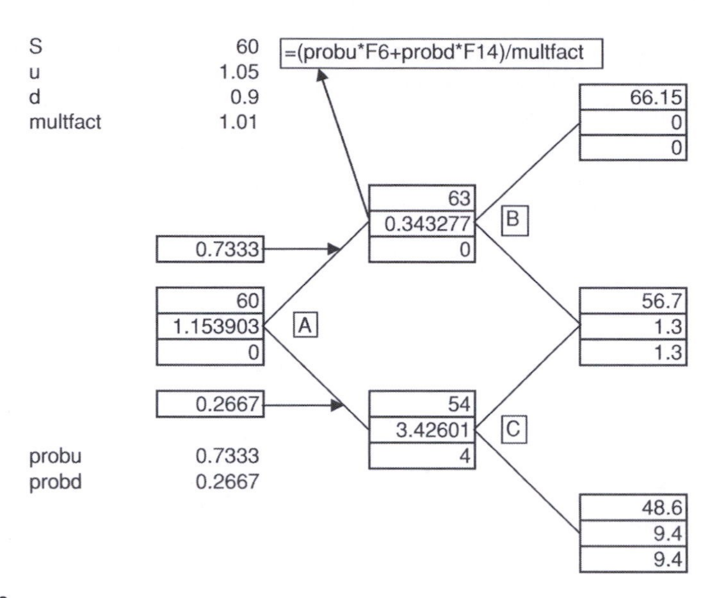

Figure 7.40

For the portfolio at A:

$$a = \frac{0.3433 - 4}{63 - 54} = -0.4063 \quad b = \frac{1}{1.01} \times (0.3433 - (-0.4063) \times 63) = 25.6834$$

Initially, the portfolio has value: $-0.4063 \times 60 + 25.6834 = 1.3054$

After a down move, the value is:

$-0.4063 \times 54 + 25.6834 \times 1.01 = 4.0000$

For the portfolio at C:

$$a = \frac{1.3 - 9.4}{56.7 - 48.6} = -1 \qquad b = \frac{1}{1.01} \times (1.3 - (-1) \times 56.7) = 57.4257$$

Initially, this portfolio has value: $-1 \times 54 + 57.4257 = 3.4257$

After an up move, the value is: $-1 \times 56.7 + 57.4257 \times 1.01 = 1.3000$

After a down move, the value is:

$-1 \times 48.6 + 57.4257 \times 1.01 = 9.4000$.

The portfolio established at A is worth £4.0000 at C. (Buy 0.4063 of one share and cash in the investment for 1.01×25.6834: this is as expected.) But the portfolio set up at C is worth, initially, £3.4257.

So £4 is received from cashing in the old portfolio and £3.4257 is paid out to set up the new one. This gives $£(4 - 3.4257) = £0.5743$ in pure profit. This is money to be consumed: it is money the seller of the option would not have had if the owner had exercised the option when it was optimal to do so.

Observe that, at maturity, the portfolio set up at C has value £1.3000 after an up move and £9.4000 after a down move. So this portfolio does indeed hedge what is to be paid out at maturity.

With the holder of the option not exercising when it was optimal to do so, the seller received £0.5743. Since we are operating in a zero-arbitrage world, the holder of the option must, therefore, have lost money. **An option loses money if the holder fails to exercise the option when it is optimal to do so.**

We are even closer to the end.

There are other ways of setting up a model:

- Three (or more) branches could be used at each vertex.
- We could allow the up-factor u and the down-factor d to vary as time progressed and/or with changes in the asset value.
- The interest rate could be allowed to vary.
- In all the above, the underlying portfolio consisted of one asset (usually a share) and an amount of cash. We could introduce more randomness into the model and a measure of correlation by introducing a second asset. The hedging portfolio would then 'look like' $a_1S_1 + a_2S_2 + b$.

So what have we done? We have described and priced a number of options. We have shown how options can be replicated – so the variation in value can be tracked through time and matched, costlessly, by a portfolio consisting of the asset and some cash. We have created a risk-free world. Using q-probabilities, we have created, entered and worked in an environment where all activities are indifferent to risk. No compensation for risk is asked for or offered. In this world, the prices that are calculated are fair to all. It seems, in these troubled times, that mathematics, through risk neutral systems, might be one of the few safe environments. Perhaps this is an important use for probability theory. Rather than trying to model existing situations by importing named and well-known probability distributions, we could calculate individual probability systems to create required environments. However, our risk-free world is created by choosing for ourselves the probabilities $\{q, 1 - q\}$ for change. Because all that we have altered are the probabilities of up, down movement, the prices that have been calculated will hold also in the risky world (so long as the defining conditions continue to hold and these are, for our purposes, constant interest rates and constant volatility). These calculated prices compare well with prices in the market place and this represents a satisfactory measure of experimental verification.

The mathematics described above is elegant, philosophically attractive and useful in an important area of human activity. This is a young and a vigorous subject. There is more, much more for the reader to investigate and explore. But not here. The references listed in the Introduction indicate the ways forward.

Appendix 1

Value of option (today) = aS + b

But $a = \dfrac{X - Y}{S(u-d)}$ $\quad b = \left(\dfrac{X(-d) + Yu}{u-d}\right)(1+r)^{-1}$

Substituting these values:

$$\text{Value of option} = \frac{(X - Y) \times S}{S(u-d)} + \left(\frac{X(-d) + Yu}{u-d}\right)(1+r)^{-1}$$

Cancel the S in the first term and make $(1+r)^{-1}$ a common factor:

$$= (1+\mathrm{r})^{-1}\left[\frac{(X-Y)}{(u-d)}(1+r) + \left(\frac{-Xd+Yu}{u-d}\right)\right]$$

$$= (1+\mathrm{r})^{-1}\left[\frac{(X-Y)(1+r) - Xd + Yu}{u-d}\right]$$

Collect together the pay-off terms, X and Y:

$$= (1+\mathrm{r})^{-1}\left[\frac{X(1+r-d) + Y(u-(1+r))}{u-d}\right]$$

$$= (1+\mathrm{r})^{-1}\left[\frac{1+r-d}{u-d} \times X + \frac{u-(1+r)}{u-d} \times Y\right]$$

And this is: $(1+\mathrm{r})^{-1}[qX + (1-q)Y]$

Appendix 2

Suppose that the share prices over successive intervals of time δt are: S_0, S_1, S_2, S_3, ... The return on a share that starts the interval at S_0 and ends at S_1 is: $\frac{\textit{increase}}{\textit{original}} = \frac{S_1 - S_0}{S_0}$

We use the result:

$\sigma\sqrt{\delta t}$ is approximately equal to the standard deviation of the return on the share price.

The first step is to calculate the returns on the share prices. Write these returns as u_1, u_2, u_3, and so on.

$$u_1 = \frac{S_1 - S_0}{S_0}, \quad u_2 = \frac{S_2 - S_1}{S_1}, \quad u_3 = \frac{S_3 - S_2}{S_2}, \ldots$$

Next, calculate the standard deviation of the $u_1, u_2, u_3, \ldots$ The standard deviation is given by:

$$SD = \sqrt{\frac{\sum(u - \overline{u})^2}{n - 1}}$$

(But this is probably best calculated in Excel – see the example below.)

The result quoted at the beginning of this section says that: $\sigma\sqrt{\delta t}$ is approximately equal to SD

So σ is approximately $\dfrac{SD}{\sqrt{\delta t}}$.

This calculates a value for σ.

A very good question is: how many share values, $S_0, S_1, S_2, S_3, \ldots$ should be used in this calculation? If too many are used, we might be admitting data from a period before present market conditions came into being and this would distort the result. If too few are used, we might not include sufficient data to create a realistic picture of the market. A widely used rule of thumb is to take the time t over which the data are collected to equal the time t for which the volatility is to apply. So if we were valuing a six-month call option, we would take six months of data. If valuing a put option with maturity in five weeks, we would take five weeks' data.

An example will illustrate the method. However, we have not included the full amount of data recommended in the previous paragraph. The idea here is simply to illustrate the calculation – which is easily carried out in Excel – as Figure 7.41 will illustrate.

Example 13

The share price of HX Furnishings, taken at the close of the market over seven successive days, is shown below.

	S_0	S_1	S_2	S_3	S_4	S_5	S_6
Share price	5.48	5.54	5.64	5.68	5.67	5.52	5.58

Estimate the volatility of this share price over the following six days.

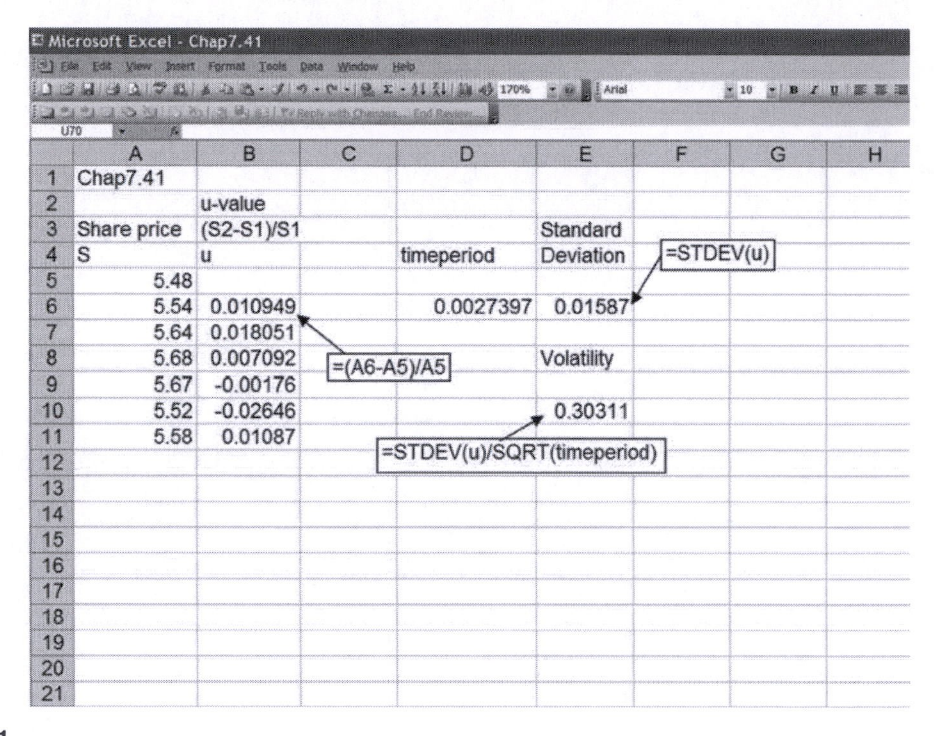

Figure 7.41

Solution

1. Calculate the successive returns:

$$u_1 = \frac{S_1 - S_0}{S_0} = \frac{5.54 - 5.48}{5.48} = 0.0109489$$

$$u_2 = \frac{S_2 - S_1}{S_1} = \frac{5.64 - 5.54}{5.54} = 0.0180505$$

$$u_3 = \frac{5.68 - 5.64}{5.64} = 0.0070922 \qquad \text{and so on through to } u_6$$

2. Calculate the mean $\overline{u}$ of the u values:

$$\overline{u} = \frac{0.01095 + 0.01805 + 0.00709 - 0.00176 - 0.02646 + 0.01087}{6}$$
$$= 0.00312$$

3. Calculate the standard deviation of the u values:

$$\text{St. Dev.} = \sqrt{\frac{\sum(u - \overline{u})^2}{n-1}} \quad \text{This comes to } 0.01587$$

4. In this case, δt is one day. So $\delta t = \dfrac{1}{365} = 0.0027397$ (years).

   Write $\sigma\sqrt{\delta t} = \text{St. Dev}$: giving $\sigma = \dfrac{St.\,Dev}{\sqrt{\delta t}}$

   σ is approximately equal to $\dfrac{0.01587}{\sqrt{0.0027397}} = 0.303109$

   The volatility over the following six weeks is estimated to be just over 30.3%.

   This calculation is shown in Figure 7.41.

   Note that the u values are entered under the range name u and that Excel functions STDEV (standard deviation) and SQRT (square root) are used.

Appendix 3

If the underlying share pays no dividend, it is never a good idea (optimal) to exercise the call option before maturity.

Proof

Consider two portfolios.

Portfolio A:
Initially this portfolio contains:
one call option:

the underlying asset has value S_t at time t,
strike price = K,
time to maturity = T,
interest rate (continuously compounded) = r.

an amount of cash equal to $K \times e^{-rT}$.
Portfolio B:
This portfolio consists of one unit of the underlying asset. The value at time t is S_t.
Consider what happens if the call option is exercised at time t, before maturity.

At time t:
Portfolio A:
Since the call option is exercised, we can assume that $S_t > K$. So the value of the call option at time t is the pay-off, $S_t - K$. The cash component will

have grown (under investment at rate r) to $K \times e^{-rT} \times e^{rt} = K \times e^{-r(T-t)}$. So the value of portfolio A at time t is: $S_t - K + K \times e^{-r(T-t)}$.

Since $e^{-r(T-t)} < 1$, $K \times e^{-r(T-t)} < K$ this means that at time t, the value of portfolio A is less than S_t.

Portfolio B:

This portfolio is worth S_t at time t.

Hence, if the portfolio is exercised at time $t < T$, then portfolio A is worth less than portfolio B.

Suppose now that the call option is not exercised early and consider the values of the two portfolios at maturity.

At maturity ($t = T$):

Portfolio A:

The cash component will now be worth $K \times e^{-rT} \times e^{rT} = K$.

If $S_T > K$, the option will be exercised. The cash component will be used to buy the share for K. So the value of portfolio A at maturity is S_T.

If $S_T \leq K$, the option will not be exercised. The call option expires worthless and at maturity, portfolio A is worth K.

In either case, portfolio A expires with value greater than or equal to S_T.

Portfolio B

This expires with value S_T. This shows that:

value of portfolio A $<$ value of portfolio B, if the call is exercised early

value of portfolio A $\geq$ value of portfolio B, if the option goes through to maturity.

This suggests that a European call option should not be exercised early.

Exercise 7

1. The value of a share today is \$10. It is thought that in two weeks' time the share will be worth either (i) \$12 or (ii) \$9. An option will pay off \$0.5 if the share has value \$12 and \$0.05 if the share has value \$9. The risk-free interest rate over the two-week period has multiplying factor 1.001. Set up a portfolio to replicate this option and hence calculate the value of the option today.

2. A one-month call option on BU Self shares has strike price \$50. The value of a BU share today is \$50. In one month's time the share price might be

(i) \$55 or it might be (ii) \$48. The interest rate multiplying factor over a one-month period is 1.01. Set up a one-stage binomial tree and calculate a replicating portfolio for the call option. Calculate the value of the option today.

3. A put option on TTZ shares has strike price £32 and matures in three months' time. The value of a TTZ share today is £30 and the risk-free interest rate (over a three-month period) has multiplying factor 1.025. Use a one-stage binomial tree with up factor $u = 1.1$ and down factor $d = 0.95$ to calculate (i) a replicating portfolio, and (ii) the value of the put option.

4. For each of the shares described in questions 1, 2 and 3, write down the up and down multiplying factors u, d, and calculate the risk neutral probability distributions.

5. An asset has value \$12. The up/down multiplying factors, u and d, over a one-month period are given as $u = 1.015$ and $d = 0.99$. The risk-free interest rate (over one month) has multiplying factor 1.01.
   (i) Calculate the risk neutral probability distribution for a one-stage binomial tree extending over one month.
   (ii) An option pays \$1.5 after an up move and \$0.1 after a down move. Use the risk neutral probabilities to calculate the value of this option.

6. The risk-free interest rate is 5.5% continuously compounded. An asset is selling today for \$9 and it is thought that in one month's time its value will be either \$10 or \$8.5. An option will pay out \$1 if the asset value is \$10 and \$0.5 if the asset value is \$8.5. Calculate the risk neutral probabilities for a one-stage binomial tree and calculate the value of the option today.

7. An asset has value \$30. The risk-free interest rate is 4%, continuously compounded, and volatility is estimated to be 30% per annum.
   (i) Using $u = e^{\sigma\sqrt{t}}$, $d = \frac{1}{u}$, construct a one-stage binomial tree for the asset value in three months' time.
   (ii) A three-month put option has strike price \$28. Calculate the risk neutral probabilities for this one-stage binomial tree and the value of the put today.

8. Suppose that an asset initially has value S and the safe interest rate, over a certain time period, has multiplying factor 1 + r. At the end of this time period the asset values are Su and Sd.
   (i) Show that the risk neutral probabilities are given by:

$$q = \frac{1 + r - d}{u - d} \qquad 1 - q = \frac{u - (1 + r)}{u - d}$$

   (ii) Show that $0 < q < 1$ if and only if $d < 1 + r < u$.

9. An asset is valued today at \$S. In a one-stage binomial tree with up and down factors u and d, and risk neutral probabilities q and 1 − q respectively, the interest rate multiplying factor over the period of the tree is 1 + r.
   (i) Show that: $S = \frac{1}{1+r}[qSu + (1 - q)Sd]$.
   (ii) Show that: S = E[discounted value of the asset, at maturity] under the probability distribution {q, 1 − q}.

10. Today, an IP1 share is priced at £18.50. Over a one-month time period, the up, down multiplying factors are given as: u = 1.08 and d = 0.93.
   (i) Generate a two-stage binomial tree for an IP1 share.
   (ii) The risk-free interest rate is 5.5%, continuously compounded. Calculate the value, today, of a two-month call option on IP1 shares with strike price £18.

11. In a two-year, two-stage binomial tree:

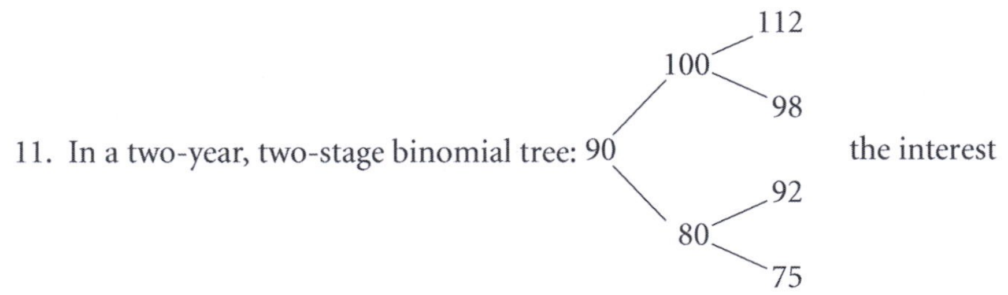

the interest rate over the first year is 5.5% and over the second, 6%, both interest rates compounded annually. Calculate the risk neutral probabilities in each of the one-stage binomial trees. A call option has strike price 91. What is the value of this option today?

12. A share costs \$50 today. Volatility is thought to be 25% per year. Set up a three-stage binomial tree to model the growth over three months of the share.

An option with maturity in three months pays out as shown below:

Share value	Option pay-out
More than $55	$3
More than $50 but less than or equal to $55	$2
More than $45 but less than or equal to $50	$1
Otherwise	0

The interest rate is 6% per year, compounded annually. Calculate the value of this option today.

13. Today, a 4-2-1 share costs £10. Volatility is estimated at 20%. The interest rate is 6% (compounded annually). I sell a three-month call option with strike price £8.50.
    (i) Draw a three-stage binomial tree to model growth over three months in 4-2-1 shares.
    (ii) Calculate replicating portfolios for a path ddu.
    (iii) Calculate the value of the option at each vertex.
    (iv) Verify that the portfolios are self-financing.
    (v) Calculate the value of the option.

14. A call option has six months to maturity. The strike price is £25, volatility is 25% and the safe interest rate is 6.5%, compounded annually. If the value of the asset today is £24, use the Black–Scholes formula to calculate the value of the call option.
    Complete the table:

Value of asset	18	20	22	24	26	28
Value of call option						

Hence plot the graph of the value of the call against the value of the asset.

15. A put option with strike price $35 has three months to maturity. Volatility is 30% and the safe interest rate is 10%, compounded annually. The value of the asset is $40.
    (i) Use the Black–Scholes formula to calculate the value of the put option.

(ii) Complete the table:

Value of asset	25	30	35	40	45	50	55
Value of put option							

(iii) Draw a graph illustrating the value of the put, three months from maturity, for a range of asset values.

16. A stock has value \$20. I buy a three-month call option with a strike price of \$18 and sell a three-month call option with a strike price of \$21.
    (i) Draw a profit diagram for this portfolio. What name is commonly given to such a portfolio?
    (ii) The safe interest rate is 6%, compounded annually, and volatility is estimated at 20%. Use the Black–Scholes formula to calculate the value of both call options and hence the value of the portfolio.

17. A stock is selling today at \$36. The up/down multiplying factors for each month are given by $u = 1.05$, $d = 0.96$.
    (i) Set up a three-stage binomial tree to model growth in the stock over a three-month period.
    (ii) A put option with strike price = \$40 expires in three months' time. The interest rate is 8% per year, continuously compounded. Use a three-stage binomial tree to calculate the value when (a) the put is European, and (b) this is an American put.

18. An EFP share is valued at \$60 today. The up/down factors for each month are $u = 1.03$, $d = 0.96$. Calculate a three-stage binomial tree to model the asset over a three-month period.
    I sell an option on EFP stock that pays out as shown below:

Stock value, S	Pay-off
$S > 65$	0
$60 < S \leq 65$	2
$55 < S \leq 60$	1
$S \leq 55$	0

The interest rate is 7% per year, compounded annually. Calculate the difference in price between a European option and an American option.

19. A stock costs \$50. The up/down factors each month are given by $u = 1.1$, $d = 0.96$ and the interest rate is 5% per year (compounded annually). I buy

a European straddle by buying a two-month call and a two-month put, both with the same strike price of \$50. Use a two-stage binomial process to price this straddle.

20. In a strangle, a trader buys a call and a put with the same maturity and with the put having a lower strike price than the call. Suppose the asset today has value £18 and that the call has strike price £18.50 while the put has strike price £18. Both options have three months to maturity.
    (i) Draw a profit diagram to illustrate a strangle. Why might a trader want to buy a strangle?
    (ii) The monthly up/down factors are given by $u = 1.05$ and $d = 0.98$. Construct a three-stage binomial tree for the asset.
    (iii) The interest rate has monthly multiplying factor 1.008. Calculate the value today of the strangle.

21. The price of a share over the previous five months is given by:

	S_0	S_1	S_2	S_3	S_4
Share price, S	16.5	17.8	19.1	18.7	19.6

    (i) Use these dates to estimate σ, the volatility of the share price.
    (ii) Construct a three-stage binomial tree to model growth in the share over a three-month period.
    (iii) The value of the share today is £20 and the risk-free interest rate is 7% per year, compounded continuously. A three-month American put option on this share has strike price £19.50. Find the value of the put.

22. I start with 'my fortune' of £100 and I play a game with my sister. I throw a fair coin: if it comes down heads, I win £1, if tails, I lose £1.
    (i) Draw a tree diagram to illustrate all possible outcomes for three throws of the coin. Write in the probabilities and at the end of each branch, write in the value of 'my fortune' (e.g. with TTH, my fortune would be £99).
    (ii) Calculate the expected value of my fortune after (a) one game, (b) two games. Show that if F_0 is the initial value of my fortune (= £100) and F_1 is my fortune after one game, then $F_0 = E[F_1]$. How would you describe the probabilities on each branch? Is this a fair game?
    (iii) Draw, in Excel, a tree illustrating one result when 100 games are played (see Figure 7.17). Does this look like the movement of a share value?

(iv) My sister (who works for a large, international bank) produced her own coin. Prob(H) = 0.4 and prob(T) = 0.6. What does the Excel graph look like now? Do we still have $F_0 = E[F_1]$?
(v) Repeat for different heads and tails probabilities.
(vi) Suppose that prob(H) = 0.3 and prob(T) = 0.7. I still lose £1 if tails is thrown. How much should I receive on heads for this game to be fair?

23. Explain carefully why, in an option, the pay-off at maturity is the value of the option at maturity.

24. Describe carefully why the cost of an American option is always greater than or equal to the cost of a European option. When could the two options have the same value?

25. (i) In section 7.6, it is stated that there is no financial advantage in exercising early an American call option. Use Figure 7.34 (modified for a call option) and a three-stage binomial tree with different values for the initial value of the asset S, different values of the strike price K and different volatilities σ to convince yourself that this statement is true.
(ii) Now take S = \$18, K = \$18 and σ = 25%. The safe interest rate changes at the end of each month and is given by:

Month	Safe interest rate (continuously compounded)
1	6%
2	6.5%
3	6.9%

What is the value today of this call option?
(iii) Test a different sequence of interest rates. Is there an advantage in exercising early an American call option?

26. The price of a PQQ share is £20. A client walks into your office. The client has a strong belief that the value of a PQQ share will not alter substantially in the coming three months. Describe four options you would recommend.

27. Sell a one-month call option with strike price £30. Buy a three-month call option with strike price £30. Draw a profit diagram for the time when

the one-month option expires. This portfolio is called a calendar spread. How could a calendar spread be set up using put options? Describe why a trader might want to buy a calendar spread.

28. Jim sells a two-month American put option with strike price \$39.50. The present value of the underlying asset is \$40 and the up/down monthly multiplying factors are $u = 1.03$, $d = 0.94$. The risk-free interest rate is 6% per year, compounded continuously. Jim wants to hedge his risk. What sum of money should he put aside now to ensure that he will have enough cash to meet all eventualities?

29. Jim's stockbroker is useless and this morning his computer shut down completely. As a result, Jim missed the opportunity to exercise early the American put option described in question 28. What were the consequences?

8 Credit derivatives

In all the pricing, with all the products considered so far, it has been assumed that all obligations will be met, in full and without delay. It has been assumed that bonds will pay their coupons, in full, on coupon dates. Shares would pay out their dividends as required. The holders of forward contracts and futures contracts, swaps and options will all pay up what they owe on the day payment is due. But what if we remove this assumption? What if we admit the possibility of default, of firms going into bankruptcy or administration and being unable to meet their financial obligations? These things certainly happen in the real world. Bankruptcies and defaulted payments might be comparatively rare events, but when they do occur, their effects can be dramatic. Setting up procedures to cope with events such as these is a major activity in the financial world. In this chapter, we offer a glimpse of the problems forming the subject matter of one of the most exciting recent developments in financial mathematics.

We will consider two problems.

(1) How can we measure the likelihood (probability) of a company experiencing some form of financial difficulty?

(2) What measures can a company take to protect itself against the event that an organisation which owes it money falls into financial difficulties?

Before we can answer these questions, we need to know what is meant by 'financial difficulty'. We will consider two areas where problems can arise, **default** and **credit spread.** We will show how to measure risk in each of these areas and by so doing we will answer (1) above. Answers to (2) appear in section 8.3. To keep the subject matter as simple as possible, we will look mainly at bonds. We now look at each of these areas in turn.

8.1 Default risk

Default risk is the risk that a company (or individual) contracted to make a payment will be unable or unwilling to make that payment in full on the date it falls due. The company might be bankrupt or in administration. Or the company might be experiencing cash flow problems. In the case of a bond, the issuing company might not pay a coupon in full on the day it fell due. In such a situation, the holder of the bond might lose the full value of the bond. Or they might receive, on a later date, a percentage of what they are owed. The amount that is recovered in the event of default is usually expressed as a percentage of the total amount: this is known as the **recovery rate.**

Each default event has two components. One is the timing of the event (when it happened) and the other is the magnitude of the event (roughly, how much is lost in the default).

How do we measure default risk?

Look at two bonds. One is issued by the US government and is a very safe investment indeed; the other is issued by B&K Rupt Ltd and this is a considerably more risky investment. To keep the calculations simple, we will look at two-year $100 zero coupon bonds. The prices and yields are as shown below.

Bond	Face value	Time to maturity	Price	Yield to maturity (continuously compounded)
US government	100	2	94	0.03094
B&K	100	2	90	0.05268

Both bonds promise to deliver $100 in two years' time. So why does one bond cost $4 less than the other and what does this difference represent? It might be argued that the $4 is a reward offered to the owner of the B&K bond for the greater risk he faces from a default in the payment(s) from the bond. So the information we require should be contained in the difference in value of the bonds. There is almost no risk attached to the US government bond, so the difference in value could represent a measure of the likelihood of default within the next two years in the B&K bond. If this were the case, the difference in value divided by the value of the risk-free bond could be the probability of default by the more risky bond.

This would give:

$$\text{Probability of default} = \frac{\text{price of risk-free bond} - \text{price of risky bond}}{\text{price of risk-free bond}}$$

$$= \frac{94 - 90}{94}$$

$$= 0.04255$$

We can express this in a way that will provide additional useful information. As in Chapter 4, we are interested in the yields of the bonds.

Let r represent the yield of the risk-free bond (continuously compounded).

Let R represent the yield of the corporate bond (continuously compounded).

The prices of the two bonds are given by:

US government bond: price $= 100 \times e^{-r \times 2}$

B&K bond: price $= 100 \times e^{-R \times 2}$

$$\begin{aligned}\text{Probability of default} &= \frac{\text{difference in value}}{\text{value of risk-free bond}} \\ &= \frac{100 \times e^{-r\times 2} - 100 \times e^{-R\times 2}}{100 \times e^{-r\times 2}} \\ &= \frac{e^{-r\times 2} - e^{-R\times 2}}{e^{-r\times 2}} \\ &= 1 - \frac{e^{-R\times 2}}{e^{-r\times 2}} \\ &= 1 - e^{-(R-r)\times 2}\end{aligned}$$

More generally: probability of default by a corporation within T years is:

$1 - \exp(-(\text{corporation bond yield} - \text{risk-free bond yield}) \times T)$

Example 1

In the data shown above, the yield of the risk-free bond (r) is 0.03094. The yield from the corporate bond (R) is 0.05268.

$$\begin{aligned}\text{Probability of default by the risky bond} &= 1 - e^{-(R-r)\times 2} \\ &= 1 - e^{-(0.05268-0.03094)\times 2} \\ &= 0.04255 \text{ (as shown above)}\end{aligned}$$

We can approach this in another way.

Let q = probability corporation X will default within T years. Assume that if a bond issued by corporation X does default, then the bond loses all its value. So if the bond does default, its value becomes \$0. If the bond does not default (with probability 1 − q), the bond's value at maturity is \$100.

We have a table with associated probabilities.

Value of bond at maturity	0 (after default)	100 (no default)
probability	q	1 − q

Expected value of the corporation X bond at maturity =
$q \times 0 + (1 - q) \times 100 = (1 - q) \times 100$.

Expected value of corporation bond today (using the risk-free discounting rate r (continuously compounded))

$$= (1 - q) \times 100 \times e^{-rT}.$$

But the value of this bond today is $100 \times e^{-RT}$. (The correct discounting rate for this bond is its yield to maturity.)

This gives:

$$(1 - q) \times 100 \times e^{-rT} = 100e^{-RT}$$

Hence: $$1 - q = e^{-RT} \times e^{rT} = e^{-(R-r)T}$$

So: $$q = 1 - e^{-(R-r)T}$$

The fact that both approaches deliver the same result is encouraging. But note that to achieve this result, we discounted the expected value of the bond using the risk-free rate, r. This will be important later.

Note 1: we have assumed that if the bond defaults, the pay-off is zero. So 100% is lost. In practice, this is not always the case and there will be a recovery rate, R^{ec}, which will ensure that the bond owner receives $R^{ec} \times 100\%$ of the value of the bond. In this case, the calculation of q shown above should include this recovery rate. See Appendix 8.1.

Note 2: the probability of default q depends on R − r (and the time to maturity, T). This quantity, R − r, the excess of the corporate bond yield above the yield on the risk-free bond, is called the **credit spread** of the corporate bond. We meet credit spread again in the next section.

Example 2

A five-year £100 zero coupon bond issued by M&JJ Productions has yield 0.7% (or 70 basis points) above the yield from a risk-free bond. Calculate the probability the bond will default within five years.

Solution

In this case, the credit spread of the bond (R − r) is 0.7% = 0.007. T = 5 and $q = 1 - e^{-0.007 \times 5} = 0.03439$.

There is a second way of calculating the probability that a company will default in a given period of time. This method is based on historical data and begins with an estimate of the creditworthiness of the company.

8.2 Credit ratings, credit spread, credit spread risk and default probabilities

Credit ratings

There are many organisations which assess the creditworthiness of large companies. Perhaps the largest are (in the US) Moody's, Standard & Poor (S&P) and Fitch and (in the UK) Dun & Bradstreet. These organisations (known as credit rating agencies) assign a credit rating to the company. The credit rating will be based on many factors, but the factors will include:

- the financial position of the company (balance sheet, orders, cash flow)
- quality of management
- an assessment of the company's ability to meet its financial obligations
- an assessment of the overall health of the sector in which the company operates.

A company will receive a credit rating A, B, C or D. But there are many important intermediate grades. The table below shows some of these grades with some comments which characterise these grades. We give some of the grades awarded by S&P and by Moody's.

S&P	Moodys	Characteristics
AAA	Aaa	Highest quality. Extremely strong capacity to meet obligations. Risk factors negligible
AA	Aa2	High quality. Very strong. Lower than AAA because protection margins not as large
A	A2	Strong capacity to meet obligations. More susceptible to adverse changes
BBB	Baa2	Adequate capacity to meet obligations. Suitable for prudent investment
BB	Ba2	Overall, likely to meet obligations. Speculative elements
B	B2	Highly speculative. High risk
CCC	Caa2	Substantial risk. Currently vulnerable to default
C	Ca	Extremely speculative. In, or approaching, bankruptcy or default
D		In default

A company rated 'investment grade' is deemed to have high creditworthiness. Such companies would normally have a credit rating AAA/Aaa down to BBB/Baa2. The remaining grades are described as 'speculative'. A company whose credit rating is 'speculative' will normally be subject to non-ignorable risk. A company receiving a rating C or D (S&P) or Ca (Moodys) would be in, or will be approaching, bankruptcy.

As I write, bonds issued by the UK government carry an AAA rating (S&P). Bonds issued by Severn Trent Water carry an AA rating. Marks and Spencer is rated BBB.

Credit spread

Credit spread is the additional premium in excess of the risk-free rate demanded by the market for accepting a certain type of risk. In the notation used above: credit spread = R − r.

Example 3

Company Y and company Z each issue a five-year $1000 (zero coupon) bond. The yield on the Y bond is 0.0673; the Z bond has yield 0.0489. It is known that a comparable, risk-free bond is selling for $900. Find the credit spreads for the Y and the Z bonds. Find the probability the Y bond defaults and the value of the Y bond. Find the probability the Z bond defaults and the value of the Z bond.

Solution

First we find the yield for the risk-free bond.

$$1000 \times e^{-r\times 5} = 900$$

$$e^{-r\times 5} = 0.9$$

$$r = -\frac{\ln(0.9)}{5} = 0.02107$$

The credit spreads (R − r) for the two bonds are:

Y bond: $0.0673 - 0.02107 = 0.04623$

Z bond: $0.0489 - 0.02107 = 0.02783$

The probabilities of default are given by:

Y bond: $1 - e^{-0.04623\times 5} = 0.2064$

Z bond: $1 - e^{-0.02783\times 5} = 0.1299$

The values of the two bonds are:

Y bond: $1000 \times e^{-0.0673\times 5} = 714.27$

Z bond: $1000 \times e^{-0.0489\times 5} = 783.10$

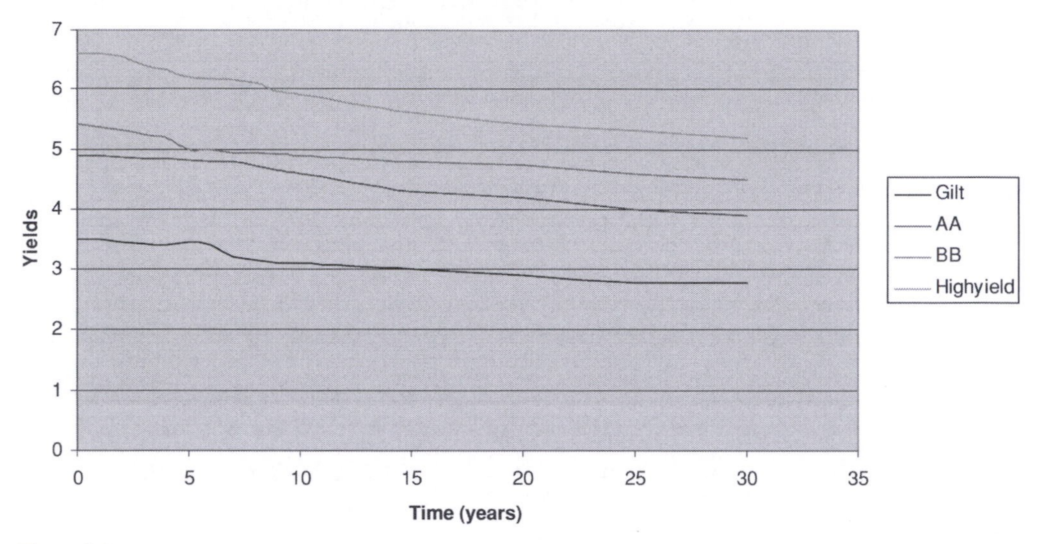

Figure 8.1

This example illustrates that an increased credit spread brings with it:

(i) greater probability of default.

(ii) a lower value for the company bond.

A company carrying a high credit rating attracts only a small amount of risk and we would expect bonds issued by such a company to have a yield reasonably close to the risk-free interest rate. The credit spread from such a company would be small. A company with a lower credit rating would be subject to greater risk: the price of a bond issued by this company would be lower and the yield on the bond higher. The credit spread for this bond would be greater than the credit spread for a company with a higher credit rating. A company with a low credit rating might expect to see its bonds carry a large credit spread. A credit spread for four companies is illustrated in Figure 8.1.

An increase in the credit spread of its bonds is not viewed favourably by the company issuing the bond. Such an increase reflects a loss of creditworthiness and this is the subject of the next section.

Credit spread risk

Credit spread risk is the risk faced by a company of being given a different credit rating (and hence a different credit spread).

The credit rating of a company is kept constantly under review. An up move (to a higher credit rating) is generally welcomed by the company. A down move would certainly not be welcomed. So it is of interest to the company and to potential investors to know the likelihood of a company moving to a higher or to a lower credit rating. Credit rating agencies produce a rating transition matrix. This gives the probability (percentage) of a bond moving from one credit rating to another during a given period of time.

The table below illustrates how the transition probabilities might look for a one-year period.

	Rating at end of year							
Initial rating	AAA	AA	A	BBB	BB	B	CCC	D
AAA	93.29	6.17	0.41	0.08	0.05	0.00	0.00	0.00
AA	0.59	91.73	6.98	0.51	0.08	0.07	0.03	0.01
A	0.06	2.22	91.68	5.27	0.48	0.19	0.05	0.05
BBB	0.05	0.24	4.61	89.43	4.40	0.74	0.28	0.25
BB	0.03	0.18	0.41	6.30	83.01	7.54	1.22	1.31
B	0.02	0.10	0.29	0.43	5.37	82.73	4.36	6.70
CCC	0.11	0.0	0.26	0.77	1.67	10.06	58.61	28.52
D	0.00	0.00	0.00	0.00	0.00	0.00	0.00	100.00

The table suggests that the probability a bond with an AA rating at the beginning of the year will still have an AA rating at the end of the year is 0.9173 (91.73%). A bond rated BB at the beginning of the year has a probability of 0.0122 (1.22%) of being rated CCC by the end of the year. Tables such as these are calculated from historical data. Over perhaps 20 years, the number of bonds that started the year with a BB rating and ended the year with a CCC rating would be recorded. From these data, the above probabilities are calculated. Observe that D is an 'absorbing state'. If a bond moves from any rating to D, that is where it stays. There is no movement to another state from the default state.

In a similar way, the probabilities of a bond defaulting within one year can be calculated. From the above table, the probability that an A-rated bond will default in one year is 0.0005 (or 0.05%). Similarly, the probability that a B-rated bond will default within one year is 0.067 (6.7%). Using similar methods (and some mathematics), probabilities that bonds of different credit ratings will default after two, three or more years can be calculated. Such probabilities are illustrated in the table below.

Cumulative default rates as percentages						
	Years					
Credit rating	1	2	3	4	5	10
AAA	0.00	0.00	0.03	0.06	0.11	0.71
AA	0.01	0.03	0.09	0.17	0.27	0.94
A	0.04	0.11	0.19	0.34	0.55	1.79
BBB	0.23	0.51	0.85	1.49	2.19	5.14
BB	1.08	3.49	6.79	9.98	12.67	18.86
B	5.55	12.97	18.97	23.18	26.71	41.01
CCC	27.43	36.84	45.71	51.49	58.63	68.29

Probability that a bond will default before a given future date

The table shows how we can answer question 1 at the beginning of the chapter. From the table, the probability an AA-rated bond will default within three years is 0.09%, or 0.0009. The probability a BB-rated bond will default within five years is 12.67%, or 0.1267.

We can draw other useful information from this table. Suppose we want to calculate the probability a bond with a BB rating will default in its fifth year. The probability a BB-rated bond will default within four years is 9.98% (0.0998). The probability a BB-rated bond will default within five years is 12.67% (0.1267). So the probability a BB-rated bond will not default in its first four years but will default in its fifth year is $0.1267 - 0.0998 = 0.0269$.

We have now achieved our aim of calculating the probability of default. We have used two methods: we have investigated bond prices and we have used an historical method based on credit ratings. An obvious question presents itself: how closely do the two methods agree? The answer is surprising.

A \$100 three-year zero coupon bond is issued by XYZ, a bank currently A rated. The bond is priced at \$88.93. A corresponding bond issued by an AAA-rated company costs \$90.

(i) Using bond pricing, estimate the probability XYZ will default within three years.

(ii) Using the previous table, estimate the probability XYZ will default within three years.

(i) From bond pricing:
probability of default within three years $= \frac{90-88.93}{90} = 0.0119$.

(ii) From the table, the probability that an A-rated company will default within three years is 0.19% or 0.0019.

This is not what we might have hoped for. The probability derived from bond prices is more than six times greater than the probability derived from historical data. And this phenomenon is widely observed. Some authors have suggested that default probabilities calculated from bond prices might be almost ten times greater than default probabilities calculated from historical data. E. I. Altmann (1989) was one of the first to notice that bond pricing consistently gave higher default probabilities than historical data. Why should this be so? We recommend the paper 'Bond Prices, Default Probabilities and Risk Premiums' by John Hull, Mirela Predescu and Alan White (www.rotman.utoronto.ca/~hull/DownloadablePublications/CreditSpreads.pdf) to anyone interested in pursuing this question. The paper is easy to follow and very informative. Some of the points the authors make are contained in the following.

Why are default probabilities taken from bond prices apparently higher than probabilities calculated from historical data?

- The probabilities drawn out from bond prices use a risk-free discounting factor e^{-rT}. So these might reasonably be regarded as 'risk neutral' probabilities. The probabilities obtained from historical data are calculated from real events and so might reasonably be regarded as 'real world' probabilities. Hence, one set of probabilities are 'risk neutral' probabilities; the other are 'real-world' probabilities. As we saw earlier, these two sets of probabilities will generally be different. But it is surprising that the probability of default in a risk neutral world is much greater than the probability of default in a real-world environment.
- It is possible that bond traders build into their pricing mechanism a compensation for possible default and this is more severe than the default possibilities considered by those producing the tables. If the table makers shared the traders' pessimism, the thinking goes, the probabilities implied by the tables would be higher.
- Banking regulations require that banks maintain a certain percentage of their assets in 'safe' investments. Government bonds are about as safe as you can get, so it is possible that a large investment by banks in government bonds will drive up the price of these bonds and so drive down their yield. This would make the government bond yield *less* than what might reasonably be regarded as the market safe interest rate. Observe that if the risk-free rate r is increased, the credit spread of the corporation bond will decrease and a lower credit spread means a smaller probability of default.
- There is additional evidence that the market risk-free rate is higher than the yield provided by government bonds. Hull et al. suggest that if a corporate bond provides a yield of 6% and five-year protection can be bought from

a credit default swap (see section 8.3a) for 150 basis points per year, then the investor is receiving a risk-free rate of 4.5% (and this is likely to be greater than the yield from a government bond). The authors suggest that a working market risk-free rate might be the swap rate (Chapter 5) minus 10 basis points.

We can calculate the amount by which the risk-free rate r needs to be increased to ensure the default probability calculated from bond prices agrees with the default probability calculated from historical data. We use the above example to illustrate.

The $100 three-year zero coupon corporation bond priced at $88.93 has, it may easily be seen, a yield of 0.0391. The corresponding risk-free bond, costing $90, carries a yield of 0.0351. The probability of default, calculated from historical data, is $Q = 0.0019$.

Let $\widehat{r}$ be the 'safe' interest rate which gives the corporate bond a probability of default Q. Then:

$$1 - e^{-(R-\widehat{r})\times T} = Q \qquad \text{or} \qquad 1 - e^{-(0.0391-\widehat{r})\times 3} = 0.0019$$

$$e^{-(R-\widehat{r})\times T} = 1 - Q \qquad\qquad e^{-(0.0391-\widehat{r})\times 3} = 1 - 0.0091$$

$$-(R - \widehat{r}) \times T = \ln(1 - Q) \qquad\qquad -(0.0391 - \widehat{r}) \times 3 = \ln(0.9909)$$

$$\widehat{r} = \frac{\ln(1 - Q)}{T} + R \qquad\qquad \widehat{r} = \frac{\ln 0.9909}{3} + 0.0391 = 0.0361$$

Since $r = 0.0351$, the risk-free bond yield needs to be increased by $0.0361 - 0.0351 = 0.001$, or 0.1% to give a probability of default of 0.0019.

8.3 Credit derivatives

A credit derivative is a contract in which the pay-off is materially affected by credit risk.

We offer four examples of credit derivatives. In the first three, the credit risk is focused on one single company or company bond. In the fourth, we look at credit risk in a portfolio.

Credit default swaps

Jack Webster, the chief financial officer of A2BB Investments, was concerned that bonds issued by Dodgem Motors formed a very high percentage of company assets. That morning, he was reading the financial pages as his wife cooked breakfast.

'If anything goes wrong with Dodgem Motors,' Jack told his wife, 'and these bonds tumble in value, we could be in hot water.'

'So is that boiled or poached, then?' his wife asked.

Jack decided to talk to his bank.

A credit default swap (CDS) is a contract designed to provide the holder with protection against the risk of default by a particular company. Over the next five years, Company A will be exposed to the risk of default by Company C. Company A approaches Company B (Company B is usually a bank) and enters a five-year credit default swap with an agreed notional principal ($10 000 000, say). The terms are:

- A will make a fixed annual payment to B in each of the next five years or until C defaults. This annual payment will be an agreed number of basis points of the notional principal. In most CDSs, this amount is paid semi-annually or quarterly.
- If C does not default within the next five years, A will make the payments for the full five years and the contract will terminate at the end of the five years. B makes no payment to A.
- If C does default before the five-year maturity:
  A will pay B the fraction of the next payment that has accrued since the previous payment (using an agreed day count convention, usually actual/360).
  B will make a payment to A. This payment might be (a) delivery or (b) cash.
  (a) With a **delivery** payment, A will deliver to B bonds issued by C and having a face value of the notional principal. B will pay A the notional principal.
  (b) With a **cash** payment, a calculation agent samples traders to determine a middle-value price for the C bond a number of days after the default. Let this price be $P per $100. The cash settlement is then (100 – P)% of the notional principal. B pays this amount to A.

Observe that in the event of default by C, Company A is in possession of the notional principal of the bonds (Figure 8.2).

Example 4

On 24 March 2006, A2BB Investments purchased a credit default swap to provide insurance against Dodgem Motors defaulting in the next five years. (Company A is A2BB Investments, Company C is Dodgem Motors.) The

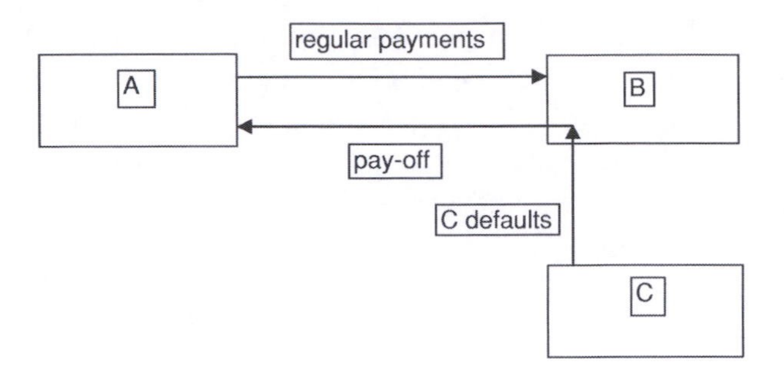

Figure 8.2

notional principal was \$50 000 000 and A2BB agreed to pay 160 basis points of \$50 000 000 each year, semi-annually, for the next five years or until Dodgem Motors defaulted.

160 basis points $= \frac{160}{100}\% = 1.6\%$. So A2BB was agreeing to pay, each year until default, $\frac{1.6}{100} \times \$50\,000\,000 = \$800\,000$. Paying semi-annually, A2BB would pay Company B (the bank) \$400 000 every six months for five years or until Dodgem Motors defaulted.

If there was no default, A2BB would pay \$400 000 to the bank on 24 September 2006 and again on 24 March 2007 and so on through to the final payment on 24 March 2011, when the contract would expire. The bank would make no payment to A2BB Investments.

Now suppose Dodgem Motors defaulted on 6 May 2008. A2BB would pay the bank the fraction of the \$400 000 that had accrued up until 6 May 2008. (Assuming an actual/360 day count convention, this would be $\frac{43}{360} \times 800\,000 = \$95\,555.56$.)

The bank would make a payment to A2BB Investments. If the payment was by 'delivery', A2BB would deliver to the bank Dodgem Motors bonds with face value \$50 000 000 and the bank would pay \$50 000 000 to A2BB for these bonds. If the payment was by 'cash', a calculation agent would take sample prices of Dodgem Motors bonds an agreed number of days after the default and declare a value (\$54 per \$100, say). The bank would then pay A2BB $(100 - 54)\%$ of \$50 000 000, or \$23 000 000.

Observe that in both cases, A2BB is left with approximately \$50 000 000 after default.

Some notes:

(1) Most credit default swaps have a maturity of five years. But many banks will quote prices for maturities of one out to ten years. (See the table below.)

(2) Rather than use the word 'default', it is usual to say, or write, that C experiences a 'credit event'. A credit event may involve one or more of the following:
 bankruptcy or insolvency
 financial or debt restructuring arising from going into receivership or administration
 default on obligations (for example, failure to pay a bond coupon in full on the due date)
 a downgrade in credit rating
 a change in credit spread on the part of Company C taking its spread above an agreed maximum.

(3) The notional principal can vary from \$1 000 000 to several hundred million dollars. The notional principal on investment-grade companies or bonds might be \$10 000 000 to \$100 000 000, but this could be lower if the company has a lower credit rating.

(4) The institutions which sell (and buy) credit default swaps will usually be large banks. The company whose default is feared, the reference entity (C), will not usually be a party to the contract. Indeed, Company C may not even be aware that a CDS has been set up.

(5) It is unclear what might happen if during the period of the contract C is taken over or merged with another company or split into several smaller companies.

(6) There is no mathematical procedure (as I write) to calculate a price (the number of basis points of the notional principal) that is fair to both A and B. This is a very new financial development. Work, as they say, is in progress.

Quotes for credit default swaps

Quotes for credit default swaps issued by a bank (Bank B) in the CDS market might be shown as follows:

Company	Rating Moodys/S&P	3 years bid/ask	5 years bid/ask	7 years bid/ask	10 years bid/ask
Safe Bank Ltd	Aa2/AA	25/44	45/60	46/87	62/105
PowerZ Corp	Baa1/BBB+	107/130	120/140	124/165	185/245
Dodgem Motors	Ba1/BB+	118/150	122/160	225/250	265/298
Night Spots UK	B/B	140/181	155/196	255/300	305/370

Column 2 gives Moody's/S&P credit rating. Column 3 shows the bid/ask quotes in basis points for a CDS with a maturity of three years. Columns 4, 5 and 6 give the bid/ask spreads in basis points for a CDS with maturity five, seven and ten years respectively.

Recall that the bid price is the price at which Bank B would buy a CDS and the ask price is the price at which Bank B would sell a CDS.

So if a company wanted to buy a seven-year CDS on PowerZ Corp, it would be paying 165 basis points per year. (For the company to buy the CDS, Bank B must sell. Hence, we look at the ask price.) If a company wanted to sell a ten-year CDS on Night Spots UK, it would be receiving 305 basis points per year. (For the company to sell a CDS, Bank B must buy.)

Who would buy/sell a CDS?

Jack Webster at A2BB was concerned about the exposure of his company to problems in the motor industry (and problems at Dodgem Motors in particular). By buying a CDS, Jack was transferring some (perhaps all) of that risk to the seller of the CDS.

But Jack could have been more subtle. He might have been concerned that $800 000 per year was a large amount to pay for insurance. His research department might have advised Jack to transfer some of this exposure to another sector of the market. To do this, A2BB could buy a five-year CDS on Dodgem Motors and sell a five-year CDS on Safe Bank Ltd. Since A2BB sold, Bank B would buy. From the table, selling a five-year CDS on Safe Bank Ltd would (in the absence of a credit event) bring A2BB an income of 45 basis points per year or $225 000 per year with a notional principal of $50 000 000. A2BB would pay out $800 000 and receive $225 000, giving a cash outflow of $575 000 per year. This would reduce A2BB's cash outflow and transfer some of A2BB's Dodgem Motors exposure to Safe Bank Ltd. So, by buying and selling CDSs in different sectors of the market, A2BB would be diversifying its credit risk.

We showed in previous chapters how movements in commodities, shares and interest rates could be utilised to create profits or to hedge risk. Credit derivatives can do the same sort of thing for credit risk. Using credit derivatives, credit can be isolated, examined and traded. Just as in previous chapters, trading can be entered into for profit or for hedging risk. Banks are interested in credit derivatives: by buying and selling credit derivatives, they are extending their portfolios into many more sections of the market.

A total return swap

Burden Industries wants to borrow \$10 000 000 from Arrico Bank to invest in a bond issued by ComPlanC Ltd. The bank is wary. It would like to have this loan on its books, but Burden's credit rating has raised a few questions: if Burden Industries defaults on this loan, the bank will lose money. So Arrico Bank and Burden Industries enter a total return swap (TRS) on a ComPlanC bond.

In a **total return swap**, A and B agree to exchange, over the time of the swap (usually one to three years), all payments from two investments. One of the investments is subject to default (we shall let this investment be a bond issued by company C) and the other is a safe investment yielding LIBOR plus a number of basis points. The number of basis points is called the **spread** of the swap. We shall suppose that A buys the C bond and that the swap and the C bond have identical payment dates.

On the regular payment dates (the coupon dates of the bond), A pays to B:

the coupon issued by the bond

any appreciation in value by the bond since the last payment date.

A is the **payer** in the TRS.

B pays to A:

LIBOR plus basis points on the face value of the bond

any depreciation in value by the bond since the last payment date.

B is the **receiver** in the TRS.

If the bond defaults, the swap is terminated and:

A pays to B the recovery value of the bond

B pays to A the face value of the bond (Figure 8.3).

Since A is compensated for any depreciation in the value of the bond, A is said to be 'buying protection'. B is said to be 'selling protection'.

Illustration

Burden Industries wants to arrange a loan from Arrico Bank to buy ComPlanC bonds with a face value of \$10 000 000. Burden's credit rating makes Arrico uneasy. Arrico Bank buys five-year ComPlanC bonds with a face value of \$10 000 000. The bonds pay six-monthly coupons. Arrico and Burden Industries enter a three-year total return swap. The spread is 60 basis points per year.

Arrico is the payer in the swap. It hands over, on coupon payment dates, the coupons paid out by the bonds and any increase in value by the bond since the previous payment date.

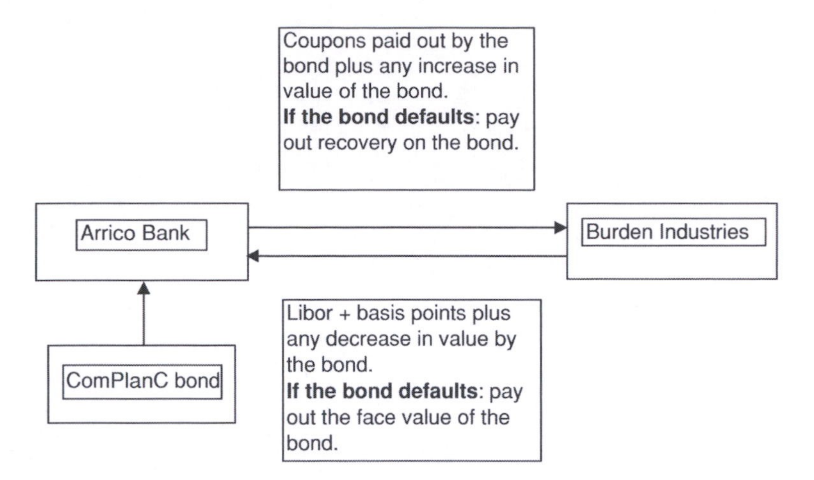

Figure 8.3

Burden Industries is the receiver. On coupon payment dates, the receiver hands over six-monthly LIBOR plus 30 basis points on a notional principal of $10 000 000. As in the swaps described in Chapter 5, LIBOR is set on one payment date and paid out the following payment date. If the bond has fallen in value since the previous payment date, Burden Industries hands over the amount by which the bond has fallen.

If the bond does not default, the swap terminates after three years. If the bond defaults, Arrico Bank, as the owner of the bond, will be paid the recovery value of the bond ($P per $100). This, it pays to Burden Industries. Burden Industries pays $10 000 000 to Arrico Bank.

Burden Industries (the receiver) enjoys the privileges of ownership of the bond. It receives the cash flows from the bond without having had to spend $10 000 000 to buy the bond. This money might profitably have been used elsewhere. Observe, however, the six-monthly LIBOR plus 30 basis points it pays every half year to Arrico Bank could look very like interest payments on a loan of $10 000 000.

Arrico Bank has protection against default by Burden Industries and by ComPlanC. Arrico Bank owns the bond, so if Burden Industries should experience a credit event, the swap is terminated and Arrico Bank will not lose the $10 000 000 it might have loaned Burden Industries to buy the bond. Arrico Bank also has protection against the bond defaulting. If the bond should default, Burden Industries would pay $10 000 000 to Arrico Bank. So a TRS does seem to give both parties what they want.

A TRS might be easier to understand and to price if we consider an extended sequence of payments in which the maturities of the swap and the bond coincide. If the bond does not default, the cash flows can be deduced from:

Time	Payments
Initially	A buys a \$10 000 000 C bond B invests \$10 000 000 in an account paying six-monthly LIBOR + 30 bps
each coupon date	A pays B the coupon and any increase in the value of the bond since the previous coupon date B pays A six-monthly LIBOR + 30 bps and any decrease in the value of the bond since the previous coupon date
additionally, at maturity	A pays \$10 000 000 to B (the return of principal on the bond) B pays \$10 000 000 to A

This illustrates a way in which the payments in the TRS could be hedged. In reality, it is rare for a TRS to proceed through to the maturity of the bond.

Who would buy/sell a TRS?

- A large part of what banks and other financial institutions (e.g. venture capital companies) do is lend money. A TRS allows the payer (A):
  - (i) to have loans on its books (the bonds)
  - (ii) to receive a stream of payments from the receiver (B) (looking for all the world like interest payments on a loan)
  - (iii) to reduce its exposure to default by investing the money that might have gone to Company B in the more creditworthy Company C.
- A has reduced its exposure to default in the C bond.
- A TRS allows the receiver (B) to enjoy the privileges of owning the bond without the inconvenience of having to buy it. This means the receiver has more ready cash available for other investments. (It can obtain greater leverage with available resources.)
- Changes in the value of the bond are received or paid out on each payment date. So price changes in the value of the bond become cash flows on each payment date. This is similar to marking to market in a futures contract. So entering a TRS is similar to taking out a futures contract on a C bond.

Credit spread options

A hedge fund owns a five-year \$50 000 000 bond in the emerging markets. The bond is currently yielding 8.5%. The comparable five-year US Treasury bond yields 4%. The fund's analysts believe there will be a major economic upturn in the country issuing the bond and the credit spread of 8.5 – 4 = 4.5% will be reduced. If the hedge fund managers are prepared to invest in their belief, they could buy a credit spread option.

Credit spread options are designed to capitalise on or to hedge against changes in credit spread.

We are looking at a particular bond – a defaultable bond – with a significant amount of risk attached. Suppose this bond has yield R and matures in five years. If an otherwise identical non-defaultable bond (a government bond, say) has yield r, then the credit spread of the defaultable bond is $R - r$. In a credit spread option the pay-off is based on whether the credit spread on the exercise date is greater than or less than a strike credit spread K. Of course, the option must be exercised before the bond matures. So the option will have an exercise date in T years' time where $T < 5$.

The pay-off:

(i) Suppose it is thought the credit spread of the bond, on the exercise date, will be greater than the strike credit spread K (known as the strike spread).

In this case, buy a credit spread option with:

$$\text{pay-off} = \text{face value of bond} \times \text{bond duration} \times \max(CS_T - K, 0)$$

where CS_T is the credit spread on the exercise date.

The option ceases to exist if the bond defaults.

Example 5

A £1000 bond issued by a BB-credit rated company matures in six years and today has yield 7.2%. A comparable bond issued by the UK government has yield 4.5%. Sarah thinks the credit spread (7.2 – 4.5 = 2.7%) will widen over the coming 12 months. What should she do?

Solution

Sarah bought a credit spread option on the bond with exercise date in one year ($T = 1$) and strike spread $K = 2.7\%$.

In one year's time, the bond showed a yield of 7.9% while the government bond yielded 4.7%. The bond duration was 4.2 years. In this case, $CS_1 = 0.079 - 0.047 = 0.032$. The pay-off is $1000 \times 4.2 \times \max(0.032 - 0.027, 0) = 1000 \times 4.2 \times 0.005 = £21$.

If $CS_1 - K \leq 0$, the pay-off is zero.

The option ceases to exist if the bond defaults within the year.

(ii) If it is thought the credit spread of the bond, at time T, will be less than the strike spread K, then buy a credit spread option with:

$$\text{pay-off} = \text{face value of bond} \times \text{bond duration} \times \max(K - CS_T, 0)$$

where CS_T is the credit spread on the exercise date.
The option ceases to exist if the bond defaults.

Example 6

Consider the position of the hedge fund described at the beginning of this section. The credit spread, today, in the emerging market bond is 4.5% and it is thought the spread will be less than 4.5% in three months' time. What should the hedge fund do?

Solution

The hedge fund could buy a three-month credit spread option with strike spread $K = 4.5\%$ and pay-off $= \$50\text{m} \times \text{duration} \times \max(0.045 - CS_{0.25}, 0)$.

Three months later, the bond showed a yield of 8.1%, while a comparable US Treasury bond was yielding 4.1%. The duration was 4.55 years. The credit spread ($CS_{0.25}$) is $0.081 - 0.041 = 0.040$ and the pay-off is:

$$\$50\text{m} \times 4.55 \times \max(0.045 - 0.040, 0) = \$50\text{m} \times 4.55 \times 0.005 = \$1\,137\,500.$$

Notes:

(1) It is possible also to have a credit spread option that gives the holder the right to buy (call option) or sell (put option) the defaultable bond on the exercise date for the pay-off price.

(2) Credit spread options have not been as successful in the financial markets as was hoped when the product was introduced in the early 1990s. Possible reasons for this might be:
   - Credit spread options are difficult to price
   - The enormous popularity of credit default swaps. It is possible to reduce exposure to changes in credit spread by entering the CDS market. CDSs are generally cheaper than credit spread options.

Who would buy/sell a credit spread option?

If it is thought the credit spread on a defaultable bond will **increase**, buy a credit spread option with
pay-off $=$ face value of bond $\times$ bond duration $\times \max(CS_T - K, 0)$.

If the feeling is that the credit spread will **decrease**, buy a credit spread option with pay-off = face value of bond × bond duration × max(K − CS_T, 0) where CS_T = credit spread on exercise date and K = strike credit spread.

The credit spread options illustrated above are European options and can be exercised only on the exercise date of the option. However, these options exist as American options (exercise at any time prior to the exercise date) and as Bermudan options (exercise only at certain, predefined times prior to the exercise date).

Collateral debt obligation

Fiona is a fund manager. This morning, she is looking with great interest at the yields on some junk bonds she would like to have in her portfolio. Alas, the regulating authorities prohibit fund managers from adding bonds with certain low credit rating to their portfolios. Yet these bonds are offering excellent returns. If the risk of default could somehow be reduced, they would make a very welcome addition to her portfolio. Fiona books an appointment with the firm's head quant. (In financial institutions, mathematicians are often referred to as 'quants' – quantitative analysts.)

A collateral debt obligation (CDO) is a structure designed to offer different ranges of risk to a portfolio of defaultable assets.

So we have a portfolio. The portfolio can consist of bonds or it could consist of loans. It could even consist of credit default swaps. To demonstrate the basic structure, we will consider a portfolio containing only bonds.

A company is set up. The sole asset of the company is the bond portfolio. Such a company is called a special purpose vehicle (SPV). Investors are invited to buy bonds issued by this company. These bonds (*obligations*) are *collaterised* by the *debt* portfolio: hence the name.

The key idea lies in the pay-off scheme for the bonds issued by the special purpose vehicle. Suppose the value of the bonds issued by the SPV is $10 000 000. Each bond issued by the SPV lies in a well-defined band or tranche. The first, lowest, tranche might make up 5% of the $10 000 000. There will be bonds with a face value of $500 000 in this tranche. This is called the equity tranche. Then there are several higher tranches. We will consider a CDO with three higher tranches. The next two tranches (known as mezzanine tranches) might each contain 10% of the $10 000 000. Finally, there is the highest tranche holding, in this case, 75% of the $10 000 000 (or bonds with a face value of $7 500 000). This is known as the senior tranche (Figure 8.4).

On all payment dates, the senior tranche is serviced first. Then payments are made in order of seniority. The highest mezzanine tranche is serviced second,

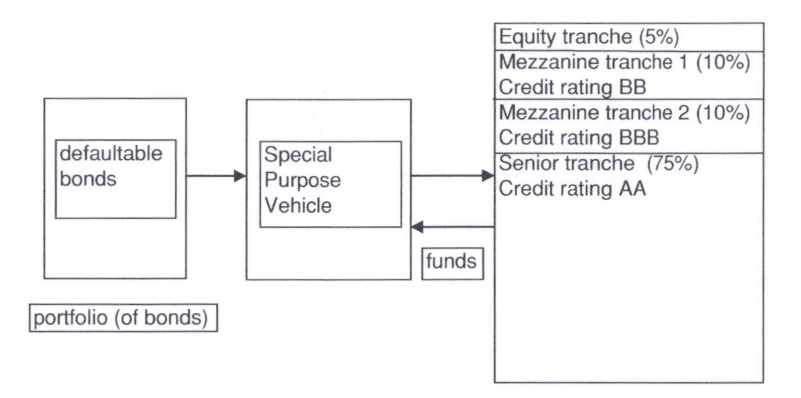

Figure 8.4

followed in descending order by the lower mezzanine tranches, with the equity tranche serviced last. At maturity, the CDO is liquidated and the proceeds are distributed to the tranches, with precedence given to seniority as described above. Bonds in the senior tranche are serviced first. If the senior tranche is repaid in full, bonds in the most senior mezzanine tranche are then paid off. If all these bonds are paid off in full, the next most senior mezzanine tranche is serviced and so on, working down through the tranches in strict order of seniority. Finally, bonds in the equity tranche are paid off with whatever funds remain.

To see more clearly the purpose of a CDO, we view the negative side. Losses hit the equity tranche first. If total losses at maturity are less than 5% of the portfolio's value, all the losses in the portfolio are absorbed by this tranche. If the portfolio loses 5% of its value, the first tranche loses 100% of its value. (This tranche is sometimes known as 'toxic waste'.) In such cases, the more senior tranches will then pay out in full. However, if losses exceed 5%, the most junior mezzanine tranche will take a hit – and if total losses exceed 15%, the second mezzanine tranche will be affected.

Bonds issued by the mezzanine and senior tranches will usually carry a credit rating. Since the senior tranche should be safe from default, bonds from this tranche will normally carry a credit rating A up to AAA. Mezzanine tranche bonds will normally be B to BBB. So even if the original portfolio contains junk bonds (credit rating BB/Ba or lower) or other bonds without a high credit rating, an investor buying a bond from the senior tranche will be holding a bond with a high credit rating. The tranches of lower seniority provide loss protection cover for the more senior tranches. The interest paid by the items in the various tranches will reflect this system of credit rating. Bonds issued by the senior tranche, being least likely to default, will pay the lowest coupons. This is illustrated in Figure 8.5.

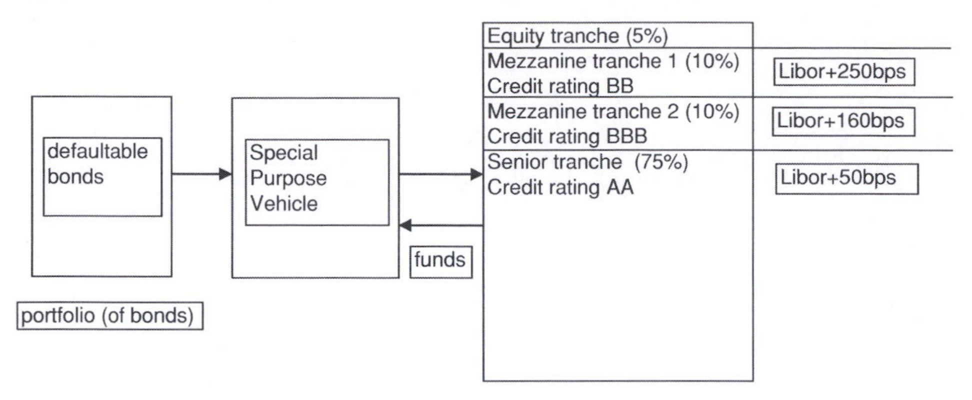

Figure 8.5

It might be said that the market maker who set up the CDO has sold 'loss layer protection' on some of the losses in the portfolio.

Who would buy/sell a CDO?

- The fund manager wanting to invest in junk bonds and prevented from doing so by industry regulations can buy bonds of a suitable seniority issued by a CDO. In this way, a portfolio of debt with a poor credit rating (below investment grade) can be repackaged into tranches, some of which will receive an investment grade rating.
- Banks can create a portfolio of loans and use a CDO to 'transform' these loans into bonds. Using a CDO, low credit rated debt can be repackaged and sold off as highly rated bonds. A CDO will allow a bank to remove a loan from its balance sheet, yet still maintain contact with borrowers. In 1996, NatWest transferred $5 billion from its balance sheet to an underlying loan portfolio. This was the first recorded example of a CDO. In the same way, through a CDO, junk bonds can be 'transformed' into bonds with a high credit rating.
- It is thought that CDO tranches offer a higher yield on bonds with identical ratings. Hence they are attractive for the interest they provide.
- A CDO can offer an investor a stake in a diversified portfolio while making an investment in bonds from just one tranche.
- The issuing bank usually keeps all or a large part of the equity tranche to itself. This is in part because it might be difficult to sell bonds from this part of the SPV, but also because by maintaining ownership of part of the SPV the issuing bank can benefit from any revenues that remain after repayment on the issued bonds. However, some investors would prefer to buy bonds from the equity tranche. Their thinking would be: they would receive a sufficient

number of generous coupon payments to recoup their investment before defaults brought coupon payments to an end.

Notes:

(1) If, during the lifetime of the CDO, one of the bonds in the portfolio defaults, all recovery payments are re-invested in default-free securities and brought back into the portfolio.
(2) A CDO that has only bonds in the original portfolio is called a collateral bond obligation (CBO). A CDO that has only loans in the portfolio is called a collateral loan obligation (CLO).
(3) The purchaser of a bond from either a mezzanine tranche or the senior tranche is hoping there will not be too many defaults among the bonds or loans in the underlying portfolio. If the level of default is less than 5% of the notional principle (as we have shown), such investors will be paid in full. So there is interest in how defaults in the portfolio are correlated. A low default correlation would suggest that losses might be limited to the equity tranche. A high correlation, on the other hand, might indicate that if one item in the portfolio defaulted, so might others. So in a sense, investors in a CDO are buying into low correlation risk. How to measure and price correlation, or dependency, is a very important topic in credit risk research.

It was estimated (the website is: http://www.celent.com/PressReleases/20051031/CDOMarket.htm) that by the end of 2006, the investment worldwide just in CDOs would have been around US$2 trillion. Truly, an investment tool of great interest and immense importance.

The world of credit derivatives is a hugely exciting area of research, packed with intriguing ideas and enormous potential. We hope you are encouraged to look further.

Appendix 8.1

Let $q =$ probability corporation X will default within T years. Assume a recovery rate R^{ec}. So if the bond does default, its value becomes $\$R^{ec} \times 100$.

We have a table with associated probabilities.

Value of bond at maturity	$R^{ec} \times 100$ (after default)	100 (no default)
probability	q	$1 - q$

Expected value of the corporation X bond at maturity
$= q \times R^{ec} \times 100 + (1 - q) \times 100.$

Expected value of corporation bond today (using the risk-free rate discounting rate r (continuously compounded)

$= (q \times R^{ec} \times 100 + (1 - q) \times 100) \times e^{-rT}$.

But the value of this bond today is $100 \times e^{-RT}$.
This gives:

$$(q \times R^{ec} \times 100 + (1 - q) \times 100) \times e^{-rT} = 100e^{-RT}$$
$$q \times R^{ec} + (1 - q) = e^{-(R-r)T}$$
$$q(R^{ec} - 1) = e^{-(R-r)T} - 1$$

Hence:

$$q = \frac{e^{-(R-r)T} - 1}{R^{ec} - 1}$$

and $$q = \frac{1 - e^{-(R-r)T}}{1 - R^{ec}}$$

Exercise 8

1. (i) A three-year $1000 zero coupon bond issued by M&M1 Constructions costs $781.53. A similar bond issued by the US government costs $883.47. Calculate the probability M&M1 will default within three years.
   (ii) M&M1 has a BB credit rating. What does this tell you about the company?
   (iii) The table below gives default probabilities (expressed as percentages) for organisations with different credit ratings.

	Years					
Credit rating	1	2	3	4	5	10
AAA	0.00	0.00	0.03	0.06	0.11	0.71
AA	0.01	0.03	0.09	0.17	0.27	0.94
A	0.04	0.11	0.19	0.34	0.55	1.79
BBB	0.23	0.51	0.85	1.49	2.19	5.14
BB	1.08	3.49	6.79	9.98	12.67	18.86
B	5.55	12.97	18.97	23.18	26.71	41.01
CCC	27.43	36.84	45.71	51.49	58.63	68.29

   Find the probability that an M&M1 bond will default within three years.

(iv) If your answers to (i) and (iii) differ significantly, give three reasons why the two methods might give such different answers.

2. Peter was concerned that his firm would make large losses if bonds issued by BJL Conglomerates defaulted. On 30 April 2006, Peter's firm entered a five-year credit default swap with MLM Bank. The notional principal was $10 000 000 and payments would be made semi-annually. The table below gives the bid/ask prices issued by MLM Bank on credit default swaps.

Company	Rating	3 years	5 years	7 years	10 years
	Moody's/S&P	bid/ask	bid/ask	bid/ask	bid/ask
IDSB Distillery	Aa2/AA	28/47	51/68	45/89	66/110
NRB Universal	Baa1/BBB+	104/140	100/140	114/155	173/238
BJL Conglomerates	Ba1/BB+	119/163	128/168	221/270	261/305
BMSH Bank	A2/A	66/83	75/107	85/133	115/175

(i) The firm bought a five-year CDS on BJL Conglomerates. Describe the cash flows assuming BJL does not default in the five years.

(ii) BJL defaulted on 1 July 2008. The day count convention is actual/360 and payment is 'delivery'. Describe the cash flows from the CDS.

(iii) Peter felt that NRB Universal was safe and responsible. How could Peter reduce his firm's CDS payments? Why by selling a CDS is Peter diversifying his firm's risk?

3. Benson Inc would like to buy a $50 000 000 bond issued by CCC Industries. It approaches Alpha1 Bank with a proposal to borrow $50 000 000. Alpha1 Bank would like to have this loan on its books, but it is uneasy with Benson's credit rating. On 3 August 2006, Benson and Alpha1 enter a total return swap on a $50 000 000 CCC Industries bond. The bond pays 5.5% per year, in semi-annual coupons. The spread of the TRS is 70 basis points.

(i) Assuming no default in the bond, and assuming that bond prices and six-monthly LIBOR rates are as shown below, describe the payments up until 3 February 2009.

Date	Bond value (per $100)	Six-month LIBOR
3 Aug 2006	82.53	0.048
3 Feb 2007	85.14	0.042
3 Aug 2007	84.92	0.046
3 Feb 2008	82.11	0.049
3 Aug 2008	82.39	0.0483
3 Feb 2009	83.81	0.0481

(ii) If the bond defaulted on 28 November 2007 and the recovery value was 45%, describe the payments on 28 November 2007.

4. The republic of Beelzebub has experienced many years of internal upheaval. A government-backed ten-year zero coupon bond yields 9.16%. Then a new government takes power. Susan feels that a period of greater stability lays ahead and that the spread over a US government rate will be reduced. A US government ten-year zero coupon bond is yielding 4.08%. Susan enters a six-month credit spread option on a $5 000 000 bond with a strike spread of 0.0508.
   (i) Describe the pay-off.
   (ii) Six months later, the Beelzebub bond is selling for $43.76 per $100 of face value and the US government bond is yielding 4.10%. The duration of the Beelzebub bond is 9.2 years. Calculate the pay-off.

5. Explain how a junk bond (credit rated BB or lower) can be repackaged as an A-rated bond.

6. (i) What is a collateralised bond obligation?
   (ii) Why does the senior tranche in a CBO have a high credit rating?
   (iii) Why might a bank setting up a CBO keep the bonds in the equity tranche?
   (iv) Explain why a low default correlation between issuers of the bonds (debts) in the portfolio leads to a high credit rating for the higher tranches.
   (v) Why might a bank set up a CDO based on a portfolio of loans?

Solutions

Solutions 1

1. 3.938%

2. 3.732%

3. 5.870%

4. 4.778%

5. 5.069%

6. 8.16%, 7.844%

7. 6.4% compounded daily.

8. (i) AAABank: £25 541.67
   (ii) FriendlyBank: £25 521.20
   (iii) InvestandGrow: £25 505.84
   (iv) MoneyValue: £25 523.26

9. (i) 5.6% compounded semi-annually, (ii) 5.5% compounded quarterly.

10. £81.25

11. 5605 days.

12. (i) £4408.30 (ii) 9690.03 (iii) 7298808.37

13. \$89 583.41

14. £12 781.13

15. £7427.65

16. 6.68% compounded monthly.

17. \$52 061.06

18. 1.77168%

19. 7.1085%

20. Buy in London at £7.38. Sell in NY for £7.4028. No transaction costs.

21. Buy 1 000 000 yen in London for £5000. Sell in Frankfurt for £5035. Heavy buying in London and selling in Frankfurt will cause the price differential to disappear.

22. In Moscow, spend 27.98 RUB and buy \$1. Sell this dollar in NY for 29.9145 RUB. This is an arbitrage opportunity.

23. In the absence of transaction costs and assuming the prices remain as described, this is an arbitrage opportunity. Risk-free profit = £841.53.

24. Do not buy the bond. Sell this bond for £95.50. Invest £95.50 for nine months at 6.53%. In nine months' time receive £100.22. Pay £100 to the bond holder. Profit = £0.22.

25. (i) (a) If £1 is changed: pounds $\rightarrow$ yen $\rightarrow$ euro $\rightarrow$ pounds, the product gives the value of £1 at the end of this chain.
    (b) 1.00043. There is an arbitrage opportunity in buying pounds, changing currencies as shown in the chain and selling pounds at the end of the chain.
    (ii) (a) Buy pounds. Change currencies as shown in the chain. Sell pounds at the end of the chain.
    (b) Do nothing.

(c) If abc $< 1, \frac{1}{a} \times \frac{1}{b} \times \frac{1}{c} > 1$. Then as above (reversed). Buy pounds. Pounds $\rightarrow$ euros $\rightarrow$ yen $\rightarrow$ pounds. Sell pounds.

26. Suppose not. Investor A borrows the amount needed today to buy the portfolio at the lower price. The amount borrowed must (or an arbitrage opportunity will arise) increase in value to the value of the portfolio at maturity. Investor B borrows enough to buy at the higher price. This loan must also increase in value until at maturity it matches the value of the portfolio. But at maturity, the portfolios have equal value. Contradiction.

27. (i) $\frac{2}{7}, \frac{5}{7}$
(ii) $\frac{2}{7}[-4000 \times 2.5 + 8000] + \frac{5}{7}[-8000 \times \frac{2}{5} + 4000] = 0$
(iii) BB wins.
(iv) BB: 2 to 1 against (probability $\frac{1}{3}$).
SI: 2 to 1 on (probability $\frac{2}{3}$).

29. (i) 6.65476% (ii) 7.4701%

Solutions 2

1. Net income today = £0. To avoid arbitrage, net income at maturity must also be zero. Hence K = value of investment at maturity.
$K = 900 \times 1.05^{\frac{1}{4}}$

2. £3.56

3. $2245.87

4. Enter a long two-month forward contract: delivery price = £101 218.43.

5. The forward price is the price that would be agreed today for the delivery of the asset on a specified future date.
The forward price is the delivery price in a forward contract. The delivery price causes the forward contract to have, today, zero value.

6. (i) £10.76, (ii) £10.88. Same as (ii).

7. (i) £35 557 783. 56. Same.
   (ii) (a) Same, (b) 32 887 687.67

8. (i) 0 (ii) £16.17 (iii) £16.17, £18.38

9. (i) £19.29 (ii) £20.69, £1.35 (iii) £20.05, £0.74

10. £147.56

11. £9.69

12. (i) $19.07, 0 (ii) $15.81, $3.10 (iii) $24.06, −$4.78

13. Forward price should be £33.71.
    Today: Borrow $D = 2.5 \times 1.073^{-0.25}$ for three months.
    Borrow $35 - D$ for six months.
    Buy one share.
    Enter a short forward contract on this share with delivery price £34.
    At maturity: pay £33.71. Receive £34.

14. £0.5334. Because the UK interest rate (4.8%) is less than the US interest rate (5.3%).

16. £11912.51

17. Forward price = $0.7653.
    (i) Today: borrow $1. This is 1.3103 AUD. Invest at 4.23% for six months. Enter six-month forward contract to sell 1 AUD for $0.7700.
    At maturity: repay $1.02419. Investment pays out 1.3383 AUD. Use the forward contract to sell 1.3383 AUD for $1.0305. Profit = $\$6.31 \times 10^{-3}$.
    (ii) Today: borrow 1 AUD. This is $0.7632. Invest at 4.78% for six months. Enter six-month forward contract to buy AUD at rate 1 AUD = $0.7600.
    At maturity: repay 1.021375 AUD. Investment pays out $0.78166. Using the forward contract, buy AUD at rate 1 AUD = $0.7600. This gives you 1.0285 AUD. Profit = 7.13×10^{-3} AUD.

18. (i) (a) $R = 0.04475$, (b) $Q = 0.03961$, (ii) £5.73

19. Discrete: £15.34. Continuous: £15.36.

20. 13.86%

21.

Asset pays	Forward price	Value of short forward contract with delivery price K
No dividend	$S_0 e^{RT}$	$Ke^{-RT} - S_0$
Discrete (known dividend)	$(S_0 - D)e^{RT}$	$Ke^{-RT} - (S_0 - D)$
Continuous yield	$S_0 e^{(R-Q)T}$	$Ke^{-RT} - S_0 e^{-QT}$

22. (i) £52.67, 0

(ii)

Month	Asset value	Value of contract
0	55.00	0
1	59.32	4.09
2	64.15	8.69
3	62.70	9.52
4	60.08	6.68
5	58.44	4.81
6	54.88	1.03
7	51.90	−2.18
8	48.60	−5.70
9	44.70	−7.32
10	46.88	−5.35
11	50.80	−1.65
12	52.50	−0.17

Solutions 3

1. A complete answer must contain a description of margin accounts and marking to market.

2. See section 3.1.

3. Enter a long futures contract if you think the price of the asset is going to rise. Enter a short futures contract if you think the price of the asset is likely to fall.

4. Usha is contracting to sell gold in June 2005 at a price agreed on 11 November 2004. Enter a short June futures contract in gold. Set up a margin account. Set maintenance margin.

5.

Ex3.5answer							
		Futures	Contract	Daily	Cumulative	Margin account	Margin
No. contracts	Day	price	value	gain	gain	balance	call
3	1	2.68	13400			1300	
	2	2.65	13250	-150	-150	1150	0
Contract size	3	2.61	13050	-200	-350	1300	350
5000	4	2.54	12700	-350	-700	1300	350
	5	2.59	12950	250	-450	1550	0
	6	2.63	13150	200	-250	1750	0
Initial margin	7	2.62	13100	-50	-300	1700	0
1300	8	2.57	12850	-250	-550	1450	0
Maintenance margin							
975							

Overall loss $550 per contract or $1650 on the three contracts.

6. On Day 6, the margin account balance should be $21 600. The calculation performs a margin call when the margin account falls below the level of the initial margin. A margin call should be made when the margin account falls below the maintenance margin.

7.

Ex3.7answer							
		Futures	Contract	Daily	Cumulative	Margin account	Margin
No. contracts	Day	price	value	gain	gain	balance	call
5	1	4.78	47800			5000	
	2	4.5	45000	2800	2800	7800	0
Contract size	3	4.36	43600	1400	4200	9200	0
10000	4	4.47	44700	-1100	3100	8100	0
	5	4.59	45900	-1200	1900	6900	0
	6	4.78	47800	-1900	0	5000	0
Initial margin	7	4.96	49600	-1800	-1800	5000	1800
5000	8	5.16	51600	-2000	-3800	5000	2000
Maintenance margin							
3750							

Overall loss £3800 per contract or £19 000 on the five contracts.

8.

Ex3.8answer							
Contract							
		Futures	Contract	Daily	Cumulative	Margin account	Margin
No. contracts	Day	price	value	gain	gain	balance	call
3	1	0.9513	39954.6			12000	
	2	0.9011	37846.2	-2108.4	-2108.4	9891.6	0
Contract size	3	0.8798	36951.6	-894.6	-3003	12000	3003
42000	4	0.8948	37581.6	630	-2373	12630	0
	5	0.8969	37669.8	88.2	-2284.8	12718.2	0
	6	0.8371	35158.2	-2511.6	-4796.4	10206.6	0
Initial margin	7	0.8049	33805.8	-1352.4	-6148.8	12000	3145.8
12000	8	0.9713	40794.6	6988.8	840	18988.8	0
Maintenance margin							
9000							

Overall gain $840 per contract or $2520 on the three contracts.

9.

Ex3.9answer							
		Futures	Contract	Daily	Cumulative	Margin account	Margin
No. contracts	Day	price	value	gain	gain	balance	call
3	1	0.8537	21342.5			2000	
	2	0.8481	21202.5	140	140	2140	0
Contract size	3	0.8948	22370	-1167.5	-1027.5	2000	1027.5
25000	4	0.8911	22277.5	92.5	-935	2092.5	0
	5	0.8792	21980	297.5	-637.5	2390	0
	6	0.8899	22247.5	-267.5	-905	2122.5	0
Initial margin	7	0.8219	20547.5	1700	795	3822.5	0
2000							
Maintenance margin							
1500							

Overall gain £1700 per contract or £5100 on the three contracts.

11. For example:

Buy shares:	Buy futures:
Buy 3225 shares	Each contract is for $20 380. Put up 10%
Profit = $1515.75	Buy 24 futures contracts
	Gain of $80 per contract or $1920 overall

12. (i) Buy two long December futures contracts in silver.
    (ii) Two cases:
        (a) the price of silver rises (to \$6.20, say). Gain approx. $2 \times 5000 \times (6.20 - 5.97) = \$2300$ on the futures contracts. Pay $\$10\,000 \times 6.20 = \$62\,000$ for the silver, giving an outlay of $\$62\,000 - 2300 = \$59\,700$ altogether. This represents a price of approximately \$5.97 per troy oz.
        (b) The price of silver falls (to \$5.50, say). From the futures contracts: (approx) $2 \times 5000 \times (5.50 - 5.97) = -\$4700$.
            From the purchase of the silver: $\$10\,000 \times 5.50 = \$55\,000$
            This represents a total cost of approx \$59 700: again, approx \$5.97 per ounce.

13. Buy two short August heating oil futures contracts.
    Roughly, if the price falls (to \$0.80, say), the company gains from the futures contracts (approximately $\$0.14 \times 84\,000 = \$11\,760$) and loses from its purchase of heating oil ($\$0.07 \times 90\,000 = \$6300$). This gives a profit of \$5460. $\$0.87 \times 90\,000 + 5460$ gives, approximately, a cost of \$0.94 per gallon.
    Similarly, if the price rises (above \$0.94 per gallon), the company will lose from the futures contracts and gain from their purchase. This, too, gives a price for the company of approximately \$0.94 per gallon.
    These calculations yield approximations because (a) the futures contracts did not match exactly the heating oil purchase, (b) we are assuming that when the contracts are closed out, the futures price is close to the spot price, and (c) we are assuming that the cost of heating oil No2 is highly correlated with Hothomes' brand of heating oil.

14. (i) Enter a short hedge if you have to sell an asset in the future and you want to lock in a price now.
    (ii) Enter a long hedge if you have to purchase an asset in the future and you want to lock in a price now.

15. Hedge ratio $= \dfrac{\text{size of position in futures contracts}}{\text{size of asset to be hedged}}$

$0.8 = \frac{N \times 4.05 \times 5000}{5\,000\,000} \qquad N = 197.$

16.

Ex3.16answer							
					=CORREL(D8:D16,E8:E16)		
	F value	S value	x	y			
						0.833555	
	148.45	32.78			=VAR(E8:E16)		
	149.54	33.5	1.09	0.72			
	150.32	33.97	0.78	0.47		0.320128	
	150.04	33.98	-0.28	0.01	=VAR(D8:D16)		
	149.55	33.05	-0.49	-0.93			
	148.97	32.69	-0.58	-0.36		0.72185	
	147.79	32.13	-1.18	-0.56			
	148.23	32.75	0.44	0.62	=G5*SQRT(G9/G12)		
	148.74	32.8	0.51	0.05			
	150.07	33.18	1.33	0.38		0.555101	

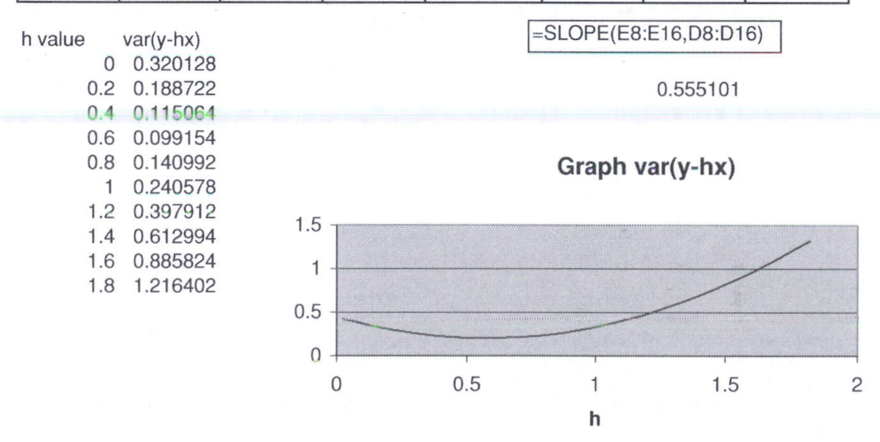

h value	var(y-hx)
0	0.320128
0.2	0.188722
0.4	0.115064
0.6	0.099154
0.8	0.140992
1	0.240578
1.2	0.397912
1.4	0.612994
1.6	0.885824
1.8	1.216402

=SLOPE(E8:E16,D8:D16)

0.555101

See figure. $h = 0.551$: $N = 186$ (calculated from $(0.5551 \times 5\,000\,000)/(149.17 \times 100)$ where the average futures price has been used in the calculation. 186

17.

Ex3.17answer						
						var (x) =VAR(D7:D13)
Time	F value	S value	x value	y value		
					4.175524	
					0.263095	
0	45.67	14.85				
0.083333	47.94	14.97	2.27	0.12		var (y) =VAR(E7:E13)
0.166666	48.25	15.12	0.31	0.15		
0.249999	46.74	15.01	-1.51	-0.11	0.869632	
0.333332	44.26	14.11	-2.48	-0.9		
0.416665	41.38	13.27	-2.88	-0.84		=CORREL(D7:D13,E7:E13)
0.5	42.61	13.25	1.23	-0.02		
0.583333	44.01	13.7	1.4	0.45	0.218291	=F9*SQRT(F5/F4)
					0.218291	=SLOPE(E7:E13,D7:D13)

h value	var(y-hx)
0	0.263095
0.1	0.122554
0.2	0.065524
0.3	0.092004
0.4	0.201994
0.5	0.395495
0.6	0.672507
0.7	1.033029
0.8	1.477061
0.9	2.004604
1	2.615657

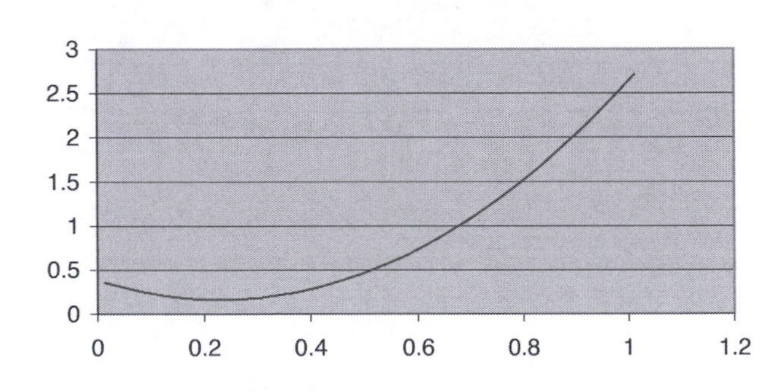

See figure. $h = 0.2183$: $N = 97$ (calculated from $(0.2183 \times 10\,000\,000)/(0.4511 \times 50\,000)$ where the average futures price has been used in the calculation. 95

Solutions 4

1. £88.17

2. £820.92

3. Today: borrow \$97.36 for six months at 5.4%. Buy a bond.
   At maturity: repay $97.36 \times 1.054^{0.5} = \$99.95$. Receive \$100.

4. £101.86

5. (i) 8.8%. (ii) \$989.42. (iii) The bond pays less than the safe interest rate.

6. (i) 7.5%. (ii) \$524.10. (iii) The bond pays more than the safe interest rate.

7. (i) The bond pays a coupon rate less than the safe interest rate.
   (ii) The bond pays a coupon rate more than the safe interest rate.

8. (i)

Interest rate	3.5	4	4.5	5	5.5	6	6.5
Value of bond	103.63	102.45	101.29	100.14	99.02	97.91	96.82

9. (i) \$1.7901 (ii) \$1.8 (iii) \$1.7778

10. (i) $\frac{209}{360}$ (ii) $\frac{210}{360}$

11. (i) \$21.8478 (ii) \$22.1667

12. Dirty price = quoted price + accrued interest.
    Clean price = quoted price.

13. (i) (a) \$2.9144 (b) \$2.9431
    (ii) \$104; \$106.9144, \$106.9431

14. See quotations in section 4.4. (i) £112.3984 (ii) £112.425
    (iii) £112.4

15. 8, 7.5472, 8.80613, 0.03882

16. (i) 5 (ii) 5.2632 (iii) 54.26386 (iv) 0.06991

17. 6.106768, 0.02643

18. 48.58, 0.003127

19. 5.9880, 36.664, 0.05990

20. 10.482, 0.0967621

21.

Bond value	90	95	100	105	110	115
Par yield	5.4264	5.4264	5.4264	5.4264	5.4264	5.4264
Yield to maturity	0.1210	0.08973	0.0609	0.03422	0.009433	−0.01367

(iii) The price of £115 is too high to support a positive yield to maturity.

23. 0.03273, 5.2274

24.

Bond	YTM
1	0.02439
2	0.02484
3	0.02491
4	0.02232

Buy bond number 3.

25. See section 4.6.

26. See section 4.6.

27. (i) $\frac{5}{1+R} + \frac{5}{(1+R)^2} + \frac{5}{(1+R)^3} + \frac{5}{(1+R)^4} + \frac{100}{(1+R)^4}$ is the value today of all payments made by the bond. In the absence of arbitrage, this must be the value of the bond today.

(ii) $\frac{5}{1+R} + \frac{5}{(1+R)^2} + \frac{5}{(1+R)^3} + \frac{5}{(1+R)^4} + \frac{100}{(1+R)^4} = 100$. Multiply through by $(1 + R)^4$.

$5[(1 + R)^3 + (1 + R)^2 + (1 + R) + 1] = 100[(1 + R)^4 - 1]$

Use the GP result: $1 + x + x^2 + x^3 + \cdots + x^{n-1} = \frac{x^n - 1}{x-1}$

$5[\frac{(1+R)^4-1}{1+R-1}] = 100[(1 + R)^4 - 1]$

This gives: $\frac{5}{R} = 100$ and so $\frac{5}{100} = R$. This gives: coupon rate = current yield = YTM.

(iii) $\frac{5}{1+R} + \frac{5}{(1+R)^2} + \frac{5}{(1+R)^3} + \frac{5}{(1+R)^4} + \frac{100}{(1+R)^4} = B$

As above: $5[\frac{(1+R)^4-1}{R}] = B(1 + R)^4 - 100$ **

If $B < 100$, $\frac{5}{100} < \frac{5}{B}$.

It remains to show that $\frac{5}{B} <$ YTM

From **, $\frac{5}{B}[\frac{(1+R)^4-1}{R}] = (1 + R)^4 - \frac{100}{B} < (1+R)^4 - 1$ (since $\frac{100}{B} > 1$)

This gives $\frac{5}{B}[\frac{1}{R}] < 1$ or $\frac{5}{R} < R$.

(iv) Proved similarly.

28. (i) 0.08194 (ii) 0.03816

(iii) Low bond price indicates a high interest rate; high bond price indicates a low interest rate.

30.

Price	Gain	Accumulated gain	
117468.75			
117906.25	437.5	437.5	
118593.75	687.5	1125	Margin account
119500	906.25	2031.25	remains above 7500
121625	2125	4156.25	
122937.5	1312.5	5468.75	
122187.5	−750	4718.75	

no margin calls. Gain is 4718.75 per contract.

31. $1000

32. $109.41

33.

Bond	quoted − (quoted futures × conversion factor)
1	1.7244
2	0.8694
3	1.7299

Bond 2.

Solutions 5

1. 0.065

2. (i) 0.0555 (ii) 0.059 (iii) 0.06067

3. 0.07612

4. 0.06447

5. (i) Today: borrow £P with six-month maturity, invest £P with two-year maturity.
   (ii) 0.055. Borrow $23 733.22 at 5.35% for two years. Invest $23 733.22 at 5.2% for one year.
   (iii) Borrow $97 482.24 at 5.1% for six months. Invest $97 482.24 at 5.35% for two years. Rate = 0.0543.

6. (i) 0.07405. Borrow P for three years at 6.2%. Invest P for four years at 6.5%.
   (ii) Borrow £8348.85 for four years at 6.5%. Invest £8348.85 for three years at 6.2%.

7. See section 5.2.

8. £7527.48

9. The value of an FRA, initially, is zero.

11. If interest rates rose, an FRA offering a lower rate of interest would become more valuable. If interest rates fell, an FRA offering a higher rate would become less valuable.

12. To fix, today, an interest rate over a future time period.

13. (i) Enter a payers FRA.
    (ii) 0.06091.
    (iii) It would not.

14. (i) Enter a payers FRA.
    (ii) 0.05621.
    (iii) −£1745.91.

15. See section 5.3.

16. (i) The interest at the current six-month floating rate is exchanged for the interest at the fixed rate.
    (ii) Ten years.
    (iii) (a) Pay fixed, receive floating. (b) Receive fixed, pay floating.
    (iv) Accrual period = six months.

17. (i) 0.05063
    (ii) (a) 26 447.68 (b) 26 780.35

18. (ii) 0.05390 (iii) −$36 730.93 (iv) −$132 659.80

19. (i) Enter a receivers swap.

20. 0.04815

21. (i) AA borrows at a fixed rate, BB borrows at a floating rate. AA enters a receivers swap, BB enters a payers swap.
    (ii) $x = 1.3$, $y = 0.8$, $x - y = 0.5$. Total gain $= 0.1$ (AA) $+ 0.4$ (BB) $=$ 0.5
    (iii) AA pays L + 0.115%, BB pays 9.915%.

22. Enter a cap; strike rate = 7.5%.

23. See caplets and caps, section 5.3.

25. Change by $25.

Solutions 6

1. See section 6.1. Less than $21.5.

2. Both will today fix a future exchange rate.

   Forward contract: advantage – costs nothing to enter; disadvantage – potential for large losses.

   Call option: advantage – losses are bounded; disadvantages – there is an initial cost, prices from an asset rising in value are less than those from a forward contract.

3. (i) pay-off (ii) profit

(i) pay-off	(ii) profit
(a) 2.70	1.50
(b) 1.20	0
(c) 0	−1.20

4. See section 6.2. Enter a put option if you think the asset will fall in value (below the strike price plus cost of the option).

5. (i) pay-off (ii) profit

(i) pay-off	(ii) profit
(a) 0	−2.00
(b) 1	−1
(c) 2.01	0.01

9. (i) $11.147 < 11.16$: not arbitrage free.
   (ii) Today: borrow one share, sell the share, write one put option, buy one call option.
   (iii) Profit = £0.0134. Approx 75 000.

10. See section 6.4. Buy a call option. Sell a call option with a higher strike.

11. (i) 3
    (ii) 1
    (iii) −0.5

12. Buy a put option. Sell a put option with a higher strike price.

13. See section 6.4.

14. (i) −6.5
    (ii) −1
    (iii) 3.50

15. Buy a put option. Sell a put option with a lower strike price.

16. (ii) (a) 0
         (b) 4
         (c) 2
    (iii) They expect the price to stay close to £30. The portfolio leads to a small loss if there is a significant move either up or down.
    (iv) Butterfly spread.

17. Buy a put (low strike). Buy a put (high strike). Sell two puts (intermediate strike).
    If all options are European (see Chapter 7, section 7.6), cost is the same.

18. (i) 0.5
    (ii) −3.5
    (iii) 0.5
    Investor believes the value of the asset will change significantly (up or down). A straddle.

19. See section 6.4.

(i) 0
(ii) −3
(iii) 5

Expect significant change in the value of the asset. Believe that a fall in value is more likely than a rise. One situation: I come to believe that a rise in value is more likely than a fall, so then I buy a strap.

20. \$80 −\$120: expect price to stay close to \$100. −\$293 918 750

21. Buy a call option, strike price K; sell a put option, strike price K; both options having a maturity of three months.

22.

S = asset value at maturity	Pay-off (call)	Pay-off (put)	Pay-off
$S \leq K_2$	0	$K_2 - S$	$K_2 - S$
$K_2 < S < K_1$	0	0	0
$S \geq K_1$	$S - K_1$	0	$S - K_1$

Buy a strangle if you think there will be a large change in the value of the asset but you are not sure whether the change will be an increase or a decrease. A strangle, in that respect, is similar to a straddle. But the penalty for being wrong is less with a strangle than with a straddle.

24. For a put option: $P \leq K$ (in fact, $P \leq Ke^{-RT}$): $P \geq Ke^{-RT} - S_0$

25. (i)

Stock price at maturity	Pay-off
$S \leq K_1$	$K_2 - K_1$
$K_1 < S < K_2$	$K_2 - K_1$
$S \geq K_2$	$K_2 - K_1$

(ii) $(K_2 - K_1)e^{-RT}$

(iii) $C_1 + K_1e^{-RT} = P_1 + S$

$C_2 + K_2e^{-RT} = P_2 + S -$

$C_1 - C_2 + (K_1 - K_2)\,e^{-RT} = P_1 - P_2$

Solutions 7

1. (i) $= 0.15$, (ii) $= -1.2987$, 0.2013

2. (i) $= 0.7143$, (ii) $= -33.9463$, 1.7687

3. (i) $= -0.7778$, (ii) $= 25.0407$, 1.7067

4. Q. 1: $u = 1.2$, $d = 0.9$, $q = 0.3367$, $1 - q = 0.6633$
   Q. 2: $u = 1.1$, $d = 0.96$, $q = 0.3571$, $1 - q = 0.6429$
   Q. 3: $u = 1.1$, $d = 0.95$, $q = 0.5$, $1 - q = 0.5$

5. (i) $q = 0.8$, $1 - q = 0.2$ (ii) 1.2079

6. $q = 0.3611$, $1 - q = 0.6389$, 0.6774

7. (ii) $q = 0.4960$, $1 - q = 0.5040$, 1.0872

10. (ii) 1.1646

11. First stage: $q = 0.7476$, $1 - q = 0.2524$. Second stage after up move: $q = 0.5714$, $1 - q = 0.4286$. Second stage after down move: $q = 0.5765$, $1 - q = 0.4235$. Value $= 10.1576$.

12. 1.5247

13. (ii) $a = 0.9827$, $b = -8.1949$: $a = 0.9611$, $b = -8.0303$, $a = 0.9122$, -7.6339
    (v) 1.6329

14.

Value of asset	18	20	22	24	26	28
Value of call option	0.0706	0.2748	0.7504	1.5881	2.7954	4.3086

15.

Value of asset	25	30	35	40	45	50	55
Value of put option	9.2054	4.6856	1.6818	0.4197	0.0768	0.0111	0.0013

16. (i) Bull spread. (ii) $0.5103 - 2.3661 = -1.8558$

17. European put: 3.4371. American put: 3.7558

18. European: 1.1055. American: 1.7852. Difference $= 0.6797$.

19. Call: 2.2304: Put: 1.8255. 4.0559.

20.

	Call	Put	Value
European	0.4127	0.2232	0.6359
American	0.4127	0.2526	0.6653

21. (i) $\sigma = 0.158565$ (iii) 0.3329. If Leisen parameters are used, $u = 1.0380$, $d = 0.9472$ and put value = 0.3357.

22. (ii) (a) $\frac{1}{2} \times 101 + \frac{1}{2} \times 99 = 100$ (b) $\frac{1}{4} \times 102 + \frac{1}{4} \times 100 + \frac{1}{4} \times 100 + \frac{1}{4} \times 98 = 100$
(vi) $x = £\frac{7}{3}$

23. The pay-off at maturity is the amount the holder receives at the expiry of the option. If the value of the option was different to the pay-off, an arbitrage opportunity would arise.

24. An American option offers its holder a greater opportunity for profitable exercise over the holder of a comparable European option. The holder must compensate the seller for the greater possibility of profitable exercise. The options would have the same value if, at all vertices, the calculated value of the option was greater than the intrinsic value of the option.

25. (ii) \$1.115

26. Buy a butterfly spread. Sell a straddle, a strip, a strap.

27. A calendar spread makes a profit if the asset value at the maturity of the one-month option is close to the strike price. The option will make a loss if the asset value is significantly above or below this strike price.
   To create a calendar spread using put options, buy a long maturity put option and sell a shorter maturity put option. Both options will have the same strike price.

28. \$0.6785

29. The initial (a,b) portfolio is $a = -0.4685$, $b = 19.4185$. Sell 0.4685 of the asset and receive \$18.74. Receive the cost of the option, \$0.6785. Invest

the total income \$19.4185 at 6% for one month. At the end of the month, buy 0.4685 of one share and cash in the investment. Whether the asset rose or fell in value, this money will match the value of the option. If the asset fell in value, to \$37.60, the option should be exercised. One share is exchanged for the strike price of \$39.50. The money received from the sale of the old portfolio (\$1.90) funds the difference. If, however, the option is not exercised, we have an interesting situation. The option continues and a new (a,b) portfolio is needed: $a = -1$ and $b = 39.303$. This new portfolio costs \$1.703 to set up. This portfolio will replicate the option value at maturity, but \$1.90 was received from cashing in the old portfolio. Hence, the seller has \$0.197 to consume. Since the seller has made money from the non-exercise of the option, the buyer must have lost money.

Solutions 8

1. (i) 0.1154
   (ii) The bond has speculative elements. Future not well assured.
   (iii) 0.0679
   (iv) (a) US government bonds might be bought as safe elements in a portfolio, so their price (and yield) might not reflect the true market rate.
   (b) Traders might build compensation for possible default into the bond price.
   (c) Other market products (CDSs) might be used to calculate a more realistic market 'safe' interest rate.

2. (i) The firm pays \$84 000 every six months to MLM Bank.
   (ii) Peter's firm pays MLM: \$84 000 on 30 October 2006, 30 April 2007, 30 October 2007 and 30 April 2008. On 1 July 2008, it pays $\frac{62}{360} \times 168\,000 = \$28\,933.33$ and delivers BJL bonds with a face value of \$10 000 000. MLM pays \$10 000 000 to Peter's firm.
   (iii) Sell a five-year CDS (notional principal = \$10 000 000) on NRB bonds. This would bring in per year (until default) 100 basis points on a notional principal of \$10 000 000. So Peter's firm would be paying out, every six months, \$34 000. Peter has reduced its exposure to default by BJL. The firm is paying less but is exposed to risk of default by NRB.

3. (i)

Date	Alpha pays	Benson pays
3 Feb 2007	1 375 000 + 1 305 000	1 375 000
3 Aug 2007	1 375 000	1 225 000 + 110 000
3 Feb 2008	1 375 000	1 325 000 + 1 405 000
3 Aug 2008	1 375 000 + 140 000	1 400 000
3 Feb 2009	1 375 000 + 710 000	1 382 500

   (ii) Alpha paid Benson 45% of the par value (= $22 500 000) and Benson paid Alpha the par value (= $50 000 000).

4. (i) Pay-off = $5m × bond duration × max[(strike spread – actual spread), 0].
   (ii) Six months later, the Beelzebub bond is yielding 8.699%. The spread of this bond over a US government bond is 0.04599. The pay-off = $5m × 9.2 × max[(0.0508 – 0.04599), 0] = $221 260.

5. Include the bond in the portfolio of a collateral bond obligation. When the special purpose vehicle issues bonds, the senior tranche bonds will be A rated.

6. Answers in section 8.3.

Index

3417040R00222

Printed in Great Britain
by Amazon.co.uk, Ltd.,
Marston Gate.